Racial and Ethnic Relations in America

S. Dale McLemore
The University of Texas at Austin

Allyn and Bacon, Inc.
Boston / London / Sydney / Toronto

Credits for photographs

The Bettmann Archive Inc., *facing page 1;* Mark Chester for Stock, Boston, *22;* John Dunning for Stock, Boston, *50;* D. Krathwohl for Stock, Boston, *100;* R. P. Angier for Stock, Boston, *154;* Peter Menzel for Stock, Boston, *202;* Harry Wilks for Stock, Boston, *254;* Steve Hansen for Stock, Boston, *322*

Printed in the United States of America.

Library of Congress Cataloging in Publication Data

McLemore, S   Dale.
  Racial and ethnic relations in America.

  Bibliography: p.
  Includes index.
  1. Minorities—United States. 2. United States—Race relations. I. Title.
E184.A1M16   301.45′1′0973   79–16359
ISBN 0–205–06827–8

To Pat and Jean and Scott

Contents

List of Illustrations   *x*

List of Tables   *xi*

Preface   *xiii*

One   Natives and Newcomers   **1**

A Popular View of Americanization   *2*
Some Factors Affecting Inclusion   *6*
From Tradition to Modernity   *12*
Theory and Practice   *15*
A Note on Values   *17*
Key Ideas   *18*

Two   A Model of Inclusion   **23**

The Cycle of Race Relations   *23*
The Formation of the White Protestant   *25*
Majority in America
     Indian-English relations   *31*
     The Anglo-Conformity ideology   *33*
The Colonial Irish   *35*
     Scotch-Irish assimilation   *38*
The Colonial Germans   *39*
The Revolutionary Period   *41*
Key Ideas   *46*

Three   Anglo Conformity and Its Challengers   **51**

The First Great Immigrant Stream   *53*
Nativism   *59*
     Changing patterns of immigration   *63*
The Second Great Immigrant Stream   *64*
     Nativism and restriction   *70*

Assimilation and Race	*71*
Race Differences	*77*
Race, intelligence, and immigration restriction	*79*
Black-white intelligence test differences	*84*
The melting-pot ideology	*89*
The ideology of cultural pluralism	*91*
Key Ideas	*96*

Four   Prejudice and Discrimination **101**

Theories of Prejudice	*105*
The cultural transmission theory of prejudice	*105*
Personality theories of prejudice	*109*
The group-gains theory of prejudice	*114*
The group-identification theory of prejudice	*120*
Theories of Discrimination	*124*
The cultural-transmission theory of discrimination	*126*
The group-gains theory of discrimination	*128*
The situational-pressures theory of discrimination	*129*
Institutional discrimination	*133*
Reducing Prejudice and Discrimination	*134*
The educational approach	*135*
The legal approach	*143*
Organized social protest	*147*
Conclusion	*148*
Key Ideas	*149*

Five   Japanese Americans **155**

Japanese Immigration and Native Reactions	*157*
The Japanese Family and Community in America	*164*
Japanese occupations and the alien land laws	*168*
Exclusion	*170*
The second-generation period	*171*
War, Evacuation, and Relocation	*173*
The relocation program	*175*
Legal issues	*182*
Japanese American Assimilation	*184*
Cultural assimilation	*184*
Secondary structural assimilation	*187*
Primary structural assimilation	*188*
Marital assimilation	*189*
Japanese American "Success"	*191*
Value compatibility	*191*

Community cohesion   193
A comparison of success theories   195
Key Ideas   198

Six   The Chicanos   **203**

The Colonial Analogy   204
The Immigrant Analogy   215
Mexican Immigration and Native Reaction   219
Generation and Assimilation   230
 The census reports   231
Chicano Assimilation   234
 Cultural assimilation   234
 Secondary structural assimilation   237
 Primary structural assimilation   242
 Marital assimilation   243
Chicano "Success"   245
Key Ideas   249

Seven Black Americans   **255**

Servants and Slaves   256
 Immigrant or colonized minority?   265
 Emancipation and reconstruction   267
 The restoration of white supremacy   270
 Migration, urbanization, and employment   275
The Civil Rights Movement   277
Black Power   293
Black American Assimilation   298
 Cultural assimilation   298
 Secondary structural assimilation   303
 Primary structural assimilation   312
 Marital assimilation   312
Black American "Success"   314
Key Ideas   316

Eight Ascending Pluralism   **323**

An Ethnic Revival   325
When Is Soon?   329
Primary and Secondary Ethnic Groups   333
The Future of Ethnicity in America   334
Key Ideas   341

References   **345**

Index   **365**

List of Illustrations

1.1   *Majority and Minority Reactions to Inclusion*   *8*

3.1   *Ideal Assimilation: The Melting Pot*   *90*

3.2   *Ideal Assimilation: Cultural Pluralism*   *93*

4.1   *A Possible Relationship Between
Prejudice and Discrimination*   *103*

4.2   *Major Direct Causes of Prejudice and
Indirect Causes of Discrimination*   *104*

4.3   *Major Direct and Indirect Causes of
Prejudice and Discrimination*   *127*

List of Tables

3.1   Immigration into the United States from
       Selected Countries, 1880–1909   64

6.1   Percentage of Chicano and Anglo Workers in
       Selected Occupational Categories, 1950,
       1960, and 1970   238

6.2   Median Years of Schooling of the Chicano
       Population by Year, Nativity, and Sex   239

7.1   Percentage of White and Nonwhite Workers in
       Selected Occupational Categories, 1950,
       1960, and 1970   304

Preface

One of the biggest problems faced by the beginning student of racial and ethnic relations is the scope and diversity of the field. The United States alone has so many different racial and ethnic groups, each with a different history and problems, that it is difficult to gain an overview of the subject. Moreover, scholarly specialization within sociology, anthropology, psychology, history, government, economics, ethnic studies, and other disciplines focusing on racial and ethnic problems has expanded our knowledge so rapidly and along such varied lines that the materials to be presented become richer by the day. This is fundamentally a happy state of affairs, but it does complicate the task of giving the introductory student a coherent picture of this exciting field.

The strategy of the present volume is to join two of the broadest, most illuminating approaches to the study of American racial and ethnic relations: the sociological analysis of intergroup processes and the history of ethnic groups in America. These two approaches combine nicely because the study of processes such as competition, conflict, segregation, stratification, accommodation, and the various subprocesses of assimilation is inherently temporal in character. The flow of these processes in the interactions of racial and ethnic groups is most readily grasped through an examination of the history of the relations of these groups.

A "processual-historical" approach, if we may call it that, also enables us to place within a broad narrative context many of the customary topics of interest to beginning students. Such conventional topics as race and race differences, stereotyping, social distance, prejudice and discrimination, vertical mobility, and methods of social change are introduced as elements in the general development of the relations among racial and ethnic groups in the United States. The IQ controversy, for instance, is discussed briefly in relation to the rise of "scientific racism" and the movement to restrict immigration at the turn of the twentieth century.

At the most general level, our story and analysis proceed from the beginnings of contact among different groups in the New World to the pressing racial and ethnic issues of contemporary America. We deviate from this general thrust, however, to encompass several special topics, for example, prejudice and discrimination, and a more detailed exploration of three non-white American groups. After a brief introduction focusing on the question "How do people acquire an American identity?" we move, in chapter 2, to the development of the dominant Anglo-American group, its ideology of group inclusion, and the first major challenges to this group by the colonial Irish and Germans. We also present in this chapter a discussion of the four subprocesses of assimilation around which much of our later analysis revolves.

In chapter 3, we review the major nineteenth-century challenges to the dominant group and the development of alternative ideologies of group adjustment. Chapter 4 discusses the most prominent theories of prejudice and discrimination and considers briefly some of the main approaches to change. This chapter also serves as a transition to the examination of the Japanese American experience (chapter 5), the Chicano experience (chapter 6), and the black American experience (chapter 7). Chapter 8 considers the re-awakening of ethnic consciousness in America during and following the turbulent 1960s. The chapter also proposes a solution to a major puzzle posed by the preceding chapters. We close with some conjectures, suggested by our analysis, concerning the future of ethnicity in America.

Although the ideas presented here are potentially applicable to racial and ethnic settings anywhere in the world, the book is not expressly comparative. Some comparative materials are introduced very briefly in the discussions of the Spanish and English colonization and slave systems, and certain ideas stemming from comparative research are crucial to the development of the book's materials and to the suggested resolution (in chapter 8) of the debate over the immigrant and colonial analogies. The reader is often alerted to the important effects of the international context on the patterns of racial and ethnic relations existing within a given multicultural society.

There is, however, a special sense in which the book is definitely comparative. The primary aim of this volume is to reveal to the student a set of "key ideas" concerning racial and ethnic relations; these ideas are developed and illustrated mainly through comparisons of the experiences of different racial and ethnic groups within the United States. Twelve groups in all are discussed, eight of them all too briefly. The eight are the English, the Indians, the colonial Irish and Germans, the nineteenth-century Irish and Germans, the Italians, and the Jews.

As mentioned above, the Japanese Americans, Chicanos, and black Americans are the subjects of complete chapters; the dominant Anglo-Americans are discussed throughout. This choice of groups and of emphasis should not, of course, be construed as slighting the many other groups that might have been included. There is no intention, in any case, to present complete profiles of the groups in question. The choices were dictated chiefly by an interest in presenting and illustrating the key ideas listed at the end of each chapter. The student may find, in fact, that it is useful to read the key ideas pertaining to a given chapter both before and after reading the chapter itself. This procedure should help the reader distinguish more clearly the central points under discussion from the many details that are useful in understanding those points.

My debts to others are incalculable. I am especially conscious of my debt to the scholars who have generated the stimulating ideas and conducted the numerous studies on which I have relied in the preparation of this volume. I am grateful, too, to the many fine teachers who aroused my interest in the field of racial and ethnic relations and to the hundreds of students who, over the years, have challenged and sharpened my thinking concerning the complex issues of this field. I wish to express thanks also to Mr. Gary Folven and Mr. Al Levitt, Editors of Allyn and Bacon, Inc., and their staff for their support throughout the writing of this book. Finally, I wish to thank Pamala Bockoven, Olivia Becerra, Celia Clattenburg, Linda Joseph, and Sharon Moon for the many hours they spent typing the manuscript.

Racial and
Ethnic Relations
in America

One

Natives
and Newcomers

Send these, the homeless, tempest-tossed, to me:
I lift my lamp beside the golden door.

*Emma Lazarus**

The United States of America frequently has been described as a nation of nations, a mixture of immigrants from all over the world. Most Americans cannot trace their stay in this land to more than five or six generations, and only the Indians can claim to have been here for more than a few centuries. As a result, many Americans still think of themselves as having a "nationality" (or ethnicity) in addition to their identity as Americans. Despite the somewhat romantic insistence that Americans are the product of an international melting pot, that they are the first "self-created People in the history of the world" (MacLeish, 1943:115), newspapers, magazines, and television bring us daily reminders that the fabric of modern American society consists of Italian Americans, Polish Americans, Irish Americans, Chicanos, black Americans, white Americans, Chinese Americans, Puerto Rican Americans, and many others.[1] This diversity of nationalities, races, and religions has been a source of pride and of problems.

The basic problem has been to answer the question "What is an American?" How can we accomplish what Glazer (1972:175) has called "the difficult task of fashioning a single national identity?" If an American citizen's national origin is Italian or Polish or Irish, is the person *first* an American and *then* a member of an ethnic group? Or is the order of priority and loyalty reversed? These questions ask us to think about what people consider to be their basic group attachments or identities. When people speak of "my people" or "we," what group or groups do they have in mind? Behind questions such as these lie some others of critical importance. If many people in the United States have divided group loyalties, how is the underlying unity of the nation affected? What should be the official policy of the United States toward these citizens who feel primarily or significantly loyal to some subgroup within the

---

* These lines are inscribed on the pedestal of the Statue of Liberty.

1

American nation as a whole rather than to the nation itself? Should racial, ethnic, and religious differences and loyalties be encouraged as sources of variety and strength or be discouraged as sources of disunity and distrust? What official and unofficial actions strengthen or weaken racial and ethnic groups? Whether they are discouraged or not, will these types of groups naturally disappear with the passage of time? Some of those perplexing questions call for factual answers. Others are concerned mainly with the goals, values, and purposes of American society as a whole and of the various groups within it. Together, they have been, and continue to be, the subject of an enormous amount of public and scholarly attention and controversy.

For more than half a century, sociologists have had an active interest in the issues raised above; during that time, a substantial body of ideas and findings relating to these issues has accumulated. Although most of the materials considered in this book are taken from the work of people who are identified as professional sociologists, the thinking of sociologists has been influenced by the work of historians, psychologists, anthropologists, economists, political scientists, journalists, novelists, social critics, and many others. Additionally, different sociologists who have worked in this interesting and difficult field have chosen to emphasize various issues and approaches. When one examines the broad outlines of this field of study, however, certain major trends are visible. Many of the assumptions, theories, topics of study, and suggestions for social change that were in the forefront during the 1940s and 1950s lost some of their intellectual appeal as the racial and ethnic protests of the 1960s developed and intensified. Beginning with those same events, many competing ideas have attracted attention and have been the focus of new and illuminating discussions.

Let us begin our exploration of the ideas that have been prominent in sociological thought on the subject of racial and ethnic groups in America (and the ideas that have been emerging to challenge them) by tracing very briefly a popular view of how a person's identity may be transformed from that of a "foreigner" to that of an "American." The plan of presentation is to start with ideas and terms that are to a large extent a matter of common sense concerning this subject. But this approach can take us only so far. The problems of racial and ethnic relations are too complex to be analyzed fruitfully entirely in everyday terms. When simplification threatens to become oversimplification, the ideas with which we began will be refined. As the discussion moves from its common-sense beginning toward a more technical level, special terms will be introduced as needed.

A Popular View of Americanization

The principal stages through which a newcomer to our shores generally is presumed to travel have been portrayed in many biographies, novels, plays, movies, and scholarly books and articles. Both in fact and in legend, millions of people have crossed the oceans in search of economic, religious, and other opportunities in the United States. The central image is very familiar: a ship enters New York harbor within view of the Statue of Liberty; the weary and awe-stricken immigrants are cleared through Ellis Island ("The Gateway to the New World") for entry into the United States; after clearance, they disperse and begin a new life in the Italian, Polish, Hungarian, or Greek section of the city.

The life of the "greenhorn," though exciting, is filled with problems to be solved and obstacles to be overcome. He or she must find a place to live, find a job, and manage to cope with the countless difficulties that arise daily when one is trying to learn a new language and adopt a new way of living. The "old-country" ways and ideas are no longer appropriate. The newcomer must do his best to learn rapidly the "American way" to speak, dress, think, and act. Gradually, the greenhorn begins to "learn the ropes," to speak and act less like an Italian, Pole, Hungarian, or Greek and more like an "American." But even an immigrant who wishes to do so probably will not be able completely to make the transition to the new way of life. His or her name, speech, dress, manner, religious observances, food preferences, place of residence, or type of occupation may continue to mark the person as "foreign." In many cases, of course, newcomers do not want to be divorced entirely from the old-country ways. They may wish to be accepted as Americans in all of those ways that are essential to their livelihood and immediate welfare; they may wish for the members of their families to be able to participate as fully as they like in the "mainstream" of American life; but they may find life's greatest pleasures and satisfactions in the sights, smells, sounds, and companionship that exist only in the "Little Italy," "Little Poland," or "Little Hungary" that those of the same nationality have constructed in "their" section of the city. Nevertheless, these new, first-generation Americans who have been unable or unwilling to give up certain elements of the foreign culture may hope that their children will move further in the direction of losing their identities as foreigners and become completely "American."

The children of the immigrant, the second generation, may have learned so many of the old-country ways from their parents that they, too, are unable or unwilling to drop all vestiges of their parents' culture. They, of course, probably will become much more fluent in English than their parents, and they may fail to learn or may actively reject certain features of the old-country culture. When these second-generation Americans are grown, they may move out of the old neighborhood or take a job in another city. They may even marry someone of a different "ethnicity" or change their name to something more "American." Still, many elements of the old culture may remain either by preference or by necessity, and the person may be regarded by himself or by others as still remaining in some significant way Italian, Polish, Hungarian, or Greek. Such a person is "marginal," having one foot in the "host society" and one in the immigrant society.[2]

Finally, according to the familiar view being sketched, the grandchildren of the immigrant (the third generation) will move completely into the "mainstream" of American life. Their parents have not transmitted to them a noticeable portion of the old culture. This failure of transmission may occur partly because the parents do not wish to have the children maintain an ethnic identity (other than American) and partly because the parents do not themselves know enough of the old culture to transmit it. The children of the third generation, of course, may learn to speak a few words of the old-country language, especially if the grandparents are still alive, and they may learn certain old-country recipes, folk songs, and proverbs. But they will speak English without an accent, and questions concerning their "nationality" will seldom arise. The third-generation Americans will have completed, for all practical purposes, the process of Americanization set into motion by their grandparents. At this point, the individual's national origin becomes essentially invisible. The grandchildren of the immigrant think of themselves as "Americans" and are so regarded by other "Americans" (who may themselves be the children or grandchildren of immigrants). The individual has now become a full member of the host society, sharing equally with the "charter" members in the distribution of social rewards. No racial or ethnic restrictions on the individual's participation in the society exist. He or she may "rise" to any position the society has to offer.

A number of different terms are current in both popular and scholarly language to refer to the transformation of a person's identity from foreign to American. Some of the more prominent of these are *acculturation, assimilation, integration,* and *absorption.* The idea that the foreigner becomes an American through a process of "melting" or "fusing" is frequently suggested. For the moment, though, let us postpone a discussion of the exact meanings of such terms and refer to the experience of Americanization simply as one of inclusion.[3] When a person first enters a society, he or she may be included only in a physical sense. The person may be "in" the society but not be included as a participant in a social sense. Of primary interest to us here is how a person does or does not become more nearly "fitted into" the various parts of a society.

The particular process of inclusion outlined above is usually called *the three-generations process.*[4] It is one description of the sequence of stages through which members of successive generations may pass to become "completely American" and may be summarized as follows: "Except where color is involved . . . The specifically *national* aspect of most ethnic groups rarely survives the third generation in any significant terms" (Glazer and Moynihan, 1964:313). However, even if this account is accepted as a general description of the way immigrants have been fully included within American society, certain aspects of it must be altered before the description will fit many other cases. For example, many immigrants have gone directly to farms or small towns rather than remain in a large city. Also, the process under discussion may appear to have been completed in some of these cases by the end of the second generation, or it may seem to be continuing into the fourth. With certain changes in the locations or the exact length of time involved, then, the process that has been outlined can be extended to cover a wider range of actual instances. Another interesting phenomenon is that in many instances the grandchildren of immigrants attempt to recover the heritage of the first generation. This phenomenon, in which "what the son wishes to forget the grandson wishes to remember," is usually referred to as Hansen's "law" or thesis (Hansen, 1938:9). The basic idea is that if the second generation successfully "forgets" its heritage, the third generation has a feeling of having lost its roots and, therefore, attempts to fill the void through cultural revival.

But even greater alterations in the suggested picture of the inclusion of the immigrant are needed. All of the examples given refer to people from southern or eastern Europe, and though no time period was specified, the examples actually suggest the experiences of those who came to the United States from Europe during a particular period of high immigration, the years 1880–1920. What assumption is to be made, however, concerning the process of including immigrants from other parts of the world? And what is to be assumed in regard to other periods of immigration to the United States? More specifically, has the same process of inclusion (with the appropriate geographical and temporal modifications) been at work among all of the different peoples who comprise the present population of the United States and within all of the different periods of its history? Let us pursue these questions briefly by turning away from illustrations taken from the experiences of the European ethnic groups and consider instead illustrations from the experiences of black Americans, Chicanos, and Indian Americans.

Since the grandparents (or earlier ancestors) of most black Americans came to the United States as bonded servants or slaves, they obviously did not "emigrate" to the United States in the sense being discussed. While much human migration involves to some degree both voluntary and involuntary elements, it is clear that the involuntary element was enormously greater in the migration of the ancestors of most black Americans than was true of any other group that has come to the United States.[5] It also is clear that after many more than three generations (in most cases), the black Americans have not reached the expected end point of the three-generations process. Black Americans have not entered fully as a group into the mainstream of American life and become simply "Americans." The process of inclusion has not been completed.

In a similar vein, it is plain that the Indian Americans did not enter American society as "immigrants" at all. Since they preceded American society, one may say that American society has "migrated" to them! Moreover, as has been true for the black Americans, the Indian Americans have for the most part been brought into American society involuntarily, in this case through conquest and the occupation of their territory.

The Chicanos present a similar, but in some ways more complicated, case. Like the Indian Americans, many of the ancestors of the Chicanos were brought into the United States involuntarily through conquest. The ancestors of some others, however, had joined in and supported the military operations that resulted in the transfer of enormous tracts of land to the United States, while the ancestors of still others—and this is the largest category—migrated more or less voluntarily to the United States from Mexico. Many of those in the latter group, however, have not necessarily thought of themselves as "immigrants" to a "foreign" country. Although the lands along Mexico's northern border are within the political boundaries of the United States, a vigorous variant of Mexican culture preceded American occupation and has continued there to the present. Consequently, many Mexicans and Chicanos do not find the border between the two countries to be very important psychologically (Alvarez, 1973). Like the black Americans and the Indian Americans, most Chicanos have not completed the process of inclusion within three generations.

The experience of the black, Indian, and Chicano groups should leave little doubt that the three-generations process (even with some fairly large temporal modifications) does not describe very well what has happened to some of the groups that have been brought into American society. Why is this true? Is it likely, given still longer periods of time, that even these groups will gradually be included fully? Stated more broadly, the question is this: what factors affect the extent to which the members of a particular group are included within American society and the *rate* at which inclusion occurs?

Some Factors Affecting Inclusion

The simplified sketch presented so far has suggested that the members of some groups appear to be more likely to approximate the three-generations process of inclusion within American society than others. The discussion also has implied that at least two factors may increase or decrease the speed of inclusion. The first of these factors is whether people have entered American society mainly voluntarily or involuntarily. Those who have chosen to come to the United States may exert special efforts to learn English and to alter many other established ways of acting. Their *goal* may be full inclusion. On the other hand, people who have been enslaved or conquered may be less willing to become members of the society that has been responsible for those acts. Their goal in this case may be to escape the new society and return to the homeland.[6] Please note, however, that even though a voluntary entrance into the society may initially lead people to be more favorable toward the adoption of American ways, and an involuntary entrance may favor rejection of Americanization, the two types of entrance do not necessarily lead to different results.

Americanization may be viewed even by those who have migrated voluntarily as having both desirable and undesirable aspects. For example, full inclusion within American life may be viewed by the members of a particular racial or ethnic group as a process of erosion or cultural destruction. From the latter standpoint, inclusion represents a gradual decline of a cherished way of life rather than progress. From this same standpoint, a major problem for the minority group members may be their inability to resist inclusion. As we shall see, many groups of this type have been described by Americans as being "clannish," as refusing to give up their "foreign" or "un-American" ways of living.

A second factor implied above as having an effect on inclusion is the racial identification of the individual or group. This point will be discussed much more fully later, but certain assumptions should be noted here. Most observers have assumed, for instance, that the inclusion of people who are distinguished by racial features is necessarily slower and more difficult than is the inclusion of people who are distinguished "merely" by cultural differences. The argument usually is based on the reasonable view that those who are culturally different may become socially invisible through learning, while those who are physically different generally cannot alter that fact.

Two points concerning this argument are of special interest. First, it assumes that people who have entered the United States, whether voluntarily or involuntarily, will *want* to relinquish those traits that make them dstinctive so that they may "disappear" socially. As suggested already, this assumption may be false. The members of a given group may disagree with one another regarding whether, or in what ways, inclusion should be sought. Nearly all Jews, for example, may agree that the members of their group should learn English and be permitted to attend the public schools, but they may disagree sharply concerning the extent to which their religious ceremonies should be conducted in English. Second, the argument that racial groups will be the slowest to be included calls attention to a very important point: although white Americans have generally shown some hostility toward all foreigners, they have been more willing to accept the members of some groups than others. In particular, the history of the United States shows that white resistance to the inclusion of different groups is greater against those who are defined as "nonwhite" than against those who are considered to be "white." For reasons to be discussed later, white Americans generally have considered those labeled as "nonwhite" to be especially inferior and unacceptable as social equals.[7]

The latter point focuses on the wishes of white Americans (rather than some other group) for a simple, but most important, reason. White Americans have been not only the numerical majority throughout most of the history of the United States; they also have been the most powerful group in the society. The racial and ethnic groups to be included, on the other hand, have been minorities in power as well as in numbers. For our purposes, the latter point is primary. Racial and ethnic relations, not only in the United States but throughout the world, may usefully be viewed as one among a family of human relationships in which one group is more powerful and dominates another. In all human societies, some group or groups will have greater power than others, and the kinds of relations these more or less powerful groups have with one another represent a crucial element in the operation of the society.

The power of many groups is accepted as legitimate by those below them, and their commands are willingly obeyed; however, powerful groups sometimes are not willingly obeyed by subordinate groups, and then concealed or open conflicts may erupt between the dominant and subordinate groups. Hence, the relative power or degree of dominance of various racial and ethnic groups, rather than their sheer size, is of paramount sociological significance. Indeed, one of the most important facts about numerical majorities is that their large size frequently lays the foundation for the exercise of superior power. When the terms *majority* and *minority* are used to refer to power differences, therefore, rather than merely to differences in size, we are encouraged to pay close attention to the extent to which the minority group's behavior and life circumstances are related to the superior control exercised by the majority. We also are alerted to the possibilities for conflict between groups as well as for cooperation.

These ideas suggest that the rate of a group's inclusion within American society may be affected by the extent to which its members seek inclusion, by the extent to which the white Americans desire or resist their inclusion, or by the combined effects of these forces. It seems likely that in the case of a racial minority, the resistance of the majority will be stronger than in the case of a white minority. Figure 1.1 depicts these possibilities in a highly simplified form.[8]

One may speculate on the basis of Figure 1.1 that if either the majority or the minority rejects the desirability of inclusion (as in cells b and c of Figure 1.1), then the rate of inclusion will be slower than if both groups accept inclusion as a goal. In a situation in which both groups reject the desirability of inclusion (as in cell d of Figure 1.1), then the rate will be the slowest of all. Whether in the case of a particular minority a slow rate of inclusion reflects a rejection mainly from the side of the majority, the side of the minority, or both sides is a question that can be settled only by specific research.

FIGURE 1.1

		Majority	
		Accepts	Rejects
Minority	Accepts	+ + (a)	+ − (b)
	Rejects	− + (c)	− − (d)

Majority and Minority Reactions to Inclusion

So far, it has been noted that a voluntary entrance into our society may dispose a person to seek inclusion and that a racial identification may dispose the majority to resist a person's inclusion. Without any further investigation, one might well believe that a satisfactory reason has been found for the comparative slowness of the inclusion of the black, Indian, and Chicano groups. The argument might be advanced that a group such as the German Americans illustrate the situation described in cell a of Figure 1.1. Since the members of this group were not forced to come here, strictly speaking, and since they are considered to be white, both the minority and the majority probably have accepted inclusion as a desirable goal. Black and Indian Americans, by contrast, did not generally enter the society voluntarily, and they generally are regarded as members of nonwhite races. Therefore, on the basis of the discussion thus far, the assumption seems to be supported that these two minorities and the majority have rejected full inclusion as a desirable goal. This is the situation depicted in Figure 1.1, cell d. To illustrate further, the Japanese Americans, though racially nonwhite, may nevertheless be viewed as voluntary immigrants. Hence, we might expect that the Japanese Americans would be included more rapidly than the black and Indian groups, as shown in cell b.

The case of the Chicanos, as before, requires some additional qualifications. The extent to which Chicanos are in this country voluntarily and the extent to which they are regarded by the majority group as members of a nonwhite race are both so subject to question that we cannot assume, even tentatively, that cell b, c, or d of Figure 1.1 affords the most useful description. It is not difficult to argue, though, that one or more of these three cells is more nearly appropriate for the Chicanos than is cell a. From this standpoint, it is still possible to understand the more rapid and more nearly complete inclusion of the German Americans than of the Chicanos.

The above explanation seems to describe, in rough outline at least, the actual situation existing in the United States. Regrettably, however, the apparent "fit" between the suggested explanation and the facts may be no more than accidental. Please remember that a voluntary entrance into a country does not guarantee that the minority will wish to be included, certainly not in every respect. Many German Americans, as we discuss later, wished originally to set up a separate state or nation within the United States. Even though that effort was unsuccessful, many German American communities were established and have continued to this day to maintain a distinctive German "flavor." For this reason, one may wish to place the German Americans in cell c of Figure 1.1 instead of cell a, as suggested earlier. Similarly, as mentioned above, an involuntary entrance into a country does not guarantee that the minority will wish to remain apart.

Although the point is currently in dispute, there are many reasons to suppose that large numbers of black Americans have worked vigorously at various times to achieve full inclusion despite the involuntary entrance of their ancestors. From this perspective, black Americans illustrate cell b of Figure 1.1 rather than cell d. These shortcomings, and others that may occur to the reader, indicate that we must know a great deal about a particular minority and about its relation to the majority before Figure 1.1 can be very useful. It is absolutely essential in this regard that we study the historical sequences that have created the dominant-subordinate group relations of interest to us. In this way, we will gain an appreciation of the part played by many other factors affecting inclusion.

In addition to voluntary or involuntary entrance and to the way the dominant whites receive different racial and ethnic groups, certain additional factors affecting inclusion spring readily to mind. For example, the size of the minority (both absolutely and in relation to the size of the majority) is of considerable importance. It is familiar knowledge that majority group members are much more concerned about the presence of minority group members and give much more evidence of rejecting them in those places in which the minority is relatively large and in which the minority group has grown rapidly in size.[9] Of course, if the minority group actually becomes larger than the majority group, the concern of the majority group members may be greater still. Many towns in the southern United States illustrate the latter point in regard to black and white Americans. Many towns in the southwestern and western United States afford illustrations of comparatively large concentrations of Chicanos and Indian Americans. Outside the United States, the position of whites in the Union of South Africa and of English-speaking Canadians in Quebec is notable. In South Africa, even though the white English and Dutch groups run the affairs of the nation, they constitute only about 20 percent of the total population. The English-speaking group is dominant in the province of Quebec but is a numerical minority.

Another factor generally believed to have a very important bearing on the rate of inclusion of a minority group within the United States is the similarity between the culture of the minority and the culture of the majority. Consider, for example, such important aspects of culture as language and religion. People whose native languages are Chinese, Hindi, or Japanese may find that learning English involves a larger adjustment in their vocabularies, speech patterns, and inflections than will those whose native languages are Dutch, German, or Spanish. Since Judeo-Christian beliefs are predominant within the United States, those who have been raised in a different religious tradition may find many "American" ways difficult to accept.[10] Much the same may be said concerning American approaches to politics, education, courtship, marriage, and many other aspects of life.

As a final illustration (among several that might be presented), consider the effect that the *timing* of a group's entry into the United States may have. When the country has been in periods of economic expansion, and more "hands" have been needed to do the work, immigrants have been encouraged to move to the United States, and they have been accepted more cheerfully than during periods of depression, when many of those already here have been out of work.[11]

The actual stage of inclusion in which a particular racial or ethnic group is found, then, is the result of many different forces acting in combination. These forces may serve collectively to strengthen or weaken the degree to which the inclusion of a minority is encouraged by the majority. A given factor may exert a predominating influence at one time but be less consequential at another. In view of the number of factors that affect the rate of inclusion and their variable effects at different times and under differing conditions, no neat formula can be offered for determining which factors are having the greatest influence on a specific minority group at a given moment. Nevertheless, it seems reasonable to assume, at least tentatively, that such factors as the historical sequence leading to the contact of the majority and minority, the minority group's racial classification, the similarity of their culture to the "American" culture, the number of generations they have been within the United States, and the size of the minority and the majority may well exert a significant influence on whether the minority and majority groups will desire inclusion. Although this discussion has been focused on the United States, it is probable that these same factors have been of importance in the contacts among peoples that have been occurring throughout the world during the past several centuries.

Now consider again the first of the questions that led us to think about factors affecting the rate of inclusion: "Why doesn't the three-generations process describe very well the experience of the black, Indian, and Chicano groups?" Even though the discussion so far has not produced a compact answer to the question, it has taken us beyond the initial assumption that if one knows a group's race or ethnicity and whether it entered the country voluntarily, the group may be assigned accurately to the cells of Figure 1.1. The discussion has yielded a checklist of additional factors that may be useful in an effort to understand what has happened, and is now happening, to any given minority group within the United States. More important, though, as we shall see, is the recognition that certain barriers to inclusion may be erected either by the majority or by a given minority.

Let us now recall the second question that led to the examination of the factors that may affect the rate of inclusion: "Even though three generations may not be long enough, will all of the racial and ethnic distinctions in modern America gradually become less important?" To put the matter somewhat differently, does the natural or normal operation of American society act so as to blur the distinctions among racial and ethnic groups? Are the "forces of history" against the maintenance of racial and ethnic distinctiveness?

Broadly speaking, both social theory and common sense have supported the view that the normal historical tendency of American society has been toward the complete disappearance of *cultural* differences between groups of people. As discussed above, the assumption has been made that as time passes, culturally different peoples become progressively less "ethnic" and more "American." The big difference between the theoretical and common-sense views in this regard has been in the reasoning underlying the conclusion rather than in the conclusion itself. However, social theory and common sense have been in less agreement concerning the future of the *racial* groups in America. Although there has been a general agreement that racial differences are a stronger barrier to inclusion than are cultural differences, social theorists have been somewhat more likely than others to argue that the social forces working toward a full inclusion of the ethnic groups will, in the long run, produce essentially the same result with the racial groups. On this point, social theory frequently has differed from common sense in the ex- pected result as well as in the reasoning involved. To understand how social theorists have tried to approach this complicated subject, let us turn briefly to some ideas pertaining to an even broader sociological problem.

From Tradition to Modernity

For many decades now, a central concern of sociologists has been to describe and understand what happens when a society undergoes the enormous shift from a premodern to a modern form of social organization. In Western Europe, for example, the transformation has been from the traditional pat- terns of social life that characterized the feudal system to the radically different patterns of life that characterize modern industrial societies. In many African nations, on the other hand, the shift has been away from what may be called a folk society and toward the modern type. Although there are some significant differences between feudal societies and folk societies, both types frequently have been described as traditional in their organization and outlook. For instance, both feudal and folk societies are regulated mainly by custom and are organized primarily in terms of kinship. The members of families work together and form the basic economic unit of the society. Since neighboring families live in essentially the same way, mutual understanding and cooperative activity are promoted, and a strong sense of community attachment or solidarity develops. In such a setting, religion is a powerful force that tends to permeate all segments of individual and community life. The pervasiveness of religion combines with the force of custom and tradition to maintain a slowly changing, comparatively static social order. The ordinary person in a society of this type lives a hard life in many physical respects and probably is poor and illiterate. Such a person is compensated for these disadvantages, however, by the continuous social support of family, friends, and religious leaders. These supports create within the individual a strong sense of belonging, community purpose, and reverence.

The essential, defining properties of modern societies frequently have been portrayed as the exact opposite of those contained or implied in the above description of traditional societies. If the main tendency of traditional societies is to create and maintain a strong family and community in which people live with a sense of belonging and purpose, the main tendency of modern societies is to weaken the bonds of family and community and to atomize the individual. Within modern societies, economic activities shift away from the family and are located in the city and the corporation. Work tasks are more likely to be divided and organized according to rational plans than according to custom. Instead of engaging in the same kinds of work, family members and neighbors usually engage in different kinds of work. In this way, the intimate knowledge and mutual understanding of one another that are cultivated when people work together at the same activities are hindered or do not develop. Even individuals who work together are less likely to develop strong personal ties within the modern setting. For one thing, people move around so frequently in modern societies that it is difficult to develop enduring personal bonds. Life, in general, becomes more hurried and more bureaucratic. The individual's sense of commitment to his family and community declines.

Some version of this comparison of the traditional and modern forms of social life probably is already familiar to the reader. In the form given here, the comparison suggests mainly the losses that individuals suffer in the shift from the former to the latter. But the picture may also be painted primarily in terms of the ways in which individuals gain. The term "modern," in fact, usually connotes improvement and progress. Modernization frequently is advocated as a way to decrease poverty, disease, and death rates. It is a way to increase material abundance and the enjoyment of life. Modern life is seen by many as more enlightened and efficiently organized than traditional life. Moreover, those who emphasize the advantages of modern life frequently assume that the individual's attachment and loyalty to kinship and community groups will be transferred to other groups within modern societies. This capacity to transfer one's allegiance frees the individual from the accidental restraints of birth and tradition, enabling him or her to pick and choose personal attachments on the basis of more "rational" considerations. Hence, the individual's place in society and his or her group memberships are not determined primarily by who the individual *is;* they are determined primarily by what the individual can *do.* From this standpoint, a loyalty to the family, clan, tribe, or village that interferes with one's ability to change group memberships is "irrational" and "inefficient."

With these ideas as a background, some of the reasons why many sociologists have believed that both racial and ethnic distinctions would become decreasingly important in the modern world may be more understandable. It has been assumed frequently that the historical trend of American society is away from tradition and toward modernity. From this perspective, social distinctions based on racial as well as ethnic differences are "leftovers," so to speak, from the traditional form of social organization. The ties that bind individuals to racial and ethnic groups in American society, therefore, are expected to continue to become progressively weaker. Racial and ethnic loyalties and "consciousness" should decline. At the same time, the ties that bind individuals to some other groups, especially to the nation as a whole, are expected to become stronger. It follows from this that if a nation wishes to modernize, both kinship (racial) and cultural (ethnic) loyalties are interferences that should be discouraged or, if possible, eliminated. Consequently, those who have a strong commitment to national unity and modernization are likely to view racial and ethnic differences as interfering with the proper functioning of society. They may advocate, therefore, either the full inclusion of the racial and ethnic groups existing within a country, their expulsion, or their annihilation. If full inclusion has not occurred or is occurring slowly, this fact is likely to be seen as a "problem" that needs to be solved.[12]

Several questions are raised by the ideas just presented. For instance, even though there is much evidence to support our general description of the positive and negative changes that accompany modernization, one still may wonder whether such changes must occur. Is it possible that traditional loyalties to family and tribe are compatible with the efficient operation of a modern nation? Even more intriguing, is it possible that the retention of traditional loyalties may afford a necessary anchorage for people facing the "future shock" of rapid social and cultural change? Please notice that questions such as these direct attention to issues both of fact and of human values. They suggest the possibility that the results of modernization may be more varied than usually has been believed.

It should be emphasized that the various views being described and questioned here are in many cases unstated assumptions. Frequently, in fact, those who accept a particular view may not be aware they have accepted it. In any event, the view, whether stated, unstated, or below the level of awareness, represents a particular philosophy concerning the status of racial and ethnic problems. This philosophy has a profound influence on the way racial and ethnic issues are defined and analyzed.

The idea that racial and ethnic differences gradually will decline in importance because the organization of modern society requires it has been shaken to some extent by the rise of the civil rights protest movements in the United States during the 1960s. The kind of theorizing that has been outlined did not predict the occurrence of the numerous confrontations, conflicts, and "consciousness raising" activities associated with these movements. Hence, it would seem that some kind of a change is needed in this view of the organization of modern American society and the direction in which it is changing. At the moment, however, it is unclear whether or to what extent the basic idea is incorrect or in what ways it may be altered constructively. The range of possibilities is quite large. For example, it is possible that the racial and ethnic problems of the present are little more than a temporary fluctuation in the long-term trend toward full inclusion. If this were true, the basic idea of a shift from tradition to modernity could be expanded to include an explanation of why this fluctuation has occurred during this period; perhaps the expanded explanation would be useful in predicting future fluctuations.

Another possibility is that the theory is essentially correct as an explanation of the experiences of some groups but not of others. In this case, it might be modified to explain the experiences of the groups that are considered at present to be exceptions. Or, in this same vein, an entirely different theory might be constructed to explain why some groups do not fit the pattern of inclusion that has been discussed. In this case, the two resulting theories might be used alternatively according to which racial or ethnic group is under consideration.

But all this is quite abstract. What difference does it make, really, whether one adheres to one or another of these views? Isn't it more important to direct people's efforts toward practical solutions to our racial and ethnic problems than to continue theorizing about what may happen in the future?

Theory and Practice

In the minds of many people, theoretical activity is the opposite of practical activity. It frequently is remarked that something "is all right in theory but not in practice." Or it may be said that people should be "less theoretical and more practical" in their efforts to solve a particular problem. In fact, the discussion above has focused intentionally on an instance in which theory and practice may be to some extent opposed. Surely the continuing (or even rising) importance of racial and ethnic groups in America does not seem consistent with the ideas of inclusion that have been presented. Perhaps surprisingly, however, scholars do not generally see theory and practice as necessarily opposed even when the actual events do not support a given theory. Indeed, a discrepancy between a particular theory and "the facts" may lead to an increase in the effort to construct a more nearly satisfactory theory rather than to the abandonment of theorizing. The reason for this is simple. Both common experience and the history of science and discovery strongly suggest that a *correct* theory is very useful. Only when the most important factors that precede or lead to the occurrence of something of interest to us have been identified do we feel that we have an understanding of it. If one knows the principles that lie behind a particular phenomenon or that regulate the occurrence of a particular event, then it is possible to predict and possibly to control that phenomenon or event. Most people would concede, for instance, that a person has a better chance to repair an automobile engine if he or she understands the principles of internal combustion than if he or she merely approaches the matter through trial and error. At a more sophisticated level, people easily recognize that such "miracles" as the Salk polio vaccine and manned space flights would have been extremely unlikely had researchers not possessed well-established principles of immunology and aerodynamics. Consequently, the rejection of "theory" that is frequently expressed is more often a rejection of a particular theory than of theorizing as an activity.

There are substantial differences, to be sure, between human societies and automobile engines, vaccines, and space flights. Moreover, it is by no means clear that the operation of human societies will ever be understood in quite the same way as automobile engines, etc., are understood at the present time. It also is possible that the role of trial and error in the development of these miracles of technology has been underestimated. Nevertheless, it would be naive to believe that social policies toward racial and ethnic groups are not presently guided (perhaps inconsistently) by some kind of theory or theories. Similarly, it would be a mistake to assume that the best way to improve our policies is to stop theorizing and to start a deliberate program of trial and error. The question is not really whether we shall theorize; the question is whether we shall theorize well or poorly.

To bring these matters down to earth, suppose it is expected that the Chicanos who have been in the United States for at least three generations should have achieved an average level of education roughly equal to that of the average for native whites. But suppose that, in fact, there is an average difference between the two groups of about three years. Why does this difference exist, and what is to be done about it? If the ideas concerning the three-generations process are correct, then one's reasoning about this problem may run somewhat as follows: (1) many Chicanos learn only Spanish in the home; (2) when the children go to school, they do not understand English well enough to learn the lessons they are given; (3) they gradually fall behind children who are better prepared in English, and they are more likely to drop out of school; (4) this process produces a lower educational level among Chicanos; therefore, (5) efforts should be made to help Spanish-speaking children (a) learn English before they start school and (b) discontinue the use of Spanish once they are in school. This line of reasoning suggests such "practical" measures as preschool English programs for Spanish-speaking children and rules to prevent the use of Spanish at school. Here may be seen two assumptions of considerable importance. First, this is an example of the way specific practical actions may be suggested by a particular theoretical position and, at the same time, how certain solutions to a problem may be ruled out. For instance, a person holding the view just described probably would *not* agree with the idea that the teachers of Spanish-speaking children in the United States should teach the children in Spanish. Second, please notice that *behind* the argument that Spanish-speaking children should give up Spanish for English lies the assumption (mentioned earlier) that this is the "normal" course of Americanization. Notice, too, that some alternative assumption and theory must lie behind the suggestion that Spanish-speaking children should be taught in Spanish. The ideas that comprise such an alternative are discussed later in this book.

The main point of the example in the above paragraph is that a given theory may imply certain practical actions but not others. Consequently, in order to answer the many questions raised in this chapter, some of the implications of the major ideas that have been introduced must be examined in greater detail. These efforts are launched in chapter 2 through a more complete development of the theory of inclusion that has been most prominent in American thought.

A Note on Values

Sociologists have long recognized that, like all other humans, they have value preferences. They have acknowledged, too, that these values may play a part, sometimes large and unrecognized, in shaping their results and interpretations of the social world. Some serious questions for all students of society, therefore, are: "How can we study human problems objectively?" "Won't our biases, many of which are hidden even from ourselves, influence the way we gather, report, and interpret the facts?" "How can we prevent our political preferences from distorting the way we perceive social reality?"

The tradition of debate over these questions is rich and complex.[13] There is considerable agreement that the methods of social science may assist us in gaining a clearer understanding of the social world than will casual, undisciplined observation. For instance, we are obligated to look especially for evidence that goes against any theory we may hope to support. We are obligated also to search for explanations that undermine our privately held opinions. Despite these and many other precautions, the sociologist's values may nevertheless enter unintentionally into a study's results. There is considerable disagreement concerning just how serious the problem of hidden values really is and concerning what may be done about it.

An influential suggestion, proposed by Myrdal (1964:1043), is that students of society should attempt to set forth their major "value premises," to get them out into the open. When such value statements are made explicit, they should serve as constant reminders of the primary biases that are most likely to produce distortions. Although the present book is not a research study of the type Myrdal discussed, it does strive to present information in a balanced, unbiased way. The reader may wish to know beforehand, therefore, some of the author's major value premises concerning racial and ethnic relations in America. In the author's opinion:

1. The past and present discrimination suffered by America's minorities is one of our nation's saddest and most significant problems. Discrimination should be halted.
2. The maintenance of a certain level of ethnic diversity in America is both feasible and desirable. The effort to require American minorities to accept completely the standards of the majority should be discontinued.
3. The historical sketches presented in the coming chapters reveal a shocking gap between our most cherished ideals and the facts of dominant-subordinate group relations. We can and should move rapidly in the direction of our ideals.

4. American history is filled with examples of conflict between the majority group and the members of different minorities. Unfortunately, rapid social change seldom occurs in a completely cooperative, harmonious way. Therefore, in addition to becoming educated, voting, and appealing to the courts, minority group members must be prepared occasionally to use what Gordon (1978:67) refers to as "disruptive pressure." The most effective forms of disruptive pressure are nonviolent.

These views are by no means unusual. Indeed, they appear to be widely held by American sociologists (Horton, 1966). And they are quite compatible with what Myrdal (1964:3) has called "the American Creed" of democracy and equality, which is accepted by large numbers of Americans. But a viewpoint's popularity does not assure its correctness. Perhaps, if anything, a popular view should be examined with an even more critical eye.

With these understandings in mind, let us proceed at once to our exploration of racial and ethnic relations in America.

KEY IDEAS

1. Many people assume that the usual and normal course of Americanization requires three generations. In this view, the adult grandchild of the immigrant generally is and should be fully Americanized.
2. Many factors may affect the rate at which different groups move toward full inclusion within American society. Some of the most important of these factors are (1) the extent to which the group's entry into the society was voluntary, (2) the wishes and strength of the minority, (3) the wishes and strength of the majority, and (4) the racial and cultural similarity of the minority and majority groups.
3. Many scholars have assumed that as societies move away from traditional forms of social organization, loyalties based on kinship and cultural similarity tend to recede in importance or disappear. These forms of loyalty are thought to be incompatible with the requirements of modern social organization. From this point of view, the kinship and cultural loyalties that remain within a modern nation are problems to be solved.
4. The way racial and ethnic "problems" are defined and analyzed is profoundly influenced by one's assumptions concerning the compatibility of kinship and cultural loyalties with modern social organization.
5. Correct theories are no less important for an understanding of social matters than are accurate facts. Theories guide both research and practical recommendations for social change.
6. Although sociologists attempt to discover social facts and understand social reality, value preferences may be an important source of bias. One technique to decrease the effects of this form of bias is to make one's value premises explicit.

NOTES

1. There is no completely satisfactory way to identify the various racial and ethnic groups within the United States. Some Americans of African descent, for example, prefer to be called *black*. Others prefer *Negro, Afro-African, African American,* or *Colored*. Similarly, some Americans of Mexican descent prefer *Chicano,* while others prefer *Mexican American, Hispano, Mexicano, Latin American,* or *brown*. And some Indian Americans prefer a specific tribal name or the term *Native American*. Even the term *American* offends some, who suggest, rather, *United Statesian*. Whatever term is used, there is a regrettable tendency for it to gather unfavorable or insulting connotations. The practice followed here is intended to be both neutral and as close as possible to the contemporary preferences of the groups involved. For these reasons, we will describe most groups by ethnicity, race, or religion, followed by the word American. However, since the term *black* seems currently to be preferred by more Americans of African descent than any other, we generally will use it here. Although the matter of an appropriate name for Americans of Mexican descent appears to be very controversial, the terms *Chicano* and *Mexican American* appear to be the most popular. We will mainly use the term *Chicano*.

2. The problems and advantages of occupying a marginal position within a society has been a subject of sustained interest to students of racial and ethnic relations. For the classic work, see Stonequist, *The Marginal Man*.

3. The word *inclusion* also has been used in a technical sense by at least one prominent sociologist (Parsons, "Full Citizenship for the Negro American?" pp. 1009–1054). It is not being used in that way here.

4. The length of a generation varies substantially among different families. We assume here that a generation is approximately twenty-five years.

5. Schermerhorn presents a valuable classification of migrations according to the amount of coercion involved (Schermerhorn, *Comparative Ethnic Relations,* p. 98). Slave transfers are the most coercive type.

6. The most influential analysis of minority groups in terms of their goals has been presented by Wirth, "The Problem of Minority Groups," in *The Science of Man in the World Crisis,* pp. 347–372.

7. The dominant whites in America, of course, make numerous other distinctions both within the white group and among the various nonwhite groups. For instance, whites who are members of relatively dark-skinned groups are generally less acceptable to the dominant group than are whites from groups with generally light skins. People who represent a mixture of white and Oriental ancestry are generally less acceptable than dark-skinned whites but are more acceptable than Orientals, and so on. For an excellent discussion of these points, see Warner and Srole, *The Social Systems of American Ethnic Groups,* pp. 285–286.

8. For a comprehensive depiction of these possibilities, see Schermerhorn, *Comparative Ethnic Relations,* p. 207.

9. This principle is expressed by Williams, *The Reduction of Intergroup Tensions,* pp. 56–57, as follows: "Migration of a visibly different group into a given area increases the likelihood of conflict; the probability of conflict is the

greater (a) the larger the ratio of the incoming minority to the resident population, and (b) the more rapid the influx."

10. For a careful statement of the way language and religious differences are generally appraised against the accepted American standards, see Warner and Srole, *American Ethnic Groups*, pp. 286–288.

11. Some additional factors affecting the rate of inclusion may be found in the useful discussion presented by Berry, *Race and Ethnic Relations*, pp. 263–271. Andrew M. Greeley suggests three broad categories of factors affecting the inclusion of immigrants: (1) the social and cultural conditions of the old country; (2) the reception of the host country; and (3) the organization and sophistication of the immigrants (Greeley, *Why Can't They Be Like Us?* p. 32).

12. For an excellent brief analysis of the biases that may lie beneath the view that ethnic groups are problems, see Enloe, *Ethnic Conflict and Political Development*, pp. 7–8.

13. For an introduction to this literature, see Homans, "What Kind of a Myth is the Myth of a Value-free Science?" pp. 530–541.

Two

A Model
of Inclusion

> They must cast off the European skin, never to resume it.
> They must look forward to their posterity rather than
> backward to their ancestors.
>
> *John Quincy Adams*

The process through which many immigrants and their descendants appear to have passed to become full members of American society has been described briefly in chapter 1. This process appears frequently to have required a period of about three generations; however, the description given so far is too rough or approximate to afford satisfactory answers to the many questions that have been raised.

The purpose of the present chapter is to develop the ideas that have been introduced by examining the experiences of some of our earliest immigrant groups. As the discussion proceeds, it will become apparent that the common-sense language of chapter 1 is inadequate for our purposes. So, in order to improve our understanding of these pressing matters, our vocabulary will begin to shift in a technical direction. Let us begin with some of the ideas of an influential thinker on this subject, Robert E. Park.

The Cycle of Race Relations

Park was deeply interested in the experiences of racial and cultural groups throughout the world. His professional work on this subject covered a span of more than thirty years. The framework of his thought was presented in the form of his now-famous "cycle of race relations."

> In the relations of races there is a cycle of events which tends everywhere to repeat itself.
>
> The race relations cycle . . . contacts, competition, accommodation and eventual assimilation, is apparently progressive and irreversible. Customs regulations, immigration restrictions and racial barriers may slacken the tempo of the movement; may perhaps halt it altogether for a time; but cannot change its direction; cannot at any rate, reverse it (Park, 1964:150).

The four main stages of this cycle, according to Park (1964:104) are "the processes by which the integration of peoples and cultures have always and everywhere taken place." Groups of people first come into *contact* through exploration or migration. Once they are in contact, a *competition* between the groups is set into motion for land, natural resources, and various goods and services, a competition in which violent conflict frequently erupts. After a period of time, overt conflict becomes less frequent as one of the two groups establishes dominance over the other. The groups develop some fairly regular or customary ways of living together; at this point, they are said to have *accommodated* to one another.[1]

During all this time, beginning with the first contacts, various individuals within the two groups are spontaneously learning some of the language, customs, sentiments, and attitudes of those in the other group. Although this latter process is initiated in the contact phase of the groups' relations with one another, it gains momentum after the more or less stable period of accommodation has been reached. As the groups continue to live together, there occurs, according to Park (1964:205), a "progressive merging" of the smaller group into the larger. The members of the smaller group increasingly adopt the language, manners, and public customs of the larger group. Except in the case of physical differences, this process has "erased the external signs which formerly distinguished the members of one (group) from those of another." When the external signs have been erased, the members of the smaller group are said to be *assimilated*. Although *eventual* assimilation is listed by Park as the final stage in the cycle, the assimilation process occurs throughout the cycle, reaching its completion when all distinguishing external signs of group membership have been "erased."

Now please compare the cycle described by Park with the popular view of Americanization presented in chapter 1. Park, of course, was attempting to understand the results of racial and ethnic contacts "always and everywhere," while our interest is centered on the United States. However, even though the account presented in chapter 1 and Park's differ in a number of ways, they appear to be entirely compatible in their main features. In this sense, the popular view of Americanization may be regarded as a "special case" of Park's general theory. For example, the account given previously of the three-generations process is consistent with Park's description of the way groups gradually "merge" in the use of language, manners, and so on. And the term *assimilation* as used above seems to cover entirely the terms *Americanization* and *inclusion* as they have been used here.

Why, then, has the term assimilation been avoided in the discussion so far, especially since it appears frequently in newspapers, magazines, and radio and television reports? Strangely enough, Park himself has supplied an answer in his earliest paper on this topic. "The race problem," Park (1964:204) said, "has sometimes been described as a problem in assimilation. It is not always clear, however, what assimilation means." Unfortunately, Park's observation is even more appropriate today than at the time it was written. Unfortunately, too, this is no mere terminological quibble of interest only to scholars in their ivory towers. As mentioned in chapter 1, when a person speaks of assimilation, we frequently cannot be sure what assumptions are being made or how to evaluate the practical policies that the person may suggest or attempt to put into effect. Even though the word assimilation has a precise ring to it and is used in technical discussions, people with quite different or incompatible ideas may use it to describe their particular points of view on racial and ethnic problems. As a result, many of the programs that are intended to improve racial and ethnic relations or to combat inequality and injustice are confused from the beginning.

Many scholars since Park's time have criticized, amended, and extended his ideas. He has been criticized particularly for seeming to advocate accommodation, while giving insufficient attention to conflict. In the course of these criticisms, many valuable contributions have been made to our knowledge of this subject. Although we will discuss several of these at various points, the framework of our discussion is heavily indebted to the outstanding work of Milton M. Gordon (1964). Gordon has effectively made the point that it is useful to view assimilation as a *collection of subprocesses* rather than as a single process; and he has identified several important subprocesses.[2] Some of these will be presented shortly. He also has identified three main *theories* or *ideologies* of assimilation that have been significant in the development of the United States as a nation, and these will be introduced soon.[3] Since the fullest appreciation of the value of these ideas can be gained by considering them in relation to certain events in our country's history, the initial approach is mainly historical. So, without further delay, and following Gordon's illuminating lead, let us turn now to the circumstances underlying the creation of one of the main ideologies of assimilation.

The Formation of the White Protestant Majority in America

It is familiar knowledge that the discovery of the Western Hemisphere was followed by a long period of competition among European nations for control of the land and resources of the new territories. Well known, too, is that the Spanish and Portuguese led the way in the exploration and colonization of the New World. As successful colonists, they preceded the English by more than a century. Nevertheless, the English were the first to carry out large-scale colonization of what is now the Atlantic seaboard of the United States. The first successful steps in this comparatively large migration were taken at Jamestown, Virginia (1607), and Plymouth, Massachusetts (1620); by the middle of the next century, the thirteen American colonies of the English were well established. By that time, the English language, English customs, and English ideas of commerce, law, government, and religion were predominant throughout the region. But all of these elements of English culture had been modified in myriad and complex ways. After all, the colonies were a long way from the mother country, and the conditions in the New World promoted, and sometimes required, new ways of doing things. The colonies also were generally a long way from one another, and the kinds of problems that arose in different colonies encouraged different solutions. Of special importance is that, even during the colonial period, many immigrants came to the Atlantic coast of North America from Ireland, Germany, Scotland, Holland, Sweden, and France, as well as from England. Additionally, large numbers of black people were imported as slaves, and, of course, the Indians were here from the first. The resulting complicated mixture of peoples and cultures produced the new "American" society and culture.

A consideration of some early developments within this new society—English in broad outline but with many non-English elements—is crucial to an understanding of racial and ethnic relations in America today. To illustrate, let us first review how certain legal and political traditions were transplanted from Europe to America.

The monarchs of England, Spain, Portugal, Holland, and France had several reasons for wishing to colonize their New World empires. They sought precious metals and stones, of course, and they wished to increase their own spheres of control and to limit the power of rival nations. They also wished to develop new markets for finished goods, new sources of raw materials, and new jobs for the many people who were forced out of rural occupations as Europe moved from a feudal to an industrial form of social organization. These general desires for colonization, however, were counterbalanced by some other considerations. For example, during this period, many economic theorists believed that a nation could only become rich if it exported more than it imported and that, to accomplish this, a growing domestic population was necessary. For this reason, many rulers were alarmed if the population of their country declined; so they discouraged or prevented the migration of their people. Not to be ignored either is that most people did not wish to migrate regardless of the preferences of the rulers. Fortunately for the development of the New World territories of the English, several factors combined during the early decades of the seventeenth century to encourage the colonization of the Atlantic coast.

It may sound strange and unexciting to the modern ear, but some of the most important factors to be considered here concern the changes that were taking place in the way European trade and commerce were organized. During that time, the nations of Europe were becoming generally stronger and more unified. Their monarchs were reaching out in many directions in an effort to consolidate and centralize their power. However, while these rulers could *claim* authority, sometimes over vast empires, they actually could exert their authority only in fairly limited ways. They had neither the money nor the manpower to regulate closely all of the activities that were taking place in their domains. Consequently, the rulers were faced with practical questions such as these: who will supply the funds and skills that are necessary to conduct trade over extremely long distances? What kinds of authority shall be granted to those who engage in trade? How can the traders be held within the limits of their authority? As an answer to these questions, many rulers granted royal charters—a kind of monopoly—to various individuals and groups. A charter typically granted to an individual or to a group of merchants the exclusive rights to trade or colonize in a particular area for a given period of years; however, the exact terms of the charters tended to vary considerably among the different monarchs. Many of the charters, especially those granted by the Dutch and English rulers, provided that the individual or company receiving it would have powers that we today might expect only of a national government. For example, the famous Dutch East India Company, founded in 1602, not only had a monopoly (so far as the Dutch were concerned!) over certain rights in the Far East, but they also had the right to conclude treaties, establish colonies, pass laws, build forts, make war, and coin money. Generally speaking, the Dutch charters tended to grant greater privileges than did the English charters; however, the Dutch and the English were quite similar to one another in this respect. The rulers of both countries tended to grant the recipients of charters greater powers than did the rulers of the other main competing nations.

The increase in the granting of royal charters for commercial purposes, however, is only one significant aspect of the changes that were taking place in business organization during this period. Of equal interest is the growth of profit-sharing arrangements, including the issuance of stock. Although direct ocean trade was less expensive in the long run than was overland trade, ocean trade required greater initial expenses and, in certain ways, involved greater risks. Hence, it was difficult for individual merchants to raise the money and assemble the supplies that were required for lengthy ocean voyages. This meant that the merchants who held a charter in common were now more likely to pool their assets for a given share of the entire group's profits. It also meant, as is true today, that, in some instances, individuals who were not named in the charter were permitted to purchase shares in a particular venture and to receive a proportional amount of whatever profits were earned. With these points regarding commercial organization in mind, the founding of Jamestown and Plymouth and the subsequent spread of English colonial America are easier to understand.

Both Jamestown and Plymouth were established by commercial companies operating under a charter granted by King James I. This particular charter gave the members of the companies very broad powers, including the right to colonize, but did not initially give them control of the government of any colonies they might establish. The king at first appointed a royal council to govern from London. These companies set to work immediately, with varying degrees of success, to colonize some portion of the territories granted to them. The London Company landed some settlers in 1607 at the site of Jamestown. As would be true for hundreds of thousands of others, these settlers were mostly indentured, that is they were expected to work for a specified number of years in order to pay for their passage. The story of the misery and suffering of these first settlers is too well known to be recounted here. It should be noted, though, that the conditions were such that the investors in the London Company were not making the profits they had hoped for, and the entire enterprise was in danger of failing. Clearly, something had to be done to save this attempt at colonization.

Three important changes were made in the organization of the Jamestown colony. First, the king for a time discontinued his direct control of the colony through the royal council. Second, the company (now called the Virginia Company) began to grant settlers land and stock in the company so that they, too, would have a "stake" in its success—what we today call "profit sharing." Third, in 1619, the company permitted a representative assembly to be established. This assembly, which has been widely hailed as the beginning of representative democracy in America, became, in 1624, the famous House of Burgesses. The House of Burgesses could enact any law that was not contrary to the laws of England. Although the king retained veto power, the Virginia settlers had a great deal of control over their own affairs.

One other event of special importance helped to secure England's first toehold in North America. As has been said, the investors of the London Company were hoping for profits; and, like most other Europeans, they thought it possible that such things as gold and silver would be discovered by the expeditions they financed. They also hoped to establish a profitable trade in furs and other goods with the Indians and to use products from the forests to supply England's navy. However, no riches in precious metals were to be found in the Chesapeake Bay area, and factionalism threatened the very existence of the colony. After several turbulent years, though, it was discovered that Virginia was an excellent place to grow tobacco. This discovery provided the economic underpinning that was needed in order for the colony to survive.

Many investors in the London and Virginia companies suffered financial losses; understandably, they may have regarded their efforts in America as a failure. Yet it can easily be seen from the vantage point of the present that the events at Jamestown were of the greatest significance for English colonial development. Less than twenty years after the initial landing there, an enduring sprig of English life had been transplanted. Although many of the ideas and ways of doing things were not exclusively English or of English origin, they were nevertheless distinctively English. The language, of course, was English. The laws followed English precedents and could range over vast areas of human endeavor as long as they did not contradict English laws. Also, English ways of organizing business and government were established. As time passed, to be sure, all of these and many others features were gradually changed in detail; but the framework within which these changes occurred was one inherited from England.

The second early success in the colonization of English America also occurred under the sponsorship of the Virginia Company: the founding of Plymouth by the Pilgrims. In this case, though, as is well known, the colonists who agreed to cross the Atlantic in the *Mayflower* were looking for freedom from religious persecution as well as for improved economic conditions. And so it is not surprising to learn that the variation of English life that they founded emphasized not only English ideas and ways but also those of their particular Protestant religious group. This fact played an extremely important role in the subsequent English immigration to America.

A famous illustration of the English Protestant approach to human relations took place soon after the Pilgrims reached America. Although the expedition was conducted under a patent from the Virginia Company, the *Mayflower* accidentally landed beyond the northernmost boundary of the company's land. So the colonists had no title to the land they wished to settle, and the rules under which they had sailed from England were no longer binding. To place their activities on a more nearly "legal" footing (whether the Indians or the king of France thought so or not), the Mayflower Compact was drawn up and signed. Under this agreement, a governor was elected, laws were passed, and the Plymouth Colony was brought into being. The Pilgrims did not continue to govern themselves on this basis alone, however. During the next year (1621), they received a patent from the company that had the English rights to the land they had settled.

Another patent came into the hands of a group of Puritans who migrated to Massachusetts Bay in 1630. This group established several colonies (including Boston) that were more religious than commercial in nature; and many people were attracted to them for religious reasons. During the first ten years, approximately 20,000 immigrants reached the Massachusetts Bay Colony. Possibly twice that number had arrived in other portions of the lands claimed by England, making this the first period of heavy immigration to America.

That the English immigrants came in comparatively large numbers at this time is significant. Consider, by contrast, what happened in New Netherland. This colony (which, in time, included New Sweden) was established between Massachusetts and Virginia. As was true for the English colonies, it was founded by commercial trading companies. The Dutch companies were attempting to colonize at roughly the same time as the English, but their efforts to increase the population were not very successful. At one point, the famous Dutch West India Company offered large grants of land along the Hudson River to members of the company who would finance the passage of fifty families to New Netherland. Some who accepted the offer were given, in addition to the land, extremely strong control over the lives of those who settled there. These inducements did not, however, lead to the volume of immigration that was taking place in the English colonies. When the English king "gave" the duke of York the lands occupied by the Dutch and the Swedes (1664), the population of the English colonies may have been six or seven times as large as the combined Dutch and Swedish populations. The task of placing this territory under English rule, therefore, was greatly simplified. New Amsterdam (renamed New York) was captured without a struggle, and English control of the land stretching from Massachusetts through Virginia was now uninterrupted.

The case of New Netherland is of interest for more than one reason, however. The capture of this colony represents the first important instance in English America in which the dominant white English Protestant population was confronted with the problem of including sizable numbers of people from European nations other than England. The Dutch were the dominant group, but numerous other nationalities already were represented in New Amsterdam.[4] In addition to the Dutch, there were Swedes, Frenchmen, Portuguese Jews, Spaniards, Norwegians, Danes, Poles, Germans, Africans, and others. The extension of the English language and English law to New Netherland, therefore, did not erase the influence of the Dutch or radically alter the cosmopolitan flavor of New Amsterdam. Nevertheless, beneath this diversity lay several crucial similarities that enabled the process of inclusion to proceed in a fairly smooth way.

Although the English and the Dutch are of unmistakably different ethnicities, they have been made alike in certain ways by their joint participation in the cultural history of Western Europe. At the time the Virginia, Massachusetts, and New Netherland colonies were founded, both countries were populated almost exclusively by people who are regarded as white. Both countries were predominantly Protestant in religion. The rulers of both countries relied heavily on private trading companies in their efforts to establish settlements and colonize the extensive overseas lands they had claimed. The two countries had been for centuries in comparatively close contact with one another through trade and war, thus exchanging many ideas and ways of doing things. In short, the differences in backgrounds of the English and Dutch colonists in America were small enough that the two groups were able to understand one another fairly readily and to establish many forms of cooperation. Hence, even though the Dutch language was maintained in some families far beyond three generations, and even though Dutch place names and family names have survived in New York down to the present, the inclusion of the Dutch minority did not confront the English majority with a very difficult problem. The English group was certainly affected in specific ways by the inclusion of the Dutch, but the main burden of change lay on the shoulders of the conquered minority.

These considerations support a very important point: by the last quarter of the seventeenth century, the Anglo-Americans had become established as the dominant, "host," or "native" group along the Atlantic seaboard from Massachusetts to Virginia. Now, obviously, this statement does not mean that the Anglo-Americans were "natives" in the same sense that the Indians were "natives." It does mean, though, that they had displaced the Indians as the principal occupants of the land, that they had established their own ways of living as dominant, and that those who entered their society from the outside were likely to be regarded as "foreign." In this way, the *standards* of "American" life were set, at least in a tentative way. The extent to which someone was American or foreign could now be determined in a rough way by a comparison with the Anglo-American pattern. The more nearly a person approximated the Anglo-American ethnic model, the more nearly American he or she was judged to be.[5]

The standards involved more than ethnicity, however. They also involved race. Throughout the Christian era, Europeans had been taught that all people are brothers. Therefore, there was little support for the idea that physical differences among groups of people were very significant. It is true that there was a great deal of hostility toward the Jews, who frequently were persecuted as if they were a "race apart" (Gossett, 1963:8–11). In general, though, neither religion nor science claimed that racial differences were of great importance. As the white Europeans expanded their explorations and colonies throughout the world, however, they began to wonder whether something about "whiteness" conferred superiority on them. It is practically universal, of course, for a given group of people to regard their culture as superior to the cultures of other peoples.[6] Various European groups exhibited this kind of group pride or vanity in their relations both with one another and with the "primitive" peoples, but this common tendency to reject the members of all out-groups was intensified toward the world's nonwhite peoples as the European successes in conquest and enslavement mounted. Groups like the Indians and blacks seemed so "different," physically as well as culturally, that even some ardent believers in the unity of mankind doubted that these groups could possibly be assimilated into the society of the "superior" whites. Gradually, the belief developed that the military and economic successes of the whites were a result of biologically inherited differences among the racial groups, and people began to seek out Biblical and scientific support for it. This *doctrine of white supremacy* (to which we return in chapter 3) has been elaborated mainly in the last two centuries and, thus, is mainly a product of the modern era.

Indian-English Relations

The doctrine of white supremacy was fairly slow to develop, however, and was a reflection of quite divergent experiences with nonwhite groups. Consider, for instance, the relations of whites and Indians on the Atlantic coast. To begin with, there were whites from several different European colonial countries—particularly, Holland, France, and England—coming into contact with a large number of different Indian tribes at different points in time and in various locations. The Indians, after all, were not a single ethnic group. They were Delaware, Iroquois, Massachusett, Penobscot, Pequot, Powhatan, Wampanoag, and so on. They spoke different languages, had different religions, and varied in their levels of economic and political organization. Hence, the interactions among the different groups resulted in a bewildering array of specific and changing relationships.

The Iroquois confederacy, for example, consisted of an alliance of five tribes: the Cayugas, Mohawks, Oneidas, Onandagas, and Senecas. This political organization probably had been formed before the arrival of the Europeans as a defensive measure in a long-standing conflict between the Iroquois and the Algonkians. By the time the Europeans arrived, the Iroquois were among the most politically and militarily active people in the Northeast. They had achieved dominance over a large region and had established an active trading network throughout it (Nash, 1974:13–25).

A different confederation of Indian tribes was present in the Chesapeake Bay area when the English founded Jamestown. These tribes, under the leadership of Powhatan, already had had some unpleasant contacts with Europeans and were, therefore, somewhat suspicious of these newcomers. The Powhatans did not, however, attempt immediately to expel the English settlers. For one thing, they were as curious about the English as the English were about them. For another, the Powhatans were engaged in warfare with other Indian tribes, and they had hoped to form an alliance with the English. Besides, the English were greatly outnumbered, and the Indians had no way of knowing about the dangers of European diseases or the size of the immigration to come.[7] Had the Indians wished to end Jamestown, they could easily have done so. In fact, the colony would not have survived its first winter without the Powhatans' help.

The Indians' role in saving the colony did not prevent relations between the two groups from deteriorating rapidly. Numerous raids and counterraids took place during the next several years. Despite the continuous intergroup hostility, however, each group had a substantial impact on the other's way of life. The Indians quickly adopted many of the metal utensils and implements of the English. The English, in turn, learned from the Indians how to fish and use canoes as well as how to grow corn, beans, pumpkins, wild rice, and so on. The main advantages of the English were their ocean-going vessels and their knowledge of metals. In many other respects, the English and the Powhatans represented agricultural societies at a similar level of development (Nash, 1974:56–60).

As the English colony jumped in size, and the Indian population began to decline, the Powhatans realized they had made a serious mistake. In 1622, they launched a full-scale effort to drive the English out. They killed almost one-third of the invaders but did not succeed in ending the colony. They did succeed, however, in convincing the English that there could be no accommodation between the groups. The hope of Christianizing and "civilizing" the "savages" was abandoned as an official policy.[8] Beyond this point, the English sought to seize the Indians' lands and to subjugate or eliminate the Indians themselves. The Indians responded in kind. In 1644, they tried again— though by now they were much weaker—to drive the English into the sea. Again, they inflicted heavy casualties on the whites but could not end English colonization. At the end of this conflict, the English signed a treaty with the Powhatans that, in effect, initiated the reservation system. The treaty, in

Nash's (1974:65) words, "recognized that assimilation of the two peoples was unlikely and guaranteed to the indigenous people a sanctuary from white land hunger and aggression." In this way, the whites set into motion a method of conquest that was used repeatedly for the next three and a half centuries. Each major conflict was ended by assigning the Indians certain "reserved" lands, which, after a while, would be infiltrated, seized, and occupied. Each time, new reservations would be created over which the Indians would be guaranteed permanent control. After a while, however, a new round of encroachment would begin.

The result of the contacts between the Indians and the English at Plymouth differed only in detail. As the size of the English colonies there grew, and as the desire of the English for the Indians' land also grew, friction between the groups mounted. Various efforts to Christianize the Indians continued throughout the seventeenth century, but most Plymouth Bay colonists accepted the conclusion of those in Virginia: despite their differing tribal languages and organization, all of those in America at the time of the European "discovery" were considered to be essentially alike. They were all given the label "Indian," and they soon were regarded as permanently alien, unassimilable, and ineligible for full membership in the new host society being created.

The Indians, of course, had shown strong resistance to becoming a part of Anglo-American society. From their viewpoint, *they* were the hosts, and the whites were simply invaders. Their societies had existed long before the whites had arrived, and they were not dependent on white society for the satisfaction of their economic and social needs. They wished to retain their own tribal identities, traditions, and institutions; moreover, they had many resources to assist them in the pursuit of this goal. Although the diseases of the whites were taking a fearful toll of Indian lives, and although the whites possessed firearms, the Indians had the advantage of knowing the territory. Moreover, the tribes with hunting and gathering economies had the capacity to recede before the invaders and still maintain their groups intact for long periods of time.

The situation of Indian-English contact in the Northeast represents our first illustration of a vital point to be developed later: minority groups that are highly solidary and socially self-sufficient, especially at the time they become subordinate, are likely to resist assimilation strongly for long periods of time. Minorities of this type are highly unlikely to pass in only a few generations through the stages described by Park's race cycle theory.[9]

The Anglo-Conformity Ideology

The preceding sections suggest *one* early answer to the questions "What is an American?" and "How does a person become an American?" From this standpoint, an American is someone who fits exactly (or closely resembles) the pattern of life and racial type preferred by the members of the Anglo-American ethnic group in colonial America. He or she should speak American English without a "foreign" accent, be of a Protestant religious persuasion, be of the so-called white physical type, have an English surname, and prefer the customs and manners of the Anglo-American way. Viewed in this light, assimilation is a process of inclusion through which a person gradually ceases to conform to any standards of life that differ from the dominant-group standards and, at the same time, learns to conform to all of the dominant-group standards. Assimilation is complete when the foreigner merges fully into the dominant group.

The Indians, of course, not only would not adopt the ways of the English, they could not satisfy the requirement that they be racially white. In this respect, they were like the blacks, who began arriving in Virginia as slaves in 1619 and who also became excluded as candidates for full membership in the society. As we discuss in chapter 7, this fact was not completely due to their original status. There is strong evidence that the first blacks in Virginia, like many whites, were purchased as indentured or bonded servants rather than as absolute slaves.

The notion that alien groups should assimilate into Anglo-American society by "disappearing" within it has been labeled the *Anglo-conformity ideology* (or theory) of assimilation. This phrase is generally accepted and will be used in this book.[10] But it should be understood that the "Anglo" standards to which foreigners were expected to conform are Anglo-*American* not English. Note, also, that the theory we have described may be applicable to any dominant-subordinate group setting. Hence, the idea that everyone in Russia or Germany should conform to the dominant group's standards may be called Russification or Germanization, respectively.

The argument presented so far is that the English colonial efforts during the seventeenth century created an Anglicized version of the very meaning of the word "American" and that Anglo conformity was established tentatively as the accepted way to achieve full inclusion. Those who championed this idea looked down on the members of any group that departed very much from the Anglo-American ideal or who appeared not to be trying to become Americans. If a person believed that Anglo-American standards of behavior were normal and desirable, then, clearly, he or she probably would believe, also, that the standards of others were *ab*normal and undesirable.

Here we have an example of the way a group's underlying philosophy concerning racial and ethnic problems influences their definitions and analyses. By the latter part of the seventeenth century, the Anglo-Americans commonly regarded their own pattern of living and race as the correct ones for the entire society. From this standpoint, Anglo-American culture and membership in the white race were not simply characteristics of the dominant group; they were the standards against which any other group's location and "progress" could be measured. Hence, groups could be graded as more or less desirable according to how closely they resembled the Anglo-American pattern at the outset, how rapidly they departed from their own cultural patterns, and how successful they were in becoming socially invisible. As noted in chapter 1, groups that are unwilling or unable to fit into the majority pattern in a developing nation frequently are viewed as "problem" groups. Either the "clannish" refusal to accept the "superior" way of life of the majority or the possession of undesirable physical traits will brand a minority group as being in some way deficient.

These ideas received some severe tests during the eighteenth century. One of these tests came from a very heavy immigration to America of the Irish, particularly the so-called Scotch-Irish of Ulster.[11] A second test came from a heavy immigration of Germans, and a third test was the revolutionary war of 1776.

The Colonial Irish

The Irish began to arrive in the American colonies of the English almost at once. Within two years of the founding of Jamestown, according to Adamic (1944:315), hundreds of the Irish were present. Throughout the seventeenth century, many more fled from the troubled Emerald Isle to the Atlantic colonies.

The largest and most discussed prerevolutionary immigration from Ireland to colonial America, however, consisted mainly of Presbyterians from Northern Ireland (Ulster). A large number of those living in Ulster were descendants of immigrant Scots who had been brought to Northern Ireland by the English early in the seventeenth century to work the Plantation of Ulster. In contrast to the other citizens of Ireland, who were predominantly Catholic, the Irish of Scots descent were mainly Presbyterians. Although the Presbyterianism of these people was involved in their departure from Ireland, economic reasons were probably much more important. The lands on which they lived and worked were generally leased from absentee English landowners. When the landowners began to raise the rents on these leases, a large number of the Ulster Irish, particularly those of Scots descent, decided to go to America (beginning markedly around 1717) rather than pay the higher rents. This heavy immigration of the Scotch-Irish (who were generally referred to simply as the Irish) continued up to the revolutionary war.[12]

More important to us than their reasons for leaving, however, is the reception that awaited them in the colonies. At first, the Scotch-Irish headed mainly for New England, where, in general, they were met with reserve. Although these people were from the British Isles, were mainly Protestants, and were needed to help settle the frontier, they definitely were not accepted wholeheartedly by the "native" Americans. They clearly were regarded as "foreigners," who deviated in certain undesirable ways from the Anglo-American ideal pattern of behavior. They were said to drink too much, to fight too much, and to be generally ill-tempered, troublesome, and coarse of speech. These presumed differences created friction between the Americans and the Scotch-Irish. In one case, for example, a Scotch-Irish Presbyterian meeting house was destroyed (Hansen, 1945:49). In another instance, "a mob arose to prevent the landing of the Irish" (Jones, 1960:45). A Boston newspaper stated, in 1725, that the difficulties created by the newcomers "gives us an ill opinion of foreigners, especially those coming from Ireland" (Jones, 1960:46).

Pennsylvania soon became the most frequent destination of the Scotch-Irish immigrants. The way they were treated in New England had something to do with this, of course. But also William Penn was actively advertising in Europe for settlers, especially for the frontier areas; so the Ulstermen were greeted in a much more friendly way in Pennsylvania. Even here, though, as the number of Irish immigrants mounted, certain interethnic problems arose. For example, it was said that unless something was done, the Scotch-Irish would "soon make themselves Proprietors of the Province" (Jones, 1960:46).

The newcomers apparently were not great respectors of property; they frequently "squatted" on land without paying for it. There was also a strong mutual antagonism between the German and Scotch-Irish settlers of Pennsylvania that led to numerous disturbances. Before long, the Pennsylvania authorities began to discourage the continuation of the Scotch-Irish immigration, so this particular migrant stream began to move heavily into the frontier regions of Virginia and the Carolinas.

The case of the Scotch-Irish affords an early example of the mixed reactions exhibited by Americans toward most later arrivals. On the one hand, immigrants frequently have been actively recruited to meet labor shortages and populate frontier areas; on the other hand, Americans have been afraid that the newcomers would not conform to Anglo-American traditions and standards. Perhaps they would, instead, establish an alternative pattern of life or, worse yet, establish themselves as a new dominant group. This ambivalence has usually been displayed in various acts of violence and other forms of discrimination against members of the minority ethnic groups. Some of the difficulties encountered by the colonial Scotch-Irish require us to consider them one of the first American immigrant minority groups.[13]

The feelings of rejection and the acts of hostility were not one-sided, however. The Scotch-Irish came to America mainly in groups, and they tended to "stick together" after they arrived. They were quite conscious of themselves as a distinctive nationality group and did not mingle easily with the host Anglo-Americans. And, as mentioned previously, they surely did not get along well with the other noticeable minority group of the day—the Germans. Perhaps the most emphatic indication of the Scotch-Irish's sense of ethnicity is that they apparently distinguished themselves fairly sharply even from the Scots who had immigrated from Scotland.

Given this outline of the entry of the Scotch-Irish into American society, what may be said concerning the course of their inclusion into American life? As Park's formulation of the cycle of race relations would lead us to expect, the contacts between the Scotch-Irish and the other main groups in American society at that time—majority and minorities alike—produced a certain amount of competition and conflict. A gradual accommodation was achieved, however, aided by the migration of the Scotch-Irish to the frontier areas in large numbers. So far, so good; but this description provides information concerning only the first three stages of Park's race relations cycle. Little has been said regarding the way the cultural and social barriers between the Scotch-Irish and the other groups were maintained or eroded as time passed.

The research evidence on these matters is far from complete. Most writers agree, though, that the culture of the Scotch-Irish was very similar to that of the Anglo-Americans in terms of religion, occupational experience, family organization, educational levels, and political traditions. The second-generation Scotch-Irish, the children of the immigrants, found it easy to adopt the ways of the Anglo-Americans and generally were eager to do so. Thus, those elements of culture (e.g., speech, dress, manners) that served readily to distinguish the Scotch-Irish from the Anglo-Americans were fairly rapidly laid aside. This cultural transformation does not mean, however, that the second-generation Scotch-Irish (or even the third) simply disappeared or were "erased" as a group. Many, if not most, of these Americans were still aware that they were Scotch-Irish. On the frontier, they were likely to select friends who were Scotch-Irish, to marry someone who was Scotch-Irish, and to maintain some kind of attachment to the Presbyterian church.

The example of the Scotch-Irish may serve to illustrate something of the complexity of the idea of assimilation. By the standards of Anglo conformity, discussed earlier, the Scotch-Irish were a "normal" and "desirable" group of people. And, in a very real sense, the descendants of the early Scotch-Irish immigrants were well mixed into the Anglo-American population by the time of the revolutionary war. They had been included sufficiently to be for many, if not most, practical purposes a functioning part of the Anglo-American host group. Nevertheless, to state, as many writers have, that the Scotch-Irish were at this point thoroughly assimilated into American society is to ignore or downgrade excessively the importance of the remaining social distinctions we have just noted.[14]

There is an interesting solution to this puzzle. The discussion so far has referred to inclusion or assimilation as if they occurred only by degrees; in some respects, this is entirely appropriate. For example, one may presume that the Scotch-Irish immigrants gradually learned to speak American English; that their children spoke more English and with less accent; and that the third generation spoke still more English and with little accent. Here inclusion or assimilation appears to have occurred along a continuum ranging from zero to completion. But when the end of this particular path was reached by the Scotch-Irish, had full inclusion or assimilation taken place? If so, why were the Scotch-Irish still more likely to select their marriage partners primarily from within their own group even in the third generation?

Scotch-Irish Assimilation

Gordon's (1964) method of treating assimilation as several subprocesses may now be applied to some extent. The ability to speak excellent American English is an example of what Gordon (1964:71) has called *cultural assimilation;* the extent to which the members of a given group formed friendships with one another is an example of *structural assimilation;* the extent to which the members of a given group intermarry with the members of the majority group illustrates *marital assimilation.* Hence, in terms of the above description, the Scotch-Irish appear to have become well assimilated culturally by the end of the third generation. It was noted, however, that they continued for some time to prefer members of their own group as friends and marriage partners. Structural and marital assimilation, therefore, occurred at a much slower rate than cultural assimilation. Finally, the point was made that relatively high levels of cultural assimilation did not prevent the Scotch-Irish from thinking of themselves primarily as Scotch-Irish. Indeed, the rejection they experienced from the dominant group despite their cultural assimilation may well have increased the strength of their ethnic identity.[15]

The meaning and value of these distinctions will become progressively clearer. For the moment, though, let us make four observations concerning them. First, each of the subprocesses of assimilation "may take place in varying degrees" (Gordon 1964:71). Second, although the subprocesses are distinctive and relatively independent, Gordon hypothesizes that the rate of change in each one will correspond to its position in the list given above. The Scotch-Irish afford only a partial illustration of these two points. Cultural assimilation apparently proceeded most rapidly, as expected, but we have reached no conclusions concerning the different rates of change among the latter three types of assimilation. Third, it is possible for a group to assimilate culturally without assimilating in the other respects mentioned. Gordon (1964:77) has stated that "this condition . . . may continue indefinitely." However, Scotch-Irish assimilation was not stopped at the cultural level. Some degree of each of the other forms was occurring throughout the eighteenth century.

Our fourth observation on Gordon's subprocesses of assimilation concerns the structural type. As defined above, structural assimilation does not focus on the kinds of human relationships that people experience most frequently on the job, in schools, at political meetings, and in places of public recreation. In these settings, most of our contacts with others are not of the warm, close, personal type that sociologists call "primary." They are, rather, of the relatively cold, distant, impersonal type called "secondary." Consequently, our analysis will be greatly aided by dividing structural assimilation into two more refined subprocesses, each focusing on one of these two different types of settings. *Secondary structural assimilation,* therefore, will be used to refer to nondiscriminatory sharing (even if it is cold and impersonal) by subordinate- and dominant-group members of occupational, educational, political, neighborhood, and public recreational settings.[16] *Primary structural assimilation* will be used to refer to warm, personal interactions between dominant- and subordinate-group members in churches, "social" clubs, neighborhoods, families, and so on.

To return to the Scotch-Irish, we see that as they moved into farms and jobs alongside the Anglo-Americans, into public schools attended by the children of the dominant group, and into various political offices, they were experiencing aspects of secondary structural assimilation. When the contacts of the subordinate- and dominant-group members led to exchanges of visits to the home and admission to the dominant group's private schools, clubs, and churches, primary structural assimilation was occurring. Notice that because people typically interact with one another in impersonal ways before they become close friends, we should expect that secondary structural assimilation will occur before primary structural assimilation.

With this refinement, we now have four subprocesses of assimilation: cultural, secondary structural, primary structural, and marital. Gordon's theory leads us to expect that even though all of these subprocesses may be underway simultaneously, the rate at which each type of change occurs depends on its place in the above list. But, in sharp contrast to Park's view, a group may assimilate culturally without necessarily proceeding through the remaining stages. However, past a certain point (and in this way Gordon's theory resembles Park's), full assimilation becomes inevitable. The crucial point in the process for Gordon is the formation of primary group relations. Once the minority group enters "into the social cliques, clubs, and institutions of the core society at the primary group level" marital assimilation will follow (Gordon 1964:80).

The Scotch-Irish were not completely assimilated into the Anglo-American majority, even culturally, by the end of the eighteenth century; nevertheless, the various types of assimilation mentioned above were all underway. The main results of these different processes was to help solidify the American majority as a white, Protestant group, originating in the British Isles. Even though the Scotch-Irish had created certain difficulties for the dominant Anglo-Americans, there was never any widespread doubt that the Scotch-Irish would and could conform to the Anglo-American pattern. The case of the colonial Germans, however, presented a more serious problem to the majority.

The Colonial Germans

At approximately the same time the Scotch-Irish settlers were coming to New England and Pennsylvania, a large number of Germans and German-Swiss were moving to America. As was true for the Scotch-Irish, Pennsylvania proved to be the most popular destination, although some members of the German group went originally to New York, Virginia, the Carolinas, and

Georgia. These people, generally referred to as the "Dutch" or the "Palatines," were quite noticeable to the Anglo-Americans. Many of those to arrive were members of various Protestant religious sects (e.g., the Mennonites), who dressed distinctively, settled together in rural areas, and did their best to maintain the language and customs of the old country.[17] Although the majority of those who came later were less militantly Protestant, they still usually clustered in farming regions and held themselves apart from all other groups.

The primary area of settlement lay to the west of Philadelphia. Here the Germans, or "Pennsylvania Dutch," as they are still frequently called, established prosperous and well-managed farms. They quickly earned a reputation for thrift, diligence, and farming skill that has continued to the present. And their numbers grew rapidly. The German population of Pennsylvania may have reached 45,000 by 1745; by 1766, Benjamin Franklin estimated that one-third of the colony's people were German (Wittke, 1964:71).

This large immigration of people who spoke German, who differed clearly from the Anglo-Americans in culture, and who tended to settle "clannishly" in isolated areas aroused a strong suspicion among many of the "old" Americans. Some of the complaints against the Germans were identical to some lodged against the Scotch-Irish. They were said to "squat" illegally on other people's land, and their manners and morals were frequently thought to be rude and unseemly. To a much greater extent than the Scotch-Irish, however, the Germans posed an apparent threat of disloyalty. It was feared that they might set up a separate German state or even, as Benjamin Franklin put it, "Germanize us instead of our Anglifying them" (Anderson, 1970:86). At one point, a law was passed requiring immigrant Germans to take an oath of allegiance, and during the so-called French and Indian War, many among the Anglo-American and Scotch-Irish groups suspected the Germans of sympathizing with the French.

An important result of these differences and suspicions was to intensify the Germans' determination to survive as a group and, thereby, to slow the rate at which they and their descendants adopted the traditions of the Anglo-Americans. The German language, only slightly modified by contact with English, was transmitted quite faithfully from the first to the second generation and even from the second to the third. The Germans did not wish to attend English-speaking schools or to participate in the political affairs of the dominant group. Indeed, they did not even strive especially to be "good citizens." The sect Germans, in particular, refused to bear arms, to hold public office, and, sometimes, to pay taxes.

Since German farmers tended to build stone and heavy wood houses and barns, to buy adjacent lands, and to establish orchards and raise large families, they did not move readily. Hence, they were likely to remain in close contact with others of their nationality. They organized publishing houses, German-language newspapers, and fairs and other celebrations to bring their people together on a regular basis. Although the sect Germans (such as the

Mennonites) were more cohesive than were the church Germans (such as the Lutherans), a German's friends were highly likely to be Germans, and marriages outside the group were uncommon. Consequently, the Germans, in many cases, maintained their sense of ethnic distinctiveness beyond the third generation.

Given the above, it seems fair to say that in terms of each of the four subprocesses we have identified, the assimilation of the Germans into the majority group was slower than that of the Scotch-Irish and was accompanied by greater friction and hostility. This resistance to assimilation meant that the Germans were viewed with greater suspicion by the Anglo-Americans. Nevertheless—and this is an important qualification—the German presence in large numbers in American society *did* strengthen further the dominant position of the white Protestants. Suppose, for example, that the Germans had succeeded in "Germanizing" the Anglo-Americans and the Scotch-Irish. The dominant group in American society still would have been white and Protestant. It also still would have been European in culture, even if not specifically British. This is another way of noting that there were important similarities as well as differences between the Anglo-American and German groups, similarities that, through time, enabled the Anglo-American majority to maintain its basic pattern of life as the "official" and preferred pattern.

The Revolutionary Period

Some interesting evidence bearing on the solidarity of the colonial Germans and the Anglo-Americans as well as on the solidarity of the Anglo-American group itself is afforded by the alignments that took place during the revolutionary war. As is well known, those favoring the Revolution probably were in the minority at the beginning of the war and may never have been a substantial majority. Of greater interest to us here is that both revolutionaries and loyalists were to be found within the different ethnic groups then present in America. Even though many claims have been made that particular ethnic groups were solidly behind Washington and the Congress, it appears that the lines of cleavage varied from colony to colony.[18]

The Scotch-Irish of Pennsylvania, for instance, evidently were strongly behind the patriot cause, but they were more or less divided among themselves in other parts of the country. In New England, members of the Scotch-Irish group served on both sides. In the back country of the southern colonies, the picture was complicated by some religious disagreements among the Scotch-Irish. Some of them were on the patriot side, some were on the loyalist side, some fought at one time or another for both sides, and many of those on the same side fought among themselves!

Despite their more intense ethnic identification, the Germans also present a mixed picture. In Pennsylvania, many of the Germans subordinated their dislike of the Scotch-Irish and joined with them against the local loyalists.

In Georgia, on the other hand, most of the Germans supported the British. And while most of the leaders of the German Reformed church favored the Revolution, most of the leaders of the Lutheran church and the sectarian churches supported the British. Perhaps most significant, though, is that in all probability the majority of the ordinary German settlers were largely indifferent to the Revolution. As stated previously, they were not really a part of the Anglo-American core group and had tried, in general, to remain outside the orbit of its affairs.

The cleavages within the Anglo-American group were regional to some extent. For example, there were many more supporters of the Revolution in Massachusetts and Virginia than there were in New York and New Jersey; but the principal line of demarcation appears to have been social and economic rather than regional. There were, of course, some wealthy and influential people behind the Revolution; but most of the people in these groups were loyal to the crown. The revolutionaries were mainly those on the frontier and those who were not very prosperous. Hence, one may see that even though the Anglo-Americans possessed a common language, religion, race, and legal tradition, they still did not constitute a unitary social, economic, and political group. The decisive point for the present discussion, though, is this: The majority of those who participated actively in the Revolution, who led the Revolution, and who held the reins of government when the Revolution ended were members of the Anglo-American group. This group had become dominant during the seventeenth century and had successfully met the challenges posed by the Scotch-Irish and the Germans during the colonial period. Now a sizable portion of this group had gained full control of the political institutions of the country, thus strengthening still further their claim to represent the ideal pattern for all Americans to follow. More than ever before, to become fully American one had to conform to the Anglo-American model of behavior and appearance.

The events of the first three decades of the existence of the United States worked generally in the direction of consolidating the acceptance of Anglo-American ethnicity as the "official" ethnicity of America. One important factor in this trend was a greatly decreased flow of immigrants to the United States between 1793 and 1815. The Napoleonic Wars in Europe interfered markedly with the free flow of international traffic and were the primary cause of the decline in immigration. Additionally, four acts of Congress, passed in 1798, reflected a growing resistance to foreigners and foreign influences in America. These acts, known as the Alien and Sedition Acts, increased the length of time required to become a naturalized citizen from five to fourteen years, gave the president extraordinary powers over aliens, and made illegal many public criticisms of the president. Since the existing ethnic groups were not being reinforced by sizable infusions from their homelands, the pressures on them to conform to the dominant Anglo-American pattern were more effective than might otherwise have been the case.

Another important factor assisting the trend toward the equation "Anglo-American" equals "American" was a comparatively high birth rate among those who by now had become "native" Americans. Even before the Revolution, when the Scotch-Irish and German immigrations were very large, it is estimated that approximately two out of three people were *not* first-generation immigrants (Faulkner, 1948:50). Under these conditions, people who were not of Anglo-American ethnicity were becoming a decreasingly small proportion of the population.

A third significant factor aiding the consolidation was the success of the Anglo-American leaders in strengthening the powers of the postrevolutionary central government. Under the Articles of Confederation, the federal government was quite weak. At that time, it did not even have the authority to levy or collect taxes! This and many other powers that most of us today consider normal (or even "natural") for a national government to have were reserved to the separate states. This weakness of the federal government was of special concern to those in the owner, merchant, or capitalist segment of society. From their viewpoint, a stronger central government was needed to protect their interests both at home and abroad. And since many of the men of property had also been leaders of the Revolution, such a government could help to create the new, united, and independent *nation* for which they had fought. Many leaders, such as Washington, Madison, and Hamilton, feared that under the Articles of Confederation this effort at nation building might fail. In the famous *Federalist Papers,* Hamilton (1961:66) argued that unless the national government was strengthened, the states would soon become separate nations and would, as frequently happens among nations, begin to make war on each other. Concerns of this sort led Congress to convene a meeting of leaders in 1787 to consider the drafting of a new and stronger Constitution.

Practically all the delegates who came to the Constitutional Convention represented the dominant white Protestant Americans, in general, and the wealthier portion of that group, in particular. It is not surprising to learn, therefore, that the members of this convention were especially concerned about the kinds of problems that they and people like them were experiencing and that they wished to strengthen the central government in ways that would help solve these problems. This is not to say, of course, that these men were thinking only of their advantage or even that they generally thought of the matter in this way. Furthermore, to the extent that most Americans, whether rich or poor, had a stake in the survival of the country as an independent nation, the Constitution that was finally approved by the states benefited many groups that were not specifically represented in the convention. Still, there were economic tensions between those who were property owners or merchants, on the one hand, and those who were poor and in debt, on the other; and these economic differences led to some lengthy, occasionally violent, conflicts (Rubenstein, 1970).

But this is not the place to engage in the debate over the motives of the members of the Constitutional Convention. The point, rather, is this: During the first five years of the postwar period, many internal divisions threatened the very existence of the United States and, simultaneously, the shaky dominance over this vast territory that the white Protestant Americans had achieved. The ratification of a new Constitution, written and supported by some wealthy representatives of the white Protestant group, was an important step in the direction of consolidating the dominant position of this group.

Let us review the argument that has been presented. The Anglo-Americans increased numerically following the Revolution. Their numbers increased absolutely and relatively because of a high birth rate, because the descendants of those from other ethnic groups had undergone some forms of assimilation, and because the flow of immigrants fell sharply after the Napoleonic Wars commenced in Europe. However, the Anglo-Americans were divided, especially in terms of wealth and the ownership of property; so those who championed the new Constitution as a means to save the nation were by no means a representative cross-section of the Anglo-American group. They nevertheless were able to establish an "American" ethnicity that was a derivative of English culture.

The effects of the events commencing with the original settlement of Jamestown and Plymouth by people of English ethnicity combined to establish an American nation that was primarily a "fragment" of English culture and society. Outstanding among these events, to repeat, were the conquest of New Netherland; the assimilation, of various types and degrees, of a large number of Scotch-Irish and German immigrants; the successful revolutionary war against Britain; the decreased flow of immigrants following the Revolution; and the successful beginning of constitutional government. In addition, it has been argued by some that the frontier was a powerful force acting to "melt" European ethnic and social-class distinctions and to create a new American ethnicity (a point to be considered in chapter 3). The contention here, however, is that the pattern of behavior preferred by those of English origin was established as the "ideal" pattern during the seventeenth century and retained this position through the comparatively heavy immigration of the eighteenth century.

This is not a claim, however, that the events affecting the development of Anglo-American ethnicity may be understood completely by focusing on the events occurring in North America. It is obvious, of course—and we have stressed the point—that events such as the religious persecutions in England, Ireland, and Germany played an important role in the process. But the matter may really go deeper than this. It is significant, for instance, that the groups that fled from Europe thereby escaped the social forces that previously had restricted the development of their preferred patterns of behavior. In the New World, these preferred patterns could begin to unfold and elaborate in a way that would have been impossible within the framework of the old country. Hence, the nature and direction of the new society's development may have been more than innovation within the new setting. It may also have represented the conservation of a specific European tradition. From this perspective, the Puritan and capitalist values that took root in New England and Virginia were more effective in meeting internal challenges because they were partially insulated from their well-organized—we may say their "natural"—enemies in Europe.[19]

In any event, the identification of the Anglo-American standard as *the* nationality of Americans climbed following the revolutionary war and was accelerated during the War of 1812. Paradoxically, even though these wars were fought against the English, the essentially English framework of American society was not obviously threatened. The wars seemed to serve, rather, to conceal the underlying similarities between the two peoples and to intensify and exaggerate their more obvious differences.[20] All this is reminiscent of Churchill's famous observation that the English and the Americans are separated by a common language.

The upshot was that by 1815 the Anglo-conformity ideology was more firmly established as the normal and accepted view of assimilation than ever before. At this point, the white Protestant Anglo-Americans were the unquestioned majority in American society both in numbers and in political and economic power. The other principal European ethnic groups, which also were white and mainly Protestant, had generally accepted the desirability or the necessity to learn to speak American English and to adopt Anglo-American ways of acting, that is, to assimilate culturally. On the surface at least, it may have seemed only a matter of time until practically all of the Europeans and their descendants would be completely assimilated culturally and, perhaps, in every other way. In theory at least, the ethnic barriers that remained between the Anglo-Americans, the Scotch-Irish, and the Germans (not to mention the numerous smaller groups) would not be strong enough to prevent these groups from rapidly becoming practically or totally indistinguishable from the majority group. Please notice, though, that under the Anglo-conformity ideology all, or nearly all, of the social and cultural changes occur as the minority groups move toward the adoption of the majority group's standards. From this perspective, it is assumed that the majority pattern will remain essentially unchanged throughout the process. One might expect, of course, that as a minority assimilates culturally, there would be some influence on the majority culture—perhaps a few new words added to the language, a few new food recipes, a new fashion in dress, or a new technique in farming. For the most part, however, the minority group was expected to do the changing.[21]

The most apparent obstacles to a realization of the goals of those who believed that Anglo conformity was the proper (or inescapable) route to Americanization were the blacks and Indians. Oddly enough, however, even though these groups seemed to pose the most serious threats to the Anglo-conformity theory, they did not. Paradoxically, these groups were such enormous exceptions to the theory that they lay beyond its scope or intentions.

Hence, that blacks and Indians were not assimilating did not mean something was wrong with the Anglo-conformity theory. It meant, rather, that these groups were not pertinent to the theory. In short, it was assumed that America was to be "a white man's country." Americans and potential Americans were *by definition* white and Protestant.

Much more difficult to explain than the nonassimilation of blacks and Indians was the continuing visibility of certain European groups, such as the sect Germans. As mentioned earlier, a number of the Mennonite groups lived largely apart from all others and clung jealously to their own traditions, language, and religious observances. One who believed in the goals of the Anglo-conformity theory could argue, of course, that it was wrong for these groups to resist assimilation. The resistors could argue, for their part, that it would be wrong not to maintain their own group life and culture. But goals aside, the fact was that the "natural" process of "melting" into the Anglo-American majority did not seem to be operating as it was supposed to.

The example of the Mennonites and of others we shall encounter later on indicates strongly that the discussion so far has revealed only a part of what we need to know before we can understand fully the meaning of assimilation. We have seen so far how the white Protestant American majority came into being. We have seen, too, that the members of this group typically have accepted a theory of assimilation that requires potential Americans to cast off their prior heritage, to accept the Anglo-American heritage, and to disappear into the core group. Although this theory had met the main eighteenth-century challenges to it both in its ideals and in fact, we have noted that its victory was not total. Even at this early date, the seeds of two rival ideologies had been planted. One of these, the melting pot theory, reached fruition during the last decade of the nineteenth century. The second and more important ideology, cultural pluralism, has reached maturity in our own time. In chapter 3, these ideologies are examined against the background of the great nineteenth- and early twentieth-century immigrations to the United States.

KEY IDEAS

1. Several scholars have maintained that when racial or ethnic groups come into contact, a specific sequence of events is set into motion. Robert Park, for example, believed that racial and ethnic contact led to competition, accommodation, and assimilation, in that order.

2. The subject of assimilation is complex. It is important to think separately about the facts of assimilation and the goals that should be pursued. In regard to facts, it is helpful to view assimilation as a collection of subprocesses. In this way, one may observe that the members of a particular group are assimilating culturally, say, more or less rapidly than the members of some other group. The positions of the two groups may be reversed, however, in relation to some aspect of

secondary structural assimilation, say, participation in education. In regard to goals, the dominant view in American society has been that those who wish to join the society should conform to the Anglo-American pattern of living. This perspective on assimilation is called the Anglo-conformity ideology or theory.

3. The Anglo-conformity ideology was created as those of English ethnicity settled along the Atlantic seacoast and gradually extended their political, economic, and religious control over the territory. Some of the characteristic elements of this ideology may be traced to (1) the English system of law, (2) the organization of commerce during the sixteenth century, and (3) English Protestant religious ideas and practices, especially Puritanism.

4. By 1700, the Anglo-Americans had replaced the Indians as the "native" American group along the Atlantic seacoast. Those who came from the outside were likely to be regarded as "foreigners." The more nearly aliens resembled the Anglo-Americans in appearance and in patterns of behavior, the more nearly "American" they were thought to be.

5. The position of the Anglo-American majority and, consequently, the preeminence of their pattern of living were challenged during the eighteenth century by heavy immigrations from Northern Ireland (Ulster) and from the German states of central Europe. Even though these groups exhibited many of the cultural and social characteristics of the Anglo-American majority, they both became to some extent the objects of hostility and discrimination. They were the first significant immigrant minorities in American history.

6. The complete assimilation of the Scotch-Irish and German groups did not occur within three generations. Although each subtype of assimilation occurred more rapidly among the Scotch-Irish than among the Germans, the secondary structural, primary structural, and marital assimilation of the Scotch-Irish was probably incomplete well into the nineteenth century.

7. The experience of the Scotch-Irish and Germans illustrates the point that groups may complete cultural assimilation but remain unassimilated in some other respects.

8. Although the Scotch-Irish and German groups posed challenges to the Anglo-Americans and their version of the "official" pattern of American life, the outcome served to strengthen the main features of the ideology of Anglo conformity. The experience seemed to prove that white Protestant Europeans could and would conform to the Anglo-American pattern.

9. The results of the revolutionary war and, later, the Constitutional Convention left the Anglo-American majority in firm control of American society. This position was strengthened further by a decrease in European migration during the Napoleonic Wars and an increase in American nationalism during the War of 1812.

10. By 1815, the Anglo-conformity ideology was practically unchallenged. To become fully American, one had to be white and had to be, or become, Protestant. By this definition, nonwhite peoples such as the blacks and Indians were not, and could not become, full-fledged Americans.

NOTES

1. Park and Burgess define accommodation as acquired adjustments that are socially transmitted (Park and Burgess, *Introduction to the Science of Sociology,* p. 664).
2. Gordon is not the first to suggest the usefulness of analyzing assimilation in this way. Galitzi, for instance, analyzed the economic, cultural, and marital assimilation of Roumanians in America (Galitzi, *A Study of Assimilation Among the Roumanians in the United States*).
3. The terms *theory* and *ideology* are used interchangeably here. However, in general, we will prefer "ideology." This term suggests the emotional fervor, commitment, and sense of moral rightness that usually accompanies a person's view of assimilation.
4. Hansen reports that eighteen languages were spoken in New Amsterdam at the time it was annexed by the English (Hansen, *The Atlantic Migration, 1607–1860,* p. 39).
5. Although it is useful for comparison to think of Anglo-Americans as sharing a single set of standards, there obviously was—and still is—a substantial diversity within this "host," "charter," or "core" group. Gordon, for example, employs one term, the *core subsociety,* to refer to middle-class Anglo-American standards and another term, the *core group,* to refer to the standards of the entire Anglo-American group (Gordon, *Assimilation,* p. 74).
6. This group pride, called *ethnocentrism* by Sumner, is discussed further in chapter 4 (Sumner, *Folkways,* p. 27).
7. No one knows, of course, how many Indians were present in the Western Hemisphere during this time. Some scholars estimate that in 1500 there may have been as many as 20 million. See, for example, Wagley and Harris, *Minorities in the New World,* p. 15.
8. The Spanish, in contrast, maintained a major missionary effort for over three centuries.
9. Francis suggests that minorities of this type be called *primary ethnic groups* (Francis, *Interethnic Relations,* pp. 167–171).
10. Gordon attributes the term to Cole and Cole (Gordon, *Assimilation,* p. 85; Cole and Cole, *Minorities and the American Promise*).
11. The estimates of the size of the early immigrations vary considerably, depending on the methods and sources of the historian. There also is sharp disagreement concerning the religious composition of the Irish immigration. Most students of the subject seem to agree that approximately 250,000 Ulstermen of Scots descent and between 100,000 and 200,000 Germans came to America before the Revolution. See, for example, Dinnerstein and Reimers, eds., *Ethnic Americans,* p. 2; Faulkner, *American Political and Social History,* p. 49; and Jones, *American Immigration,* pp. 22 and 29.

12. Some people resent the use of the term Scotch-Irish to refer to the Ulster Irish. It is argued that the term creates the impression that the "old" or Catholic Irish contributed little to the development of colonial America. No such implication is intended here.

13. In Leyburn's opinion, the Scotch-Irish were not a minority group. They were "full Americans almost from the moment they took up their farms in the back-country" (Leyburn, "Frontier Society," in *The Aliens*, pp. 65–76).

14. Dinnerstein and Jaher state, for example, "Within three generations . . . (the) Scotch-Irish dropped their 'foreign' characteristics, assimilated to the dominant culture, and disappeared." (Dinnerstein and Jaher, eds., *The Aliens*, pp. 4–5).

15. In Gordon's language, this illustrates incomplete identificational assimilation. Gordon also distinguishes three other subprocesses of assimilation that will not appear directly in our analysis. These are attitude receptional assimilation (the absence of prejudice), behavior receptional assimilation (the absence of discrimination), and civic assimilation (the absence of value and power conflicts).

16. This is the type of assimilation that is most prominent in discussions of "integration." Public school integration or desegregation is a type of secondary structural assimilation.

17. The *Mayflower* of German immigration, the *Concord*, arrived in Philadelphia in 1683. The small group of immigrant families aboard was led by Franz Daniel Pastorius, an extremely able and well-educated man who was the first to issue a public protest against slavery in America (Adamic, *A Nation of Nations*, pp. 168–169).

18. Adamic argues that "the Germans just naturally supported the Revolution." He also presents evidence to show that between 38 and 50 percent of the rebel army was of Irish birth or extraction and suggests that the long-standing Irish hatred of the English aided measurably to foment the Revolution (Adamic, *A Nation of Nations*, pp. 174, 321).

19. This thesis of the indissoluble links between American and European history has been presented by Hartz, *The Founding of New Societies*.

20. Some have maintained that the anti-English sentiment strengthened a bid by the Irish to take control of the country away from the Anglo-Americans, but there is little evidence to support this contention (Adamic, *A Nation of Nations*, p. 328).

21. It is assumed also, however, that *as they adopt the host culture*, the assimilating groups will make an enormous contribution to the development of the general society (Gordon, *Assimilation*, 73).

Three

Anglo Conformity and Its Challengers

As a nation we began by declaring that "all men are created equal." When the Know-Nothings get control, it will read "all men are created equal except Negroes and foreigners and Catholics."

*Abraham Lincoln**

What, then, is the American, this new man? He is neither a European nor the descendant of a European. . . . Here individuals of all nations are melted into a new race of men.

Jean de Crevecoeur

Thus "American civilization" may come to mean the perfection of the cooperative harmonies of "European civilization" . . . a multiplicity in a unity, an orchestration of mankind.

Horace Kallen

The greatest human migration in the history of the world has occurred since 1815. Uncounted millions of people have left their ancestral farms and villages to live in cities and cross the oceans. Although the specific reasons for migration varied substantially according to the time and place, some of the general factors contributing to this great movement of people may easily be identified. They include rapid changes in agriculture, population size, and industrial production. A significant effect of the workings of these three great factors has been to reduce large numbers of farmers to a condition of poverty and, thus, simultaneously, to "push" them off the land and "pull" them toward jobs in other places.

---

* From a letter to Joshua F. Speed.

Two results of the improvement of agricultural methods were especially important. First, the surplus of food made possible a rapid growth in population. In fact, during the seventeenth and eighteenth centuries, the population in Europe more than doubled. Second, the new methods made possible and profitable the farming of larger areas of land with fewer workers. These facts increased the efforts of the more powerful landowners to enlarge their lands. Consequently, many small private farms and much land held in common were gradually "enclosed" by the large landowners. With their farms gone, many people faced the choice of remaining as paupers where they were or moving in the hope of finding work and better living conditions elsewhere. The choice was by no means easy. People in many cases did not have the money required to make the journey and stay alive until work was found. Even if there were enough money to send one person ahead (usually a young male), the family members left behind frequently remained in desperate condition. To be sure, the increasing numbers of factories and the growth of cities created jobs for large numbers of the rural poor. But the growth of the population was so rapid that there were seldom enough jobs for those who wished to work. In addition, just as is true today, the number of jobs available fluctuated with the ups and downs of business activity.

The millions of people who were uprooted by these great changes from a preindustrial to an industrial form of social organization comprised the migrant "streams" or "waves" that flowed out of their native lands and into other countries. The United States has been, overall, the most popular destination. Since 1820, when the U.S. government began keeping official records on immigration, approximately 47 million newcomers to this country have been counted. And many other countries—Russia, Canada, Argentina, Brazil, Australia, to name only a few—have received millions of other immigrants. Whether people chose to go to one country or another depended to a large extent on such things as the likelihood that work would be found, the availability of transportation, and the presence of friends and relatives in the country of destination.

The waves of immigrants arriving at America's shores tended to peak when economic conditions within the United States were good and to recede when there were economic downturns. But as has been suggested already, much more than the "pull" of the American economy was involved in the uprooting and movement of so many people. The convergence of many different forces led to two fairly distinct and astonishingly large immigrant streams to the United States. During the century from 1820 to 1920, many different factors combined to determine which countries provided the largest numbers of immigrants comprising the streams. For reasons to be discussed later, certain generalizations concerning the peoples represented in the immigrant streams have become the subject of heated debate. For the moment, let us merely note that the Irish, Germans, English, and Scandinavians were predominant during the period of the first stream (from 1820 to 1889); and the Italians, Austro-Hungarians, Poles, and Russians (primarily Jews) were the largest groups during the second (from 1890 to 1920). The decade 1880–1889 combined high immigration from both of the two great streams and represents a period of transition from the first to the second.

The First Great Immigrant Stream

America was not really a very popular destination during the decade of the 1820s. For one thing, the economic panic of 1819 destroyed many of the opportunities the immigrants were seeking. For another, many Americans were becoming less hospitable to the newcomers and more concerned about some of the problems associated with immigration. This growing concern was foreshadowed, in fact, by the enactment, in 1819, of the United States' first federal law to supervise immigration and the collection of official statistics relating to it. The comparatively small immigration of the 1820s also was due in part to the fact that Russia and Brazil were being heralded in Europe as desirable places to go. Whatever the exact reasons, though, their effects apparently had diminished by the 1830s. During this decade, the number of immigrants to the United States was over 538,000, which was nearly four times as many as in the previous decade (U.S. Bureau of the Census, *Historical Statistics,* 1960:57). The heavy immigration in the 1830s stimulated the dissemination of information and the development of hiring and travel arrangements. These improvements facilitated the still-heavier immigrations of the 1840s and 1850s. The decade of the 1840s saw the arrival of around 1,427,000 people, while the 1850s produced approximately 2,800,000. Although even larger numbers of people arrived in some later years, this wave of immigrants was the largest ever in comparison to the existing total population of the United States.

As had been true in colonial times, most of the immigrants during this period came from Ireland and Germany. Also, as in the previous century, the large immigration of the Irish preceded that of the Germans. Even during the 1820s, over 50,000 Irish immigrants moved to the United States as compared to less than 6,000 Germans. During the next two decades, the Irish continued to be more numerous than the Germans, though the totals for both groups rose sharply. As this movement of people reached a peak during the 1850s, however, the German immigration became heavier than the Irish, and it remained so throughout the following decades of the nineteenth century.

To understand these large migrations, it is necessary to consider what was happening to many small farmers in Europe during this time. The basic problem consisted of a combination of a high population density, an unsound system of land tenure, and a high reliance on the potato.

In 1815, Ireland was the most densely populated country in Europe (Jones, 1960:107). The end of the Napoleonic Wars brought about a deflation of land values, a decline of foreign markets for wheat, and a decrease in the number of jobs available. The saving feature in the situation for the Irish was the potato. Many people believed that the potato had insured Ireland forever against the dangers of famine. It was fairly easy to cultivate, and small amounts of land yielded large crops. It took only an acre or so to support a family. As future events proved, however, this heavy reliance on the potato was ill advised. The potato could not be preserved; it was hard to transport; and it was very hard on the soil. Farmers with sufficiently large land holdings alternated the potato with wheat and oats. However, the potato depleted the soil nonetheless and caused a gradual falling off of the grain crops.

A foreshadowing of later events occurred in the year 1821 when the potato crop failed and famine followed. Although this famine was not nearly so severe as the one that led to the heavy Irish immigration of the 1840s and 1850s, many of those who were able left the country at this time. Despite this famine (and a relaxation of Irish immigration restrictions), the vast majority of the Irish preferred to remain in their homes; for the moment, there was apparently enough food to go around. But a series of disagreements between landowners and tenants made it more difficult for people to lease land on which to support their families, leading to an increase in the tempo of out-migration around 1830. At this time, a majority of the immigrants to America still, as in colonial times, came from Ulster. However, during the 1830s, an important change occurred in the character of the movement, and by the latter part of the decade, most of the immigrants were Roman Catholics from the south and west of Ireland.

By 1845, the land system that prevailed in rural Ireland had become the source of considerable tension. The majority of the Catholic Irish were entirely at the mercy of the landowners because of the existing system of rent payments. Each landlord rented a portion of his land to a tenant, who, in turn, sublet parts of his portion to still other tenants. In this way, a hierarchy developed wherein each person depended on receiving rent in order to pay his own rent. During good economic times, this system worked fairly well, although it did encourage misunderstandings and bickering. When this system failed, and the chain of rent payments was broken, large numbers of people were then forced off the land and were left with no way to earn a living.

The decisive turn of events for this rickety economic system occurred in a series of blows beginning in the autumn of 1845. A particularly virulent form of potato rot struck the Irish crop, destroying not only the potatoes in the ground but many of those already stored. Apparently between one-third and one-half of the Irish potato crop was destroyed by the disease. The fear of another crop failure encouraged many people to leave at that time in what was soon to become a general "flight from hunger."

The worst fears of the people were realized in 1846 when the potato crop failed again. In the space of a few days early in July 1846, potato gardens all over Ireland withered and died. Never before had the crop failed in two consecutive years; at this point, people finally realized that Ireland simply could not support so large a population.

The reactions of the people to this disaster were pathetic. Some simply waited patiently in their cottages to die. Others took to the road, wandering from place to place begging for food. Those who could arrange passage to England or America did so. By 1847, at least 500,000 people had starved to death, and those who survived were in desperate condition. During the following several years, the total number of Irish immigrants—the so-called famine Irish—reached unprecedented figures. Each year, approximately 200,000 people left Ireland for America during the years 1847–1850 (Wittke, 1964: 131). By 1854, approximately 1,500,000 people, representing all social classes, had left Ireland as a result of the famine (Jones, 1960:109).

Most of those who arrived in America, however, were poverty stricken. They had no money to proceed westward on their own, and they usually got out of the coastal cities only when they were needed in inland factories and mines and to help construct canals and railroads. Consequently, the conditions in the "little Dublins" and Irish "shanty towns" that sprang up along the East Coast were very poor (Wittke, 1964:134). People were crowded together in tenements, and sometimes twenty or more families lived in a single house. The houses tended to be poorly lighted and ventilated, and diseases such as cholera were rampant. Amidst all this, the "drink menace" increased in severity, and the Irish reputation as ruffians and brawlers grew. Another effect of these conditions was that family ties were weakened. All of these things contributed to the native Americans' image of the Irish as an ignorant, practically uncivilized people, leading to a marked increase in hostility toward them.

Aside from their high concentration in the eastern cities and towns and their generally offensive behavior, two features of the social organization of the Irish worried the native Americans. The first of these was their conspicuous Roman Catholicism. The Irish have always dominated the Catholic hierarchy in America, and the spread of Catholicism in the United States before 1825 and 1855 was due primarily to them. Wittke (1964:152) reports that "in 1836 the diocese of New York and half of New Jersey contained about 200,000 Catholics and of the 38 priests 35 were Irish and 3 were German." By 1852, "there were 6 archbishops, 26 bishops, and 1,385 priests in the United States." As Irish laborers were drawn from the East Coast to work on canals and railroads, new Roman Catholic parishes were created to serve them.

The Irish attracted the unfavorable notice of the native Americans in still another way. They were very active in politics. The Irish peasants had a history of conflict with their English overlords, and they were well acquainted with many of the techniques of organizing and carrying through political campaigns. The Irish, says Adamic (1944:344), "took to politics like ducks to water." In most cities, they were solidly behind the Democratic Party and tended to vote as a block on most issues. In cities like New York and Boston, the "Irish vote" became increasingly important. As their numbers grew, the

Irish became increasingly visible in various public service jobs and political offices. It was frequently claimed by angry natives that the Irish sold their votes to the Democratic city political machines in return for jobs and other favors.

The Irish reacted to the hostility of the Protestant Americans and to the problems of adapting to their new environment in much the same way as have most immigrants before and after them. Immigrants need, first of all, to solve the problem of making a living; to do that, they frequently rely on others of their nationality group for help. Moreover, the strange and hostile world of the natives typically stimulates the immigrants' desire to associate in a reassuring and friendly way with others of the same nationality—to eat together and engage in familiar recreational or religious activities. These forces encourage the members of a given nationality group to seek one another out, to form benevolent societies, churches, patriotic organizations, newspapers, and social clubs. The ethnic group that is formed through this process, in the words of Francis (1976:169), is "exclusively the result of processes originating in the host society itself."[1] The group is dependent on the host society for the satisfaction of almost all its basic needs and is under strong pressure—both from within and without—to move toward a mastery of the host group's culture.[2] Although the ethnic society that has been constructed within the host is intrinsically valuable to its members, and although they make vigorous efforts to retain it, its major purpose is to establish a place for its members *within* the host society.

The Irish ethnic group formed along these lines and began to experience, to some extent, all of the subprocesses of assimilation we have described. But their efforts were met by an intense outburst by the native Americans, to which we return after a brief discussion of the German immigration during this same period.

As was true for the Irish, the majority of German immigrants were small farmers who had been driven from their lands by widespread crop failures and financial difficulties. The German land system resembled that of Ireland. As the population increased, large tracts of land increasingly were subdivided, and the farms became smaller and smaller. Also, the potato was rapidly becoming the main food, and the system of money payments had economic consequences similar to that of the Irish rent system. By 1845, the situation of many small farmers in Germany had become desperate. Weather conditions had been poor, and the price of food was rising. Many small farmers were deeply in debt. According to Hansen (1945:225) "overpopulation, hunger and employment were the topics that dominated all discussions of social conditions."

In 1846, the potato crop failed in Germany just as it did in Ireland. Although the crop failure created a social crisis in Germany, the situation was not nearly so bad as in Ireland because the Germans had not relied quite so heavily on a single crop. Nevertheless, many people were eager to leave before things became still worse. The fear that waiting longer might be a mistake was heightened by a widely circulated rumor that the United States was on the verge of prohibiting immigration. This rumor encouraged many people to leave immediately. Hence, even though hunger was involved, the "America fever" that developed in Germany at this time was not so directly a flight from famine as was the case in Ireland.

As large numbers of people in Germany became interested in immigration, several colonization societies were formed on both sides of the Atlantic. One of the most famous of these organizations made an effort to settle German immigrants near St. Louis in the 1830s. In the 1840s, another organization sent thousands of German settlers to Texas with the "avowed object of peopling Texas with Germans" (Hansen, 1945:231). And, in the 1850s, an effort was made to Germanize Wisconsin.

During this time, travel literature concerning America had become very popular in Europe, especially in Germany. In addition to guidebooks, periodicals, and pamphlets published and disseminated by travel agents, there were books written by those who had traveled in America or had already migrated. Most important of all were personal letters. These letters were generally very encouraging. When letters arrived, they were community as well as family affairs. They generally were read aloud in the midst of audiences, and their impact on the hearers ordinarily was great. The widespread interest in America within Germany and the increasing availability of travel literature led to the formation of village reading clubs throughout the country. At weekly meetings, members of these clubs would read and discuss various things concerning America. In this way, many people received information concerning the United States and were stimulated to consider moving there.

As in the eighteenth century, the efforts of the Germans to preserve their ethnic distinctiveness in America was very noticeable. And their reasons were the same. The Irish differed markedly from the Germans because of their prior familiarity with the language and the institutions of the Anglo-Americans and in their knowledge of political organization. Although the Germans were distributed throughout the United States much more than were the Irish, they, too, built up large concentrations in cities like New York. For example, by 1850, most of the large German population of New York lived in an area lying just north of the Irish district. Within this area, nearly all of the businesses were owned and operated by Germans, and German was the principal spoken language. There were in this district German schools, churches, restaurants, saloons, newspapers, and a lending library. And the Germans, no less than the Irish, formed numerous mutual-aid societies and benevolent associations to assist the immigrants in dealing with the complexities of the strange new environment.

One of the most important differences between the German and Irish immigrations concerned politics. Germany at this time was still not a unified nation. The governments of the separate states were controlled by hundreds of princes. As the economic conditions of the country worsened, there was an increasing desire, especially among intellectuals and young people, for large-

scale reforms. The demands for solutions to the problems of hunger and unemployment and for a more democratic form of government led to a series of
revolutions during the year 1848. These uprisings were crushed, and their
leaders, many of whom were distinguished people of property, education, and
high social standing, fled from the country and eventually made their way to
the United States. Although the so-called "Forty-Eighters" numbered only a
few thousand and represented only a small proportion of the German immigration to the United States during this period, they played an important
role in determining the reaction of native Americans to the German immigration.

Many of the Forty-Eighters were radical reformers who were disappointed
to find that the United States was not a democratic utopia. They were
shocked by slavery, by the movement to prohibit alcoholic beverages, and
by many defects in the operation of American democracy. They also thought
there were too many churches and in general regarded American life as
"half-barbarian" (Wittke, 1964:192). Additionally, they were in a good
position to make these views known throughout the country. By 1852, they
controlled half of the 133 German-language newspapers in the United
States (Wittke, 1964:193).

The radical reformers within the German American community, generally referred to as the "Greens," were sharply opposed by the large
majority of German Americans who reached the United States before the
1840s. This large group, referred to as the "Grays," shunned the "Greens"
and were not at all interested in the latter's efforts to bring about sweeping
reforms relating to the church, the presidency, the Constitution, slavery,
prohibition, and so on. The vast majority of the Grays were farmers and
craftsmen who had come to the United States primarily for economic rather
than political reasons. Many of them looked forward to a rapid assimilation
into the economic, educational, and political sectors of American life.

The question of assimilation itself created another kind of split within
the ranks of the German Americans. By the 1840s, many of the German
Lutheran immigrants of the preceding century had moved very noticeably in
the direction of Anglo conformity in their church services. The American
Lutheran church had substituted English for German as the language of
worship, and the traditional Lutheran beliefs and practices also had been
modified. These modifications led to violent feuds between colonial and
nineteenth-century German Lutherans. The Missouri Synod, formed by the
more recent Lutherans, emphasized the preservation of the German language
and the traditional beliefs and practices.

Another important development among the German Americans at this
time served not only to divide the German American community itself but
also to increase the suspicion of native Americans toward all Germans. A type
of organization that was closely related to the German liberal movement was
transplanted to America in 1848. These organizations (called *Turnvereine*)

initially were gymnastic societies, emphasizing both physical and mental development, but they gradually expanded their activities to include broader intellectual and cultural objectives, including reading rooms, discussion groups, libraries, and singing and dramatic societies. They became known as centers of radical reform, advocating many measures that were considered socialistic at that time. In addition to their support for social welfare legislation, tax and tariff reform, and direct popular election of all public officials, the *Turnvereine* were centers of abolitionism and militant opposition to prohibition.

Although the arrival of the Forty-Eighters and the establishment of the *Turnvereine* made German participation in the American political process a subject of controversy, this was by no means the beginning of German political activity in America. As early as the 1820s, the importance of the German vote was recognized by the Democrats, who made a concerted effort to woo German Americans in the presidential campaigns of Andrew Jackson. Since the Democrats consistently opposed making the qualifications for naturalization more difficult, the Germans were just as devoted to the Democratic Party as were the Irish. But after the Republican Party was formed in 1854, many of the Forty-Eighters switched from the Democratic Party and became very active in the new party's program. The Republican's stand on slavery and the treatment of foreign-born citizens were especially attractive to many German intellectuals and idealists. Germans, such as Carl Schurz, were so conspicuous during Lincoln's campaign for the presidency in 1860 that many observers have claimed his victory in the middle western states was due to a block vote by the Germans. Although this claim underestimates the deep divisions among the Germans, it highlights the extent to which they had become identified as active in politics (Jones, 1960:162).

Nativism

We have noted that from the time the Anglo-Americans became consolidated as the "native" or host group in America, their reactions to immigrants usually contained an element of rejection. On the one hand, immigrants were welcomed as needed additions to the labor force; but, on the other hand, their "foreign" ways and their competition for jobs and political power were resented and feared. We have seen also that the extent to which the host group reacted to immigrants depended on such things as the size of the immigrant group, the rate at which they arrived, their concentration, and the similarity between their culture and the Anglo-American culture. If a group arrived in large numbers and behaved in ways that the members of the host society regarded as "too" different, the Anglo-Americans became alarmed and reacted in "protective" ways. Under such conditions, the usual levels of anti-foreign activity were greatly increased.

Large numbers of Americans considered the first great immigrant stream of the nineteenth century to be an extremely serious threat to the American way of life and acted accordingly. The reaction included vitriolic attacks on Catholicism and the pope, on the pauperism and illiteracy of the immigrants, and on the political rights of naturalized citizens. It also included an increasing number of proposals that laws be passed to restrict immigration, limit the rights of immigrants, and increase the length of time needed to become a naturalized citizen.

As the Irish population in America grew in size, and many of its members moved into various political and municipal jobs, there was an outburst of anti-Catholic propaganda. Many Americans believed the authoritarian organization of the Catholic church was incompatible with the democratic institutions and ideals of American society. An increasing number of newspaper accounts, books, pamphlets, and speeches claimed that the Irish Catholics were emissaries of the pope who were working to undermine American traditions and overthrow the government of the United States. In 1834, for instance, the famous inventor Samuel F. B. Morse wrote a widely publicized statement claiming that the papal conquest was underway (Jones, 1960:150).[3] Anti-Catholic sentiments were expressed also in conflicts over the Catholics' opposition to the use of the King James version of the Bible in public schools and to their demands that state funds be used to support parochial schools.

The opposition to Catholicism was fused with a frequent, not completely untrue, complaint that Europe was using America as a "dumping ground" for its paupers and criminals. There was widespread fear that the immigrants did not understand the American political system and, therefore, could easily be manipulated by corrupt leaders. The Irish were accused of using rough, unfair, "un-American" methods to rig the outcomes of elections. Instances of block voting, electoral fraud, and the intimidation of voters were cited to show that the very foundation of American democracy was being undermined. Apparently, in some of the large cities, it was common practice for immigrants to be illegally naturalized the day before an election (Jones, 1960: 154). Moreover, even though the Irish were rapidly becoming naturalized citizens, they maintained an active vocal and financial interest in political affairs in Ireland. Their interest in foreign politics increased the fear that they were really not loyal to the United States.

Although the Irish were the principal targets of the complaints against Catholics, the Germans shared in the growing antiforeign sentiment of the native Americans. The Germans were feared because they were presumed to be revolutionaries. Even Americans who did not accept many of the generally exaggerated charges against immigrants and naturalized citizens nonetheless did not like the Forty-Eighters. They were considered to be atheists and radicals who were contemptuous of American traditions. The so-called Louisville Platform of 1854 was widely publicized as an example of German radicalism. The platform called for the abolition of slavery, the United States Senate, and the presidency. Even so, it was moderate when compared to the demands of the Communist Forty-Eighters, who advocated complete social revolution (Jones, 1960:155).

The fear of Irish Catholicism and German radicalism seemed to have other justifications. The members of both groups were (as usual) considered to be clannish and resistant to Americanization. Not only did they form all sorts of associations (including militia units and secret societies); many of their members worked energetically to support political reforms and revolutions in their native lands. It seemed clear to many Americans that these immigrants had little intention to become loyal Americans.

The idea that immigrants were destroying the basic fabric of American society was made to seem even more realistic by the rising controversy between the North and the South over slavery, westward expansion, economic policies, and so on. As the possibility increased that the Union would collapse, various political parties were formed to protect the rights and privileges of natives and to combat immigration and immigrants. For example, in 1845, the Native American Party was formed. This new party's stated purpose was to devise "a plan of concerted political action in defense of American institutions against the encroachments of foreign influence . . ." (Feldstein and Costello, 1974:147). The party's "Declaration of Principles" argued that the natives were rapidly becoming "a minority in their own land." And it recited some of the charges mentioned above: the newcomers were working for foreign governments; they were comprised disproportionately of Europe's unwanted criminals, paupers, and imbeciles; they sought unfair political advantage by organizing along ethnic lines; and they "offered their votes and influence to the highest bidder" (Feldstein and Costello, 1974:153). The Native American Party did not succeed on a national scale. It was soon followed, however, by one that did—the American or "Know Nothing" Party.

The Know Nothing Party's name came from the fact that its members answered "I know nothing" whenever people sought information concerning its principles (Faulkner, 1948:345). The party's slogan was "America for the Americans" (Jones, 1960:157), and its platform urged that only native Americans be permitted to hold public office. The Know Nothings opposed the admission of paupers and criminals into the country, and they believed that the period required for naturalization should be extended to twenty-one years.

The Know Nothing Party grew out of a secret nativist organization, the Order of the Star-Spangled Banner, founded in 1850. By 1854, the party had gained enough strength to elect a number of state governors and U.S. congressmen and to dominate several state legislatures. But the party crashed down as rapidly as it had risen. Its presidential candidate in 1856, former President Millard Fillmore, was soundly defeated.

The failure of the Know Nothing Party did not reflect the end of nativist sentiment so much as it did the increasing importance of the conflict between the North and the South. As the election of 1860 approached, sectional conflict overshadowed immigration as a threat to national life. Since the nativists who supported the Know Nothing movement lived in both the North and South, the party was split over sectional issues. The simple alignment of natives versus foreigners was no longer possible to maintain.

One other complication must be mentioned in passing. The nativists' cause in the North gradually had become allied with the abolition movement. Because the Irish were rabidly opposed to abolition, this alliance greatly intensified Irish-nativist conflict in the North but gave them some common ground in the South. The Irish were in direct competition with free blacks for jobs in both sections of the country, and the use of blacks as strike breakers heightened the desire of the Irish to see slavery maintained.

The cross-pressures on the Know Nothings were too great. When the Civil War finally began, the problem of union overshadowed the question of immigration. Numerous foreigners

> became members of both the Union and confederate armies and, as such, they were able to demonstrate that their loyalties and commitments lay in the New World rather than the Old. In both sections of the country immigrants responded to the call to arms as readily as did the natives (Jones, 1960:169–170).

But two incidents during the war showed that the immigrant groups had not disappeared into the American mass and that antialien feelings were still present.

In the first instance, General Grant ordered all Jews out of his part of Tennessee. It was alleged that they were responsible for illegal cotton trading with the South. Although President Lincoln required Grant to rescind the order, it is clear that the Jews had been suspected as a group.

The second incident consisted of a triangle of ethnic hatred. The Irish in New York, in 1863, staged three days of violence directed against both the white Republican establishment and against blacks. These so-called Draft Riots were a protest against the practice of permitting rich draftees to avoid military service, which the largely poor Irish were unable to do. However, most of the rioter's attacks were on blacks. A wave of anti-Irish reaction followed the Draft Riots, suggesting again that the war had not submerged all nativist sentiment.

Although the level of nativism was dramatically lower during and immediately following the war than it had been at the zenith of the Know Nothing agitation, most Americans still believed that immigrants should give up their foreign ways and adopt the basic pattern of American life as soon as possible. Anglo conformity had met the challenge of the first great immigrant stream, and the fears exploited by nativism remained alive, waiting to be whipped again into a fury at some later time.

Changing Patterns of Immigration

The Civil War created a comparative lull in immigration but certainly did not stop it. Well over 2 million immigrants arrived during the decade in which the war occurred, and still more arrived during the succeeding ten years. More significant than the sheer numbers, however, is that during the 1870–1879 period, a noticeable change began to occur in the national origins of the newcomers. Before the war, the largest numbers of immigrants were from Germany, Ireland, England, and Scandinavia. And the predominance of these groups continued after it. In fact, the numbers coming from Scandinavia almost doubled. However, the comparative increases among those arriving from southern and eastern Europe—particularly Italy, Austria-Hungary, and Russia—were far more dramatic than that. Although their total numbers were not large, almost five times as many Italians arrived during 1870–1879 as had arrived in the previous decade. Roughly seven times as many came from Austria-Hungary; and over ten times as many came from Russia.

The following decade, 1880–1889, was very significant both for the absolute volume of immigration and because it represents the high point of the first immigrant stream. More immigrants came from Germany, England, and Scandinavia than ever before or since, and more came from Ireland than at any time since the peak in the 1850s. At the same time, however, the immigrant stream from southern and eastern Europe continued the rapid increase started in the previous decade. The Italian immigration almost quadrupled, and the Austro-Hungarian and Russian arrivals were about five times as great as before.

During the 1890s, the second immigrant stream became absolutely larger than the first. For the first time, more newcomers arrived from southern and eastern Europe than from northern and western Europe. This preponderance of the second immigrant stream continued and increased during the next two decades. As shown in Table 3.1, each of the old immigrant countries had higher levels of immigration to the United States during the 1880s than in either the 1890s or the 1900s. At the same time, immigration from the new immigrant countries increased steadily in each of the decades shown. Although the second immigrant stream continued its domination during the decade 1910–1919, the previous decade proved to be its highest point.

Another noticeable change occurring during the rise of the second immigrant stream was that a numerically small but socially significant number of Japanese immigrants began to arrive. As we shall see, the continued large size and the shifting social and racial composition of immigration to America sparked a resurgence of nativism. When combined, these forces again lifted questions of racial and ethnic relations to a high level of national attention.

TABLE 3.1
Immigration into the United States from Selected Countries, 1880–1909[a]

First-stream (Old) Immigrant Countries	1880–1889	1890–1899	1900–1909
Germany	1,445,181	579,072	328,722
Great Britain	810,900	328,759	469,518
Ireland	674,119	405,710	344,940
Scandinavia	670,783	390,729	488,208
Second-stream (New) Immigrant Countries	1880–1899	1890–1899	1900–1909
Austria-Hungary	314,797	613,001	2,001,376
Italy	267,660	691,522	1,930,475
Poland	42,910	107,793[b]	—[c]
Russia and the Baltic states	182,698	490,101	1,501,303

[a] Calculated from U.S. Bureau of the Census, *Historical Statistics,* 1960:56–57.

[b] Does not include immigration figures for 1899.

[c] From 1899 to 1919 the immigration statistics for Poland were included with those from Austria-Hungary, Germany, and Russia.

The Second Great Immigrant Stream

When Ellis Island opened in 1892 as the federal government's receiving station, officials soon began to comment on the change in the "types" of newcomers who were arriving (Novotny, 1974:104). In addition to the Austrians, Hungarians, Italians, and Russians, the second immigrant stream contained significant numbers of Bohemians, Bulgarians, Croatians, Greeks, Jews, Moravians, Poles, Serbians, Slovaks, and Slovenes. All of these "new" southern and eastern Europeans seemed even more foreign to Americans than the "old" foreigners from northern and western Europe.[4]

What was so new about the second-stream immigrants? Their languages, of course, were further removed from English than was true of most of the old immigrants. Their religions, too, either were not Christian or were so different from the prevailing Protestant and Anglicized Catholic services as to seem un-Christian. Their dress, manners, and foods also seemed especially alien. In addition to these cultural differences, many Americans soon came to believe that there was something "unnatural" or "artificial" about this new immigration. Rapid improvements in ocean travel had greatly increased competition for passengers among steamship lines, and their agents were working feverishly throughout the southern and eastern European areas to encourage immigration to America. Hence, many more people could arrange passage than had ever been able to in the past. Furthermore, American employers were eager to tap these large pools of cheap labor. But these differences conceal another very important one: America herself had changed. The people who were leaving southern and eastern Europe were, like most of their predecessors, poverty-stricken peasants who were being forced off the land by industrialization; but these people, accustomed to life in small villages and farms, arrived in a "new" America, an America that was rapidly changing from an agrarian to an industrial and urban nation.

The frontier had been declared officially "closed" after the census of 1890. There was no more free land for immigrants to clear and settle. As the demand for land increased, so did the price; and the immigrants increasingly could not escape the port cities in which they had landed. Given the closeness of Ellis Island, New York, in particular, was flooded with immigrants. Even when they were able to leave port cities like New York, Boston, Baltimore, Philadelphia, or New Orleans, the immigrants usually wound up in inland cities like Cleveland, Chicago, Pittsburgh, or St. Louis (Novotny, 1974:133). The main forms of work available were as unskilled laborers on the railroads or in factories. In nearly all cases, the immigrants could afford only the least expensive housing available. Under these conditions, a variety of ethnic slums began to develop in all of America's major cities. Disease was rampant. Novotny (1974:138) reports that "nearly 40 percent of the slum dwellers suffered from tuberculosis." The promise of a new life in America thus became a bitter joke for large numbers of immigrants. Not surprisingly, many of these disappointed people returned to their homelands at the first opportunity.

Probably the most prominent group of newcomers and slum dwellers at this time were the Italians. Several factors made this group particularly conspicuous. First, of course, were their sheer numbers and the rate at which they arrived. Well over 3 million Italians reached the United States during the thirty-year period beginning in 1890. Second, a large majority of the Italians arriving at this time were from the southern regions. The people from these regions were overwhelmingly *contadini*—poor, ignorant, landless, peasants—who were escaping from a harsh physical climate, primitive living conditions, and an oppressive social-class structure (Lopreato 1970:25–33; Schermerhorn, 1949:232–237; Wittke, 1964:441–442). Third, and surprising to many, these agricultural people did not move in large numbers directly into farming occupations when they reached America. To be sure, the changing American economy offered fewer encouragements than previously for those wishing to leave the cities. However, despite their lack of industrial skills, the southern Italians seemed to prefer to remain in the cities. Fourth, the southern Italian immigrants consisted, to an unusual degree, of males who did not intend to remain in America—the so-called birds of passage who wished to make their fortunes and return with honor to the homeland (Lopreato, 1970: 14–15; Schermerhorn, 1949:246.) As Lopreato (1970:110) observes, the Italians' "zeal for assimilation in American life left something to be desired." Wittke (1964:442) reports that, in fact, nearly 1,216,000 Italians actually returned to Italy between 1908 and 1916. Finally, since the Italians were "too many and too late" (Schermerhorn, 1949:232), they had to accept jobs that no one else wanted and to occupy housing that was in many instances unfit for human habitation. The conditions in the Italian slums were frequently so terrible that they were widely publicized. Since many Americans did not understand the circumstances giving rise to the squalid conditions in the slums, the residents themselves were often blamed. As had been true of the Irish in an earlier period, it was assumed that the Italians were "just naturally" depraved.

Among the American mental images or stereotypes of the Italians, one received special notoriety. The Italians acquired a reputation for criminality. Newspapers throughout the country described in lurid detail the extortions and murders attributed to the Black Hand (Mafia). Many Americans feared that this notorious criminal organization had been imported by the southern Italians and now posed a serious foreign threat to democratic methods of assuring law and order. While there is little doubt that Mafia-like organizations did develop among the Italians in America, there is substantial disagreement concerning the reasons for this development and the extent to which there was anything peculiarly Italian about it. Among the first-generation Italians, for example, crime rates were no higher than among other immigrant groups; and they were actually lower than those of the native Americans (Schermerhorn, 1949:250). Moreover, many sociologists believe that the pressures toward material success within American society are so great that criminal behavior typically has developed among the second-generation of our immigrant groups (see, e.g., Bell, 1960; Lopreato, 1970: 123–134).

Peculiarly Italian or not, the idea that America's Little Italys were "seething hotbeds of crime" (Schermerhorn, 1949:250) was commonly believed. This belief helped to fuel a resurgence of American nativism during this period. It also had another effect of considerable interest to us. It helped to awaken among the Italians a sense of ethnic identity.

As in the cases of the Indians and the blacks, Americans tended to lump all people from Italy into the same category. But the immigrants themselves had a very different view of the matter, at least at first. The immigrants who left Italy came not as Italians but as representatives of particular villages, cities, or regions. The cleavages among the "Italians" themselves were very deep. The country had only recently become united, and the cultural and economic differences between the northerners and southerners were wide. The people in the north felt and acted superior to the people in the south. And even among the southerners, the social differences among the peoples from different villages and regions were pronounced. Consequently, as Lopreato (1970:104) has stated, "When the Italians came to the United States they imported a pitiful tendency to mistrust and avoid all those who did not share their particular dialect and customs." This identification of the individual with groups smaller than the Italian nation was evident in the residential patterns in New York.

Various Little Italys developed, each one exhibiting village, provincial, or regional loyalties (Wittke, 1964:441). As had been true for immigrant groups to America from the earliest days, this method of organizing enabled the immigrant to give and receive help from people like himself and to bask in the warmth and security of their friendship. Here a person could speak his native language, eat food prepared in the "proper" way, and escape the insults and inconveniences encountered in the "outside" world. The ethnic slum, for all its terrible faults, served in certain ways to shield and protect the immigrant. But, to repeat, the Americans did not usually recognize the distinctions that existed among the immigrants from Italy, and hostility and rejection were directed at the "Italians." They were called "Wops," "Dagos," and "Guineas" and were referred to as "the Chinese of Europe" (Dinnerstein and Reimers, 1975:40). Hence, in Schermerhorn's (1949:250) words, "The Sicilians, the Neapolitans, and Calabrians thus became conscious of their common destiny as Italians in America . . ."; or as Lopreato (1970:171) notes, the hostility of the dominant group "*Italianized* them."[5]

If the Italians were the most conspicuous portion of the second immigrant stream, the Jews were only slightly less so. Although Jews had been present in the United States since the colonial period, the largest wave arrived during the period of the new immigration. The earliest Jews (the Sephardim) had come from Spain, Portugal, and Holland. The Sephardim were few in number, but they had a noticeable impact on the subsequent development of Jewry in America. A second and much larger wave originated in Germany and areas dominated by German culture (Sklare, 1975:263). Many of the Forty-Eighters mentioned earlier were representatives of this group. The German Jews so outnumbered the Sephardim that they soon became the primary force within Jewish American life.

The rise of the German Jews was not due entirely to their numbers, however. Of great importance, also, is that the German Jews had undergone a high degree of cultural assimilation in Germany. The identification of the German Jews as Germans continued in the United States. According to Wittke (1964:329), the Jews participated in the activities of the *Turnvereine* and generally supported German cultural activities. Hence, the political and social characteristics of the German Jews were more prominent than their religion; and their religious practices were themselves much less distinctive than those of the Orthodox Jews who had arrived earlier.

Most of the German Jews were participants in the Reform movement. The Reform synagogue differed from the Orthodox in such things as using little Hebrew in religious services, seating men and women together, celebrating Sunday as the Sabbath, approving intermarriage, and omitting prayers for the restoration of the Jewish state (Schermerhorn, 1949:391). When combined, these factors stimulated the rapid cultural and secondary structural assimilation of the German Jews in the United States. The members of this group spread out across the country, and many of them rose rapidly into the middle and upper classes. The education, wealth, and social position of the

German Jews established them as the elite of American Jewry (Sklare, 1975:263; Wittke, 1964:327). This rapid movement toward the mainstream of American life suggested that in time—perhaps the fabled three generations —the German Jews would proceed through the remaining phases of assimilation and would disappear as a distinctive group.

That the full assimilation of the Jews did not occur may be due to the arrival of the extremely large and culturally distinctive Jews of the new immigration. Between 1.5 and 2 million Jews arrived in the United States as a part of the second immigrant stream.[6] Since most of the eastern European Jews came from Russia or countries under Russian influence, they usually are referred to as Russian Jews. Like the German Jews, the Russian Jews had at one time lived in Germany; and their main language was Yiddish, a mixture of Hebrew and German. Because of this historical unity, these two groups are both referred to as the Ashkenazim; but after centuries of comparative separation, the German and Russian groups were markedly different. Unlike the German Jews, the Russian Jews had been forced to live apart from the dominant group in certain parts of the country known as the Pale of Settlement. They had been oppressed by various restrictive laws (such as the military draft) and by organized violence (pogroms). Under these conditions, they had remained strongly united and had maintained their native culture and language to a high degree. Moreover, in contrast to the German Jews, the Russian Jews had every intention to keep their culture intact in the New World. Most of the men wore beards, they organized Jewish schools to teach the ancient religious ways, they held strictly to the Sabbath and the dietary laws, and they dressed in distinctive ways. Even the German Jews considered these newcomers to be social inferiors and did not wish to associate with them (Schermerhorn, 1949:393).

Like the Italians, the Russian Jews were largely trapped in the port cities of the East, especially the Lower East Side of New York. Despite the efforts of Jewish Americans to assist the newcomers in relocating to other parts of the country, most of them remained in the newly formed urban ghettos. The Russian Jews also resembled the Italians in having had little previous experience in urban living. Most of them had come from small villages. Finally, the members of these two new immigrant groups did not come to America with the desire to assimilate.

These similarities between the Italians and the Russian Jews did not, of course, mean that their reactions to the new environment were identical. For example, although neither group wished at first to assimilate in America, their reasons were quite different. The Italians, as we noted previously, typically did not bring their families, planning instead to make a fortune and return with it to the homeland. The Russian Jews, however, while bringing their families and planning to remain permanently in America, did not wish to give up the ancient culture they had so jealously defended in eastern Europe.

Two other differences between the Italians and Russian Jews are noteworthy. The first of these has to do with the psychological impact of American urban living on the members of the two groups. It is an understatement to say that thousands of people in all of the new immigrant groups were bitterly disappointed by the conditions they found in the New World. They were exploited at every turn not only by the Americans but by many of their own countrymen who "knew the ropes." They were forced to work at unfamiliar jobs, at low wages, and with no job security. Usually, they had no choice but to move into the tenement slums with their crowding, noise, filth, lack of sanitation, and crime. Understandably, many people felt beaten, homesick, and lonely. Both the Italians and the Jews were subject to these tremendous pressures. The Jews, however, were somewhat more insulated than the Italians. Bad as the conditions were, the Jews found in America a degree of freedom from persecution unimagined under the rulers of eastern Europe. They were extremely eager to make use of their new freedom and, consequently, embraced the opportunities that existed in public education and politics much more rapidly than did the Italians. Moreover, that the Jews had come over in families and had quickly erected a cultural tent, so to speak, gave them added protection against the insults and deprivations that were common in the lives of immigrants.

The second notable difference between the two largest groups of the second immigrant stream concerns the types of skills they possessed. Although neither group was really familiar with the requirements of urban-industrial living, more Jews than Italians happened to possess occupational skills that could be put to quick use in such a setting. Ironically, some of the varied restrictions that had been placed on the Jews in eastern Europe had forced them into activities that now were of some value. Approximately two out of every three Jews had skills that enabled them to work in the "needle trades" (Novotny, 1974:138; Schermerhorn, 1949:410). They began making all types of clothing, and the garment industry in New York was soon run disproportionately on Jewish labor.

While it was advantageous to the Jews, relative to the other immigrant groups, to have readily salable skills, they nonetheless worked under poor and oppressive conditions. The garment industry was so competitive that it was very difficult for its workers to eke out a living. They worked extremely long hours for very low wages. The work week ran between 80 and 108 hours per week and the workers seldom earned more than $200 per year (Novotny, 1974:139). In addition to the long hours and low wages was the further fact that the garment shops frequently were extremely dangerous places to work. In one notorious instance, over 140 workers were killed when a garment company in a New York building was gutted by fire (Novotny, 1974:141).

There was another deplorable side to all of this that affected the members of many non-Jewish as well as Jewish immigrants. Several industries, including the garment industry, subcontracted or "farmed out" sizable shares of their work to people who could only work at home, primarily women and children. The workers were paid according to the number of items they completed. Not only were the working conditions in these home "sweatshops" frequently worse than those in the factories, but also the contractors frequently exploited an especially vicious aspect of the piecework payment arrangement. They gradually reduced the prices paid for each piece of work, thereby forcing the workers to increase their productivity in order to keep their earnings at the same level. A frequent result of this method was to force women and children to work as many as eighteen hours a day (Novotny, 1974:141–142).

The human suffering engendered among the immigrants of all nationalities by the conditions of slum life in America is truly incalculable. Nevertheless, and despite great odds, the new immigrants endured. The members of the various groups gradually made niches for themselves in American society, and, eventually, as the story of their courage and determination became widely known, they became models of what one may accomplish in America through hard work and perseverance. At the time their struggle was most intense, though, native Americans generally did not see the new immigration as a confirmation of the American dream. They saw instead a massive renewal of the assault by aliens on the standards and ideals of American life. Among all their other problems, the new immigrants were met by the most serious outburst of nativism in American history.

Nativism and Restriction

The conflicts between the native Americans and the peoples of the first great immigrant stream subsided markedly during and immediately following the Civil War. Even when the old immigrants resumed, and then exceeded, their prewar rate of arrival, the hostility of the natives toward the newcomers did not revive proportionately. The people from northern and western Europe had proved they could and would fit into the dominant Anglo-American mold, that they were assimilable. Indeed, many of those whose fathers and mothers had arrived during the 1840s and 1850s now exhibited high levels of cultural and secondary structural assimilation and had for many practical purposes joined the ranks of the natives, while those whose grandparents had arrived during the 1820s and 1830s had completed the three-generations process and were undergoing primary structural and marital assimilation. The continuation of the first immigrant stream, therefore, no longer raised in the imaginations of the natives the specter of foreign domination. The beginning of the second immigrant stream, however, aroused doubts anew. As its volume first overtook and then surpassed that of immigration from northern and western Europe, many people became alarmed.

As we have noted, the peoples of the new immigration seemed to many Americans to be much more foreign than the usual foreigners. Their manners and customs appeared to many to threaten the very basis of Americanism. And their arrival in large numbers as a part of America's shift from an agrarian to an industrial economy made it seem that the newcomers were directly responsible for the many problems associated with that shift. For example, following the Civil War, workers began to organize labor unions in an attempt to assure employment and decent working conditions. These organizational efforts were, to put it mildly, not well received by the owners and managers of industry. Working men's strikes and picket lines were met by private armies and strike breakers. Sabotage, assassinations, and open warfare were increasingly common in coal mines, steel mills, and railroads (Rubenstein, 1970:29). Since many of these conflicts involved immigrant workers, nativist fears began to revive.

The bombing of Haymarket Square in Chicago in 1886 aroused widespread fears that immigrant radicals were plotting a revolution. Following the conviction of some foreign-born anarchists, the idea that all immigrants were wild-eyed radicals was disseminated throughout the country. Less than a month later, the leaders of a new nativist political party argued that immigrants were primarily responsible for the violent strikes and riots that had rocked the country (Jones, 1960:253). The nativists' demand that heavy restrictions be placed on immigration added impetus to a new trend in American policy that had started in 1882.

The year 1882 was a watershed year in American immigration history. The number of immigrants reaching America in that year has been exceeded only by the peak of the new immigration in 1907; 1882 is important, too, because the U.S. Congress expanded the restrictions on certain types of immigrants (which had been started in 1875) to include convicts, lunatics, and idiots. But of special relevance to us at this point is that Congress, in 1882, voted to exclude from America the members of an entire nationality! Until this time, the nativism of the post–Civil War era had not been very different from the prewar variety. But with the passage of the Chinese Exclusion Act of 1882, a new element had gained official recognition. Previous exclusions had been based on the personal characteristics of different individuals. But now, for the first time, American policy accepted the idea that an entire group may be undesirable because of its race or nationality. At first, this change in immigration policy represented a victory for the doctrine of white supremacy; but it led to further governmental actions, leading to the rise of the even narrower doctrine of Anglo-Saxon supremacy. From this time forward, America's traditional open-door policy was under increasingly heavy attack. The golden door was starting to close.

Assimilation and Race

We have stressed that the Anglo-conformity ideology of assimilation holds that the children and grandchildren of immigrants should leave behind their ethnicity and move into the mainstream of American life as rapidly as possible. Full assimilation is achieved when the descendants of the immigrants blend into the majority group and are no longer distinguishable from it. We have noted, too, that from the very beginning of Anglo-American society, these requirements for full membership have raised serious questions about the ideology of Anglo conformity.

During the colonial period, the status of the Indians and blacks was a subject of controversy. People wondered about the possible significance of differences in skin color, head shape, eye form, hair texture, and so on. Was there, for example, any necessary connection between the physical features of nonwhite peoples and the patterns of living they had developed? And since the white colonists were forcibly replacing the Indians and holding most of the blacks in bondage, was there any necessary connection between social dominance and physical features?

Then, as now, the principal line of division in answering the questions occurred between those who believe the social differences among groups mainly reflect hereditary differences and those who believe social differences arise mainly because of different environmental circumstances. This important—though imprecise—line of division between hereditarians and environmentalists has appeared repeatedly in human thought as people have tried to explain the differences in human behavior and patterns of living. The division between hereditarians and environmentalists also has figured prominently in the effort to explain and justify the unequal distribution of desired goods, services, and privileges. Many Greek and Roman aristocrats, for example, were sure that they owed their position in society to their "natural" superiority. Many common citizens and slaves, on the other hand, were just as sure that the aristocrats owed their positions to differences in opportunity, including the good fortune to have been well-born. In a similar fashion, from colonial times to the present, white Americans have been inclined to believe their social dominance is a reflection of natural differences in ability, while nonwhite Americans have been inclined to reject this idea. The doctrine of white supremacy has been the source of some of the most persistent, complicated, and emotional argumentation ever to occupy the attention of American citizens, policy makers, and social scientists.

Any discussion of the differences among racial groups, much less the superiority of one over another, requires that we give some attention to the meaning of the term *race*. So far, we have used this term in a general, colloquial way to refer to the main socially recognized color groups within the United States. In everyday experience, this rough definition seems to work well enough. People routinely assign themselves and others to racial categories without too much confusion. However, because the racial distinctions we make in everyday settings are based on visible physical characteristics (*phenotypes*), many people assume these distinctions are biologically significant, clear-cut, and fixed. In fact, the relationship of phenotypes to *genotypes* (i.e., genetic constitution) is quite complicated; and races based on phenotypes are much more arbitrary than most people seem to realize.

To understand why this is true, let us consider a definition of race that is frequently presented by scholars: *races are subspecies of mankind,* that is, they are subdivisions of the genus species *Homo sapiens.* The simplicity of this definition has much to recommend it. However, to grasp its full meaning, we must know something about the scientific classification of living things and human genetics. What, for instance, are species and subspecies? How do they differ? For our purposes, the following definition of species should suffice: a species is a group of individuals who interbreed freely with other members of their own group but who do not interbreed with members of other groups. Another way of expressing the main idea here is to say that a species is a complete or nearly complete *isolated breeding population.* By this definition, various species are quite distinct from one another, although to the untrained eye they may not seem to be. For instance, even though the Indian elephant and the African elephant may not appear to be very different, they actually are members of isolated breeding populations and, therefore, represent two different species. The distinction between these phenotypically similar animals is genotypically quite sharp.

The same cannot be said for subspecies or races. Although races, like species, are breeding populations, they are only more or less isolated from one another. In some geographical areas, in fact, they may exchange genes freely (i.e., interbreed). The boundaries of races, therefore, overlap and are blurred in many ways. The extent of overlap and blurring becomes evident when we attempt to answer the apparently simple question "How many human races are there?" Possibly the most common and widely accepted answer to this question has been four or five. For instance, in 1738, Linnaeus (Dunn and Dobzhansky, 1964:109) distinguished the African (*afer*), American (*americanus*), Asian (*asiaticus*), and European (*europeaus*) subspecies or races of mankind. In 1795, Blumenbach (Gossett, 1963:37) presented the set of labels that has been most influential. This scholar, generally considered to be one of the "fathers" of anthropology, distinguished the black (Ethiopian), brown (Malayan), red (American), white (Caucasian), and yellow (Mongolian) races. The classifications of Linnaeus and Blumenbach have in common an emphasis on the geographical location of the races they recognize, while Blumenbach's adds skin color as a basic criterion. Both systems are convenient and fairly comprehensive. But they do not lead to identical results. Both the numbers of races identified and the criteria underlying the identifications are different.

These differences reveal an exceedingly important point: the division of the human species into still narrower groupings introduces an element of human choice and preference far greater than exists at the species level or any higher level of classification (e.g., genera, families, etc.). The most frequently chosen defining trait, skin color, obviously varies by degrees. Some "white" people have skins that are as dark as, or darker than, the skins of some "black" or "brown" people. Furthermore, few "white" people have skins that are literally white. Hence, although the concept of race usually is taken to refer to categories of people who are set off sharply from one another, the most common defining trait (skin color) cannot be used to establish sharp boundaries among races. Since most of the other commonly employed phenotypical traits (hair texture, nose shape, etc.) suffer this same defect, any effort to establish sharp boundaries among the races on the basis of any of these common "racial" traits is bound to be imperfect and arbitrary. Blumenbach, indeed, appreciated this point far better than have many later observers. In his words, the "innumerable varieties of mankind run into one another by insensible degrees" (King, 1971:113).

This problem cannot be surmounted by combining the various traits, either. It is true that in the United States people who are judged to have "black" skins are more likely to have "broad" noses than are people who are judged to have "white" skins (i.e., skin color and nose shape are *correlated*); but some people who are regarded socially as white have broader noses than some people who are considered to be black. As a third trait is added, and then a fourth and a fifth, the probability that *all* of the traits will lead to the same racial assignments declines. For instance, although Swedes are thought typically to be tall, long headed, blond, and blue-eyed, a study of a large sample of Swedish people found only 10.1 percent of those studied to have *all four* of these traits (Loehlin, Lindzey, and Spuhler, 1975:22). Consequently, before we can agree on the number of races, as well as many other important matters regarding them, we must recognize that different rules or criteria of grouping lead to different results. This circumstance explains why scholars who have employed the criteria of geographical location, skin color, head shape, nose shape, and so on, either singly or in combination, have frequently arrived at quite different numbers of races. For example, in contrast to Linnaeus's 4 races, Buffon distinguished 6 races, Denker concluded there are 29, Coon et al. constructed 30, and Quatrefages listed 150 (Dunn and Dobzhansky, 1964:110; Loehlin, Lindzey and Spuhler, 1975:33). Pursuing this line of reasoning, Loehlin, Lindzey, and Spuhler (1975:33) conclude there may be as many as 1 million "local breeding populations" within the human species!

These illustrations run directly counter to the prevalent idea that the "races" people usually distinguish on the basis of phenotypes are quite distinctive, specific, unvarying entities. As Allport (1958:106) has observed, people tend to emphasize racial identities because they seem so fixed, so final. Nevertheless, people may be grouped into the same or different races depending on the criteria that are used as defining traits. There is no scientific way to determine which defining traits should be given priority. In the United States, of course, skin color is by far the popular choice. But aside from its convenience in social matters, what compelling reason is there to prefer skin color as a criterion of classification? Evidently, many people believe skin color reveals something of great biological significance about a person. It is inferred that since skin color is inherited, the genetic makeup of people of different colors probably differs in ways that have socially important consequences. The person's "outside" is taken to be a significant clue concerning his or her genetic "inside."

The plausibility of this viewpoint rests primarily on the centuries-old observation that family members usually resemble one another more in both appearance and behavior than do unrelated individuals. Before the discoveries of modern genetics, it was believed that family resemblances were inherited through the blood. By extension, increasingly large "families," such as clans, tribes, and races, also were believed to owe their resemblances to shared blood. If a member of these groups had no known "blood" relatives outside the group, then he or she was considered to be a "pure blood." "Pure bloods" were believed to be genetically like others in their family and to be sharply different from "mixed bloods" or "pure bloods" of other clans, tribes, or races.

Among scientists, the discoveries of Mendel and others revealing the basic laws of heredity have totally discredited the blood theory of inheritance. In the process, the way has been cleared for a much more scientific view of racial differences. Instead of viewing the characteristics of offspring as resulting from the "mixture" of parental contributions, Mendel argued that each characteristic was regulated by specific "genes" within the germ plasm of the parents. Of great importance was Mendel's recognition that the genetic elements are either present or absent; they do not "mix." This is true whether one is discussing the garden pea (as did Mendel) or dogs or horses or human beings. This means, among other things, that an element may be present within the gene structure of an individual (the genotype) but find no expression whatever in the visible characteristics of the individual (the phenotype).

The unexpressed or *recessive characteristic* is nonetheless there; it has neither mixed into the expressed or *dominant characteristic* nor been lost. For example, among humans, the gene for blue eyes is recessive to the gene for brown eyes; so one would expect the children of brown-eyed parents also to be brown-eyed. Sometimes, however, the children of brown-eyed parents have blue eyes, a result that can hardly be explained by the blood theory of inheritance or by any other "mixture" theory. The solution to this puzzle lies in the fact that both of the brown-eyed marital partners may possess the gene for blue eyes even though there is no way to determine this merely by looking at them. If a child happens to receive the gene for blue eyes from both of the parents, he or she will have blue eyes. In this instance, we see that large mistakes may occur when we use the visible features of people as guides to their genetic structures.

Another interesting, more complex application of Mendelian theory concerns blood types. The pre-Mendelian belief that people of the same family have the same type of blood has been replaced with much more specific (and lifesaving) knowledge. If a person having type O blood, for instance, needs a transfusion, it is not physiologically important to know whether potential donors are members of the same family. Indeed, the donors may not only be from a different family; they may even be from a different skin-color race. What is important in this case is the proper matching of type O blood with type O blood. This is a striking illustration of two important points: (1) conventional phenotypic classifications of the races may not correspond to inner differences of great biological importance, and (2) similarities of great biological importance may occur among people representing different phenotypic races.

The Mendelian approach to an understanding of racial differences may be extended to help clarify many other matters. Consider, for instance, this question: since type O blood may be found among members of the different skin-color races, how *frequently* does it appear within each race? Studies to answer this question have shown that type O blood is the most common type for each of the white (Caucasoid), black (Negroid), and yellow (Mongoloid) races. Moreover, differences among the races in this respect are not large. The following figures show the size of the type O populations within each of these races: white, 66 percent; black, 71 percent; yellow, 64 percent (Loehlin, Lindzey, and Spuhler, 1975:21). These figures tell us that if we know a given individual has type O blood, we cannot easily guess from that fact whether the individual is black, brown, or yellow (or the reverse). It would be slightly more likely that the individual was black than either white or yellow; but the similarities among the races here are much more noticeable than their differences.

Now does this mean that we may say there are no large blood-type differences among the races? It does not. If we switch our attention away from the ABO blood system to the Rh (Rhesus) system, we find that while the Rh-negative type is fairly common among members of the white race, it is fairly rare among members of other races (King, 1971:117). This finding shows clearly how a combination of the older phenotypic approaches to the study of race and the newer genotypic approach may help us to avoid many of the arbitrary distinctions that accompany an exclusively phenotypic approach. Genotypic methods do not attempt to establish rigid borders among the races nor to attribute to all of the members of a given population the characteristics that distinguish it from some other. To say, for example, that blue eyes are a trait of the Caucasian race is arbitrary. However, if one notes that blue eyes are more frequent among Caucasians than among other racial groups, then it is correct to say that eye color may be a racial trait. In the first instance, individuals are assumed to belong to certain phenotypic races and, therefore, to possess the characteristics of that race. In the second instance, populations are observed to possess different frequencies of a particular gene. This approach emphasizes that races are, in the words of Dunn and Dobzhansky (1964:118), "populations which differ in the frequencies of some gene or genes." A given individual, therefore, may or may not exhibit a particular trait that occurs with a specific frequency within the breeding population of which he or she is a member. The only way to assure that every member of a race possesses a particular trait is to define the races in terms of the trait in question. One might, for example, divide mankind into races on the basis of blood groups. We then might refer to the type O race, the type A race, and so on; but this way of referring to races, though biologically useful, is obviously very far removed from what is socially significant (Bierstedt, 1970:73).

Once again, we are reminded that race is both a biological and a social concept. Although people commonly think of races as sharply distinguishable biological entities, their boundaries are, in fact, set by social agreement. The traits ordinarily selected to form the basis of the social definitions of race are, of course, biological. Skin color, head shape, eye form, hair texture, and so on are biologically inherited; but, as we have emphasized, none of the biological traits that most people view as "racial" can be used to establish clear-cut lines of division among the races. The sharpness of racial boundaries in the United States springs from the fact that people react to these groups in quite different, socially important ways.

Race Differences

The doctrine of white supremacy, as mentioned earlier, centers on the idea that all members of the white race are superior to or "better than" all members of the nonwhite races. As usually expressed, however, the argument is more specific than this. Many observers have been willing to grant that some of the more "primitive" groups are superior to the whites in such things as sensory and motor ability, keenness of the senses, quickness of response, perception of details, and emotional sensitivity (Tyler, 1965:300). The Indian, for instance, has frequently been portrayed as having especially keen senses, while blacks are thought by many to possess superior athletic and musical abilities. But even if these "admissions" were true—a point to which we will return later—they do not really contradict the doctrine of white supremacy. This doctrine does not hold that whites are superior in all respects. It holds, rather, that the different races are "naturally" superior or inferior to one another in certain respects and that the different kinds of superiority exhibited by the races are themselves higher or lower on the scale of desirable human qualities. That is to say, the whites claim to possess "higher" superiorities! These "higher" superiorities do not depend on physical prowess or emotional sensitivity; they depend, rather, on intellectual abilities, such as reasoning, attention, foresight, and judgment (Tyler, 1965: 300).

Physical and emotional superiorities are viewed as more "primitive" than intellectual superiorities. Hence, the "admission" that nonwhite peoples are superior in certain "primitive" ways actually serves to support the idea that the presumed superiority of white people is the more important, the more human, superiority. For this reason, the question of intellectual differences among the races has always been at the core of the race-differences controversy. Buffon (Gossett, 1963:36), for instance, concluded over two centuries ago that although blacks are "endowed with excellent hearts, and possess the seeds of every human virtue," they possess "little genius." Even Thomas Jefferson, who was very much influenced by the environmentalist thought of European philosophers, argued that black people are brave, adventuresome, musical, and have good memories but are "much inferior" in the ability to reason (Gossett, 1963:42). Despite a later friendship and correspondence with the gifted mathematician Benjamin Banneker, a black man, Jefferson apparently entertained doubts about the mental ability of blacks until his death (Bardolph, 1961:31–32).

Throughout the first half of the nineteenth century, the debate over the relative qualities and standing of the races intensified. Slavery in America, and the various justifications of it, moved increasingly toward the center of political, moral, and scientific controversy. Scientists and nonscientists, proslavery spokesmen and abolitionists, Christians and non-Christians, all struggled over whether blacks were really human or were, rather, members of a separate and inferior species. The political and moral battles were decided, in principle at least, by the emanicipation of the slaves, the victory of the northern armies in the Civil War, and the extension of full citizenship rights to black Americans. The scientific and scholarly controversy, however, was only beginning.

The fusion of several intellectual trends during the latter half of the nineteenth century fueled the dispute concerning racial differences. Darwin's theory of organic evolution profoundly affected thought in nearly every field of human endeavor. Among social thinkers, the view that individuals, nations, and races were engaged in a struggle to select the "fittest" and that social dominance was a sign of natural superiority gained many adherents. If the white people in America were the most powerful and successful, then this must be a result of an inherited capability resulting from their success in competition with other races. This "social Darwinism" was given added impetus by Galton's studies of British men of distinction. Galton sought to prove that success in worldly matters was due to inherited abilities. Nature, not nurture, was responsible for the rise of people to eminence. No social barriers could suppress the naturally talented person, and no social enrichment could cause an untalented person to become successful. Comparing the races, it was clear to Galton that "the average intellectual standard of the Negro race is some two grades below our own" (Gossett, 1963:156). Galton also believed that the rise and fall of nations was strongly influenced by the extent to which they followed breeding practices that led to superior or inferior offspring. He feared that the "Anglo-Saxon race" was sliding in the direction of hereditary degeneration. His teachings supported various "eugenic" measures to "improve" the racial stock, such as the sterilization of criminals.

The arguments of Galton and the social Darwinists were highly compatible with a very influential interpretation of American history that flourished during the period of the second great immigrant stream. The conviction grew that the tall, blond, blue-eyed peoples of northern and western Europe were the modern remnants of an extremely talented race called the "Teutons" or "Nordics," who, in turn, were descended from the ancient Aryans of India (Gossett, 1963:84–122). This theory held, more specifically, that of all the "Teutonic," "Nordic," or Germanic peoples, the Anglo-Saxons had made the most important contributions to English and American life. Although this theory contained numerous—sometimes contradictory—strands of thought, it served, in general, to foster the impression that different ethnic groups, as well as different races, exhibited different inherited traits. The Anglo-Saxons, for instance, were believed to love freedom and democracy and to be self-reliant, ethical, and disciplined. The "Teutonic" or "Nordic" group, as a whole, had a special talent for political organization that enabled its members to form representative governments and create just laws even when they were a numerical minority. From this perspective, members of *certain* white "races" are destined to rule not only over the nonwhite races but over the other white races as well. Under this more specific version of the doctrine of white supremacy, the "Nordic" or "Anglo-Saxon" element of the white race is held to be superior to the shorter "Alpines" and the darker-skinned "Mediterraneans." This idea is crucial for an understanding of the white Americans' reactions to the new immigration.

By the beginning of the twentieth century, the ideas of Darwin, Galton, and the Teutonic origins theorists had been combined into an influential body of *racist* theory. Taken together, these ideas appear to give scientific support to the view that (1) races may be ranked in a hierarchy of superiority, (2) the white race is superior to the nonwhite races, and (3) the Anglo-Saxon or Nordic segment of the white race is superior even to its other segments.

The doctrines of scientific racism developed in the nineteenth century have had a tremendous impact in the twentieth. In the United States, they have lain behind restrictive American immigration policies that were enacted in the 1920s and continued into the 1960s. On an even more devastating scale, they were used by the Nazis in Germany to justify military invasions and the effort to annihilate the Jews and some other entire groups of people.

Race, Intelligence, and Immigration Restriction

Galton's studies of heredity and "genius" stimulated a search for ways to test people to determine their levels of "intelligence." It was assumed that each person was endowed at birth with a certain intellectual capacity and that this capacity could in some way be measured. Galton and his followers developed some tests of sensory discrimination and motor ability in an effort to measure individual differences in intelligence. Bache (1895), for example, compared the auditory, visual, and tactile reaction times of three small samples of whites, blacks, and Indians. He reported that the Indians were the quickest in all three tests, while the blacks were second, and the whites were last. Bache's interpretation of these findings is fascinating. He concluded that the slow reactions of the whites meant that they were more "reflective" (and, hence, more intellectual) than the members of the other two groups! Studies by Woodworth and Bruner (Woodworth, 1910:174), however, found that whites excelled in several kinds of hearing and other sensory tests. These authors argued that differences in health and training probably explained the results.

The effort to measure intelligence soon began to move away from such things as hearing, sight, and reaction times. The inventors of the most influential type of mental testing procedure, Binet and Simon, combined and organized various ideas to produce the first "scale" of intelligence (Klineberg, 1937:323). The idea behind the Binet-Simon scale is that a child may be said to have normal intelligence or an appropriate "mental age" (MA) if he or she can answer certain questions that most children of the same age can answer. For example, if most children can give their birthday by the age of five years, children who cannot give their birthday at that age are "behind" their age group in this respect. At first, the Binet-Simon scale was intended only to determine whether a child was feebleminded. In a revision of the scale in 1908, Binet and Simon attempted to determine the intelligence of normal children, also (Klineberg, 1937:323). Stern compared children's performances by dividing each child's mental age (in months) by his or her chronological age (in months) to obtain the child's "intelligence quotient" (IQ). Thus, if a child whose chronological age (CA) is 62 months has a mental age (MA) of 62 months, a quotient of 1 is obtained by dividing 62 by 62. To remove the decimals, this quotient is multiplied by 100, yielding an IQ score of 100. If children are "ahead" of their age group, this procedure yields a score above 100; and children are "behind" their age group if a score less than 100 is obtained.

By 1910, the Binet-Simon scales were being used in various parts of the United States. When the IQ score was adopted for use in a revised version of the Binet-Simon scale (the so-called Stanford-Binet), the conviction spread that scientists had developed a mathematically exact way to measure an individual's inherited ability level. It was but a short step from this point to a widespread acceptance of the idea that this tool could be used to determine how racial and ethnic groups ranked in intelligence.

As we have seen, the Binet-Simon scale was developed at about the time the peak of the new immigration to the United States was reached. At about this time, pressure was mounting to shift away from America's policy of excluding only individuals who were considered undesirable and toward a policy of restricting admissions on the basis of racial or ethnic identity. This new principle of admission, to repeat, had been applied once already, in the Chinese Exclusion Act of 1882. But until after World War I, the idea of excluding immigrants on the basis of their group membership rather than their individual qualifications had not been extended to any other groups (Ware, 1937:592). By 1917, however, pressures from those who feared "racial deterioration" and the inundation of American institutions by "hordes" of European and Oriental immigrants had reached a very high level. In that year, the federal government passed an immigration act that included a literacy test as a requirement for entering the country. In 1921 the Emergency Quota Act restricted immigration from all European countries to 3 percent of the number of each nationality present in the United States in 1910. This legislation was intended not only to reduce the total number of immigrants but also to reduce the number originating in southern and eastern Europe.

However, the reductions effected by this law did not satisfy the strongest advocates of immigration restriction. Consequently, in 1924, a still more restrictive quota law was passed. Several provisions of the 1924 law are particularly significant. First, the law reduced the quota for all nations from 3 percent to 2 percent. Second, it changed the "base" year from 1910 to 1890. Third, it included a "national origins" provision—to take effect in 1927—that clearly showed America's official preference for people from the countries represented by the old immigration. And, finally, as we discuss more fully later, it completely cut off immigration from Japan. The quota act of 1924 immediately decreased the number of immigrants allowable under the 1921 act by more than one-half. The golden door was kept only slightly ajar.

Although the legislative success of the restrictionists was due to many factors (such as a new increase in immigration from war-torn Europe), there can be little doubt that the growing popularity of the doctrine of Nordic superiority during the decades of the new immigration aided enormously in preparing the way for such acts. It would be difficult to overestimate the extent to which IQ testing appeared to provide scientific support for the ideas of superiority that lay behind the restrictive legislation.

The main body of evidence came from a massive mental testing program conducted by the army during World War I. This program tested over 1,700,000 men, representing the first really large mental testing effort. The data gathered during the program have served ever since as an important reference point concerning many crucial questions. What, exactly, is intelligence? Do the tests actually measure it? How independent of prior training and experience are the questions and tasks used in intelligence testing? Is human intelligence a unitary thing, or is it composed of different elements? What sorts of questions or tasks truly tap or reveal intelligence?

Although many different types of tests were used in the program, the primary results were based on the findings of the army *alpha* and *beta* tests. The alpha was designed for those who were literate in English. It attempted to cover such attributes of "general intelligence" as the ability to take oral directions, to solve arithmetical problems, to give evidence of "practical judgment," to recognize synonyms and antonyms, to unscramble disarranged sentences, to complete a number series, to identify analogies, and to supply information. The difficulty of many of these tasks, obviously, may depend to some extent on the experience and training of the person being tested. In some cases, this dependence is quite marked.[7]

The beta examination was designed for those who were illiterate or did not understand English. The standard instructions and procedures for the beta examination were intended to reduce to a minimum the subjects' discomfort in the examining situation, to elicit their cooperation, and to present a task that may be understood even by those who have had little formal training in verbal or symbolic matters (Yerkes, 1921:163). The tasks selected to reveal the attributes of "general intelligence" among those who failed the alpha or were not selected to take the alpha in the first place include such things as the ability to trace a path through a maze, visualize accurately the number of cubes in a picture, complete a series of x's and o's according to a pattern that has been initiated by the tester, match or substitute the digits one through nine with certain symbols according to a code presented by the tester, decide whether pairs of numbers are identical, complete a picture by adding some missing part, and put together the pieces of a puzzle to form a square.

The first impression given by the results of the army's studies seemed very clear and had a tremendous impact on scholars, policy makers, and the lay public. In general, black people and immigrants did not score as well on the tests as native whites even when efforts to adjust for the differences in schooling and experience were made.

In terms of the average (median) alpha scores, white recruits of native birth ranked first; foreign-born white recruits ranked second; northern black recruits ranked third; and southern black recruits ranked fourth. The beta score median differences were generally smaller and more favorable for the black recruits, but the rank order of the four groups was unchanged.

In an important contribution to the developing controversy concerning racial and ethnic differences in intelligence, Brigham (1923) analyzed the army data further and presented them as "a companion volume" to *America, A Family Matter* by Gould (1922). Gould's book argues for restrictions on immigration to the United States and against "racial mixing." Gould's and Brigham's books, when considered within the context of the rising anti-immigration sentiment in the United States and the establishment of "quotas" on immigration in 1921, surely did nothing to discourage those who endorsed the even more restrictive quota legislation of 1924. Brigham's analysis showed that on the combined alpha and beta scores, the foreign-born recruits from four countries—England, Scotland, Holland, and Germany—exceeded the average (mean) for the white native-born recruits; however, even the lowest foreign-born groups—from Greece, Russia, Italy, and Poland—exceeded the average of the native-born blacks (Brigham, 1923:124).

Brigham asserted that these differences among the racial and ethnic groups could not be explained by differences in social and economic backgrounds but were due to a superior "hereditary endowment." Although he recognized that school does have some effect on intelligence test scores, he concluded that "the results which we obtain by interpreting the data by means of the race hypothesis support . . . the thesis of the superiority of the Nordic type." (Brigham, 1923:182). This interpretation seemed to confirm scientifically that the immigrants from northern and western Europe were intellectually superior to (and therefore more assimilable than) those from southern and eastern Europe. The result seemed to prove further that white men were superior to black men even when the black men had had the "advantage" of growing up in the United States.

Brigham's extreme hereditarianism quickly drew the fire of environmentalist critics. The counterattack on the seemingly overwhelming results of the army testing program took three main forms. Earlier criticisms that the intelligence tests are influenced by factors other than native ability were elaborated. Certain questions of method were explored more fully; and the army data themselves were subjected to further, and in some cases, different types of analyses.

In the short run, these criticisms did little to diminish the enormous impact of the army test results. By 1924, America had adopted a national policy of immigration restriction based on the doctrine of Nordic superiority, a doctrine that seemed to be confirmed by genetic and psychological science. Most psychologists at this time were, in Thompson's (1934:494) words, "pretty much of the opinion that the inherent mental inferiority of (immigrants and non-whites) had been scientifically demonstrated." The hereditarian perspective on intelligence seemed unassailable, and most ordinary citizens were convinced the matter had been settled once and for all.

The matter had not been settled, however. The number of studies comparing the IQ scores of different racial and ethnic groups mounted rapidly. As their results became known, many scholars began to have second thoughts. Certain contradictions and inconsistencies began to appear; and many hereditarian thinkers began to wonder if, after all, such things as a person's social status, language, educational level, and test experience might make a *big* difference in test scores. Even Brigham reconsidered his earlier position. On the basis of a reanalysis of portions of the alpha and beta tests, he concluded that "it is absurd" to combine different intelligence test scores as he had done previously (Brigham, 1930:160). In a retraction that has delighted environmentalists ever since, Brigham (1930:165) concluded:

> The more recent test findings . . . show that comparative studies of various national and racial groups may not be made with existing tests, and (they) show, in particular, that one of the most pretentious of these comparative racial studies—the writer's own—was without foundation.

Brigham was certainly not alone in the conclusion just expressed. In a study of the opinions of the views of "experts" concerning racial differences, Thompson (1934) found that only 46 percent of those surveyed believed the hypothesis of race inferiority was "reasonable." Even more surprising was the finding that 96 percent of the scientists did not accept racial superiority or inferiority as an established fact.

During this time, Adolph Hitler and the Nazi Party had assumed control of Germany and were espousing a virulent "master race" philosophy. Their persecution of "racial inferiors," particularly the Jews, was being justified as necessary to establish the "New Order" of the "Aryans." Many scientists in the United States and elsewhere were shocked by the Nazi's unscientific, grossly exaggerated, and inhumane ideas concerning racial differences. Several scholarly societies published resolutions attacking the misinterpretations and distortions involved in these applications. In 1938, for example, the American Anthropological Association (Benedict, 1961: 196) issued a statement that "anthropology provides no scientific basis for discrimination against any people on the ground of racial inferiority, religious affiliation, or linguistic heritage." And a division of the American Psychological Association stated that "in the experiments which psychologists have made upon different peoples, no characteristic, inherent psychological differences which fundamentally distinguish so-called 'races' have been disclosed."

In the period just preceding World War II, therefore, scholarly opinion (though not that of the general public) had reached a position far removed from the early 1920s. Although there were still some scientists who accepted the hereditarian thesis uncritically, most agreed that both heredity and environment affected mental test scores in some complicated, poorly understood way. For most researchers, the question was no longer "Is intelligence determined by heredity *or* environment?" The question became rather "How do heredity and environment combine to produce the results obtained on intelligence tests?"

Gradually, several other significant changes occurred. First, the scope of the debate narrowed to focus principally on the question of black-white IQ differences. Second, a consensus emerged that on the average whites do obtain higher intelligence test scores than blacks on standard IQ tests (approximately 100 versus 85). Third, it was demonstrated that a large number of blacks exceeded the average intelligence test score for whites.[8] Fourth, it was found that some blacks scored as high on intelligence tests as any whites. In the debates among scientists surrounding the proper interpretation of these points, the weight of informed opinion shifted toward an emphasis on the role of environmental factors in producing these group differences.

Black-White Intelligence Test Differences

The entrance of the United States into World War II in opposition to the Axis powers, the practice of racial segregation by the armed services of the United States, and the outbreak of race-related conflict within the United States during the war all helped to intensify the discussion of differences in intelligence-test scores. An important focus of discussion emerged from reanalyses of the army's World War I test scores. The reanalyses had established firmly that not only did northern black recruits have higher average scores than southern black recruits but also that northern blacks from certain states had higher average scores than southern whites from certain states. While the average alpha score for blacks from Illinois, New York, Ohio, and Pennsylvania was 45.4, the average alpha score for whites from Arkansas, Kentucky, Mississippi, and Georgia was 41.1 (Garrett, 1945a:344).[9] Those who favored a predominantly environmentalist view argued that these results were due to the fact that educational opportunities for both races were greater in the northern states. Those with hereditarian leanings, on the other hand, suggested that the results could stem from a "selective migration" among blacks. According to this argument, among the large numbers of blacks who have moved to the North from the South, the more intelligent individuals have preferred to move, leaving the less intelligent behind. Special studies by Klineberg (1935) and Lee (1951) attempted to test these alternative interpretations. By studying the IQ scores of black children who had lived in New York and Philadelphia for different lengths of time, these researchers compiled evidence showing that the longer the children had lived in the North, the better their average scores became. These findings argued strongly against the "selective migration" idea and for the idea that an improved environment leads to higher IQ scores.

On the basis of these and many other more detailed studies, the general trend of scientific opinion has continued to move away from the conviction that black-white intelligence score differences reflect inherited differences and toward the belief that numerous environmental factors influence the test results. Even those reputable scholars who have continued to favor a hereditarian interpretation of black-white intelligence test differences clearly recognize the importance of some environmental factors. For example, Garrett, one of the most distinguished hereditarians, observes that the blacks from some northern states obtained higher scores on the army tests than the whites from some southern states partly because of educational differences. He emphasizes, however, that the southern whites as a whole scored higher than the northern blacks as a whole, and he concludes that "such differences cannot be explained in socio-economic terms" (Garrett, 1945b:495). Similarly, the author of the most nearly complete review of black-white intelligence differences ever assembled also favors a hereditarian interpretation. It is Shuey's (1966:521) conviction that all of the studies "taken together inevitably point to the presence of native differences between Negroes and whites as determined by intelligence tests."

Some forty years after the army tests of World War I, the battle over the proper interpretation of black-white intelligence test differences no longer seemed so important. The environmentalists had definitely established that the earlier hereditarian interpretations were too uncritical and oversimplified. Factors such as the test taker's social-class position, self-esteem, and motivation may influence the test results. An important result of the years of study and argument was that hereditarians had been unable to prove their point. The earlier conviction that intelligence testing was a scientifically exact way to determine innate intellectual capacity was no longer generally accepted among scholars. Moreover, during the 1960s, many social programs, such as Head Start, were based on the assumption that if blacks and whites had equal social opportunities, their test results would be equal or nearly so. But the calm that seemed to settle over the debate was illusory. As Dreger and Miller (1960:330) observed, "It is not so much that the issues have been settled as that the contestants have become exhausted."

A refueling process was underway, however. The IQ debaters had learned many things, one of which was that the question under consideration was even more complex than had been realized. Hereditary and environmental factors are meshed in intricate ways, and the effort to untangle their relative contributions to intelligence, if possible, necessarily involves quite technical considerations. Headway in this area required a redefinition of the issues. For example, a number of researchers began to focus more carefully on the possibility that racial differences in intellectual functioning may be specific rather than general. This suggestion was not new, but little research had been conducted along this line. Instead of assuming that blacks and whites may differ in the average level of intelligence, studies of this type attempt to compare specific intellectual factors or "dimensions" such as verbal comprehension, perceptual speed, figural reasoning, memory span, numerical facility, and so on (Loehlin, Lindzey, and Spuhler, 1975:177–188). These studies hope to discover patterns of differences among the intellectual functions of racial and ethnic groups rather than to attempt to rank the groups on a single intelligence scale.

The lull in the argument ended suddenly. The result of the Head Start and some other "compensatory education" programs had not been as good as most environmentalists had expected. In the winter 1969 issue of the *Harvard Educational Review*, Jensen (1969:2) declared that compensatory education apparently had failed and argued that genetic factors play a much larger role in determining intelligence than do environmental factors. In a measured, scholarly way, Jensen discussed the nature of intelligence, how it is inherited, the way environment affects the development of different individual genotypes, the statistical methods researchers may apply in an effort to unravel the effects of heredity and environment, and a number of other issues. With these points made, Jensen then turned to the problem of racial differences in intelligence. He acknowledged that "as far as we know the full range of human talents is represented in all the major races of man" and that, therefore, "it is unjust to allow the mere fact of an individual's racial or social background to affect the treatment accorded him" (Jensen, 1969:78). He stated further that "no one, to my knowledge, questions the role of environmental factors" on intelligence test scores (Jensen, 1969:79). However, he went on, "the preponderance of the evidence is, in my opinion, less consistent with a strictly environmental hypothesis than with a genetic hypothesis, which, of course, does not exclude the influence of environment or its interaction with genetic characters" (Jensen, 1969:82). On the basis of all the evidence reviewed, Jensen concluded that heredity's effect on IQ is about twice as important as is the effect of environment. Thus, even though environmental influences are recognized by Jensen, the thrust of his argument is that the average IQ differences between black and white Americans is best explained mainly in genetic terms.

A storm of protest, public as well as academic, broke following the publication of Jensen's review. The spring 1969 *Harvard Educational Review* contained several replies to Jensen by specialists; and that was only the beginning. Apparently, so many people believed the hereditarian view had been "disproven" that it seemed an outrage for a reputable scholar to revive it. The subject had become, as Jensen (1969:80) noted, "almost tabooed." But revived it was. The dispute was again elevated to a high pitch.

It is not possible here to summarize the many technical and moral arguments that have surfaced in this round of debate. In many respects, the issues raised recapitulate the central points involved in the arguments following the army's World War I tests.[10] One outstanding new issue, however, deserves comment. Jensen has constructed his argument in large part on the fact that most estimates of "heritability" for intelligence are high. Although it is incorrect to assume that a visible (phenotypic) trait is due either to heredity or environment, population geneticists have made an effort to calculate the extent to which the expression of different genotypes depends on the environment. The extent to which a trait in a population depends on the genotype within a given set of environments is called its heritability.[11] The estimates of heritability are based on studies of relatives (such as identical twins reared apart) and unrelated individuals. These estimates may vary according to the method that is used (Jensen, 1969:50–56; Loehlin, Lindzey, and Spuhler, 1975: 286–291). A heritability estimate of 1 means than all of the observed differences in a population are due to differences in genotypes. An estimate of zero means that all of the observed differences in a population have arisen from environmental differences.

Jensen (1969:49) reviewed 141 existing studies of heritability. The heritability estimates ranged from a low of .60 to a high around .90 (Jensen, 1976:103) with most of them being near the higher figure. Jensen (1969: 51) averaged the available estimates and concluded that "probably the best single overall estimate of heritability of measured intelligence" is .81.

The new issue involved here is this: even if it were true that the figure .81 is correct as a measure of heritability of intelligence, does this mean that the average difference in IQ between two populations (in this case black and white) is due mainly to inheritance? The problem is that estimates of heritability apply only to the populations on which they were made. They do not apply to differences between populations. This means, theoretically, that no matter how heritable a trait may be within a given population (e.g., the white race), the difference between two populations (e.g., blacks and whites) may be due to environmental differences. For example, the average height of Americans is noticeably greater than the average height of the Japanese. Within both of these populations, height appears to be highly heritable (approximately .90). Does this high heritability mean that the difference between the two populations is genetic? Not necessarily. The fact is that with nutritional improvements, the average height of both Americans and Japanese is increasing. But the height of the Japanese appears to be increasing faster! At the present rate of increase, therefore, the Japanese may overtake the Americans (or pass them) without any change whatever in the heritability of height (Institute for Research on Poverty, 1976:4). Hence, intelligence may be highly heritable within the black and white populations, while at the same time the difference between the two populations may be due entirely to environmental influences.

Jensen (1976:103–104) agrees that the above argument is strictly logical and is "theoretically" true. He nevertheless believes that this logically possible interpretation is not very probable. Are we to believe, he asks, that the difference between the average height of Pygmies (under five feet) and Watusis (over six feet) is due to environmental differences? The problem with Jensen's question is that the evidence needed to answer it is unavailable. It appears to be about equally likely that the average black-white IQ difference is due mainly to genetic differences or mainly to environmental differences (Lewontin, 1976: 110). Those who argue for one or the other viewpoint are guessing.

What, then, are we to conclude concerning the latest, most technical round in the IQ debate? It appears that the conclusion presented earlier as the generally accepted opinion of scientists has not been altered. The hereditarians still have not proven their point. What is known, to repeat Jensen's view, is that all races display "the full range of human talents" and that there is no scientific justification for treating the members of different races differently. Since we must proceed on the basis of some unproven assumption, why not choose the one that is most consistent with the main thrust of America's democratic tradition? When we cannot answer a question concerning human capabilities scientifically, it is wise, in the words of Boyer and Walsh (1974: 61), to "base our policy on the most generous and promising assumptions about human nature rather than the most . . . pessimistic."

We have seen that the development of IQ testing may be traced to the period of the new immigration and that the assumptions underlying this development contributed to a vigorous revival of nativism. When combined with several other contemporary ideas from biology, anthropology, and sociology, a scientific form of racism was created. This new racism seemed to confirm that whites were superior to nonwhites and that the Anglo-Saxon "race" was superior to the other white "races." This line of reasoning strengthened the conviction of many native Americans that Anglo conformity was the only acceptable route to Americanization; that many new immigrants were "unassimilable;" and that, therefore, immigration should be limited to members of the Anglo-Saxon "race." However, the rise of scientific racism and the increasing efforts to force people into the Anglo-conformity mold also stimulated an increasing opposition to those ideas, especially among immigrants. During this period, therefore, two old but relatively unpopular alternatives to Anglo conformity began to attract significant attention. The first of these is the melting-pot ideology.

The Melting-Pot Ideology

The basic hope of the melting pot theorists was expressed by Israel Zangwill (1909): "America is God's crucible. The great melting pot where all the races of Europe are melting and reforming!" Less poetically, the idea behind the melting-pot theory is that while racial and ethnic groups should move toward the culture and society of the host, giving up their distinctive heritages along the way, the host society itself should also change. The culture of each ethnic group should be blended into the culture of the host group. In this way, the heritages of both the minority groups and the host group would come together in a unified but new and different culture. Likewise, the groups would merge in all social matters. Like Anglo conformity, the melting-pot view embraces the goal of the disappearance of minority groups in America. It adds to the Anglo-conformity idea of assimilation, however, the further idea that the host culture also will "disappear," reflecting the influence of the groups that have been assimilated into it. The melting-pot ideology is thoroughly assimilationist but rejects the idea that the Anglo-American core should remain as it was before assimilation occurred. The goal of the melting-pot theory may be depicted as shown in Figure 3.1. Although complete merger occurs here, as in the Anglo-conformity ideal, the Anglo-American core is also substantially changed. Advocates of this ideology believe the new host society resulting from the blend of the previously separate groups would be stronger and more nearly consistent with the fundamental ideals of the United States.

One of the most influential and persuasive expressions of this viewpoint is the "frontier thesis" of the historian Frederick Jackson Turner (1920). According to Turner, the western American frontier functioned as a great leveler of persons and a blender of cultures. On the frontier, people had to adapt to the harsh conditions confronting them by devising and sharing solutions to the problems presented. People borrowed freely from the various cultures there and, in the process, developed a new blend. The new American culture that arose on the frontier contained significant contributions from the various cultures but was distinctly different from any of them.

FIGURE 3.1

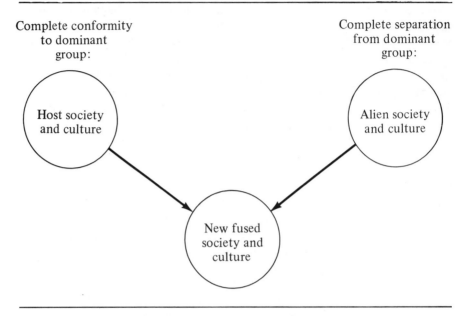

Ideal assimilation: the melting pot. (Arrows indicate the preferred direction of social and cultural change.)

When applied to the frontier experience, the melting-pot ideology seems plausible. As we have argued throughout, a new culture was created in America during the seventeenth and eighteenth centuries, and many different peoples along the Atlantic seaboard did gradually relinquish their previous heritages and social patterns and adopt the new. The crucial point, however—to repeat—is that the new culture did not represent a significant blending of the Dutch, Swedish, Norwegian, Scotch-Irish, German, and other cultures. Although the Anglo-American culture undoubtedly represented an adaptation to frontier conditions, it was still essentially English in form. Hence, the "melting" that took place was overwhelmingly toward Anglo conformity.

The melting-pot idea finds even less support when it is applied to the urban-industrial conditions that have existed in the United States since the beginning of the new immigration. As Glazer and Moynihan (1964:v) have observed in relation to New York, "The point about the melting pot . . . is that it did not happen." The same comment also seems appropriate for most parts of the country, although some instances of this type of group fusion may be found (Adams, 1934). As we have seen, even in the presence of high levels of cultural assimilation among different minorities, the other forms of assimilation have not necessarily followed at a comparable level. Moreover, the Anglo-American core, while changing in certain ways through time, seems not to have been altered in its essential characteristics.

There is one way in which the melting-pot ideology has been noticeably successful. Although the host group clearly prefers the Anglo-conformity ideology, its spokesmen frequently employ the melting-pot metaphor. For instance, St. Patrick's Day celebrations may be discussed as proof that America is a melting pot. On this day, the president may declare that all Americans are Irish. While such declarations may serve to create the impression that a fusion of the cultures of the natives and the newcomers has occurred, thereby altering significantly the host culture's society, it seems more convincing to argue that the St. Patrick's Day celebrations are a form of make-believe, illustrating less the fusion of two cultures than the dominance of one over the other.

Everything considered, it seems clear that the melting-pot ideology represents a possible alternative to Anglo conformity but does not, in fact, describe very well what has taken place in America. As expressed by Herberg (1960: 21), "Our cultural assimilation has taken place not in a 'melting pot,' but rather in a 'transmuting pot' in which all ingredients have been transformed and assimilated to an idealized 'Anglo-Saxon' model." Consequently, the melting-pot ideology has, to date, served mainly as a literary and metaphorical challenge to Anglo conformity as the leading ideology of assimilation in America.

The Ideology of Cultural Pluralism

While the idea of cultural pluralism is quite old in American thought, its formulation as an explicit ideology is usually traced to the writings of the Jewish philosopher Horace Kallen (Gordon, 1964:141; Meister, 1974: 53–61; Newman, 1973:67). Beginning in 1915, Kallen attacked the idea that it was necessary for ethnic groups to give up their distinctive cultures in order to be fully American. While all Americans should master Anglo-American culture and participate on an equal footing in such things as occupation, education, and politics, the members of each ethnic group should be free to decide for themselves how much of their ethnic heritage to retain. Neither the Anglo-conformity nor the melting-pot ideologies are acceptable goals for America. True Americanism requires us to protect the various distinctive cultures that exist within the United States. In short, the pluralist minority wishes to be equal to the majority in all matters affecting citizens but nonetheless to maintain its separate culture.

Although the general idea of cultural pluralism is simple enough, its exact goal is not as sharply delineated or as easy to describe as the goals of Anglo conformity and the melting pot. Unlike the other two ideologies, which assume or hope assimilation will end in a merger in which the distinctive groups will disappear, cultural pluralism is based on the idea that "full assimilation" will stop short of the disappearance of the respective groups. This condition involves the permanent existence of cultural and social diversity. For this reason, many people do not regard cultural pluralism as an ideology of "assimilation" at all; they regard it, rather, as a form of separatism. Indeed, in many contemporary debates concerning Americanization, "assimilation" and "pluralism" are given as the main choices.

Much of the confusion about pluralism arises because different pluralists advocate varying degrees and types of separation and merger. Hence, unlike the goals of Anglo conformity and the melting pot, there exists a range of possible pluralist solutions to the problem of dominant-subordinate group relations.

The problem of numerous pluralisms may be simplified by distinguishing two main forms or degrees of pluralism, one that emphasizes merger and has an assimilationist "tone" and another that emphasizes separation and has an antiassimilationist tone. For our purposes, complete or "perfect" pluralism of the first type exists when:

1. A minority group's members exhibit a high degree of cultural assimilation but retain a large proportion of their native heritage for use within the in-group. They are bilingual and bicultural. The differences of the majority and the minority are mutually accepted and respected.
2. The minority's members exhibit a high degree of structural assimilation in education, occupations, places of residence, political participation, and mass recreation. They have equal standing with the majority. Equality of opportunity is guaranteed. The law is color blind. It prohibits both discrimination against them and preferential treatment for them.
3. The minority's members exhibit a moderate-to-low level of secondary structural assimilation in the spheres of religion, health and welfare, and "social" recreation.
4. They exhibit low primary structural assimilation.
5. They exhibit zero marital assimilation.

This version of pluralism is depicted in Figure 3.2.[12]

Since the goals of this version of pluralism represent an acceptance of the Anglo-American culture as the "official" pattern of the country, and since there is no desire here to be separated from the society's educational, occupational, and political mainstream, it has been referred to as "consensual pluralism" (Horton, 1966:708) or "liberal pluralism" (Gordon, 1978:88). We will refer to it here simply as pluralism or cultural pluralism.

The model of "perfect" pluralism depicted in Figure 3.2, however, is not acceptable to all who consider themselves to be pluralists. Pluralists who are members of the dominant group, in particular, are likely to consider even the cultural pluralism we have described to be extreme or radical. Pluralists of this persuasion favor a still milder degree of separation in which minority-group members may maintain a few "quaint" cultural traits while generally conforming to the Anglo-American pattern. On the other hand, some pluralists desire a higher degree of separation than cultural pluralists may consider "ideal."

	Complete Anglo conformity	Complete separation
Cultural assimilation:	X (high acceptance of host culture)	X (low rejection of native culture)
Secondary structural assimilation:	X (high "integration" in education, occupations, residence, political participation, and mass recreation)	X (low "integration" in religious, health and welfare, and "social" recreational activities)
Primary structural assimilation:		X (low in out-group friendships)
Marital assimilation:		X (no out-group marriages)

Ideal assimilation: cultural pluralism (X indicates the alien group's location in regard to the characteristic in question).

They may object, for example, to the idea that only members of minority groups should be bilingual. Perhaps English should not be the only official language in all parts of the country; and perhaps the members of the majority should also be expected to be bilingual. Some who advocate an even higher degree of separation wish to establish separate school systems, separate economies, and even separate states within the United States. Whenever such separate institutions cannot be organized, the rights of the minority must be legally protected through the establishment of quotas in schools, jobs, and political offices. Equality of results, not of opportunity, is the watchword.

This second form of pluralism may be called "conflict pluralism" (Horton, 1966:708), "corporate pluralism" (Gordon, 1978:89), or "militant pluralism (Skolnick, 1975:573). In general, though, this type of pluralism appears to be what most Americans mean when they speak of separatism; and this is the term we will use here. Please notice, however, that separatism in this sense does not mean complete separation. The goal of complete withdrawal from the society is secession.

Evidently, the ideology of pluralism represents a broader range of ideas than either of the other two ideologies of assimilation. In the "ideal" form presented here, cultural pluralism does not visualize the disappearance of minority groups as do the Anglo-conformity and melting-pot ideologies. From the latter perspectives, pluralism's goal is not really "assimilation" at all but, rather, a specific form of separation. However, from the perspective of cultural pluralism, groups may retain their distinctive identities and still be "assimilated." From this viewpoint, American society actually always has been and still is a pluralist society and should strive to remain so. Many minority groups that are regarded as fully assimilated actually maintain a certain degree of separateness. As Gordon (1964:135) has stated, "cultural pluralism was a fact in American society before it became a theory."

Many critics of cultural pluralism have argued that however desirable such a solution to America's racial and ethnic problems may appear to be, it is highly unlikely to be a durable one. American life and tradition, it is said, keep constant pressures on racial and ethnic groups to "Americanize" in a way that is acceptable to the dominant group. For white ethnic groups, this means a full merger with the host group; for nonwhite groups, this means full cultural assimilation, with moderate-to-zero primary and marital assimilation. Under these circumstances, groups seeking ideal cultural pluralism may gradually lose their distinctive cultural patterns as they drift toward Anglo conformity.

The traditional pressures favoring Anglo conformity, please recall, do not represent the only forces acting to modify cultural pluralism. The forces of separation also must be taken into account. These constant opposing pressures favoring either Anglo conformity or secession suggest that ideal cultural pluralism is inherently unstable. No group, the argument runs, can stop just at the point of assimilation defined by cultural pluralist philosophy. The group must continue through the exact point of merger it prefers toward one or another of the two opposing poles. Either too much conformity to the dominant group's pattern or too much conflict between the groups is the inevitable result.

The discussion so far has attempted to show that the ideology of pluralism embraces varying degrees of merger and separation. As usually presented, the theory proposes a pluralism that is decidedly assimilationist in tone and intent. Even though cultural pluralism contains certain separatist elements, these occur mainly in the sphere of private relations. Advocates of this kind of separateness emphasize that it does not detract from the unity of the nation. They argue instead that permitting different racial and ethnic groups to retain their distinctiveness without discrimination creates especially loyal citizens. Diversity, not uniformity, is seen as the key to the maintenance of a vigorous democracy. As stated by Wirth (1945:355), its advocates believe pluralism is "one of the necessary preconditions of a rich and dynamic civilization under conditions of freedom."

Our discussion also has attempted to show that pluralism may be decidedly antiassimilationist in tone and intent. Separatists (i.e., conflict pluralists) do not accept the basic values of the dominant group, and they consider the levels of distinctiveness permitted under cultural pluralism to be unsatisfactory. The presumption is made that the supposedly "democratic" inclusion of the minority is in reality a subtle form of repression. True democracy, from the perspective of separatists, cannot occur when the majority has the power to control the destiny of the minority's members. The minority's ability to protect its rights depends, according to this line of reasoning, on a high degree of independence in economic, political, and educational, as well as in more personal matters.

The antiassimilationist view of the second form of pluralism—separatism —shades into the more extreme position of secessionism. In principle, of course, secessionism represents the ultimate challenge to Anglo-conformity ideology. One of the most important contemporary antiassimilationist theories, the theory of internal colonialism, is discussed in chapters 6 and 7.

In the present chapter, we have seen that the shift from the old to the new immigration led to an intensification of the pressures on minorities to accept Anglo conformity. This intensification was aided significantly by the elaboration of the doctrine of Nordic supremacy, which, in turn, was strengthened by the early results and interpretations of intelligence tests. Two ideologies of assimilation, the melting-pot ideology and the ideology of cultural pluralism, emerged in reaction to the increased demands that ethnic groups should rapidly merge with the dominant society. Both of these alternatives to Anglo conformity emphasize the advantages of accepting diverse elements into the mainstream of American life. In its consensual or cultural form, pluralism holds that minority groups may retain their distinctive heritages and at the same time live in harmony with the dominant society. In its separatist form, pluralism is less confident about the good will of the majority and focuses on what it believes to be basic flaws in the society. It sees majority and minority groups more as adversaries than as cooperating partners in a joint venture.

As generally expressed, all of the assimilationist views—Anglo conformity, the melting pot, and cultural pluralism—share a very important assumption: under "normal" circumstances, ethnic and racial groups in the United States should move within a few generations into the mainstream of American economic and political life. Groups that do not exhibit this pattern are considered to be failing to make progress. Hence, assimilation and success are seen as different sides of the same coin.

Various explanations for group differences in economic and political success have been offered. We have seen already, for example, that hereditarians believe genetic differences are paramount, while environmentalists point to the influence of different social and cultural factors. But there are profound disagreements even among environmentalists concerning the factors having the greatest effects on group success and assimilation. We review some of these differences in chapters 5–7.

Behind the differences among environmentalists, however, one major line of thought has stood out, in Metzger's (1971:637) words, "as a kind of official orthodoxy." The conceptual framework of this approach has been essentially assimilationist, and the principal object of research has been the prejudice and discrimination of majority-group members. Since the time this line of research began to gather momentum (soon after World War I), a large number of studies of prejudice and discrimination have been conducted. Some of this work is summarized and discussed in the next chapter.

KEY IDEAS

1. The greatest human migration in history occurred during the century beginning in 1820. During that time, millions of people came to the United States as parts of two great overlapping immigrant streams. The first great stream (the "old" immigration) consisted mainly of people from Ireland, Germany, England, and Scandinavia. The second great stream (the "new" immigration) consisted mainly of people from Italy, Austria-Hungary, and Russia.

2. Both the old immigrants and the new tended to cluster together with others from their land of origin. In the process, they formed ethnic communities for mutual aid and the preservation of their ethnic heritages. The members of both types of immigrant groups were subjected to hostility and abuse by the native Americans. In the case of both types of groups, the natives feared disloyalty, foreign "radicalism," and competition for jobs. In the case of the new immigrants, however, a new, "scientific" racism also played a crucial role.

3. Several lines of scientific thought during the nineteenth century led to the conclusion that there are a number of biologically distinct human races; but numerous problems exist in the effort to classify people into races. A basic problem is that the traits usually chosen (e.g., skin color,

hair form, nose shape, etc.) vary by degrees. Hence, the members of the races that people recognize socially do not necessarily exhibit any particular biological trait they are supposed to possess. Moreover, people in different socially recognized races may possess identical genes for biologically significant traits (e.g., blood types).

4. Nineteenth-century thought also led to the conclusion that human races may be ranked as innately superior or inferior to one another. It was assumed, in particular, that the characteristic that basically determines the superiority of one race to another is "intelligence."

5. Various efforts to measure human intellectual functions resulted in the development of "intelligence" tests that yielded a single score—the intelligence quotient (IQ). When the average IQ scores of different groups were calculated, it was found that white Americans of colonial or old immigrant stock generally ranked higher than did those of the new immigration. It was discovered further that whites generally received higher IQ scores than did nonwhites.

6. The efforts to define and measure human intelligence have raised many questions. Many scholars vigorously deny that an IQ score is an adequate measure of general intelligence. Even when IQ scores are accepted as having some well-defined meaning, however, there are many objections to the idea that the scores represent an inborn quality. Environmental as well as biological factors are known to affect people's performances on tests; and there has been no conclusive demonstration that the biological factors play the most important role. After more than six decades of debate, those who favor a hereditarian interpretation of the existing racial differences in IQ scores have not proven their point.

7. The belief that the white race is biologically superior to the nonwhite races and that the Anglo-Saxon race is superior to the other white races led the United States to enact restrictive legislation favoring the countries that contributed the most people to our colonial and old immigrant populations. In this legislation, the traditional American conviction that each individual should be judged according to his own merits was abandoned in favor of the idea that a person's worth depended on his racial endowment. People who were of white, Anglo-Saxon ancestry were considered "naturally" more desirable as citizens. The doctrine of white supremacy and the ideology of Anglo conformity were officially joined.

8. The most prominent views opposing the idea that Anglo conformity is *the* way to become an American and the idea that people of white, Anglo-Saxon ancestry make the most desirable citizens are the melting-pot ideology and the ideology of cultural pluralism.

9. The melting-pot ideology, like Anglo conformity, favors a complete merging of the majority and the minority. Unlike Anglo conformity, however, the melting pot should alter both the majority and the minority, creating a new and different blend. Although many Americans

give lip service to the melting-pot ideology, its impact on actual social arrangements in America has been comparatively small. People who adopt the melting-pot metaphor usually are referring to Anglo conformity.

10. The ideology of cultural pluralism opposes the complete merger of minorities with the majority. It seeks instead various degrees of recognition for the right of minorities to retain their heritage and separate ways of life. In its main form, pluralism stresses equality of opportunity for minority-group citizens plus the right to retain their cultural distinctiveness. In this form, the minority seeks to master the culture of the dominant group without losing its own culture. It also seeks structural assimilation. This approach, therefore, has a decidedly assimilationist tone even though some types of separation are involved.

11. A second form of pluralism, which we refer to as separatism, seeks not only the preservation of the minority's culture but a high degree of separation in many other ways as well. Advocates of this view may urge quotas in schools, jobs, and political offices. Or they may urge separate schools, economies, and governments. The resulting social arrangements would be pluralist but would involve a great deal more actual and legal separation than cultural pluralism. Although the emphasis here is on separation rather than on merger, the minority would still be an integral part of the larger society. It would not attempt to secede or to overthrow the government by force.

NOTES

1. The process through which people from the same geographical origins join together to form a new ethnic group within a different society has been called ethnogenesis. See Greeley, *Why Can't They Be Like Us?;* Singer, "Ethnogenesis and Negro Americans Today," pp. 419–432.
2. This type of group is called a secondary ethnic group (Francis, *Interethnic Relations*, p. 209).
3. The fear of Catholicism was, of course, not new. Adamic reports, for instance, that as early as 1728 a number of Pennsylvanians expressed alarm over the "Irish Papists" (Adamic, *A Nation of Nations*, p. 316).
4. The practice of calling the first-stream immigrants "old" and the second-stream immigrants "new" may be traced to the work of a congressional commission known as the Dillingham Commission. The report of this group portrayed the immigrants of the second stream as something new in American history who could not be expected to become good Americans as had the "old" immigrants. This report played a conspicuous role in the federal government's response to the second stream.
5. We see here a striking example of the process of ethnogenesis in American life.

6. The official statistics concerning the Jews are less reliable than for many other groups because some Jews are listed only as nationals of the particular countries from which they came. See Schermerhorn, *These Our People,* p. 389.

7. The alpha information test, for example, included such questions as "The author of the Raven is Stevenson, Kipling, Hawthorne, Poe" and "Mica is a vegetable, mineral, gas, liquid" (Yerkes, ed., *Psychological Examining in the United States Army,* p. 227).

8. Shuey is critical of the frequent claim made by environmentalists that there is a large overlap (25–30 percent) in the distributions of white and black intelligence test scores (Shuey, *The Testing of Negro Intelligence,* pp. 501–502). Her comprehensive review shows that overlap has ranged in various studies from zero to 44 percent, with an average near 12 percent. Nevertheless, even if one accepts the lower figure, the number of black Americans who exceed the white average would be at least 3 million.

9. One comparison of this type became the subject of a heated public dispute. The distribution to U.S. soldiers of a pamphlet containing this information was blocked by a committee of Congress. See Benedict, *Race: Science and Politics,* pp. 167–168.

10. See, for example, the exchanges between Walter Lippmann and Lewis M. Terman in Block and Dworkin, eds., *The IQ Controversy,* pp. 4–44.

11. It is important to note that the idea of heritability has no meaning when applied to an individual. Jensen states that it is "nonsense" to say that a given person's IQ is "80 points . . . acquired and 20 . . . points from his environment" (Jensen, "How Much Can We Boost IQ and Scholastic Achievement?," pp. 1–123).

12. For a related attempt to describe ideal or perfect cultural pluralism, see Murguía, *Assimilation, Colonialism and the Mexican American People,* pp. 109–110.

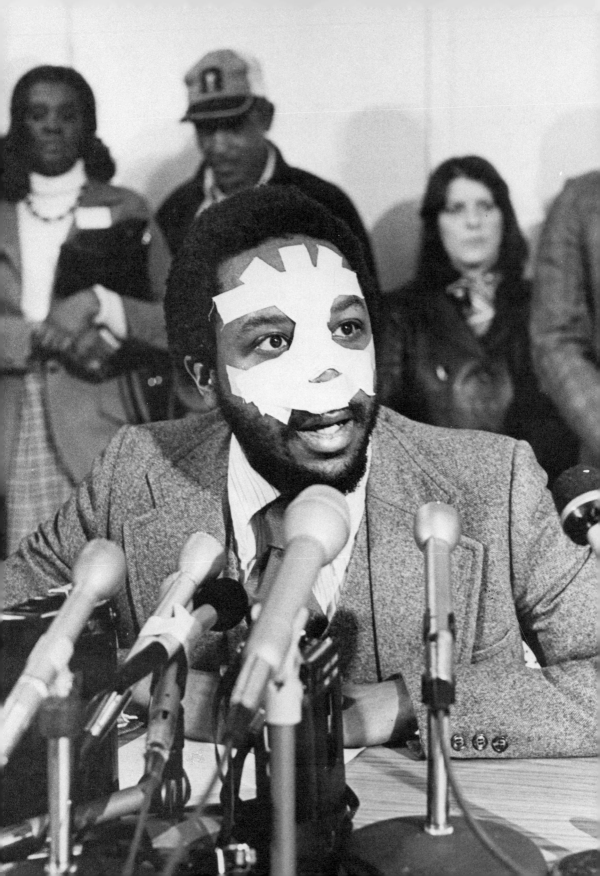

Four

Prejudice and Discrimination

> . . . we must sound the inside and see what springs set us in motion.
>
> *M. E. de Montaigne*

> Men begin with acts, not with thoughts.
>
> *William Graham Sumner*

Since the formation of the dominant Anglo-American group, its members have to some extent resented, downgraded, and harassed the members of all alien groups. We have seen, however, that aliens from countries of the old immigration have generally been more acceptable to the Anglo-Americans than have aliens from countries of the new immigration. And we have seen that regardless of their place of origin, whites have been more acceptable than nonwhites. Our analysis has shown, therefore, that the historical sequence of intergroup contacts in America created a particular pattern of social "layers" or strata among America's ethnic groups. Our analysis also has implied that the dominant group's efforts to prevent the "rise" of different ethnic groups in the stratification system were a reflection of the various group's "places" in the system. In other words, while the members of the dominant group have rated all other groups as "beneath" them socially and have tried to keep each group "in its place," they have reacted with greater *prejudice* and *discrimination* toward some groups than others. Why do people act this way? Why do prejudice and discrimination even exist?

As we turn to these intriguing questions, let us note at the outset that the key terms, *prejudice* and *discrimination,* have a variety of meanings and implications. Consider, for example, this situation: a white employer has the choice to hire a white person or a black person for a particular job. Both candidates are well qualified, but the white is chosen. Is this an example of prejudice against blacks, for whites, or both? Is discrimination involved? If so, in what direction? Now suppose, to continue the example, that the employer is overheard to say, "Most black people are lazy, and I don't like that." How does this new information affect our thinking? In addition to knowing about the employer's action in choosing the white candidate for the job, we now know something about what he or she thinks and feels. It now seems plausible to argue that the employer chose the white person because he thinks the black person may have possessed an undersirable quality, laziness. If this reasoning were correct, is the employer prejudiced? And has he or she discriminated?

Few people would feel entirely comfortable answering all of the above questions on the basis of the information presented. Among the more serious difficulties are that we have not yet agreed exactly how prejudice and discrimination should be distinguished; we do not know how prejudice and discrimination are related; and we lack several important facts about the specific case in question. The illustration nevertheless serves to highlight certain points on which there is widespread agreement. First, the term prejudice refers to an attitude or some other similar internal state or disposition, feeling, or opinion. The term discrimination, in contrast, refers to an overt action. Second, although racial and ethnic prejudice and discrimination may involve attitudes and actions that are intended to favor a particular group or its members, these terms usually refer to actions directed against certain persons. Third, prejudice usually is thought to precede, lie behind, or be the cause of discrimination.[1]

Several qualifications of these statements may be suggested. For instance, some observers have argued that an unfavorable attitude concerning a person or group should be considered a prejudice only if it is a judgment that is not based on fact or experience. This presumably is what Ambrose Bierce had in mind when he defined prejudice as "a vagrant opinion without visible means of support." Others have held that a prejudice must involve faulty logic or must perform some irrational function for the personality of the prejudiced person, while still others have stressed that prejudices are attitudes that are especially resistant to change. Discrimination, similarly, is used by some to refer only to certain forms of negative actions. Frequently, for instance, it refers only to negative actions that spring from prejudice. Luckily for our present purposes, it is not necessary to arrive at a precise or universally acceptable definition of prejudice and discrimination. It is important, though, that we explore the relationship of prejudice to discrimination; to do this, we need a working definition of these terms. Let us say, therefore, that a *prejudice* is an *unfavorable attitude toward people because they are members of a particular racial or ethnic group* and that *discrimination* is an *unfavorable action toward people because they are members of a particular racial or ethnic group.*

In the hypothetical situation of the white and black job applicants presented above, the possibility was raised that the white employer may have rejected the black applicant because the employer was prejudiced. This idea may be diagrammed as shown in Figure 4.1.

This way of viewing the relationship of prejudice to discrimination is, to repeat, very common. And it is easy to see why. Much of our everyday experience seems to confirm the idea that people are motivated to act in different ways and that their actions are an indication of the way they think

FIGURE 4.1

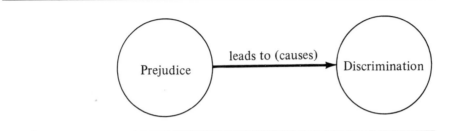

A *possible relationship between prejudice and discrimination. (Arrow indicates presumed direction of causation.)*

and feel about things. From this point of view, a person first has an attitude
or belief about something, and then he or she acts as a result of that attitude
or belief. Seen in this light, the relationship of prejudice to discrimination is
a special case of the broader relationship of any given attitude to any given
action.

Where does this line of reasoning lead? Let us assume that, as a nation,
we accept the "American Creed," containing the belief that people should
be treated according to their individual merits (Myrdal, 1964:209). Suppose
further that, on this basis, we conclude discrimination is bad and should be
abolished. The question now is, How are we to proceed? As a first step—in
purely logical terms—the answer to the question is "We must attempt to
remove prejudices." If prejudices can be removed, reduced, or prevented, so
the argument runs, then discrimination will diminish or disappear.

So far so good. But now we reach the hard part. How are people's
prejudices to be altered? Obviously, the answer given to this question will
depend primarily on what a person believes to be the cause(s) or source(s)
of prejudice. Nearly all social scientists assume that prejudice is largely or
totally learned. How it is learned, though, and the reasons for learning it are
hotly disputed. Many different sources of prejudice have been proposed; but
chief among these have been the process of learning one's culture (at home,
at school, and among peers), the process of psychological development (involving frustration, anxiety, personality "needs," and so on), the struggle of
groups to gain superiority (in income, prestige, and power), and the human
need to have a firm anchorage in a well-defined group.[2] This situation may
be diagrammed as shown in Figure 4.2.

The relative importance of the different sources of prejudice shown in
Figure 4.2 has been the subject of a great deal of controversy, and an
enormous literature has been created in the process. Some students have
emphasized only one of the sources, while others have stressed the importance
of viewing them together. Although we cannot hope to examine the many
issues that have been raised, let us consider some of the more prominent
points.

FIGURE 4.2

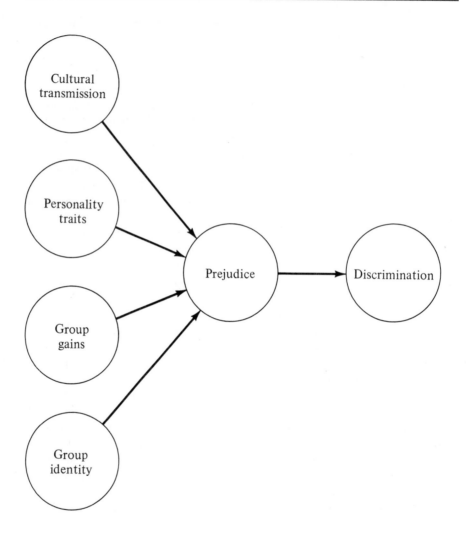

*Major direct causes of prejudice and indirect causes of dis-
crimination. (Arrows indicate presumed direction of causation.)*

Theories of Prejudice

The Cultural Transmission Theory of Prejudice

One important theory holds that children learn prejudice in much the same way they learn to speak a particular language, dress in a given manner, or use certain eating utensils. From this viewpoint, the building blocks of prejudice are contained within the society's traditions or culture and are transmitted to children in a natural way as they are exposed to those traditions in the home and community. Two aspects of a culture are particularly closely related to the extent and kind of prejudice that is found in a given society. The first of these has to do with the shared beliefs that the members of one group have about the members of the other groups in the society. The second has to do with a culture's prescriptions concerning the degrees of intimacy or "nearness" that one group's members should permit or desire from any other group's members.

To illustrate the first point, consider the kind of "information" that the children of Anglo-Americans are likely to receive regarding various other ethnic groups in America. Are they not likely to learn—by direct instruction, indirect instruction, and accidentally—that the Germans are persistent, the Mexicans are lazy, the Italians are artistic, the Irish are quick-tempered, the Jews are mercenary, and the French are amorous? Even the children of quite "liberal" parents are likely to acquire such ideas as they come into contact with a wider circle of people in the neighborhood and school. Moreover, the children usually learn that the members of different groups possess not just a single distinctive trait but a cluster of such traits. The extent to which these shared beliefs exist within a society's culture and are transmitted more or less intact from one generation to the next has stimulated a large number of studies of stereotypes. The extent to which a person accepts stereotypes is frequently used to determine how prejudiced he or she is.

The term *stereotype,* like the term prejudice, has been defined in a number of ways. Walter Lippmann has defined stereotypes as "pictures in our heads" (Klineberg, 1974:631). Ehrlich (1973:20) considers them to be "a set of beliefs and disbeliefs about any group of people." And Allport (1958:187) states that "a stereotype is an exaggerated belief associated with a category." As in the case of prejudice, these definitions call attention to certain aspects of the problem and ignore others. For example, even though none of these definitions specifies the direction of the stereotype, in practice, people use the term primarily to call attention to unfavorable beliefs. Furthermore, as a comparison of Ehrlich's and Allport's definitions shows, the term may or may not presume the accuracy of a given belief. Nevertheless, most people use the term to signify, with Allport, an exaggerated or false belief. It is seldom explained, though, just how false a belief must be before it is to be regarded as a stereotype. Indeed, even a person who rejects a given stereotype may state that "it contains a grain of truth." For our purposes, a *stereotype* is a *largely false belief, or set of beliefs, concerning the characteristics of the members of a racial or ethnic group.* It is assumed that the presence of a stereotype within a culture indicates that those who subscribe to it are prejudiced against the members of a given group. The stereotype assists to generate and to sustain prejudice.

The major research tradition concerning stereotypes began with a study by Katz and Braly (1933). These researchers compiled a list of eighty-four adjectives that may be used to describe the traits of members of a given racial or ethnic group. Each participant in the study was asked to select five words from the list that were thought to be "the most typical of the race in question." By this method, the words that are most frequently selected for a particular group are considered to be the elements of the stereotype for that group. If all of the participants in a study were to select the same five traits for a given ethnic group, the stereotype would be perfect. To illustrate, suppose each participant in a study describes the Germans as hard-working, intelligent, progressive, practical, and brave. These five traits would then comprise the stereotype of the Germans. Such a complete agreement, however, is extremely unlikely to occur. In a study on this point (Ehrlich, 1973:30), a total of twenty-three traits (including the above five) were mentioned.

To return to the theory that prejudices are learned as a part of growing up, to what extent do stereotypes exist within American culture? The evidence on this point appears to be very strong. Katz and Braly (1933), for example, found that more than half of the Princeton College students in their sample agreed that the Germans are scientifically minded and industrious; the Italians are artistic; the English are sportsmanlike; the Jews are shrewd; and the Negroes are superstitious and lazy. More than a third of the students also believed that the Germans are stolid; the Italians are passionate and quick-tempered; the English are intelligent and conventional; the Jews are mercenary, industrious, and grasping; the Americans are industrious, intelligent, materialistic, and ambitious; the Negroes are happy-go-lucky and ignorant; the Irish are pugnacious, quick-tempered, and witty; the Chinese are superstitious; the Japanese are intelligent and industrious; and the Turks are cruel. The researchers contend that these high levels of agreement cannot be understood as a reflection of the actual experiences of the study participants and must, therefore, represent the influence of beliefs that exist within the culture and are widely shared.

This conclusion may be qualified—but hardly contradicted—by a consideration of the findings of some of the other studies of stereotypes that have been conducted since 1933.[3] Two important qualifications are that the elements of a stereotype are affected to some extent by (1) contemporary events and (2) the kind of research method that is adopted. The effect of contemporary events on the composition of a stereotype has been illustrated clearly by studies of Americans' views of their allies and enemies during and after World War II. For example, public opinion polls in 1942 and 1966 showed that a large proportion of the people who were polled agreed at both times that the Germans, Japanese, and Russians were hard-working (Ehrlich, 1973:30). However, the proportion of the respondents who described the Germans as warlike fell from 67 percent in 1942 to 16 percent in 1966; the proportion who described the Japanese as sly fell from 63 percent in 1942 to 19 percent in 1966. Some other illustrations of the way stereotypes may change are presented in a study comparing the stereotypes held by Princeton undergraduates in 1950 with those found by Katz and Braly nearly two decades earlier. Gilbert (1951) discovered that the stereotypes still existed in 1950, but they appeared to have been greatly weakened. For instance, in the earlier study, 53 percent of the students believed the Italians were artistic. In the later study, only 28 percent of the students subscribed to this view. The results of a still more recent study (Karlins, Coffman, and Walters, 1969) confirm that stereotypes have continued to weaken but are still measurable.

The results of studies of stereotyping also may be affected by the research method that is used. Ehrlich and Rinehart (1965) compared the results of the usual checklist method with those resulting from the use of an "open-end" method. In the latter case, the participants were not given the eighty-four-item checklist but were asked instead simply to list the traits they thought certain groups possess. Consistent with the researchers' expectations, it was found that the respondents who used the open-end method listed fewer traits than those who used the checklist and that there was greater disagreement on the traits among those using the open-end method. The study also showed that the traits that were thought to be more characteristic of the various racial and ethnic groups were different in the two instances. To illustrate, over half (53 percent) of those responding to the checklist believed Negroes to be musical; but the trait that was most frequently listed by those using the open-end approach was dark-skinned (43 percent). Only 24 percent of the latter group believed Negroes to be musical. Similarly, among those using the checklist the trait considered to be the most characterisitc of the Japanese was loyalty to family ties (75 percent). This characteristic was mentioned by only 15 percent of those who used the open-end answer format.

Despite the existence of some variability in the results of stereotype research, depending on such things as the time of the study and the method used, it is difficult to escape the conclusion that a large number of Americans share a discernible cluster of beliefs regarding the traits of different racial and ethnic groups.

This conclusion has been supported further by a second line of stereotype research. Although children seem to learn racial and ethnic stereotypes primarily in the home and neighborhood, the mass media of communication have tended to reflect and spread the culture's stereotypes (Ehrlich, 1973:32). For instance, in a well-known study of popular fiction, Berelson and Salter (1946) found that Negroes and Jews were greatly underrepresented among the characters in the stories and were usually presented in stereotyped ways. Studies of the materials presented in movies, in magazines, on television, and in school textbooks have led to similar findings. Elson (1964), for example, has shown that elementary-school textbooks contain racial and ethnic stereotypes. His findings are consistent with the Anglo-conformity view we have emphasized previously. The ideal American is presented as a member "of the white race, of Northern European background, Protestant, self-made and . . . retaining the virtues of yeoman ancestors" (Elson, 1964). On the basis of the many studies that have been conducted, it seems safe to conclude that stereotypes are indeed an integral part of American culture and that people learn the stereotypes as an ordinary consequence of associating with other members of the society.

But is there any other evidence that prejudice is learned in the normal course of acquiring the American culture? The answer is "yes." A related but nonetheless distinct research tradition offers exceptionally convincing evidence that the very process of learning American culture teaches an individual specific prejudices. The basic idea of the line of research to be described is this: as people grow up in America, they learn more than that various racial and ethnic groups are thought to be intelligent, ambitious, dull, slovenly, and so on. People also learn that some of these traits are preferable to others and that, therefore, it is more desirable to associate with the members of some groups than others. People learn to desire social "closeness" to some groups and social "distance" from others. Stated more exactly, *social distance* refers to "the grades and degrees of understanding and intimacy which characterize personal and social relations generally" (Park, 1924:339). The idea "includes social nearness or social farness or any degree of distance between the extremes" (Bogardus, 1959:7).

The concept of social distance was discussed in 1908 by Simmel (1950) and was developed further by Park (1924). But the main research technique for the study of social distance was introduced by Bogardus (1933). Bogardus's method consists of asking people to consider a list of different kinds of social contacts they would be willing to permit with the members of various racial and ethnic groups. The types of social contacts shown in the list are selected to represent fairly evenly spaced points, running from a high willingness to permit social contact (e.g., "Would admit to close kinship by marriage") or, at the other extreme, a low willingness to permit social contact (e.g., "Would exclude from my country"). The number of the item (usually one through seven) representing the greatest degree of closeness a given person is willing to accept with the members of a particular ethnic group is the one used to calculate the group's average social-distance score. Hence, if every person in a study selected item three ("Would admit to my street as a neighbor"), the social-distance score for the French would be 3. Using this approach and modifications of it, students of social distance have shown that people who differ widely in such things as occupation, education, and geographical location are nonetheless similar in regard to the pattern of social distance they wish to place between themselves and the members of various racial and ethnic groups. The pattern discovered by Bogardus should not surprise the student of American immigration history. In general, people from the British Isles and from northern and western Europe (the old immigrants) were ranked near the top of the list. People from southern and eastern Europe were next in order, and people of the racial minorities were ranked near the bottom. In short, the general pattern of social distance that is transmitted from generation to generation in the United States is the pattern that was created through the historical sequences of intergroup contact that we already have observed.

As in the case of stereotypes, the conclusion seems warranted that the normal development of people within American society predisposes them to regard some racial and ethnic groups more favorably than others. We cannot know, of course, whether a specific individual's behavior will correspond to the answers given on a paper-and-pencil social-distance form, but we can assume, on this basis, that the person at least has learned the answers he or she is expected to give under these circumstances.

Personality Theories of Prejudice

Although the cultural-transmission theory of prejudice has received a sub-stantial amount of support, few people have supposed that, as presented, it is the whole story. Our focus so far has been on the information (or misinformation) that people learn about racial and ethnic groups as they grow up. Members of X groups are "dirty"; "they" should be kept at a great distance socially. But this is a narrow view of what a person learns during the process of growing up. It is possible that the kind of person an individual learns to be—the kind of personality he or she develops—is of greater importance in understanding prejudice than the kinds of information that the person "picks up" along the way. Why, for example, do some people accept the racial and ethnic stereotypes that are common in their home community while others reject these stereotypes? Why do some people fervently believe that their community's norms of social distance are correct and should be defended while others strongly disagree? And how, in particular, is it possible for members of the same family to disagree over these matters? Apparently, for prejudice to develop, something more is required than that people learn the content of their groups' stereotypes and social distance norms. It is one thing to learn that the members of a particular group are thought to possess undesirable characteristics and should not be selected as close associates. It is another thing entirely to feel strongly that these are matters of great importance. In the former case, the process of learning prejudice seems to be perfectly normal and understandable. Given the existence of stereotypes and social-distance norms within a culture, their acquisition is hardly more surprising than is the learning of the group's language or standards of dress. In the latter case, however, something more seems to be involved. It is as if the personalities of some people "need" or depend on prejudice. Many everyday comments concerning prejudice reflect this idea that some kind of conscious or unconscious personality need or problem lies behind racial and ethnic prejudice. We may hear, for example, that "if George didn't need someone to 'look down' on, he wouldn't say such things." Other comments may assume that a person's prejudice stems from a feeling of anxiety, fear, uncertainty, or guilt.

Such observations rest on the idea that prejudice is more than a matter of correct information or ignorance. They suggest, instead, that prejudice performs some important functions for the personality of the prejudiced person; it serves in some way to help the person cope with his inner conflicts and tensions. Although this type of theorizing about the inner causes of prejudice is now commonplace, the basic ideas have been developed primarily in the personality theories of various scholars.

One of the most popular of these theories is related to the widespread observation that a person who is frustrated in some way is likely to vent his anger in an aggressive action even if the action is only verbal (e.g., shouting, name calling, or cursing). As Baron (1977:22) notes, it is quite likely that most people consider frustration to be the main cause of human aggression.

The scholarly version of this idea, called the *frustration-aggression hypothesis,* is generally traced to the important work of Dollard et al. (1939). These researchers argued that (1) frustration always leads to aggression, and (2) aggression is always the result of frustration. Stated in this way, however, a number of difficulties arise. For example, common observation reveals that many people who seem to be frustrated do not, in fact, engage in aggressive behavior. Many frustrations (such as a rejection by a sweetheart) may result in despair rather than anger. This commonsense conclusion has been supported by numerous laboratory studies showing that while frustration is sometimes followed by aggression and that aggression is sometimes preceded by frustration, the two things are not always connected. As Berkowitz (1969: 2) and Baron (1977:22) observe, the original formulation of the hypothesis was too simple and sweeping. For these reasons, Miller (1941:30), one of the authors of the original statement, quickly revised the hypothesis and conceded that aggression could be caused by things other than frustration.

Since then, many refinements of the hypothesis (and various definitions of frustration) have been proposed and tested; and many different issues have arisen in the process. Buss (1966), for instance, has argued that attack is a much more potent cause of aggression than is frustration. While Berkowitz (1969) has maintained that although frustration alone probably will not lead to aggression, aggression is likely to result if the frustration occurs in the presence of certain other factors (called *aggressive cues*). Berkowitz argues that frustration creates an emotional readiness to be aggressive but that this readiness generally will not be translated into action unless an aggressive cue is present.

A number of studies have been designed to test this controversial revision of the frustration-aggression hypothesis. To illustrate, Geen and Berkowitz (1967) have studied the reactions of college students who were given puzzles to complete. Although the experiment is too complex to describe fully here, the central point grew out of the fact that some students (the experimental subjects) were given insoluble (hence, frustrating) puzzles to work with, while other students (confederates of the experimenters) were given puzzles that looked the same but were not. Each experimental subject was paired with a confederate, and both students were asked to solve the puzzle in one another's presence. In some cases, the confederate (who, of course, solved the puzzle) paid no attention to the unsuccessful experimental subject; in other cases, however, the confederate openly criticized the subject and boasted of his own cleverness. In both situations, the confederate was introduced as "Mr. Anderson." In half the cases, he was "Kirk Anderson"; in the other half, he was "Bob Anderson."

When the puzzle task ended, half of each group of students was shown a violent prize-fight film starring the actor Kirk Douglas, and the other half was shown a film about a foot race. Still later in the experiment, the subjects were told they had been selected to teach the other member of their pair (the confederate) a certain task. They were told, too, that they could administer electric shocks (in a special apparatus) whenever the "students" made mistakes. One of the several predictions of this study was that the confederates who had been introduced as "Kirk" would be given higher levels of shock from the frustrated subjects than would those introduced as "Bob." The association of the name Kirk with the prize fighter in the film was expected to serve as an aggressive cue. This prediction was shown to be correct, thus lending support to the idea that frustration is more likely to lead to aggression if it occurs in the presence of an aggressive cue.

Evidently, the frustration-aggression hypothesis is no longer as it was in 1939; however, the core idea—that frustration is related to aggression—has been amply supported. But what has all this to do with prejudice? Dollard et al. (1939) recognized that people frequently do not behave aggressively immediately after being frustrated. Many things may prevent a person from doing so. To use a familiar example, a person who causes frustration may be too powerful (e.g., one's boss) to attack directly or openly. In such cases, the frustration and hostility experienced by the individual may have no feasible outlet. It may, instead, be awaiting a safe or convenient substitute target. This situation leads to the frequent admonition to an angry person that he or she should not "take it out on me" (or the dog or your brother, etc.). Such a safe, convenient substitute target is called a "scapegoat" (Allport, 1958:236). Since the hostility that lies behind scapegoating may be released against a wide variety of targets, it has been described as "free-floating" (Allport, 1958:337).

Let us accept the general argument that all people experience various frustrations in their daily lives, that these frustrations give rise to hostile feelings, that the hostile feelings may lead to aggressive behavior, and that the aggression may be aimed at a substitute target. Now—with only one addition to this general line of reasoning—we may apply it to the problem of understanding prejudice. Ethnic groups in America, especially the newest arrivals and those in the racial minorities, have frequently afforded a weak and convenient target—scapegoats—for the free-floating aggressions of the majority. In this way, prejudice serves to assist the majority-group members to displace (and possibly to "drain off") their accumulated feelings without exposing themselves to a high risk of retaliation.[4]

As stated so far, the frustration-aggression hypothesis seems to fit well with much everyday experience, as well as with the more formal evidence of many studies. Still, a number of questions remain unanswered. For instance, isn't it the case that when we displace our frustrations through aggression against an innocent person or animal, we usually recognize, if only dimly, that we have not really attacked the true target of our anger? Scapegoating may serve briefly to relieve a sense of frustration, but if the real source remains unaltered, how effective can such a displacement be? Even though we may momentarily feel better after such an outburst, do we not later feel foolish or guilty? An affirmative answer to these questions may seem to suggest that a person probably would soon abandon such as ineffective method of coping with frustration and that, therefore, prejudice stemming from this source would not be very important. However, the frustration-aggression theory points in a different direction. Although the theory assumes that scapegoating creates at least some guilt in the prejudiced person, it does not assume the prejudiced person will discontinue displacement as a method of coping with frustration. The difficulty here (according to the theory) is that the guilt produced by scapegoating—the sense that one may have committed an injustice—is then itself a problem. If people believe they have acted unjustly, then their guilt may be accompanied by a fear that the injured person will retaliate. The combination of guilt and fear now becomes a new source of frustration, and this new source of frustration, like the original source, arouses aggressive feelings.[5] Once again, the fuel has been provided for a certain amount of free-floating hostility and a new round of scapegoating. In this way, a vicious circle is created. Displaced aggression appears to "feed upon" itself and to grow, rather than diminish, in strength. The "need" of prejudiced people to cope with the frustrations in their daily lives is met by directing the resulting hostility toward the members of minority groups.

Once the members of a minority group are chosen as targets, the displacement of aggression may also lead to an increase in stereotyping, as well as frustration. The possible reasons for this go well beyond our present argument; however, we may notice in passing an intriguing explanation that has attracted much interest since it was first proposed by Festinger (1957).

Festinger is one of many so-called balance theorists who maintain that humans are more comfortable psychologically when their attitudes, beliefs, or ideas ("cognitive elements") are consistent ("consonant") than when they are inconsistent ("dissonant"). The presence of dissonance, therefore, creates psychological pressure within people to change their attitudes, beliefs, or ideas. According to Festinger (1957:30), "the existence of dissonance, being psychologically uncomfortable, will motivate the person to try to reduce the dissonance and achieve consonance." For instance, if a person's behavior (e.g., smoking) is inconsistent with his beliefs (e.g., smoking is a health hazard), he might reduce dissonance either by giving up smoking or by convincing himself that smoking is not *really* bad for him. Either way, the dissonant cognitive elements will become consistent, and the psychological pressure to *do* something will be diminished. Since for many people it is more difficult to give up smoking than to reject the arguments against it, the latter is a frequent outcome. Similarly, if a frustrated person displaces hostility on to minority-group members whom he knows had nothing to do with the frustration, dissonance is created.

Two cognitive elements—the knowledge that an aggressive action has occurred and an awareness that the target was innocent—are not in harmony. Consequently, psychological discomfort results. Since the behavior already has occurred and, thus, cannot be changed, the aggressor may reduce his cognitive dissonance by accepting stereotyped beliefs about his victim. The more frequently the individual displaces hostility in this way, the more occasions he will have for dissonance reduction, and the greater will be the psychological pressure to accept the prevailing stereotypes about the victim. Whether an individual actually does accept the stereotypes, however, or discontinues his aggression instead is a very complex matter, depending on much more than we can discuss here. Later on in this chapter, we refer again to the theory of cognitive dissonance.

Everything considered, the possibility that frustration may lead to aggressive actions against minority groups makes a good deal of sense. It does, however, have some serious shortcomings. For instance, the theory does not explain why some frustrated people displace aggression on to the members of minority groups while some other, perhaps even more frustrated, people do not do so (Allport, 1958:210, 332). Similarly, the theory does not explain why some frustrated people vent their anger on the members of a particular ethnic minority while others select a completely different group as a target. But the problems do not end here. There is ample reason to question the idea that when an ethnic target is chosen, the group in question will be relatively defenseless—that, in Allport's (1958:332) phrase, the scapegoat will be a "safe goat." The members of ethnic minorities also experience frustration and become filled with aggressive impulses. Does this mean that they do not harbor prejudices against the majority or find ways to vent their anger against the majority? There is every reason to believe that some black Americans, Indian Americans, Jewish Americans, and so on, hate Anglo-Americans just as vigorously as the other way around. Moreover, the hostility that is felt against the members of the dominant group may be expressed in acts ranging from subtle sabotage to ghetto riots (Simpson and Yinger, 1972: 218–219).

We should note one final limitation of the frustration-aggression theory of prejudice. Its emphasis on the displacement of hostility turns attention away from the fact that racial and ethnic groups actually do compete with one another for many desired ends—such things as property, prestige, and power; and in the process of this competition, the groups actually do frustrate one another's ambitions to a greater or lesser degree. Our previous discussions of the reactions of Indian Americans to the successive waves of newcomers afford numerous examples of such realistic group conflicts and the antagonisms precipitated by them. Under these circumstances, it is not always easy or even possible to sort out the extent to which the negative beliefs of each group have some basis in fact. Each group in the competition, of course, will claim that the other group richly deserves to be hated. And we may assume on the basis of our review of immigration to America that the charges and countercharges are likely to be exaggerated and to be generalized unfairly to each and every member of the hated group.

So far we have attempted to explain this process of generalization—of becoming prejudiced—in terms of theories that focus primarily on the prejudiced individual. Individuals are more or less educated; individuals are more or less frustrated. But as we consider the point that realistic conflicts exist among groups, we must wonder whether this fact may also contribute to the development of prejudice, and if so, how.

Our conclusion concerning the frustration-aggression theory resembles the previous one regarding the cultural-transmission theory: it seems reasonable to suppose that some people react to life's innumerable frustrations by displacing their aggressive feelings on to the members of certain minority groups. But not all ethnic prejudices are readily explained in this way. Frustration, like misinformation, is one among many things that may lead to ethnic prejudice.

The Group-Gains Theory of Prejudice

The most influential line of analysis of this problem is associated with the name of Karl Marx. The central focus of interest is the attempt by dominant-group workers to realize economic gains by "keeping down" the workers of minority groups. Presumably, if minority-group workers are forced into the hardest, dirtiest, lowest-paying jobs, majority-group workers are freed to rise into the cleaner, higher-paying jobs (Glenn, 1966:161). Simultaneously, the possibility that minority-group workers will pose a threat of taking jobs away from the dominant-group members is reduced. Marxian writers argue that this strategy on the part of dominant-group workers is mistaken. While it may seem to the majority-group workers that they profit from such a system, this belief is an illusion. The real beneficiaries of this situation, in Marxian terms, are the members of the upper, "ruling," or capitalist class. By encouraging the hostility of white American workers toward blacks, Chicanos, and Indians, white employers benefit in several ways. They apply the ancient maxim "divide and rule." They also are enabled by the presence of a large, inexpensive labor pool to cut costs and increase profits. And they are afforded a "mask for privilege," a set of justifications for posing as the friends of the oppressed while not giving minority-group workers a larger share of the economic pie (Simpson and Yinger, 1972:127). The net result for the dominant-group workers, the argument runs, is only a relative gain. Even if dominant-group workers actually receive greater rewards than minority-group workers, their share is smaller than it would be if workers from both the majority and the minority joined together against their common oppressor. By accepting as facts the ethnic prejudices regarding blacks fostered by the white upper class, white workers are effectively separated from black workers. By believing the black workers are their enemies, the white workers do not perceive that their real enemy—the source of their own frustrations and low rewards—is the white upper class. From this perspective, the prejudice of the white workers is in two senses "irrational": it is based at least in part on non-economic motivations; second, it loses for the white worker the economic gains that could be realized by combining with black workers against the employer. This perspective also suggests that the white upper classes would gain the most from this arrangement and would, therefore, actually be more prejudiced than the white workers. Even though many white workers recognize only dimly that they, like black workers, are also oppressed by the white upper class, there is an underlying similarity in their economic situations, and their prejudices should be somewhat reduced by that fact.

Despite the Marxian criticisms, the theory that all members of the dominant group—workers as well as capitalists—profit by dominant-group prejudice seems to fit well with many of the facts of everyday experience. Although it is no longer legal in America to advertise that "Jews need not apply" or that "Mexicans and dogs are not served here," it still seems obvious that in the United States white workers benefit in some ways by their membership in the dominant group. By and large, minority workers typically have performed the hardest and dirtiest jobs, while white workers usually have earned more money for performing cleaner, easier jobs. As a consequence, white workers not only have done more pleasant work but, also have, on the average, enjoyed better houses, better health, more free time, more goods and services, and so on.

There also are theoretical as well as commonsense reasons to doubt the accuracy of the Marxian view. Many writers have argued that high prejudice levels among white workers are quite consistent with their own economic interests and serve actually to increase the white workers' economic rewards (see, e.g., Myrdal, 1964:68). This theme has been pursued in an especially telling way in a theory advanced by Bonacich (1972; 1973; 1975; 1976). Bonacich agrees with the Marxian writers that economic forces are at the root of ethnic antagonisms, but she disagrees that the conflict between white and black workers is economically "irrational." She argues that such a theory of prejudice is not adequate to explain the actual course of race relations in American history. And she attacks the Marxian notion that capitalists encourage or deliberately create a division between different groups of workers in order to subordinate them both. After all, if the employers of labor actually adopt such a strategy, then they must pay one group of workers (e.g., the whites) more than is necessary, thus increasing their operating costs and reducing their profits. Why, Bonacich (1976:44) asks, would employers adopt such a "convoluted" strategy?

Her alternative theory states that the antagonism of white workers toward black workers (among others) stems from the fact that the price of the workers' labor in the two groups differs initially (Bonacich, 1972:549) and that the capitalist class does not create but is faced with a "split labor market." A split labor market is characterized by conflict among three key groups: business people (capitalists), higher-paid labor, and cheaper labor (Bonacich, 1972:553). In these terms, the main economic interests of the two laboring groups are not essentially alike (as in the Marxian analysis); they are fundamentally different. Higher-paid labor (e.g., whites) is genuinely threatened by the presence of cheaper labor (e.g., blacks). The latter may undercut the higher-paid laborers by doing the same work at lower wages. Since it is in the interest of the capitalist class to cut costs by hiring the least expensive workers, the capitalists may substitute the cheaper workers for the higher-paid ones. Moreover, if the higher-paid workers attempt to improve their wages and working conditions by organizing and striking, the employers may easily turn to the "reserve army" of the cheaper laborers to recruit strikebreakers. By using the cheaper laborers to undercut and to break strikes, the employers may undermine the position of the higher-paid workers (Bonacich, 1972:554; 1976:40).

How can the higher-paid laborers control the quite real threat against them that is posed by the cheaper laborers? Two main methods are available. The first is simply to exclude the cheaper laborers from the territory in which the higher-paid laborers work. This method has been employed frequently by workers all over the world. We have seen already, in chapter 3, that the United States excluded Chinese labor beginning in 1882; and, as we shall see in chapter 5, the same strategy was used later against the Japanese. In both cases, the hostility of the white workers, rather than the employers, provided the force behind the exclusionist efforts.

The second main method used by higher-paid labor to combat cheaper labor in a split labor market is to reserve certain jobs for the members of the higher-paid group. Thus, certain jobs become "white jobs," while others become "black jobs." If the higher-paid group is sufficiently well organized and powerful, they may be able to gain the employers' acceptance of this division of jobs and to permit the higher-paid group to decide which jobs will be held exclusively by members of one laboring group or the other. Alternatively, they may succeed in having the members of the two groups do the same work but at different rates of pay. By these methods, a rigid, castelike system of employment is developed.

The split labor market theory has many implications, several of which we will touch on in this and the next chapter. For the moment, though, we are interested in only two questions: first, is prejudice higher among the white upper classes than among white workers? Second, do white workers actually gain economically through the subordination of black and other minority workers? Since in the light of split labor market theory employers will attempt to hire the cheapest labor (if there are no differences in skill) and higher-paid workers will attempt to maintain their higher wages, employers should be less prejudiced than higher-paid workers. Furthermore, the higher-paid workers should realize definite economic benefits from their opposition to cheaper labor.

The evidence concerning the first question—Are upper or lower class whites more prejudiced?—generally supports the following statement: social-class levels (as measured by education, income, occupation, and so on) are inversely related to prejudice levels. The higher people are in the social-class hierarchy, the less likely they are to accept ethnic stereotypes or to express the wish to hold people of a different ethnicity at a great social distance.[6]

Taken at face value, this finding supports Bonacich's position rather than the Marxian interpretation. The white lower classes, comprised of individuals who generally must compete fairly directly with blacks not only for jobs but for houses, schools, and public facilities as well are the most resentful and express the most virulent antiblack sentiments. These appear to be the classic bigots, the dyed-in-the-wool "nigger haters." This is not, of course, the only possible interpretation. Perhaps in time, the white lower classes will realize the "true" situation, as Marx predicted, and will then combine forces with the blacks and other downtrodden groups.

But let us turn now to the second question of interest here. Is the higher level of hostility among white workers justified in economic terms? Do white workers actually gain economically through the subordination of black and other minority workers? Marxian analysis, to repeat, leads us to expect that white workers would, in the long run, lose by the "irrational" subordination of minority-group workers. The "realistic" course of action from this standpoint is for the workers of all races and ethnicities to join forces against the employers. Split labor market theory, in contrast, leads us to expect that white workers know where their best interests lie and that the subordination of minority workers results in economic gains to white workers.

Studies attempting to deal with these issues have been conducted by several scholars, including Becker (1971), Dowdall (1974), Glenn (1963; 1966), Thurow (1969), Reich (1971), and Szymanski (1976). These scholars have adopted various approaches to the problem and have used several sources of information and techniques of analysis. Our treatment of the complexities that have arisen in the process, consequently, is necessarily greatly simplified. The logic of this type of inquiry may be illustrated through a brief description of studies completed by Glenn (1963; 1966) and Dowdall (1974) covering two decades of experience in the United States.

To answer the question "Do specific groups of whites gain from the fact that blacks are kept down and if so, how?" Glenn and Dowdall have examined data on a large number of cities in the United States for the years 1950, 1960, and 1970. The basic idea behind these studies is this: if white people gain in various ways from the subordination of blacks, then the whites' advantage should be greater within cities having a relatively large black population. Where the black population is relatively large, whites should hold more high-prestige jobs than in cities having relatively fewer blacks. Similarly, the incomes of whites should rise with an increase in the presence of black people. Under these circumstances, whites should also experience less unemployment.

The analyses by Glenn strongly support the conclusion that in the middle of the twentieth century, white urbanized Americans still were gaining occupationally and economically through the subordination of black Americans. These effects were greater in southern cities, where the proportions of blacks were generally larger, than in northern and western cities. The gains to whites, however, were not evenly distributed. The groups that appeared to benefit most by the subordination of blacks "are middle-class Southern housewives and white workers in proprietary, managerial, sales, and upper-level manual occupations" (Glenn, 1966:177). These advantages to whites, moreover, apparently were undiminished by the great efforts to create social changes during the decade of the 1960s. Dowdall (1974:181) reports, on the basis of data gathered in 1970, that "whites continued to benefit from the subordinate position of blacks by gaining higher occupational status, lower unemployment, and higher family income; Southern employers, overwhelmingly white, still seemed to gain from blacks in reduced labor costs."

Even though the main results of Glenn's and Dowdall's studies agree, it still is not clear whether the findings strengthen the Marxian or split labor market interpretations of black-white economic conflict. While Glenn (1966: 177) concludes that "the findings of this study do not support the Marxist view that discrimination against Negroes benefits the 'capitalist class' but hurts white workers," Dowdall (1974:182) maintains that both his and Glenn's analyses "seem completely consistent" with the view that "gains accrue more rapidly to those at the top."

The latter interpretation has been strengthened in subsequent studies by Reich (1971) and Szymanski (1976). These researchers maintain that although some aspects of black-white economic conflict serve to raise the earnings of white workers, these gains are, on balance, more than offset by the resulting weakening of the labor movement. Their studies show that the more white workers discriminate against blacks, the more the white workers are injured economically. As Szymanski (1976:412) puts it: "the more intense racial discrimination is, the lower are white earnings . . ."—a result that is brought about by the lowering of "working class solidarity." He concludes, therefore, that "the Marxist theory of the effect of racial discrimination of white workers is thus partially borne out" (Szymanski, 1976:413).

Although much of the most recent work seems mainly to support the Marxian view on this issue, the evidence is certainly not decisive or incontrovertible. For example, Glenn's "white gains" interpretation has been supported, in general, by the findings of Becker (1971) and Thurow (1969), though these authors disagree with one another in other ways. If nothing else, these studies have confirmed Glenn's (1966:160) observation that it is by no means easy to ascertain "that whites would be more prosperous and have more favorable occupations if Negroes were not present and subordinated."

Most of the controversy regarding the possibility that whites gain through the subordination of blacks and other minorities has centered on the matter of economic gains; but the debate has not been limited to this issue. In a pioneering analysis of white gains, Dollard (1957) argued that whites have gained not only economically but in other ways as well. For instance, throughout most of the history of the United States, especially in the South, white men have realized a "sexual gain" because they have had sexual access to black women, while sexual relations between black men and white women have been taboo. Citing still another advantage whites have enjoyed over blacks, the "prestige gain," Dollard (1957:173–187) emphasizes that the traditions of the South have required black people to be completely sub-missive in the presence of whites. Indeed, it has even been required that blacks smother the whites in adulation. The traditional southern "ettiquette of race relations" (Doyle, 1937) permitted any white person—no matter how young or unaccomplished—to address all black people—no matter how old or accomplished—by their first names. Blacks, on the other hand, were re-quired always to address whites by titles of respect. They were expected to say "sir" or "m'am" and to show continuous agreement "such as 'yes, Boss,' 'Sho nuff,' 'well, I declare,' " and the like (Dollard, 1957:180). Black people always were expected to defer to the wishes of white people and to praise their goodness, wit, and skill. Blacks who did not behave in these expected ways were regarded as "uppity" and "getting out of their place" (Dollard, 1957: 175). Such behavior was viewed as a challenge to the southern system of white supremacy that existed in every sphere of life. Since the overwhelming majority of blacks did in fact "knuckle under"—at least in appearance—the whites regularly received the satisfactions that come to humans who believe themselves to be superior and are so treated. All of these requirements guaranteed prestige supremacy. No matter how low a white person was in the "pecking order," he or she was still above all of the blacks.

Dollard's analysis seems quite compelling. But even here, as in the case of economic gains, it is not certain that the sexual, social, and psychological gains for whites of the white supremacy system completely outweighed their costs, especially in the long run. There are many noneconomic costs involved in maintaining a castelike system of subordination, and many of these costs are extraordinarily difficult to measure. To raise only one possibility, may it not be true that the costs to the dominant group in feelings of guilt, fear, and anxiety have been so large as to counterbalance whatever satisfactions they may have received? This theme has been pursued in many works of literature, as well as social science. For example, Lillian Smith (1963:28) states in a moving passage:

> I began to understand slowly at first but more clearly as the years passed, that the warped, distorted frame we have put around every Negro child from birth is around every white child also. . . . And I know that what cruelly shapes and cripples the personality of one is as cruelly shaping and crippling the personality of the other.

Such subtle reckonings go beyond the powers of our poor social science, but they may not for that reason be ignored.

Taken together, the results of the many studies and literary insights concerning the total effects of the system of white supremacy in the United States afford a basis for the tentative claim that, however misguided, prejudice has been used by members of the dominant group in the United States to keep the members of various subordinate groups "down." Prejudice helps to explain and justify the fact that such social arrangements are, in a very broad sense, "profitable" for many, if not all, members of the dominant group.

The accumulated evidence also appears to support the view that within the dominant group, the lower class appears to have the greatest "need" or incentive to strive to stay "above" other racial and ethnic groups and that this "need" among lower-class individuals is translated into a high level of racial and ethnic prejudice. The higher people are in the social-class hierarchy (as measured by education, income, occupation, and so on), the less likely they are to accept ethnic stereotypes or to express the wish to hold people of a different ethnicity at a great social distance.

Whether the above conclusions are correct is a matter of considerable practical importance. If white workers or white employers do not truly gain by possessing ethnic prejudices and by discrimination, then they have, in fact, a strong incentive to discontinue such beliefs and practices. From this vantage point, one may argue that when people are properly educated so as to see correctly their own true interests, they may then cooperate to bring about needed social changes. On the other hand, if any substantial segment of the dominant group is realizing actual gains from the system of subordination, then they may be expected to resist changes tooth and nail. Perhaps, as the split labor market theory suggests, those who express the most open ethnic hatreds, the classic bigots, have, in fact, much to lose by changes in the economic and social structure. If so, changes will be much more difficult to effect.

The Group-Identification Theory of Prejudice

Let us now turn to the last of the four main types of causes of prejudice shown in Figure 4.2, viz., group identification. The importance of a person's group memberships as a molding force has nowhere been stated more powerfully than by Sumner (1906) in his famous book *Folkways*. In Sumner's (1906:12) view, a fundamental fact concerning human groups is that as their members are drawn together by a common interest, they simultaneously become distinguished from other groups. In this process, those in the newly formed group come to see themselves as the "in-group" or "we-group" and to categorize everyone else as members of an "out-group" or "other-group." As our brief review of nativism in the United States has shown, the members of an in-group have feelings of loyalty and pride toward their own group and feelings of superiority and, frequently, contempt toward members of out-groups. The in-group is seen as possessing the right, the natural, the human ways of living and thinking. "We" are believed to be virtuous and civilized; "they" are believed to be vicious and barbaric. Outsiders are likely to be described in scornful and derogatory terms. In the United States, for example, such terms as "dago," "nigger," "kike," "honkey," "spick," "mick," "limey," "chink," "gringo," and so on have been applied frequently to out-groups as terms of extreme disrespect. As noted in chapter 3, this tendency to rate all out-groups as lower than the in-group is called ethnocentrism (Sumner, 1906:13).

Ethnocentrism is a pervasive sentiment. Children normally learn very early to distinguish the groups to which they belong from all other groups. And they usually have a strong attachment to and preference for their own groups' ways. Since children develop within a specific set of groups, beginning with their families, and since they usually learn only one way to behave, it is quite understandable that people should regard their groups' ways of thinking and acting as natural and good. From this point, it is but an easy step to the rejection of the ways of all out-groups and a general conviction that those ways are unnatural and bad. Thus, children's awareness of themselves as distinct individuals and their evaluations of themselves are inextricably connected to the standards and traditions of specific groups. In this way, the group's preferences become their preferences; its standards, their standards; its beliefs, their beliefs; and its enemies, their enemies. To grow up as a member of a given group, this argument states, is automatically to place the group at the center of things and to adopt its evaluations as the best. Prejudice is a predictable consequence of this natural ethnocentrism.

This theory, like the other three we have reviewed so far, is quite plausible and easily fits many of the facts of everyday experience. But it, too, has shortcomings. For example, loyalty to one's ethnic in-group is frequently accompanied by an admiration for some specific accomplishments by the members of out-groups (Williams, 1964:22). "We" may despise "them" and, at the same time, recognize that "they" are quite good at something. Even in the midst of war, for example, a hated enemy may be granted a grudging respect for his skill or daring. Such departures from perfect ethnocentrism, however, do not necessarily mean that an enemy out-group that is respected in some particular way is generally rated above the in-group. We may consider ourselves superior to them but still concede that they are very good in one particular way. Indeed, some such concession may even be expected to occur on the grounds that little glory is to be gained by defeating a markedly inferior foe. Furthermore, we sometimes admit that they are our superiors but seek at the same time to turn this fact to our advantage. For instance, when the Soviet Union successfully launched a space rocket before the United States, it was frequently claimed that they had stolen the necessary ideas and technology from us. Nevertheless, many cases exist in which in-group members may reject their own group and join another. As Williams (1964:23) has remarked, "History is replete with voluntary exiles, expatriates, out-group emulators, social climbers, renegades, and traitors."

Of greater theoretical significance is a different type of exception to the rule that ethnocentrism automatically generates prejudice in a group's members. Even though ethnic in-groups usually react to out-group hostility by becoming more solidary, more aware of their ethnic identity, and more determined to maintain their heritage, domination by an out-group may lead a number of the in-group's members to accept the oppressor's evaluation of their group and, hence, of themselves. This condition, which frequently is referred to as "self-hate," may begin to develop at an astonishingly early age.

Some very interesting discoveries have been based on the use of a technique called the "dolls test," pioneered by Clark and Clark (1939). In the dolls test, children are shown two dolls that are identical except for their skin and hair color. To learn whether children have a color preference, they may be asked to hand the researcher "the doll that is a nice color"; to learn whether children are aware of racial differences, they may be asked to select "the doll that looks like a white child"; and to discover whether children have identified their own racial-group membership, the researcher may ask for "the doll that looks like you" (Clark and Clark, 1958:602). In a study of 253 black children between the ages of three and seven, Clark and Clark (1958:603) found, in regard to race awareness, that a large majority (93 percent) of the children could identify the "colored" doll and nearly three-fourths (72 percent) could identify the "Negro" doll. Although the children's ability to distinguish the white and brown dolls was most pronounced among the seven-year-olds, over three-fourths (77 percent) of the three-year-olds were able to do this, also. Despite their high ability to distinguish the two dolls correctly, however, many of the children, particularly the three- and four-year-olds, did not identify themselves as "colored." Among the six- and seven-year-olds, approximately two-thirds did so identify themselves.

Probably the most remarkable findings, though, concerned the children's skin-color preferences. At every age level, and despite their own skin color, the majority of these children preferred the white doll to the brown doll. Most of them preferred to play with the white doll, thought that the white doll was "nice," and said that the brown doll "looks bad." These similarities among the different age groups, however, do conceal a difference of great possible significance. The greatest degree of "self-hate"—if we may call it that—appeared to be among the four- and five-year-olds. Beyond that point, the extent to which the children preferred the white dolls began to decline. When the seven-year-olds were asked to select "the doll that is a nice color," half of them chose the brown doll. This finding suggests that past a certain point, the members of a subordinate group may begin to "recover" from the numerous humiliations they experience at the hands of the dominant group. At some point, perhaps, self-hate may generally begin to give way to the more "normal" feelings of group pride and self-esteem.

A large number of subsequent studies using the dolls test have generally supported the Clarks' findings, though there have been disagreements on some other points. It has been confirmed, for example, that white children consistently display a strong, positive attitude toward the doll representing whites and a negative attitude toward the doll representing blacks (see, e.g., Asher and Allen, 1969; Fox and Jordan, 1973).[7] It also has been largely confirmed that black children begin to learn early in life that they are members of a despised group and that many of these children reject the symbols of their in-group and attempt to identify with symbols of the dominant white out-group. However, the age trend noted by the Clarks has not always been found. Some studies have found no age trend, while others have found contradictory trends.

Although the dolls test has been used in many studies, it is not the only technique developed to study the self-concepts of black and white children. Horowitz (1936) and Morland (1966), for instance, have used pictures of black and white children; more recently, Williams and his colleagues (see, e.g., Williams and Morland, 1976) have developed "a picture-story format" to study this problem. Their main tool is the Preschool Racial Attitudes Measure (PRAM). The PRAM assesses children's racial attitudes by scoring their responses "to stories containing positive or negative evaluative attitudes," such as clean, dirty, good, bad, and so on (Williams and Morland, 1976: 101–102). On the basis of several studies in different parts of the United States, researchers using PRAM have supported the basic findings of the dolls test investigations. On the average, both white and black children show a prowhite, antiblack bias. The PRAM studies have also revealed, however, that the prowhite bias of black children is lower than that of white children. Taken altogether, the main thrust of research on the self-esteem of black children has supported the Clarks' (1958:608) judgment that children who learn they are members of an inferior group and accept that opinion may experience incalculable, possibly irreversible, damage to their personalities. The U.S. Supreme Court accepted this view in the famous school desegregation case, *Brown* v. *Topeka Board of Education,* 1954. The court held that to segregate children "from others of similar age and qualifications solely because of their race generates a feeling of inferiority as to their status in the community that may affect their hearts and minds in a way unlikely ever to be undone" (Osofsky, 1968:477).

So much research has confirmed the idea that the self-esteem of black children is comparatively low that, as Heiss and Owens (1972:360) note, "The idea seems almost unassailable." Nevertheless, several authors have raised questions about this view. McCarthy and Yancey (1971), for instance, suggest that the case for low black self-esteem is very weak. Following their lead, Heiss and Owens (1972:369) analyzed the results of two large-scale surveys and found no evidence "that blacks are 'crippled' by low self-evaluations." Rosenberg and Simmons (1972) reached that same conclusions in a Baltimore study. Additionally, Lerner and Buehrig (1975:46), using open-end interviews rather than the forced-choice approach of the dolls test and PRAM, did not find that black children had negative self-attitudes, a result that stands "in marked contrast to those of most previous studies of racial attitudes." These newer findings may mean that the increasing emphasis on black pride during the 1960s has altered the way black children are socialized. Or they may mean that the methods of the earlier studies were invalid and led to mistaken conclusions. Although it seems too early to conclude with Adam (1978:48) that "the 1970s overturned the tradition epitomized by the Clarks," there surely is room for further research on this important topic.

What conclusion may be reached from this brief review regarding the causes of prejudice? Evidently, many factors are at work. The culture of a society contains within it many ideas and beliefs concerning various racial and ethnic groups, and these ideas may be transmitted more or less intact from one generation to the next. Children learn these traditions as a natural and normal part of growing up. Moreover, since these traditions are indistinguishable in children's experience from the development of their own sense of self and are rooted in their basic sense of group membership or identity, they generally embrace the group's traditions as their own. Still further, if children are members of the dominant group, the traditional arrangements work in numerous ways to their advantage. In addition to direct and indirect economic gains, the individual also receives sexual and prestige "bonuses" as well as the psychological gains afforded by the continuous presence of convenient scapegoats. Allport's (1958:212) conclusion regarding the diversity of causes of prejudice seems sound: "By far the best view to take toward this multiplicity of approaches is to admit them all. Each has something to teach us. None possesses a monopoly of insight."

Theories of Discrimination

Earlier in this chapter, we outlined some crucial assumptions concerning prejudice and discrimination. We have assumed, for example, that (1) prejudice is an antidemocratic sentiment and, therefore, should be reduced or, ideally, eliminated. We also have assumed that (2) the reduction or elimination of prejudice requires an understanding of its causes. These two assumptions, however, gain much of their importance from three additional assumptions. These are that (3) discrimination is, like prejudice, undemocratic and should be reduced or eliminated, (4) prejudice is the cause of discrimination, and, therefore, (5) to reduce or eliminate discrimination, one must first attack prejudice, its cause.

The logic of these interlocking assumptions is quite compelling. Even people who may have philosophical reservations concerning assumptions one and three ordinarily will agree that *if* it is accepted that prejudice and discrimination should be reduced, then it makes sense to attack prejudice and to do so at its roots. The choice of a particular strategy to be adopted on this basis, of course, will be guided by one's opinion concerning which theory of prejudice is most important or most nearly accurate. (See again Figure 4.2.) If it is believed that the cultural-transmission theory is most nearly correct, changes may be recommended in a way children are taught in the family and in the schools. If it is believed that prejudice is rooted in the dynamics of personality, efforts may be made to reduce frustrations or other inner forces and to train people to "cope" with their personal problems. And if one holds with Allport (1958) and Myrdal (1964) that prejudice is a matter of multiple causation, then the "prescription" for a "cure" may involve a simultaneous attack on several—or, if possible, all—of the factors causing it. In this regard, Myrdal (1964:77) states that *"a rational policy will never work by changing only one factor."*

We must now have a closer look at the assumptions on which these plans for practical actions rest. Two reservations are especially important. The first concerns what may be called the "location" and "depth" of prejudice. Without actually saying so, the various ideas we have reviewed regarding the causes of prejudice imply that while many individuals in America are prejudiced (and are to that extent undemocratic), the structure of American society itself is democratic. Stated metaphorically, the argument is that while many individuals may deviate from America's ideas (and are therefore "sick"), the basic operations of the society are in line with its ideas (and are therefore "healthy"). For this reason, the members of the dominant group frequently propose such remedies for prejudice as courses to combat group stereotypes, books and films that portray sympathetically the plight of oppressed peoples, personal counseling for people who are filled with ethnic hatreds, and "get-togethers" that enable the members of different groups to become acquainted.

Many critics of America's record in the area of racial and ethnic relations think the "solutions" proposed above are quite superficial and miss the mark entirely. From this perspective, prejudice is not an "abnormal" feature of American society; it lies at the society's very core. It is an inevitable product of America's normal operations. Prejudice, in this view, cannot be eliminated through any of the means that are popularly proposed. Only a substantial reorganization of the society's basic institutions will do. This important theme is common in separatist and secessionist philosophies.

The second reservation is of a very different sort. It does not focus on which one of the different sources of prejudice is most important, nor does it concern the location or depth of prejudice. The reservation in this case concerns the extent to which prejudice is, in fact, a *cause* of discrimination. From this vantage point, the pattern of causation depicted in Figures 4.1 and

4.2 is seriously deficient. Instead of placing all of our emphasis on the effect prejudice has on discrimination, we should place at least equal emphasis on the reverse pattern, included in Figure 4.3. Figure 4.3 suggests two conclusions that run counter to the idea that prejudice is the sole cause of discrimination. First, although two of the factors shown as a cause of discrimination on the right side of Figure 4.3 (i.e., cultural transmission and group gains) also have been discussed as causes of prejudice, the remaining factors on each side are different. This indicates that certain causal factors may generate discrimination directly rather than indirectly through a prior effect on prejudice. Another important point to notice in Figure 4.3 is the arrow pointing from discrimination to prejudice. This suggests the uncommon conclusion that discrimination is a cause of prejudice!

The Cultural-Transmission Theory of Discrimination

We have seen previously that prejudice may be learned as a normal part of a person's "upbringing" or *socialization*. Children just seem to absorb the "knowledge" that different ethnic groups possess specific traits and therefore occupy given rungs on the ladder of social importance. Although it frequently is assumed that the prejudice thus formed lays the basis for discrimination, there is ample reason to believe that much discriminatory behavior is learned directly in the process of cultural transmission. There are reasons to believe, also, that the discrimination that is learned in this natural way may then lead to prejudice, as well as the other way around. A simple illustration from everyday life should assist to clarify this idea.

It frequently is observed that children learn an enormous amount through imitation. They see their parents, older siblings, and neighbors performing certain acts, and they mimic those acts. In many of these cases, children literally "don't know what they are doing." More important for our argument, though, is that, in many cases, children's actions are not accompanied by the same emotion and feelings that are present in the person they are imitating. Children "go through the motions," so to speak. They do not necessarily understand why the action is being performed and may have inner experiences during the act that are quite unlike those of the "model."

Applying this observation to the matter of prejudice and discrimination, we see that children frequently learn to hurl an epithet (or a rock) at the members of an out-group *before* they know whom they are "hating" or why. The discriminatory act in this instance precedes the "appropriate" or expected internal condition. Only gradually, through direct and indirect instruction, does the child come to experience the prejudice he is supposed to feel. Once the prejudice has been learned, the child may then experience it as coming before a given act of discrimination. The individual, thus, may say to others that he has discriminated because he thinks or feels in a particular way. Although this may be an accurate account of the temporal sequence, so far as it goes, the problem is that it doesn't go far enough. From a broader per-

FIGURE 4.3

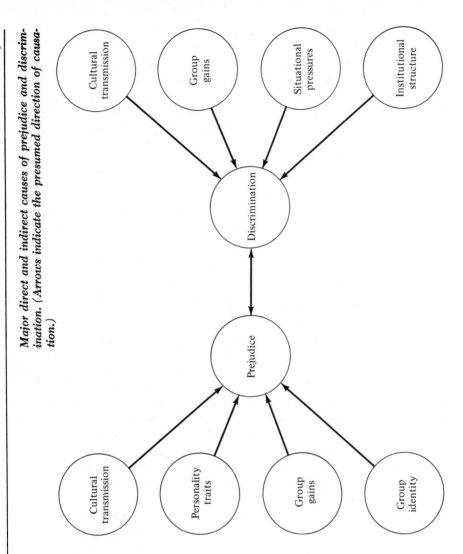

Major direct and indirect causes of prejudice and discrimination. (Arrows indicate the presumed direction of causation.)

spective, the feeling of prejudice that precedes a given act of discrimination may itself have been preceded by certain acts of discrimination.

But this is not the only (perhaps not even the main) way that discrimination may lead to prejudice. Please recall that such authorities as Allport (1958) and Myrdal (1964) maintain that an understanding of prejudice and discrimination requires the idea of multiple causation. To this we may now add Myrdal's (1964:1066) insistence that our approach must be *dynamic*. To illustrate the meaning of this latter point, let us examine some of Myrdal's assumptions.

To begin, he assumes that the relationship of the white and black groups in America is determined *in part* "by a specific degree of 'race prejudice' on the side of the whites, directed against the Negroes." Next, he assumes that the standard of living among blacks is substantially lower than among whites and that this fact is due to discrimination by whites against blacks. Then he argues that the discrimination employed by whites is caused mainly by the substandard living of the blacks. Hence, Myrdal (1964:1066) contends, prejudice and discrimination among whites form a vicious circle: "The Negroes' poverty, ignorance, superstition, slum dwellings, health deficiencies, dirty appearance, disorderly conduct, bad odor and criminality stimulate and feed the antipathy of the whites for them." In this view, whether one starts an analysis of race relations in America with prejudice or with discrimination, the result is the same. Prejudice among the whites causes discrimination, which lowers the plane of living of the blacks; the low plane of living among the blacks, in turn, generates and maintains the whites' prejudices, and so on. Each side of our prejudice-discrimination equation "feeds back" on the other side, thus maintaining a back-and-forth movement. Each side, then, "causes" the other in a circular and—from the standpoint of democratic values—vicious way.

Myrdal was not interested primarily in the "hen and egg" problem of whether prejudice or discrimination came first at some time in the past. At the very least, though, the place of the discrimination factor is as important in his theory as the prejudice factor; and discrimination is learned in part directly through cultural transmission.

The Group-Gains Theory of Discrimination

Our previous discussion of group gains focused on the way prejudices are generated by real or presumed conflicts between the interests of different groups and how these prejudices, in turn, produce various forms of discrimination against minority groups. A crucial assumption of this line of reasoning is that prejudices serve as an important "cause" of discrimination. Practically speaking, this means that if prejudice levels can be lowered, discrimination levels should follow suit.

We must now examine this implication somewhat more carefully. Consider, for instance, this question: when prejudices are created by true conflicts of group interests, may not discrimination continue even as the prejudices that support it decline? Put differently, isn't it true that as people learn not to hate the members of a different ethnic group, they may nonetheless continue to discriminate where genuine gains are at stake?

Many observers believe the answer to these questions is "yes." Thurow (1969), for instance, believes that both white workers and employers benefit economically from discrimination and that the discrimination of whites toward blacks does not stem mainly from prejudice. Bonacich's (1972) analysis of split labor markets (though it does not address this specific question) appears clearly to support the idea that discrimination could continue during a time when prejudice levels were declining. Indeed, since, from her perspective, prejudice, discrimination, and all other forms of intergroup conflict (collectively called "antagonism") arise fundamentally from genuine economic conflict, there is little reason to suppose that any one of these forms of antagonism (e.g., discrimination) would necessarily decline simply as a result of lowered prejudice levels. And Glenn's (1966:178) analysis, though not based on the assumption that prejudice and discrimination are mainly an expression of economic conflict, supports the view that "Negro-white antagonism in the United States is and will long remain partly a matter of realistic conflict."

The recognition that discrimination has important sources other than prejudice is exceptionally important in the present period. Many white Americans now recognize that their forefathers profited from discrimination against blacks and other minorities; and some even acknowledge that the effects of past discrimination have not been entirely erased. It is not always easy to see, however, that present discrimination is also profitable to the dominant group. Consequently, the complaint is frequently heard "I haven't discriminated against anyone, so why should I pay for the mistakes of the past?" The answer supported by the studies presented is that various groups of contemporary white Americans still receive a direct "bonus" for being white even if this gain is seldom noticed.

The group-gains theory alerts us to the fact that discrimination may currently be profitable whether or not prejudice levels are high and that it is likely to continue as long as the profits last.

The Situational-Pressures Theory of Discrimination

This theory of discrimination is based on two common observations. The first is the well-known fact that people's "preaching" may not always correspond to their "practicing." There frequently is a discrepancy or gap between the creed and the deed. Ordinarily, the creed-deed discrepancy arises when a person professes to have little or no ethnic prejudice but, in fact, discriminates in some social situations. A familiar example of this point is the person who feels it is necessary for social reasons not to associate openly with members of minority groups. Such a person may confide that "I am not prejudiced, you understand. But what would my friends and neighbors think!" This type of creed-deed discrepancy (or hypocrisy) is so common that people customarily assume most people will claim to be more tolerant than they really are. Such professions frequently are "taken with a grain of salt." Strangely enough, however, the gap between preaching and practicing also may arise in the opposite manner. Many people actually claim in some situations to be more prejudiced than their actions would imply! Discrepancies in either direction suggest a very important idea: whether people discriminate or not may depend more on the characteristics and demands of the social situation than on their levels of prejudice.

A landmark exploration of the creed-deed discrepancy was conducted by LaPiere (1934). LaPiere and a Chinese couple traveled some ten thousand miles together in the United States, stopping at 66 hotels and other tourist accommodations and at 184 restaurants and cafes. Despite the high level of prejudice toward the Chinese in the United States at that time, they were refused service only once in 251 instances. After the trip was over, LaPiere mailed questionnaires to all of the proprietors involved asking whether they would accept as customers "members of the Chinese race." Among those who answered the questionnaire (51 percent), 92 percent of the hotel proprietors and 93 percent of the restaurant proprietors stated they *would not* accept Chinese as guests! In short, the vast majority of a group of proprietors who already had demonstrated they were capable of not discriminating against Chinese claimed they would.

A number of other investigators have pursued the problem raised by LaPiere's study: Why do people's attitudes and actions frequently fail to correspond? What other factors enter the picture to create this inconsistency? Lohman and Reitzes (1952:242), for instance, have argued that in modern industrial society "attitudes toward minority groups may be of little consequence in explaining an individual's behavior." To test this idea, they studied the behavior of a sample of white workers in Chicago. The study was designed to compare the attitudes and behavior of workers who were members of a union that admitted blacks without reservation but who lived in a neighborhood where black residents were unwelcome. As members of the union, the workers were expected by other union members to ignore racial differences and to stand together on such common interests as wages and working conditions. As residents of the neighborhood, the workers were expected by their neighbors to act on the assumption that admitting blacks to the neighborhood as residents would lower property values. The results of the study showed that in the job situation, as predicted, the workers seemed to agree with the official view of their union and to encourage all workers to unite for their common advantage, that is, to be unprejudiced; at home, however, the workers seemed to accept the official view of the neighborhood improvement association and to reject blacks as neighbors.

The studies by LaPiere and Lohman and Reitzes, as well as a number of other studies, demonstrated that prejudice and discrimination do not necessarily go together. Discrimination may not occur when prejudice is present, and it may occur when prejudice is absent. In either case, a serious objection is raised to the presumption that prejudice is *the* cause of discrimination. To study this problem under more controlled conditions, several investigators have performed social experiments concerning the relationship of prejudice to discrimination. In one influential study, DeFleur and Westie (1958) asked forty-six white students to participate in a nationwide campaign for racial integration. Twenty-three of the students had very unfavorable attitudes toward blacks, and the remaining twenty-three had very favorable attitudes. To test the extent of a person's willingness to act in a manner consistent with their prejudice levels, the researchers asked the students to be photographed with a black person of the opposite sex and to sign release agreements to permit the pictures to be used in various phases of the campaign. The study showed that prejudice was positively related to discrimination (i.e., unwillingness to sign the releases); however, it also revealed that nine of the presumably unprejudiced students were less willing than the average to have their photographs used and that five of the presumably prejudiced students were more willing than the average to release their photographs. DeFleur and Westie interpreted these discrepancies in terms of differing peer-group pressures.

A later study by Linn (1965) followed the method developed by DeFleur and Westie. Although Linn did not find the positive relationship between prejudice and discrimination reported by DeFleur and Westie, he did find a large number of discrepant cases, that is, cases in which a person's verbal attitude did not match his willingness to sign a release to permit the photograph to be used under different circumstances. Linn (1965:364) agreed that different peer pressures were an important cause of these discrepancies but suggested further that differences in role expectations were probably also important.

A still more recent study using the photograph-release approach to measure discrimination has been conducted by Green (1972). Green found, as did DeFleur and Westie, that there is a positive relationship between prejudice and discrimination. He also found that regardless of their expressed racial attitude, white people's willingness to pose with a black person of the opposite sex diminished as the pose became more intimate. Green agreed with DeFleur and Westie that peer pressures in different social situations lead to inconsistencies between expressed attitudes and actual behavior. Warner and DeFleur (1969:154) have proposed that although attitudes do play a role in causing behavior, such things as social norms, group memberships, and other situational factors also affect the relationship.[8]

The above studies show that people may claim to be unprejudiced but, in fact, discriminate under some conditions; but they also show that people may claim to be prejudiced and not discriminate. The specific social pressures arising in particular situations seem, in many instances, to outweigh personal prejudice as a cause of discrimination. "If research has confirmed anything in this area," Schermerhorn (1970:6) argues, "it is that prejudice is a product of *situations,* historical situations, economic situations, political situations; it is not a little demon that emerges in people simply because they are depraved." Since some of the ideas expressed above depart from commonsense reasoning, let us summarize them briefly.

An illuminating way to order these thoughts concerning the relationship of prejudice and discrimination has been suggested by Merton (1949). Although people's levels of prejudice and discrimination actually range from extremely high to extremely low, we may for convenience think of them as being either high or nonexistent in each respect. By combining the two resulting dichotomies, any given individual may be classified or "typed" as (1) a prejudiced discriminator—high in prejudice, high in discrimination, (2) a prejudiced nondiscriminator—high in prejudice, no discrimination, (3) an unprejudiced discriminator—no prejudice, high in discrimination, or (4) an unprejudiced nondiscriminator—no prejudice, no discrimination. In the study by Lohman and Reitzes, the union workers who seemed to be low in prejudice but who, nevertheless, discriminated in the neighborhood setting seem to illustrate type 3, the unprejudiced discriminator. And in the study conducted by LaPiere, the proprietors who seemed to be prejudiced but did not discriminate in certain actual settings appear to illustrate type 2, the prejudiced nondiscriminator.

These observations are not intended to show that prejudice and discrimination never or seldom occur together. The existence of types 1 and 4 remind us, as is ordinarily supposed, that in many—probably most—cases, people who are low in prejudice also are low in discrimination. But notice that the existence of people who actually are high in both prejudice and discrimination does not tell us the *direction* of causation. It is just as easy to assume in such cases that discrimination has led to prejudice as it is to assume the reverse.

Each of the views presented thus far has some important implications for practical measures to reduce or eliminate prejudice and discrimination. We will return to these shortly. First, however, we must become acquainted with one further idea concerning prejudice and discrimination. It is seldom encountered in everyday thought and may, therefore, be somewhat difficult to grasp at first. However, it lies behind the remaining theory of discrimination to be presented—one, which if accepted, has profound implications for practical actions intended to reduce discrimination.

In our discussion above, we have concluded that a given person may discriminate, even if unprejudiced, in order to conform to the social expectations of those about him. In this situation, even though the individual in question is not prejudiced, some others in the situation are, and their prejudice acts indirectly to cause discrimination. But now consider this possibility: suppose that no one in the situation were prejudiced but that discrimination still occurred. Would this mean that prejudice is not a significant cause, even indirectly, of present discrimination? This unsettling question has grown out of research on what is called institutional discrimination.

Institutional Discrimination

American ethnic relations entered a critical period during the decade of the 1960s. This development, discussed more fully in the succeeding chapters, may have been generated to a considerable degree by an apparent inconsistency or paradox. The Civil Rights Movement had scored numerous successes, especially on the legal front, symbolized by the 1954 Supreme Court school desegregation order in *Brown* v. *Topeka Board of Education*. During the same period, national opinion polls showed that white Americans were becoming less prejudiced. Hyman and Sheatsley (1964:18–19), for example, found that public approval of school desegregation had risen from 30 percent in 1942 to 62 percent in 1963 and that approval of neighborhood desegregation had risen from 35 percent in 1942 to 64 percent in 1963.[9] Despite the legal gains and the increasing tolerance of the majority, however, many members of minority groups (particularly black Americans) did not feel that significant changes were taking place in their lives. At best, the rate of change seemed painfully slow.[10] The question that loomed in the minds of many people, therefore, was "How can so many changes occur in the laws and in people's attitudes but not be reflected in the actual living conditions of the members of minority groups?"

An intriguing answer to this question was presented by Carmichael and Hamilton (1967) in their influential book *Black Power*. The answer these authors suggested is that the ordinary operations of American institutions discriminate against subordinate groups. Schools, hospitals, factories, banks, and so on do not need to be staffed by prejudiced people in order to achieve discriminatory results. For example, most employers have certain formal educational requirements for hiring, such as a high school or college diploma. When these requirements are applied uniformly (and many would add "fairly") to all those who apply, the automatic result is to exclude those who have been deprived of an equal opportunity to gain the necessary credentials. If people have been subject to discrimination in the schools, then they are less likely to have graduated and, therefore, to be less qualified for a job that requires a diploma. Even if the people who conduct the hiring procedure are completely tolerant as individuals, the rules of the organization they represent will require them to accept only those who have proper diplomas, test scores, certificates, and so on. In this case, we see that the discrimination that occurs in one institutional setting may carry over into or have side effects on a related institutional setting (Feagin, 1977). To carry the matter further, a father's difficulties in finding employment may lead his son to drop out of school to go to work. The son, too, may then later encounter the same employment problems as the father. Here we see how unintentional discrimination may place a vicious circle into operation both within and between generations.

Another type of institutional discrimination in employment arises because the members of a minority "lack some ability or qualification intentionally denied to them in the past" (Feagin, 1977:189). If an employer requires that a person must have worked in one job for ten years in order to be qualified for another job, anyone who was deliberately excluded from the first job cannot possibly be qualified for the second. For instance, for a very long time, black Americans have had the experience of being "the last hired and the first fired." During periods of economic expansion, employers frequently have not hired black workers until no other workers were available. Then, during slack periods, the black workers frequently were the first to lose their jobs. Under these circumstances, it was very difficult for black workers to accumulate the years of seniority needed to qualify for many jobs. Therefore, wherever seniority rules are used in hiring and firing—even when such rules are applied evenly—the black workers are at a disadvantage. The employers in this situation may be able to say truthfully that they are not prejudiced and are not discriminating even though the application of the seniority rules may work to the disadvantage of the black workers.

Note that the main claim of this theory is that prejudice presently is not required to keep the system of discrimination intact. It acknowledges that prejudice initially may have played a key role in producing the existing system, and it does not deny that prejudice still produces some discrimination.[11]

Reducing Prejudice and Discrimination

The above discussion has emphasized that the various theories of prejudice and discrimination are important sources of suggestions of ways to attack these social problems. There is not, however, a simple one-to-one correspondence between the theories and the various strategies of social change that may be implied by them. Consider, for example, some implications of the cultural transmission theory of prejudice. One way to interfere with the transmission of racial and ethnic prejudice from one generation to another is to remove racial and ethnic stereotypes from children's school books. Minority-group members may be portrayed in certain situations and roles that run counter to the prevailing stereotypes. But the cultural transmission theory of prejudice also suggests some more "militant" strategies. Stereotypes also may be attacked by requiring children from different groups to attend the same schools and by removing barriers to neighborhood desegregation. From this standpoint, too, one may argue that required classes should be established in our public schools (especially at the primary levels) to guarantee that the prejudices children have learned at home will be challenged. These examples show that one's political stand, as well as one's theory of prejudice and discrimination, will have an important effect on the strategy of change one prefers.

Nevertheless, and despite many exceptions, a broad pattern of theoretical and strategic preferences is discernible. Dominant-group members are likely to focus on the reduction of prejudice through methods derived from the cultural-transmission and personality theories. Minority-group members, in contrast, are likely to focus on the reduction of discrimination through methods derived from the group-gains and institutional-discrimination theories. Furthermore, members of the dominant group are likely to advocate methods of change that are gradual in their effects and are not likely to result in open conflicts between groups. The members of minority groups, on the other hand, are more likely to advocate methods that promise rapid social changes even though the risk of group conflict may be higher. As a result of this broad pattern of theoretical and strategic preferences, the majority of studies in this field have focused on prejudice reduction through the use of various educational approaches. Increasingly, however, the focus of attention has been shifting toward the reduction of discrimination, especially through changes in the law and by means of organized social protest. We will briefly illustrate these methods here, giving most attention to the educational and legal approaches. Organized social protest will be treated more fully in the chapters that follow.

The Educational Approach

Many people believe that individual prejudice reflects a lack of knowledge. But what constitutes "knowledge?" And how is "knowledge" best acquired? Differences of opinion concerning the answers to these questions have led to different "educational" methods for reducing prejudice.

Since a frequent assumption has been that prejudiced people lack accurate information regarding the groups they dislike, many courses in racial and ethnic studies place a strong emphasis on replacing ethnic stereotypes with accurate information. To illustrate, it may be argued that while white Americans frequently consider black Americans to be lazy, black Americans, in fact, have shouldered far more than their share of the heavy, backbreaking labor that has been required to build our industrial civilization. If the participants believe that Chicanos are likely to put pleasure before business—the so-called *mañana* attitude—then information can be presented to show that this pattern can be found also among Anglo-Americans and that there is no significant difference in this respect between Anglos and Chicanos of similar social-class position.

There is certainly some evidence to back up the belief that people are less likely to harbor ethnic prejudices if they are well informed. There is, for instance, the fact (noted earlier) that those with a college education generally are more tolerant than those who have only an elementary education (Berelson and Steiner, 1964:515). But it is easy to exaggerate the significance of this point. The differences between the educational groups may not be as large as some other differences. In a study of white Americans' attitudes toward black Americans, Taylor, Sheatsley, and Greeley (1976:45) found that in 1976 white northerners with an elementary school education were only slightly less favorable toward racial integration than were white southerners who had completed high school; and they were noticeably more favorable toward integration than were white southerners who had attended but not completed high school. Moreover, white southerners who had not completed college were less favorable toward integration than were white northern high school graduates. It should be said, however, that there was a striking change in the pattern of regional differences during the first half of the 1970s, with southern college students and high school graduates showing a rapid acceptance of integration. Although these findings are subject to several interpretations, they are consistent with the idea that reducing prejudice requires more than formal education.

To possess knowledge, however, may mean something more or different than having been exposed to certain bits of factual information. Since prejudice appears to have a strong emotional as well as intellectual side, many people feel it is more effective to "speak to the heart than to the head." For example, instead of imparting specific facts to people, a program of intercultural education may be based on films, plays, television productions, biographies, and novels that present the members of minority groups in a sympathetic way (Allport, 1958:454). The underlying premise here is that exposure to such materials may help a person recognize and appreciate the humanness of the members of a minority group and, thus, to reduce the tendency for majority-group members to see sharp differences between "them" and "us." The participant in such a program is encouraged to "take the role of the other," to see the world from the minority person's point of view. Such a vicarious experience, it is assumed, should lead the prejudiced people to see themselves through the eyes of the victim of prejudice, to dislike what they see, and, thereby, to stimulate changes in attitudes and behavior.

Several criticisms of the approach through vicarious experience have been advanced. Some evidence suggests that prejudiced people frequently do not interpret accurately the films and books that run counter to their prejudices. They do not necessarily "get the message"; they may pay greatest attention to side issues and ignore the central point. It seems, too, that the effectiveness of a film of some other dramatic presentation in reducing prejudice depends greatly on the skill with which the "message" of tolerance is presented. Some presentations actually create a "boomerang effect" in which prejudices are heightened instead of diminished. And one may reasonably argue that it is unrealistic to assume that something as superficial as a film or a book may seriously disrupt a deep-seated ethnic prejudice.

An interesting attempt to test these ideas has been conducted by Middleton (1960). This research was designed to counter the above criticisms. Two groups of university students were selected to participate in the study. One group of 329 subjects—the experimental group—was shown an award-winning commercial film *(Gentleman's Agreement)*, while the other group of 116 subjects—the control group—was not shown the film. *Gentleman's Agreement* concerns the subject of anti-Jewish prejudice (or anti-Semitism).

It attempts to convey the twin message that anti-Jewish sentiments are despicable and are perpetuated significantly by "fair-weather liberals." The students in both the experimental and control study groups were given a questionnaire to measure their levels of prejudice against Jews and blacks. Shortly thereafter, the students in the experimental group were shown *Gentleman's Agreement*. Within a week after the showing, both groups of students were again asked to fill out the questionnaire concerning their ethnic prejudices.

Since the film in question is concerned directly with the topic of prejudice against Jews, Middleton's main purpose was to determine whether the film lowered prejudices against the members of that ethnic group. He also wished to know, though, whether a reduction in prejudice toward Jews might also be accompanied by a reduction in prejudice against blacks. Such a finding would lend some support to the idea that ethnic prejudices are not simple attitudes directed only against this or that specific group but are, rather, a complex part of the organization of an individual's personality.

Middleton's primary findings were that (1) on the average, the anti-Jewish sentiments of the experimental group—those who saw the film—were significantly reduced following the showing and that (2) the same result—though not as pronounced—was found in regard to antiblack prejudice. Hence, this study supports the idea that deeply ingrained ethnic prejudices may be significantly reduced by a particular kind of motion picture. It also supports the view that a good film aimed toward a particular ethnic prejudice (e.g., against Jews) may also reduce ethnic prejudices concerning other groups. And the study affords some convincing evidence in opposition to the various criticisms of this approach mentioned earlier.

Middleton's study is a fine example of social scientific research. It does not, however, prove that the best way to reduce ethnic prejudice is to arouse people's sympathies through dramatic or emotionally appealing presentations. As Middleton (1960:68) notes, there is no evidence that the reductions in prejudice observed in his experiment were permanent; and, as we have seen previously, it is difficult to know to what extent the participants in the study surmised the researchers' intent and adjusted their answers in a socially desirable direction. Furthermore, even if the changes in prejudice were permanent and real, there is no evidence that these changes were translated into lowered levels of discrimination.

So far, we have considered two main approaches to increasing the intercultural knowledge of prejudiced people: (1) exposing them to accurate information concerning ethnic minorities and (2) assisting them "to place themselves in the other person's shoes." It is not easy to compare the effectiveness of these two approaches in reducing prejudice and discrimination. So far as attitude change is concerned, the informational approach appears generally to be weaker than the more emotional approach using books, plays, films and so on; but little evidence exists that either approach leads to permanent reductions in prejudice or to much change in behavior. It is possible, of course, that the changes take place over a long period of time and that they are difficult to detect. Still, it seems that other methods are required if much change is to be effected.

The drawbacks of the informational approach and the vicarious-experience approach have led some people to favor a third approach to increasing the knowledge of prejudiced people about subordinate groups. As in the case of the previous two, this third approach is well grounded in everyday thought. The idea is frequently voiced that those who hate one another really do not know one another. A variation on this theme is that the parties to a conflict have experienced "a breakdown in communications." Consequently, one of the most common suggestions is that people should get together so that they may establish communications, get to know one another, participate in various activities together, and discuss their differences. When people do things together, they have an excellent opportunity to discover what the members of different groups are really like. They are enabled to see that those in other groups have the same kinds of human emotions and problems that they have; and they are in a position to learn the importance of individual differences among the members of seemingly alien groups. The opportunity arises in such a situation for a person to learn how to judge the members of other groups on the basis of their individual merits and, in this way, to apply the same kinds of standards to others they apply to people in their own group. Among sociologists this idea is known as the "contact hypothesis" (Allport, 1958:250–261).

The idea that contact is essential to the reduction of prejudice is certainly consistent with much everyday experience. Practically everyone can name at least one person whom he or she disliked at first but grew to like later on. And it is clear that many problems in human relations do, indeed, involve a failure of communication. It is also clear, however, that contacts between the members of different racial and ethnic groups may have no effect whatever on the prejudices of the groups' members or may even strengthen them (Berelson and Steiner, 1964:570). For example, when contacts between the groups involve unequal social statuses, it is unlikely that prejudices will be weakened. If the dominant-group members enjoy the higher status (e.g., employer-employee relations), the contact will serve mainly to remind them of their superiority. But if the minority-group members occupy the higher status (e.g., police-citizen relations), the contact may serve to increase the dominants' resentment. Equal status contacts, however, may lead to reductions in prejudice, especially if people do something together that is enjoyable or is of mutual significance (Allport, 1958:264).

Numerous factors in addition to social status may affect the outcome of contacts between the members of dominant and subordinate groups. Equal status contacts among people with only mild prejudices may be more successful than those involving people with strong prejudices. And even equal-status contacts among those with mild prejudices may lead to resentment if contacts occur in an "unusual" setting such as a social club or church. Moreover, many otherwise favorable contacts may not produce the desired result if those in positions of authority or social influence disapprove. For example, children involved in school-desegregation programs may become more prejudiced if parents, teachers, school administrators, and local elected officials do not make public declarations supporting desegregation.[12]

A variety of social settings within which intergroup contacts occur have been investigated, but two settings have received special research attention. These are interracial housing and desegregated schooling.[13] Along with most other studies of intergroup contact, the basic assumption of housing and school-desegregation research has been that contact (or even proximity) will lead to the reduction of prejudice and intergroup tension; however, after a thorough review of the literature, Amir (1969:319) concluded that "changes in ethnic relations do occur following intergroup contact, but the nature of this change is not necessarily in the anticipated direction."

Let us consider Amir's generalization in the light of some studies of interracial housing, beginning with some findings from the best-known study of racial desegregation in public housing (Deutsch and Collins, 1956). These researchers compared two public housing projects in New York and Newark to see how desegregated housing affected relations between blacks and whites. In two of the projects, the tenants were assigned to apartments without regard to race. In the other two projects, the tenants were assigned to racially segregated buildings. It was therefore possible to study the reactions of people living in two situations that were highly similar except for the physical closeness of the members of the two races. The researchers were interested in such things as whether the black and white families had more frequent contact with one another in the "integrated" projects or the "segregated" projects; whether interracial contacts were more friendly in one of the two settings; and whether contacts between the members of the two races led to decreases in the tenants' prejudice levels.

The study showed that white housewives who lived in the two segregated projects had many fewer neighborly relations with blacks than did the white housewives in the two integrated projects. In both of the segregated projects, in fact, there were almost no neighborly relations. Although the two integrated projects differed somewhat in their levels of neighborly relations, both were noticeably different from the segregated projects (Deutsch and Collins, 1956:26–27). The study also showed that some white housewives in both types of projects became more favorable in their attitudes toward blacks, while some became more unfavorable. However, within both types of projects, more housewives changed in a favorable than in an unfavorable direction. Furthermore, the total number of favorable changes was much larger within the integrated than within the segregated projects (Deutsch and Collins, 1956:42–43).

Although the main findings of Deutsch and Collins have been strengthened and refined by a number of subsequent investigations (see, e.g., Ford,

1973; Wilner, Walkley, and Cook, 1955; Works, 1961), some refinements have been suggested. Ford (1973:1440), for instance, found that in an interracial housing project in which racial tension was present, a longer duration of residence in the project did not increase the tolerance of whites for blacks. He found, too (contrary to the findings of Works, 1961), that equal-status contacts did not appear to reduce the prejudice of blacks for whites. Researchers also have extended the scope of the findings pertaining to residential contact through studies of middle-class neighborhoods. (See, e.g., Meer and Freedman, 1966.)

Of particular importance here is a well-designed study by Hamilton and Bishop (1976). Since most previous studies of housing desegregation have focused on public housing, and since all previous studies have examined the effects of contact after desegregation has occurred, Hamilton and Bishop studied middle-class residential neighborhoods before as well as after desegregation. They also studied middle-class white neighborhoods in which desegregation did not occur during the research period, affording them a "control" group for comparison. And because they had collected information before desegregation took place, they were able to "follow" the changes in people's attitudes by gathering data at several different times.

The researchers found (unsurprisingly) that when whites learned a black family was moving into their neighborhood, this fact attracted much more notice than when another white family was moving in. The initial reaction to having black neighbors was frequently a concern that property values would begin to decline. This concern usually lasted for several months; by the end of one year, however, most responses by the white neighbors toward the black families were positive. Moreover, whites living in the newly desegregated neighborhoods showed less prejudice than those in the neighborhoods that had not been desegregated (Hamilton and Bishop, 1976:65). However, they found also that this change toward favorable attitudes occurred whether the white residents actually had contact with the black neighbors or not. Hence, even though the attitudes of whites changed in the predicted direction, it does not appear that contact as such was responsible for it. Hamilton and Bishop (1976:66) suggested that perhaps the white neighbors were able to see their fears had been groundless and that this "disconfirmation of expectancies" led to more favorable attitudes.

Turning now to studies of school desegregation, we find an even larger and more variegated literature. An important difference between studies of housing and school desegregation is that many of the former have focused directly on the contact hypothesis. Studies of school desegregation, however, have been concerned with a number of topics, including whether the "achievement gap" between black and white children is due to different values in the black and white communities (to which we return in chapter 7), whether "deficits" in achievement values (if they exist) are reversible, whether white teachers will treat children alike regardless of ethnicity, whether the self-esteem of black children will rise following desegregation, and so on (Gerard and Miller, 1975:14–21). More generally, these studies have been classified by St. John (1975:7) as focusing on academic achievement, motivation and self-confidence, and interracial attitudes and behavior. Although the effects of contact and proximity in each of these areas is a matter of considerable practical importance, we are interested here primarily in interracial attitudes and behavior.

St. John's review of evidence relating to the contact hypothesis is based on forty-one studies. These studies were conducted during a period of about thirty-five years in different regions of the country. They included sample sizes ranging from below 100 to over 3,000 and involved children of various ages; and they were based on a number of different research designs and data-gathering methods. St. John (1975:67–68) summarizes the results of the studies by saying that

> for either race positive findings are less common than negative findings and
> . . . It is also apparent that the direction of the findings is as often con-
> tradictory as it is consistent for the two races. Sometimes desegregation is
> reported to have ameliorated the prejudice of whites but intensified that of
> blacks, sometimes the reverse.

Even among the seven studies that focused most directly on desegregation's effect on racial attitudes and employed the best research methods, the pattern of findings was still conflicting. St. John (1975:80) concludes that "comparative studies of the racial attitudes of segregated and desegregated school children are inconclusive." She reminds us, nevertheless, that the conditions under which contact is theoretically expected to lead to changes in attitudes are seldom fully realized in actual desegregation programs; and that when such conditions are met, the results are more promising. For instance, as expected under the contact hypothesis, "Several of the studies reviewed found evidence that long-term desegregation had a beneficial effect on attitudes."

This conclusion has generally been supported by the results of one of the largest and best studies of school desegregation yet performed (Gerard and Miller, 1975). This long-term study of desegregation in the elementary schools of Riverside, California, included both black and Chicano children. Among the many types of data gathered by these researchers were approximately 20,000 children's choices of friends, school-work partners, and play partners. These sociometric data enabled the researchers to make inferences not only about changes in attitudes but about changes in behavior, too. However, despite some favorable changes in attitudes (Goodchilds, Green, and Bikson, 1975), they found that "with the exception of playground interaction, little or no real integration occurred during the relatively long-term contact situation." (Gerard et al., 1975:237). These findings illustrate again that attitudes frequently do not affect behavior as much as do other factors in a social situation. Patchen et al. (1977:73) observe in this connection that "the determinants of interracial behavior are different than those of opinion change."

The evidence we have reviewed on the capacity of contact to reduce intergroup prejudice and discrimination is well summarized by Amir (1969: 319): "At present there are conflicting views and evidence regarding this problem." Obviously, intergroup contacts may not be hailed as *the* way to reduce prejudice. But, like the other "educational" methods we have considered, it has its place. Despite the limitations of attempting to reduce prejudice through interethnic contacts, the main point of the contact hypothesis has generally been supported by sociological studies: under appropriate conditions, personal contacts between majority- and minority-group members can lead to reductions in prejudice. The method seems to work best when people are, so to speak, "in the same boat." But even under apparently unfavorable conditions, contact sometimes leads to reduced antipathy.

To the extent that "educational" methods of reducing prejudice are effective, discrimination also presumably is reduced. Remember, though, this argument assumes that the most effective way to control discrimination is *through* an attack on prejudice. But remember, also, that some of the theories we have reviewed emphasize that the practice of discrimination is more or less independent of the existence of prejudice. These theories, in varying degrees, suggest it may be possible to reduce discrimination directly. Indeed, the institutional-discrimination view implies that this is the only feasible approach.

To illustrate, let us refer again to Merton's (1949) comparison of types of prejudice and discrimination. The prejudiced nondiscriminator, we have seen, fails to discriminate when an external restraint of some kind is encountered. The "external restraint" may be no more than the fear that the individual's friends may disapprove of discrimination. Or it could be a fear that one's business associates or clients will take their business elsewhere. Or it may be an awareness that discrimination is illegal and may, therefore, be punished. In addition to these fears, of course, the prejudiced nondiscriminator may hope that failing to discriminate will bring certain rewards. In short, many people who may harbor beliefs and feelings that seemingly could lead them to discriminate may, in particular social situations, behave in a nondiscriminatory way.

By the same reasoning, many people who do not discriminate in one social situation may do so in another. This fact means we cannot be sure when a person either discriminates or fails to discriminate whether the person is prejudiced. It means further that to predict whether an individual will discriminate, it may be more important to understand the features of the social situation than the individual's tolerance level. This logical possibility was shown to be an actuality in the study by Lohman and Reitzes (1952). It was shown by these researchers that the union's rules forbidding discrimination were upheld in the work place. But to what extent can we rely on the restraints of particular social situations to control discrimination in America? Wouldn't it be better if Americans were always under restraint not to discriminate? Considerations such as these touch an old and controversial question: "If we wish people to stop discriminating (or anything else), why not pass a law against it?"

The Legal Approach

For more than a century, one of the most prominent features of interethnic conflict in America has been the effort to control intergroup relations through laws and judicial decisions. At the national level, in particular, many "landmark" laws and court cases afford a veritable outline of the fight to extend equal rights to all citizens. This approach has always received a substantial amount of support in America, at least at the verbal level. Americans generally claim to endorse the "American Creed" and to believe that its ideals should be inscribed into law (Myrdal, 1964:14). In practice, however, two currents of thought have tended to undermine this approach and to support opposition to it. The first current is that Americans seem generally to couple the statement "There ought to be a law" with a low degree of respect for law (Myrdal, 1964:14). As Berger (1968:1) states, "Americans seem to want laws expressing high ideals but they seem also to want the convenience of ignoring or violating many of them with impunity." Hence, although many people appear to favor laws against discrimination in employment, schooling, housing, access to health care, and so on, such laws are not necessarily obeyed.

This fact is related to the second current of thought opposing the legal approach. It frequently is said that laws cannot enforce good conduct unless they are popular. Since laws that attempt to control private behavior or personal tastes are almost always unpopular, it is said that laws attempting to force equality cannot succeed. Of course, it may be conceded, laws may affect the blatant forms of discrimination; but such controls, at best, affect only the external form of lawful behavior. They cannot change the will to discriminate and cannot, therefore, prevent people from finding ways to circumvent the law. "Laws cannot change the hearts and minds of men," it is said. To support this view, people often cite the failure of the Prohibition experiment in America. Prohibition not only failed to prevent the manufacture, sale, and use of alcoholic beverages but also seemed actually to have encouraged it. It created a "backlash." Many people bought "bootleg" liquor and visited "speakeasies" during the Prohibition era partly because of the excitement that accompanies a popular form of lawbreaking. People seemed attracted to drinking as a way to flaunt the law. Much the same sort of thing has accompained the efforts to increase the legal restraints on the use of other drugs and on such things as prostitution. The great lesson that seems to have been learned in these efforts to control socially disapproved behavior is that "you can't legislate morality!" Effective laws appear only to express what the people regard as legitimate and will accept.

This issue has been the source of a long-standing controversy in Western thought. Among social scientists, the view that unpopular legislation is doomed usually is traced to the influential work of William Graham Sumner (1906;

Allport, 1958:429–443). Sumner's arguments concerning the effort to change society through legislation rested on his analysis of the *folkways* and *mores*. Folkways, or customs, are the practices that the members of a society have adopted as answers to life's problems (Sumner, 1906:34). These methods of doing things gradually become traditions and, as such, define the kinds of behavior that are regarded as right or wrong. Every aspect of life is regulated by the folkways, ranging from how many spouses a person may have to what kind of clothing is acceptable. Those folkways having to do with the most serious social matters are called mores.

Sumner's discussion of the relationship of the laws to the mores is not easily summarized, but the most prominent portions of it appear to support the idea that laws are ineffective tools for bringing about social change. His commentary on the effects of the laws passed during the Reconstruction period following the Civil War is frequently quoted: "Vain attempts have been made to control the new order by legislation. The only result is the proof that legislation cannot make mores" (Sumner, 1906:77). In another place, Sumner (1906:55) states that "Acts of legislation come out of the mores . . . legislation, to be strong, must be consistent with the mores."

Despite appearances, Sumner did not believe the laws could never have an effect on the mores. Indeed, as shown by Ball, Simpson, and Ikeda (1962), he believed that with proper planning laws definitely could be used to bring about fundamental changes. If laws are skillfully framed and rationally planned, he believed, then some portions of conduct could be altered; and if conduct were altered, then changes in thought and feeling would follow. However, he had little confidence that most legislators knew enough to use the law in this way (Sumner, 1906:95). As a result, many people have relied on Sumner's authority to argue that laws cannot alter people's hearts and minds and, therefore, cannot alter behavior. Whether he intended it or not, Sumner's work has been interpreted by many readers to support the idea "that social change must always be glacier-like in its movement and that mass change in attitudes must precede legislative action" (Roche and Gordon, 1965:332).

Let us acknowledge right away that there is a large element of good sense in this argument. Quite clearly, the enactment of a law cannot directly alter people's ideas and emotions. As Sumner has emphasized, the "stroke of the pen" does not, itself, produce changes in the morality of people. However, as this point ordinarily is understood, it contains two important errors. First, it misses the crucial distinction between attitudes and actions. Since most people assume that attitudes are the wellspring of action, the obvious difficulty of changing attitudes through legislation serves to discredit the idea that behavior may be altered in this way. Contemporary sociological thought on this matter generally agrees with a statement by Martin Luther King, Jr. (1962:49): "while it may be true that morality cannot be legislated, behavior *can* be regulated." Consequently, "the habits, if not the hearts, of people *are* being altered every day by Federal action."

The second important point that tends to be ignored by opponents of the legal approach is the possibility that actions—once they conform to the requirements of the law—may lead to a change in the attitudes that seem to underlie the previous actions. However, recall our findings regarding desegregated housing. Very few of the white people living in interracial public housing may realistically be described as having voluntarily chosen these living conditions. For the most part, they accepted the apartments because they had to. As Deutsch and Collins (1956:22) describe it, "Their intensive need for housing compelled them to move into a situation they would otherwise have avoided." But we saw that under the conditions studied blacks and whites who were "forced" to live together did not generally become more antagonistic. In fact, the more closely the whites were required to live with the blacks, the more favorable their attitudes generally became. While this outcome runs counter to commonsense expectations, it may readily be interpreted (among other ways) in terms of the theory of cognitive dissonance introduced earlier. If prejudiced people move into interracial housing, cognitive dissonance is produced. Since the fact of living in interracial housing cannot readily be denied or altered, the main route open to dissonance reduction is a change of attitude. Of course, our review of studies relating to the contact hypothesis has shown that many factors enter into most actual situations, so there is no guarantee that when people are "forced" to alter their discriminatory actions, they will experience a subsequent reduction in prejudice. Nevertheless, even when "their hearts are not in it," new ways of acting may lead people to new ways of thinking. As Pettigrew (1971:279) observes, "Laws first act to modify behavior, and this modified behavior in turn changes the participants' attitudes. . . . Behaving differently . . . often precedes thinking differently." Strange to say, therefore, perhaps the most effective way to reduce prejudice is *first* to reduce discrimination.

If we accept that some laws effectively alter behavior and that behavioral changes may then bring attitudes "into line," then the task of those who favor the legal approach is to estimate the probability that a proposed law to regulate discrimination will succeed. As was true in Sumner's day, there still is no scientific or mathematical solution to this problem. Although Sumner was surely right in his claim that laws are more likely to succeed if they "run with the mores," we now know something more about how they may succeed when the laws and the mores do not coincide. For instance, a number of studies of efforts to desegregate schools have discovered two important and related facts. First, if legal orders to desegregate are strongly and publicly supported by local government and school officials and other influential citizens, then the chance is greatly improved that the change will take place peacefully even when most people in the community are opposed to it. Second, officials should not be intimidated by a noisy opposition. Most people who protest a proposed change and hold up the specter of violence and retaliation will nonetheless accept the change once it has taken place. We should recognize, of course, that there are limits to the application of these ideas. The extent to which the opposition is concentrated and organized, the number of influential citizens who join the opposition, and the intensity of the opposition are a few of the factors that may contribute to the failure of a desegregation effort that is strongly supported by most of the community's leaders. But it is an advance in our thinking to see that the presence of such factors in a social situation do not necessarily mean that effective legislation is impossible.

Another very important discovery in this regard is that a law prohibiting discrimination is much more likely to succeed if it is vigorously enforced. Public officials need not only to make public pronouncements of support for a new law, but they need also to guarantee that those who violate the law—especially at the outset—are punished swiftly for doing so. The swift and certain punishment of violators has led in many actual instances to a rapid and generally peaceful acceptance of an initially unpopular law.

Still another significant point here is the capacity of public officials to enforce the law. For technical reasons, a law that is opposed only moderately may be more difficult to enforce than one that is opposed strongly. Hence, some thought should be given to this point in advance of the passage of a law. We may speculate, for instance, that the Prohibition experiment might have failed even if it had been more strongly supported by the public. As Roche and Gordon (1965:336) observe, "Home manufacture of alcoholic beverages has . . . survived in the Soviet Union, and if the M.V.D. is incapable of banning private brew, there is little reason to suspect that a democratic society could handle the job."

There is, of course, much more to be said on this complex subject; but let us conclude by noting only one additional thing. Despite Sumner's emphasis on the general resistance of the mores to change, he also stressed that under some circumstances changes in them occur rapidly. One of these circumstances occurs when two or more sets of conflicting mores exist simultaneously within a society. This conflict generates a "strain toward consistency," and the law may tip the balance in one direction or the other. In modern societies, in particular, the law seldom is required to stand alone against a monolithic set of opposing mores. More often, the law chooses between competing moral codes (Berger, 1968:219). In this way, the law is aided strongly by some existing ideas and beliefs to create a general social situation that favors obedience to the law once it has been adopted. Thus, the law, with the aid of an existing—though not necessarily predominant—moral code and strong official support and enforcement, may bring about a reduction in discrimination. Then, after people have conformed to the new law, parallel changes in their attitudes are likely to follow.

The legal approach is consistent with the thinking of all of the theorists who emphasize the possibility and importance of direct methods of controlling discrimination. There are some important differences among these theorists, however. Some who advocate direct-control methods may still place heavy emphasis on educational programs aimed at the reduction of prejudice, while others, such as the institutional-discrimination theorists, focus at least as much attention on the rules of organizations (and the way they are administered) as on the laws passed by legislative bodies. The rules governing hiring and firing by corporations and those regulating all forms of licensing and certification may be only loosely connected to enacted laws, but these rules play an enormously important role in the day-to-day lives of everyone in our society. Institutional-discrimination theorists argue that strategic changes in the countless "laws" of the large bureaucracies of modern society are necessary before any attitudinal changes that may have taken place can be made effective. For example, when minority-group members are poorly represented among the employees of a particular organization, these theorists argue that the hiring practices used are either discriminatory or reflect the effects of past discrimination. An especially important way to attack this kind of situation is embodied in the affirmative-action programs sponsored by the federal government. Under these programs, organizations found to have engaged in discrimination in the past must make "good faith" efforts to find qualified minority-group employees. Moreover, any organization may take race into account in hiring in order to make its staff's ethnic composition more nearly resemble that of the general population. In the famous *Bakke* decision of the Supreme Court, such efforts to overcome the effects of past discrimination have been found to be legal if they do not involve precise quotas.[14]

Organized Social Protest

Although the role of organized protest in the reduction of discrimination is explored later (mainly in chapter 7), some comments are appropriate at this point. The discussion thus far has rested on the assumption that the majority's levels of prejudice and discrimination may be reduced with relatively little disharmony or open intergroup conflict. The usual expectation of those who favor education, intergroup contact, the passage of laws, and affirmative action is that, grumbling and complaining aside, the majority will respond to a program of change by easing its pressure on the minorities and that the minorities, after some period of time, will become "equal" to the majority. Intergroup tensions will have been reduced with only moderate "dislocations" and "adjustments" along the way.

This assumption has been sharply challenged, usually by minority-group members. It is argued, in keeping with the group-gains theory, that equality will never be given freely by the majority. As stated by Martin Luther King, Jr. (1964:80) "Lamentably, it is an historical fact that privileged groups seldom give up their privileges voluntarily." The majority is much more likely, in this view, to reduce its levels of discrimination in the face of a boycott, a strike, or a sit-in than in response to the usual kind of educational program or even to laws prohibiting discrimination. Indeed, the majority may be unwilling to adopt laws of this type unless it is pressured to do so by organized minority groups.

From this vantage point, it is possible to claim that whenever the legal approach succeeds, this result is largely due to the power to the minorities. However desirable such things as educational programs, interracial contacts, and antidiscrimination laws may be, they must always be only a part of a larger program consisting of strong ethnic organizations and constant pressure on the majority. All efforts to reduce discrimination and to attain a social standing that is acceptable to the minority must involve some conflict. It is crucial to distinguish here, however, between nonviolent and violent conflict. Many who accept nonviolent conflict as a necessary part of social change are totally opposed to the use of violence and believe that it is indeed "counter-productive."

Conclusion

We have seen that many students assume ethnic prejudice to be the sole or principal cause of discrimination and believe, therefore, that the primary question to be answered is "What causes prejudice?" The underlying assumption here is that if the causes of prejudice can be discovered, then prejudice and, ultimately, discrimination can be reduced by attacking those causes. We have seen further, though, some evidence to suggest that discrimination has other roots. It may not arise mainly from prejudice; its reduction, therefore, may not require an attack on prejudice. Indeed, we have found that if discrimination is controlled first, a surprise extra benefit is sometimes a subsequent decline in prejudice.

The merits of these two opposing approaches—whether to attack prejudice or discrimination first—have led many observers to the view that a compromise is needed. A compromise approach emphasizes the reciprocal relationship of prejudice and discrimination and calls for a simultaneous attack at many different points in the causal chain.

From the standpoint of practical application, the main question is: "Are efforts to create social change aided more by theories that emphasize the role of prejudice, discrimination, or both?" The few illustrations we have discussed show that various educational approaches can reduce prejudice. They do not tell us, however, whether these attitude changes lead to less discrimination and toward equality among racial and ethnic groups. Our illustrations suggest, too, that discrimination may be reduced through legal means even though the prejudice levels of the dominant group have not been previously lowered. Laws against discrimination are aided by the open support of officials and other respected citizens. They also are aided by swift and certain enforcement. Nevertheless, the effort to control discrimination through law faces many obstacles and cannot be relied on solely as a solution to the problem.

Although we are very far indeed from being able to say exactly what measures are most effective in reducing prejudice and discrimination, our analysis supports the following conclusion: given our present knowledge, it is probably best to assume that prejudice and discrimination form a vicious circle and must be attacked simultaneously. However, it is likely that most people overestimate the role of prejudice as a cause of discrimination. Dominant-group members, in particular, tend to ignore or play down the possible effectiveness of strategies that focus on the control of discrimination rather than the reduction of prejudice. Legal methods and some direct-action approaches may not only be the most effective ways to reduce discrimination but also may assist, through time, in the reduction of prejudice as well.

KEY IDEAS

1. Although prejudice (a negative attitude) is usually thought to precede and be *the* cause of discrimination (a negative action), discrimination may also precede prejudice and be a cause of it. Moreover, a person may be prejudiced but not discriminate and discriminate without being prejudiced.

2. Prejudice arises from several sources. Among the most important of these are:

   a. The transmission of specific attitudes and beliefs from one generation to the next: Children learn their group's stereotypes of different out-groups. They also learn which groups are to be admired and which should be held at a great social distance. In the United States, people from countries of the old immigration are socially the least distant from the majority, while nonwhites are the most distant.

   b. The effort to manage the personal frustrations and problems of life: people frequently exhibit an exaggerated, seemingly "irrational" hostility toward the members of out-groups. Such prejudices appear to have more to do with people's inner tensions and conflicts than with the characteristics of the members of the hated group(s).

   c. The material gains and personal satisfactions that accompany social dominance: the members of dominant groups generally enjoy higher incomes, more desirable jobs, and less unemployment than the members of subordinate groups. The dominant-group members also generally receive numerous "psychic gains" or gratifications at the expense of subordinate groups.

   d. The sense of group identity, belongingness, and loyalty that people ordinarily develop toward their own group's members and culture: pride in one's own group may easily shade into or stimulate prejudice toward the groups of others.

3. Discrimination arises from several important sources, some of which do not directly involve prejudice.
   a. The transmission of discriminatory actions: just as children receive certain ideas from their elders, they are also taught directly to act in some ways rather than others. Many of these ways of acting are discriminatory.
   b. The material and psychic gains that accompany social dominance: whether or not it is due to prejudice, discrimination confers advantages on at least some segments of the dominant group.
   c. The social pressures that are exerted to ensure people's conformity to the norms of their group: even when people do not personally desire to ostracize or harm the members of an out-group, they may be expected to do so by the other members of their own group. Those who violate the in-group norms may themselves be ostracized by the in-group members.
   d. The normal operations of the society's institutions: equal opportunity and fair play within a given institutional sector (e.g., the economy) may not lead to equal results. The lingering effects of past discrimination or the existence of discrimination within a related institution (e.g., education) may lead to the disproportionate disqualification of the members of minority groups. The rules of organizations may automatically discriminate.
4. Prejudice and discrimination are related to one another in an incomplete and circular fashion. Discrimination may be reduced by attacks on prejudice, and prejudice may be reduced by attacks on discrimination. However, declines in prejudice are not necessarily translated into reductions in discrimination, and vice versa.
5. The theories of prejudice and discrimination suggest ways to attack these problems. Dominant-group members tend to focus on the reduction of prejudice, the cultural transmission and personality theories, and education as a tool of social change.
6. One important form of intergroup education is to expose people to information concerning out-groups; another is to assist people "to take the role of the other" through books, plays, films, and so on. Both of these methods appear to be useful but not powerful methods of reducing prejudice. The emotional approach seems to be somewhat more effective than the factual approach.
7. Intergroup contacts may be effective in reducing prejudice if the people involved are of similar social status and are engaged in an enjoyable or mutually significant activity. Under other circumstances, intergroup contacts may lead to increased prejudice.
8. Subordinate-group members tend to focus on the reduction of discrimination, the group gains and institutional theories, and the law as an instrument of social change.

9. Many forms of discrimination may be reduced directly rather than by attempting first to alter people's prejudices. The passage and strict enforcement of antidiscrimination laws even when these laws are not popular may bring about rapid changes in behavior. Of course, attempts to "outflank" people's opinions and to require them not to discriminate may boomerang; under many circumstances, however, they do not. Furthermore, once people's discriminatory behavior has been altered, their prejudices are, in many instances, subsequently reduced.

10. Although America's contemporary policies and noblest ideals assume that prejudice and discrimination may be sharply reduced entirely through education and the passage of laws, history shows that changes in majority-minority relations typically have required the organized protest of minorities. While organized protest necessarily involves conflict, effective conflict may be limited to boycotts, strikes, lobbying, and other nonviolent tactics.

11. Since prejudice and discrimination form a vicious circle, it is best to attack them simultaneously. The exclusive or preponderant attention given in the past to the causes and reduction of prejudice rather than directly to discrimination is unwarranted.

NOTES

1. This idea is so prevalent that in many cases discrimination is defined as the acting out of prejudice.

2. Our classification and discussion of the main theories of prejudice and discrimination are particularly indebted to the outstanding presentations of Allport and Simpson and Yinger (Allport, *The Nature of Prejudice;* Simpson and Yinger, *Racial and Cultural Minorities,* pp. 63–164).

3. For reviews of the literature on stereotypes research, see Ehrlich, *The Social Psychology of Prejudice,* pp. 20–60; Bonjean, Hill, and McLemore, *Sociological Measurement,* pp. 163–168.

4. The idea that people may "drain off" aggressive impulses by displacement is a popular one. Many people explain their enthusiasm for "contact" sports (such as football) or "striking" sports (such as bowling) by saying that it helps them to "get things out of their systems." The technical name for this process is *catharsis.*

5. Berkowitz suggests that hostile impulses will not disappear until the frustrated person actually injures the one who is responsible for the frustration.

6. The main findings concerning prejudice, however, go well beyond noting that highly prejudiced persons are more likely to be lower than upper class. Those who are highly prejudiced have been found, on the average, to display a number of other interesting characteristics. Consistent with the frustration-aggression theory, they are more likely to exhibit a high level of frustration and displaced aggression; and they are more likely to exhibit sexual repres-

sion, insecurity, and a "jungle philosophy" of life. These combined traits have suggested to many students of this subject that prejudice is not an isolated attitude but rather a part of a personality syndrome. Such a view helps to explain another general finding in this field: people who are prejudiced against the members of one racial or ethnic group tend also to be prejudiced against others (Berelson and Steiner, *Human Behavior,* pp. 502, 515). The most influential study along this line has been conducted by Adorno et al., *The Authoritarian Personality.* For a good brief discussion, see Allport, *Nature of Prejudice,* pp. 371–412.

7. For a review of many of the earlier studies, see Proshansky, "The Development of Intergroup Attitudes," in *Review of Child Development,* pp. 311–371.

8. For an excellent review of studies of the attitude-behavior relationship, see Schuman and Johnson, "Attitudes and Behavior," in *Annual Reviews of Sociology,* pp. 161–207.

9. There were substantial differences in the opinions of white northerners and southerners. By 1976, roughly 83 percent of all white Americans expressed approval of school desegregation (Taylor, Sheatsley, and Greeley, "Attitudes toward Racial Integration," pp. 42–49).

10. The question of the rate of change is a topic of the succeeding chapters. We may note in passing, however, that at the rates of change in effect between 1950 and 1960, the "gap" between white and nonwhite median years of schooling "would not close until the year 2022," while the gap in incomes "would not close until 2410!" (Broom and Glenn, "When Will America's Negroes Catch Up?" See also, Broom and Glenn, *Transformation of the Negro American,* pp. 84–88, 115–122; Lieberson and Fuguitt, "Negro-White Occupational Differences in the Absence of Discrimination," pp. 188–200). King has attacked the slowness of change more viscerally: "When you are forever fighting a degenerating sense of 'nobodiness'—then you will understand why we find it difficult to wait" (King, *Why We Can't Wait,* p. 82).

11. Although the idea that discrimination might continue even if *nobody* presently were prejudiced may seem extreme, it is not nearly as radical as it might be. In the eyes of some influential social-learning theorists (or behaviorists), attitudes or opinions never cause actions. Skinner, for instance, argues that all behavior is repeated and learned because it is rewarded (reinforced). Since the feelings that accompany a rewarding experience are themselves also rewarded, these feelings may later occur when the rewarded behavior is repeated. After a while, the feelings may occur before the behavior and appear to be the cause of it. As Skinner states: "Many of the things we observe just before we behave occur within our body, and it is easy to take them as the causes of our behavior. Feelings occur at just the right time to serve as causes of behavior" (Skinner, *About Behaviorism,* p. 10). Hence, from a behaviorist perspective, prejudice is not only not *the* main cause of discrimination, it is not even *a* cause! Please note, though, that behaviorists do not argue prejudice is unimportant. People's feelings and attitudes are important in their own right, and prejudices are undesirable psychic conditions. However, from this vantage point, one should not attack prejudice in the hope that this will lead to reductions in discrimination.

12. An important effort to explain the effects of contact has been presented in Williams, *Reduction of Tension through Intergroup Contact,* pp. 81–88.

13. Another area of special research interest has been desegregation in the armed services. See, for example, Butler and Wilson, "The American Soldier Revisited."

14. *Regents of the University of California* v. *Bakke,* 76–811 (1978).

Five

Japanese Americans

I am proud that I am an American citizen of Japanese
Ancestry. . . . Because I believe in America, . . . I pledge
to do her honor in all times and all places.

Mike Masaoka

To create a truly fulfilling identity, Asian Americans realize
they must redefine and articulate Asian American identity
on their own terms.

Amy Tachiki

Our discussions of the old and new immigrations (chapter 3) and prejudice
and discrimination (chapter 4) have shown that the less the members of a
group have resembled the Anglo-American ideal of an "American," the less
acceptable they have been to the dominant group. Our discussion has shown,
too, that although the members of all minority groups in America have
suffered significant degrees of prejudice and discrimination at the hands of
the majority, the levels of prejudice and discrimination have been greatest
toward those groups that are socially most "distant" from the majority. Groups
that are far from the dominant group's notion of the ideal American have been
considered to be low in "assimilative potential" or even to be "unassimilable."

Of all the many factors that affect the dominant group's reactions to a
subordinate group, the factor of race has been most troublesome. We have
noted that during the colonial period, blacks and Indians were defined as
standing outside of the developing Anglo-American society. As other racially
distinctive groups have entered or been brought into the territory of the
United States, they also have been viewed typically as being too distant from
the American ideal to be included as full members of American society. They
have been subjected, therefore, to levels of prejudice and discrimination
resembling those directed toward the blacks and Indians. From this perspective, nonwhite peoples in America have had fewer opportunities and
faced larger obstacles to material or worldly success than have white peoples.
The possibility for these groups "to climb the ladder of success" (e.g., to
achieve secondary structural assimilation) has been lower from the first and

has remained so. Both the level of past discrimination and the extent to which that discrimination has been carried into the present are involved.

Many Americans either reject the above argument outright or accept only a modified form of it. Some believe that the obstacles standing in the way of the success of the nonwhite groups is hardly different from those faced by their own forefathers. Others, who comprise the largest group, will agree that nonwhites have faced the highest levels of prejudice and discrimination, but they will not agree that these barriers have been large enough to explain why blacks, Chicanos, and Indians have remained conspicuously outside the mainstream of American life. Probably, most Americans believe that hard work, education, perseverance, and faith in the American dream are still the main ingredients of success in American society. From this vantage point, even those who suffer the highest levels of prejudice and discrimination should be able to succeed if they will only try hard enough. Their battle may be more difficult, so the argument goes, but if they will quietly tend to their business, opportunities will appear, and they will earn their place in American society.

The above contrast (differences in discrimination versus differences in effort) ignores the many other factors we have mentioned that affect the rate of assimilation of minorities and is, therefore, too sharp. The contrast nonetheless reflects real political differences in modern America and serves as a useful point of reference for our further consideration of the experiences of all nonwhite groups in America.

This observation is especially true of the Japanese Americans. While (as discussed later) the largest nonwhite groups in America have been comparatively unsuccessful, materially speaking, the Japanese Americans have frequently been singled out as an exception to the rule. A series of articles and books have proclaimed the Japanese Americans to be a "model minority," a nonwhite group that has overcome all obstacles through hard work and determination (Hosokawa, 1969; Petersen, 1971; *Newsweek,* 1971). One observer has said, for example, that "no other immigrant group ever faced such difficulties as the Japanese encountered in this country" and "no group ever conducted themselves more creditably" (McWilliams, 1949:155); while another has contended that among those now alive, the Japanese Americans have suffered more discrimination and injustice than any other of America's minorities (Petersen, 1971:3). Despite the odds, however, in terms of many criteria of success and assimilation, the Japanese appear to have "made it" in America. They seem to vindicate the Horatio Alger stories of the American dream. For example, the average number of years of education in the United States in 1970 was 12.1 years (U.S. Bureau of the Census, 1970:386). The comparable figure among the Japanese Americans was 12.5 years (U.S. Bureau of the Census, *Japanese, Chinese, and Filipinos in the United States* 1973:9). Similarly, among white Americans who were employed in 1970, 14.2 percent of the males and 15.3 percent of the females were in occupations classified by the U.S. Bureau of the Census (1970:31) as "professional, technical, and kindred workers." Among Japanese Americans, 21.4 percent of the males and 15.9 percent of the females are classified in these high-prestige occupations.

The extent, cost, and meaning of Japanese American success, however, has been the subject of debate. While most Japanese Americans appear to agree that theirs is a successful group, some others are not so sure. For instance, despite their high average educational level and the appearance that they have been competing successfully for jobs, their average (median) income has remained below that of the white Americans (Schmid and Nobbe, 1965). In 1970, for instance, median family income was $9,961 for whites and $9,590 for Japanese Americans (U.S. Bureau of the Census, 1970:377). This difference in earnings may indicate that the Japanese Americans do not receive jobs equivalent to their educational levels, or it may indicate that they do not receive equal pay for the same work. In either case, this fact suggests that the Japanese Americans, for all their effort, still face discrimination in America. For this reason, among others, some Japanese Americans react strongly to the description of their group as a modern American success story. They consider such descriptions to be self-serving stereotypes through which the dominant group attempts to deny the continuation of discrimination against the Japanese Americans and to prove that a lack of effort—not discrimination—is responsible for the problems of black Americans, Chicanos, and Indian Americans (Tachiki, 1971:1). Furthermore, some Japanese American scholars have concluded that it is seriously misleading even to consider the status of Japanese Americans as a question of assimilation. Takagi (1973) considers the concept of assimilation to be implicitly racist, while Kagiwada (1973:162) believes any study of assimilation processes necessarily strengthens the ideology of Anglo conformity.

The Japanese Americans, then, present a puzzling and instructive picture. Despite their nonwhite racial identification, they appear in several important respects to have followed a path of assimilation resembling that of many of the new immigrants who were arriving from Europe during the period of heaviest Japanese immigration. They surely have not disappeared as a group, however, and there is today a new questioning within the Japanese American community of its place in American society. Let us begin to explore this puzzle by examining some of the most important events that have affected the Japanese since their arrival in this country. We return later to questions concerning the types and extent of Japanese American assimilation.

Japanese Immigration and Native Reactions

The peak years of Japanese immigration occurred during the period of the new immigration from Europe. This period, please recall, was characterized by the growing hostility of native Americans to foreigners, by the development and popularization of racist ideas, and by the growth of legal efforts to restrict immigration. Therefore, even though the Japanese immigration to America was comparatively small, many factors combined to create the impression that the United States was in grave danger of being overrun by "hordes" of "Mongolians" and must be constantly on guard against "the yellow peril." Although the phrase "the yellow peril" originally had been applied mainly to the Chinese, by 1905, it referred primarily to the Japanese.[1] In that year, the war in progress between Russia and Japan ended in a resounding victory for Japan. For the first time since the Europeans had commenced to colonize the world during the fifteenth century, a "colored" nation had defeated a "white" nation. In so doing, Japan established a reputation as a first-rank military power. The belief that the United States was in imminent danger of being swamped in a sea of human waves from the East gained in popular acceptance, especially in California.

California had long been a center for anti-Asian sentiment. The basis for this hostility was created during the years following the gold rush when thousands of Chinese coolies had been accepted into the United States—as had so many other peoples before them—to assist with the hard manual labor of mining, building railroads, and so on. The concentration of the Chinese in California, however, soon became the subject of political debate and public protest. In 1852, the governor of California recommended that some action be taken to stem the "tide of Asiatic immigration" (Daniels, 1969:16). The "action" taken by many whites was the slaughter, largely unpunished, of hundreds of Chinese (tenBroek, Barnhart, and Matson, 1954: 15). Anticoolie clubs were organized beginning in 1862. When the transcontinental railroad was completed in 1869, thousands of American men were thrown out of work and into direct competition for employment with Chinese laborers. Their resentment of what they considered to be unfair competition led to demands that Chinese immigration be stopped. It also led to the formation of a Workingmen's Party that campaigned with the slogan "The Chinese Must Go!" (McWilliams, 1949:174). The issue of Chinese immigration became so prominent in California during this period that both major political parties came out against the Chinese. By 1882, the clamor in California for action reached such proportions that the Congress of the United States passed a law that suspended the immigration of Chinese to the United States for a period of ten years.

The extraordinary unity of California's working people against the Chinese (and later the Japanese and other Asians) rests on a paradox. Although California has long been an important agricultural state, it has had from the very beginning a powerful labor movement (McWilliams, 1949:128). For such a movement to exist in a nonindustrial state, many different elements had to combine. Shopkeepers, rural people, and white-collar workers have all strongly supported labor unions. The glue holding this unusual coalition together, according the McWilliams (1949:140), has been an anti-Asian "emotional class consciousness." In addition, therefore, to the usual opposition laboring immigrants have faced from their direct native competitors, Asian Americans in California have had to contend with a broadly based, powerful labor movement. In California, only the upper classes consistently favored open immigration.

Practically none of the early criticism of "Asiatics" and "Mongolians" was directed toward the Japanese. From 1638 to 1868, the Japanese government had not permitted its citizens to emigrate, so until 1868 there had been no official Japanese emigration to the United States. Previously, only a few castaways and government representatives had ever reached this country (Ichihashi, 1932:47–48). Even after the Japanese government did begin to permit emigration, those granted passports were mainly students who were expected to seek knowledge and come back home "so that the foundations of the Empire may be strengthened" (Ichihashi, 1932:3). Laborers, in particular, were still forbidden to leave the country. The Japanese government did not wish to create the impression that Japan, like China, was a reservoir of coolie labor. Consequently, until 1884, laborers did not receive permission to travel abroad (Ichihashi, 1932:6).[2] Altogether, before 1890, hardly more than 4,000 Japanese had traveled to the United States, and more than half of these had returned home (Ichihashi, 1932:53). Consequently, the U.S. census of 1890 showed only 2,039 Japanese in the whole country.

As noted previously, the Chinese Exclusion Act of 1882 marks the first time that the United States had acted to restrict immigration on the basis of national origin. It also was the first time Congress had acted to bar members of a particular ethnic group from becoming citizens. However, since the period of suspension of immigration under the act was to end in 1892, the supporters of Chinese exclusion continued to agitate, and the legislation was continued after 1892. However, as 1892 approached—the year of the renewal of the Chinese Exclusion Act—the Japanese began to arrive in larger numbers. For example, in 1891, nearly 1,500 arrived. Although these numbers were still extremely small compared to the population of the United States at that time or compared to the numbers of immigrants arriving simultaneously from several other countries, they represented a noticeable increase in Japanese immigration over the previous years. This increase, following as it did some forty years of anti-Chinese agitation, attracted the unfavorable attention of the San Francisco *Morning Call.* In a series of five articles, the *Call* launched a "crusade against Japanese contract labor" (Daniels, 1969:20). The paper claimed the Japanese immigrants were taking work away from Americans and that by 1900 their immigration would reach a yearly level of 120,000. The number of Japanese arriving during the decade of the 1890s did, in fact, rise sharply over the 1880s; in 1900, there were over 25,000 Japanese in the United States. But that number did not even come close to the dire predictions of the *Call.*

The first large anti-Japanese protest meeting in California was organized in 1900 after labor unions gained partial control of the San Francisco city government (tenBroek, Barnhart, and Matson, 1954:35). The meeting featured such prominent figures of the day as J. D. Phelan (later a U.S.

senator) and E. A. Ross, a sociology professor at Stanford University. Phelan declared, in a speech to the group, that "these Asiatic laborers will undermine our civilization" (tenBroek, Barnhart, and Matson, 1954:35). He stated also that "the Chinese and Japanese are not the stuff of which American citizens can be made" (Daniels, 1969:21). Ross wished to restrict Japanese immigration on the familiar ground that it undercut native labor, a sentiment echoed in that election year by the platforms of both major political parties.

The charge that the Japanese were a threat to American labor deserves further comment. The small numbers of the Japanese plus the vigor of the native resistance to them have led writers to assume that the hostility toward the Japanese was totally or largely without foundation, that it was an "irrational" rejection based primarily on the fact of racial and cultural differences. This position has been criticized by Bonacich (1972:551–554) on two grounds. First, she argues that Japanese workers for the most part were fortune seekers ("sojourners") who intended to return home to Japan as soon as possible. Consequently, they were willing to work for lower wages than the members of any other group and to work longer hours at the convenience of the employer. Each of these characteristics served actually to reduce the overall cost of Japanese labor. Second, one should not assume that low-cost labor must be present in large numbers in order to pose a genuine threat to native laborers. If the latter have reason to believe that a small group of low-priced laborers are merely the vanguard of a larger flow, then they have a realistic basis for opposing that flow. Bonacich (1972:555) argues, therefore, that the movement to exclude the Japanese was an understandable reaction of higher-priced labor to the split labor market created by the Japanese immigration.

After the anti-Japanese outbursts of 1900, things quieted down again until 1905. In that year, however, a sustained campaign against the Japanese was launched. The most conspicuous forces initiating this campaign were, as in 1892, a newspaper and, as in 1900, organized labor. The newspaper was the very influential, highly respected *San Francisco Chronicle*. Beginning in February 1905 and continuing for nearly a year, the *Chronicle* ran "scare" headlines and page-one articles attacking Japanese immigration. In its first broadside, the headline read: "THE JAPANESE INVASION, THE PROBLEM OF THE HOUR." Some of the subsequent headlines included "THE YELLOW PERIL—HOW JAPANESE CROWD OUT THE WHITE RACE" (Daniels, 1969:25). In the articles accompanying such headlines, the paper repeated the old claims that the Japanese immigration would become a "raging torrent" that would inundate the West Coast. Repeated and embroidered, too, were the charges that the Japanese were unassimilable and were an economic threat to native laborers. In March 1905, the California legislature passed a resolution attacking the Japanese as "undesirable" and as a "blight" that would soon descend on our shores (Daniels, 1969:27). It also asked Congress to restrict the further immigration of the Japanese. Every session of the California legislature for the next forty years considered measures against the Japanese.

The anti-Japanese barrage led to the formation, in May 1905, of the Japanese and Korean Exclusion League, which was later renamed the Asiatic Exclusion League (tenBroek, Barnhart, and Matson, 1954:35). This league, comprised primarily of labor-union representatives, was the first and most prominent organization founded for the purpose of excluding the Japanese from the United States. Its program listed both economic and racial reasons for exclusion. Among its principles, for instance, were listed the argument "We cannot compete with a people having a low standard of wages" and "It should be against public policy to permit our women to intermarry with Asiatics" (Daniels, 1969:28). Although the Asiatic Exclusion League represented the conservative wing of the American labor movement, its main goal was endorsed also by many socialists. Jack London conveyed the prevailing mood in the following: "I am first of all a white man and only then a Socialist" (Daniels, 1969:30). In 1907, the National Executive Committee of the American Socialist Party unanimously agreed to oppose the immigration of Asiatics.

One of the first actions of the Asiatic Exclusion League was to endorse the segregation of Japanese pupils in the public schools of San Francisco. This idea was not new. In fact, the San Francisco Board of Education had announced only a few days before the league was formed that such a plan was being considered. In view of the fact that the "separate but equal" doctrine of public education had been in effect by this time for nine years, such an action does not seem too strange.[3] Moreover, since the segregation would affect only a small number of pupils in only one city, we might expect no more than local interest in it. Strangely enough, though, the conflict in San Francisco concerning the segregation of Japanese pupils spiraled into a tense confrontation between the governments of the United States and Japan.

The combined agitations of the *Chronicle* and the league were followed by a rapid increase in the number of incidents of interracial violence in San Francisco. Individual Japanese were attacked. Rocks and rotten eggs were thrown at and into places of business owned by Japanese. And a boycott instituted against Japanese restaurants was ended only after the restaurant owners agreed to pay for "protection." These incidents were accompanied by periodic demands that the board of education implement the segregation plan that had been mentioned. A year and a half after the league began its agitation, the board of education ordered all Japanese, Chinese, and Korean pupils to attend a separate school for Orientals. The board defended this action by referring to a California law that permitted school boards to take such steps. Oddly, this event received little public attention at the time, even in San Francisco; however, the matter was destined to be amply noticed. Nine days after the order went into effect, various reports concerning it were published in Tokyo newspapers, and the Japanese government filed an official complaint with Pres. Theodore Roosevelt. At this point, a problem that previously had been mainly of local interest became a matter of national concern and, possibly, of national security. President Roosevelt quickly announced his grave concern about the situation and stated his intention to protect Japanese nationals in this country. He also dispatched his secretary of commerce and labor, Victor Metcalf, to San Francisco to investigate, and he authorized the secretary of state, Elihu Root, to use armed forces if necessary to protect the Japanese. In his annual message to Congress a few weeks later, the president asked that he be given more authority to protect the rights of aliens and, thereby, to prevent local mobs from committing acts "which would plunge us into war" (Daniels, 1969:39).

The school-board crisis set into motion a long and complicated series of negotiations between the governments of the United States and Japan, on the one hand, and the federal and California governments, on the other. President Roosevelt was sufficiently impressed by Admiral Togo's victory over the Russian fleet to believe that a solution must be reached that was in no way insulting to Japan. At the same time, he was eager to find some way to restrict Japanese immigration, which had fueled the anti-Japanese movement in California.

A compromise was achieved in two main steps during 1907 and 1908. First, the president promised the San Francisco Board of Education that if they would permit all Japanese children, whether citizens or aliens, to return to the regular public schools, he would move to restrict Japanese immigration. The president also urged the California governor and state legislature to reject any further efforts to pass anti-Japanese legislation. On March 13, 1907, the board repealed the school segregation resolution. The president, in turn, issued an executive order the very next day saying that Japanese workers would no longer be permitted to enter the United States through Mexico, Canada, or Hawaii unless their passports specifically entitled them to do so (Ichihashi, 1932:244–245).

The second part of the compromise was the celebrated "Gentlemen's Agreement" between the United States and Japan concerning the types of emigration the Japanese government would encourage. Under the terms of the agreement, to begin in the summer of 1908, the government of Japan would continue issuing passports to the United States only to nonlaborers; laborers who lived in America but had been visiting Japan; the wives, parents, and children of those who had settled in America; and those who owned an interest in an American farm enterprise (Ichihashi, 1932:246; Petersen, 1971:43). Additionally, on its own initiative, the Japanese government applied the terms of the Gentlemen's Agreement to Hawaii (which was now a U.S. possession) and sharply curtailed the issuance of passports to those who wished to go to Mexico. Thus, some eighteen months after the school crisis had erupted, the Gentlemen's Agreement appeared to have resolved a difficult set of problems. The anti-Japanese elements in California believed that the further immigration of the Japanese had been stopped even though no insulting restrictions had been placed by the United States on immigration directly from Japan. That matter had been handled "voluntarily" by the Japanese.

We may note here that the American exclusionists had found allies beyond the borders of the United States. Many of the points of friction between the West Coast Americans and the Japanese existed also between the West Coast Canadians and the Japanese. As a consequence, a Canadian branch of the Asiatic Exclusion League was formed in Vancouver, British Columbia, in 1907. In September of that year, a mass meeting of the league was organized to rally support for the exclusion of the Japanese and all other Asians from Canada. As the crowd warmed to its task, some of its members began to destroy property in the Chinese and Japanese sections of the city. Fighting broke out between the exclusionists and the Japanese and some blood was shed. The rioting led to a deterioration of relations between Japan and Canada. Approximately four months later, Canada concluded a gentlemen's agreement along the lines of the one negotiated by the United States.[4]

The Gentlemen's Agreement had a dramatic impact on the number of Japanese aliens admitted to and remaining in the United States and Hawaii. The peak years of 1907–1908 were followed by sharp reductions in the number of admissions (Ichihashi, 1932:58), and for the next two years, the departures actually exceeded admissions, resulting in a net decline of the Japanese population (Petersen, 1971:197). These drastic changes ended what has been called the "frontier period" of the Japanese experience in America (LaViolette, 1945:10; Miyamoto, 1972:220).

As has been generally true of the vanguard among immigrant groups, most of the Japanese who came to America before 1908 were single males in search of a fortune; so, at the beginning of this century, there were in the United States nearly seven Japanese men for each Japanese woman (Petersen, 1971:196). Consequently, the Japanese community in America contained few families and only the beginnings of ordinary institutional life. This situation changed rapidly, however, in the following decade. Since the Gentlemen's Agreement permitted those who were the wives of residents of the United States to enter, many of the men who decided to stay here sent home to Japan for wives. Even though this action was completely consistent with the Gentlemen's Agreement, many Americans nevertheless saw it as treachery.

This interpretation seemed all the more plausible to many people as the traditional marriage customs of Japan became a topic of public discussion. In Japan, marriages were considered to be more a union of two families than of two individuals. When a young man was ready to marry, and an eligible girl was under consideration, a go-between who was respected by both families would investigate the backgrounds of the prospective partners. If both met all of the tests of eligibility, the go-between then would negotiate the wedding arrangements (Ichihashi, 1932:293). Under normal circumstances, of course, the partners would meet at a specified place and time, and the wedding would be conducted. But what is to be done when the partners are, literally, oceans apart? A solution to this problem was the "picture-bride marriage" (Miyamoto, 1972:226). Under this arrangement, the prospective bride and groom exchanged photographs as a part of the agreement procedure. Then, after the go-between's work was over, the prospective bride would sail for America to conclude the marriage.

This practice of selecting marriage partners sight unseen struck many Americans as outrageous and uncivilized. Stories were circulated concerning fraudulent and "immoral" aspects of the process. It was said that the use of retouched photographs was common and that the Japanese men frequently "swapped" brides at the dock. More disturbing to many, though, was that the arrival of thousands of these "picture brides" during the next few years seemed to confirm the view that the Japanese were determined to circumvent any measure intended to keep them from "overrunning" the country. If they were unable to accomplish this feat through immigration, it was said, then they would do it through high fertility rates!

The emotional character of the reaction to the "picture brides" created the impression that many more Japanese were arriving (and staying) then really were. During the period 1911–1920, approximately 87,000 Japanese aliens were admitted to the United States; however, more than 70,000 Japanese aliens left the country during the same time. Thus, the total gain of Japanese aliens during the decade was about 17,000; and in no year did the net gain of Japanese aliens reach 3,500 (Ichihashi, 1932:62). Moreover, probably no more than one-third of this small increase was comprised of "picture brides" (Ichihashi, 1932:292). An important effect of the "picture bride" migration, nevertheless, was to reduce greatly the imbalance between the sexes within the Japanese group in America. Although the "picture bride" migration ended in 1921 when the Japanese government stopped issuing passports for this purpose, it created the conditions necessary for building families and developing institutionally balanced communities. By 1920, there were less than two men for each woman; and the Japanese—like so many other immigrant groups—had formed numerous small communities and sub-communities that recreated in many ways the institutions and culture of the homeland.

The Japanese Family and Community in America

Many immigrant groups to this country have been "clannish," have had families that (at least formally) were dominated by the father, have attached great importance to age, have given preference to male children (especially the firstborn), and have experienced a marked split between the first and second generations. While the Japanese have not been unusual in possessing this cluster of characteristics, they have exhibited them to an unusually high degree.

Consider the last point first. The different Japanese and Japanese American generations were so distinct from one another that they were identified by different names. The first-generation immigrants, the Issei, are primarily those who arrived before the legal exclusion of 1924 (described below). The second generation, the Nisei, are American-born citizens who generally reached adulthood before or by the outbreak of World War II. The third generation, the Sansei, were born mainly following World War II.[5]

The distinctiveness of the Japanese generations was created primarily by the interruption of the immigrant flow created, first, by the Gentlemen's Agreement and then, later, by exclusionary legislation. For this reason, the normal age gap that exists between generations became even more important than usual. The Issei did not continue to be enlarged by the arrival of new-comers from Japan, so the age gap was not blurred by the presence of people of intermediate ages. Consequently, the Nisei seldom encountered a young person who recently had migrated from the old country. Nearly all of their peers were, like themselves, American born. To a larger extent than is usually true of an immigrant group, therefore, the old country experiences and ways of the Issei stood in sharp contrast to the American ways of the Nisei.

While the two-stage process through which the Issei immigration was halted generated special problems for them, it did not prevent them from developing in America, as in Japan, highly interdependent and cohesive communities. The ethnic community afforded the immigrants economic support, the satisfactions of being with countrymen, and even physical protection. Within the ethnic community, a person could receive help in locating a job, finding a place to live, or starting a business. One could also speak the native language, eat familiar foods, and relax among relatives and friends. And, given the obvious hostility of so many Americans toward them, the ethnic community provided the Japanese some protection from the surrounding society. As has been true for other immigrant groups, the ethnic community was simultaneously a tool to assist the immigrant to adjust to the demands of the new setting and to sustain and embellish the way of life that had been left behind.[6]

Several aspects of Japanese family and community life are of special importance in understanding their adjustment to American life both at the beginning and later on. As noted earlier, the traditional Japanese family was not thought of merely as a union of two people who were in love but as a union of two families. The extended family unit thus created was, in turn, connected in numerous ways through other marriages to the larger community. An important effect of this pattern of interrelationships is that everyone in the community had important obligations to many others within the community. The other side of the coin was that the family could call on the larger community for assistance and support. The Issei were extraordinarily eager to reestablish this traditional pattern of family and community relationships and to transmit its sustaining values to the Nisei. To a greater extent than most other immigrant groups of this period, the Issei identified with the homeland, took pride in its achievements, and, therefore, wished their children to have a strong tie to Japan. The open display of affection for Japan was frequently used against them in later years.

The Nisei were taught Japanese etiquette, which involves a high regard for obligation and authority. Children were expected to understand that they were members of a Japanese family and community, not just unfettered individuals, and that each member had numerous duties and responsibilities. The parents were obligated to the children, but the children were expected to reciprocate. In this way, the child learned that the acts of each individual are of significance to the entire group (LaViolette, 1945:19; Miyamoto, 1972: 228–229).

In addition to the importance of politeness, respect for authority, attention to parental wishes, and duty to the community, the Issei also emphasized the traditional Japanese values of hard work, cleanliness, neatness, and honesty and the importance of education, occupational success, and good reputation. Although we turn later to an analysis of the importance of these values in the adjustment of the Japanese to American conditions, it is obvious that many of the traditional Japanese values are the same as many traditional values of the Anglo-Americans. We may presume even now, therefore, that their acceptance of these values has played an important part in the relations of the two groups.

As we have mentioned, the type of human relations stressed by the Issei within the family were synchronized with, and comprised an integral part of, the organization of the wider community. The main links between the extended family and the rest of the community grew out of the fact that people from the same areas of Japan tended to settle near one another in the United States. Those from the same *ken* (province or prefecture) felt especially close to one another. *Kenjin* (those from the same *ken*) were preferred as friends, neighbors, business associates, and marriage partners. These bonds were so strong that associations based on them often were formed (*kenjinkai*). But the purposes of the *kenjinkai* went far beyond sociable, business, and recreational activities. They published newspapers, acted as employment agencies, provided legal advice, gave money to needy members, and paid medical and burial expenses (Light, 1974:283). They also frequently sponsored a form of financial assistance known as the *tanomoshi-kō*. The *tanomoshi-kō* was an organization (usually of a few *kenjin*) through which money was pooled and then loaned in rotation to various members. This rotating pool of funds was loaned entirely on mutual trust and obligation (Light, 1974:283; Miyamoto, 1972:224; Petersen, 1971:56–57). The success of the *tanomoshi-kō* frequently is cited to illustrate both the Japanese approach to wordly success and the strength of their interpersonal bonds.

Many of the functions of the *kenjinkai* were formalized in the Japanese Association, which, according to Kitano (1969:81), "was the most important Issei group." While the Japanese Association also provided numerous social and benevolent services, its main object was the protection of the Japanese community. The Issei worked through this association to keep the Japanese community "in line" and, thereby, to reduce friction with the Americans. They also used the association to obtain legal services and police assistance. Whenever the police were unresponsive, the Japanese Association could turn to the Japanese consul and ask the Japanese government to intervene in their behalf. This latter power, as was illustrated in the school board crisis, has been of considerable significance. Everything considered, the Japanese Association has played an important role in establishing and maintaining traditional Japanese ways of life within the American setting and, consequently, of resisting cultural, primary structural, and marital assimilation (Kitano, 1969:81–82). To the extent that the association promoted Japanese-owned businesses to serve an all-Japanese clientele, it also resisted second: ry structural assimilation.

Another important form of association established by the Issei to build and strengthen the Japanese community in America was the Japanese Language School (Kitano, 1969:24–25; LaViolette, 1945:52–56; Petersen, 1971:54–58). As the Nisei began to grow and to learn English, the Issei recognized that their ability to transmit the ideals of Japanese society to their children required formal instruction in the Japanese language; so the main purpose of these schools was to teach the Nisei Japanese. However, even though most Nisei children attended such schools at one time or another, few of them learned fluent Japanese.

The Japanese Language Schools were also expected to supplement the parents' efforts to instill the traditional ethics and values of Japan. As in the family, the children were drilled on such things as the importance of industry, home, and duty to one's parents. Although the schools were not very effective as a means to transmit the Japanese language, they symbolized the desire of the Issei to assure their children a Japanese education. They also brought the Nisei together after public school hours and on Saturday, thereby strengthening the social ties among them and decreasing their contacts with other American children. Finally, the schools served as social centers for the Issei. In all of these ways, the Japanese Language Schools sought to keep the Nisei generation in close contact with the Issei generation and, simultaneously, to prevent them from becoming "too American."

All of these factors combined to accentuate the differences between the Issei and Nisei generations. Each of the two generations was unusually homogeneous with respect to age, background, and general life experiences. The center of gravity within the Issei generation was the old country and its traditions. The Nisei, like most other second-generation groups, sought increasingly to break with the old ways.

Japanese Occupations and the Alien Land Laws

As stated earlier, the first Japanese who came to America after the Japanese government permitted it (in 1868) were not members of the laboring classes; they were students (the well-known "school boys") who took part-time jobs to help pay the costs of their stay here. Most of these students worked as domestic servants; however, when the main body of Japanese immigration got underway during the 1890s, the new arrivals took a wide variety of jobs. They were found in railroad construction, canning, lumbering, mining, fishing, seasonal farm labor, and so on. As the turn of the century approached, though, the Japanese moved increasingly into agricultural pursuits. During the first decade of the present century, the number of Japanese in agriculture grew rapidly, especially in California where they were most numerous; and, by 1908, agriculture was the leading form of employment among them (Ichihashi, 1932:162–163).

As the Japanese became more conspicuous in agriculture, native Americans began to complain that the Japanese were acquiring too much land and were "taking over" food production. As usual, a persuasive charge against the Japanese was they did not compete fairly. They were willing to work for less than white laborers and, in some instances, preferred payment in crops or land rather than in wages. In this way, they were gradually gaining a toehold in agriculture and driving out some of the native farmers.

The fear that the efficient Japanese would gradually acquire all of the farming land of California led to an increase in the attempts to control them by legislation. Anti-Japanese land bills were introduced into the California legislature in 1909 and 1911. The first bill to become law, however, was the Alien Land Law of 1913. Although this law did not specifically mention the Japanese or any other nationality group, it was clearly aimed at the Japanese. Instead of saying that Japanese aliens could not own land, the law prohibited ownership by those who were "ineligible to citizenship."

This curious phrase rests on some equally curious facts about American naturalization law. When the first naturalization act was written in 1790, citizenship was made available to any "free white person," which excluded blacks and Indians. And, as noted in chapter 3, this prohibition was enlarged through the Chinese Exclusion Act of 1882. However, the ineligibility of the Japanese for citizenship was based on a different circumstance. When Hawaii was annexed in 1898, "all persons who had been citizens of the Republic were given citizenship, and no others" (Petersen, 1971:47). Since the Japanese had been denied citizenship in Hawaii, and since the Hawaiian rules of citizenship had been accepted by the United States, it was assumed, when the Alien Land Law was enacted, that the Japanese could not become citizens of the United States. As things turned out, this position was correct; but the matter was not settled until 1922 when the Supreme Court ruled in *Ozawa* v. *the United States* that the Japanese, indeed, were not eligible for citizenship.

The thinly veiled, discriminatory intent of the Alien Land Law was readily apparent in Japan. Once again, anti-Japanese activities in California precipitated an international incident. Many people in Japan favored war with the United States (Daniels, 1969:61). When the law was signed, the Japanese government was very displeased and entered a vigorous official protest in Washington. The American government denied that the California law was intended to discriminate against the Japanese. Although the controversy stirred emotions on both sides of the Pacific, it was soon overshadowed by the gathering storm clouds of war in Europe. In the summer of 1914, World War I broke out. Japan quickly declared war on Germany and joined the Allies.

As matters developed, the Japanese were particularly successful in agriculture following the passage of the Alien Land Law. The traditional techniques of reclaiming land and farming it intensively served them well. "Their skill and energy," writes Iwata (1962:37), "helped to reclaim and improve thousands of acres of worthless lands throughout the state . . . and made them fertile and immensely productive." Even though they controlled only about 1 percent of California's agricultural land, the crops they produced were valued at about 10 percent of the state's total. In Iwata's (1962:37) opinion, the Issei were "a significant factor in making California one of the greatest farming States in the union." In the first place, the Issei soon learned ways to evade the law. One common method was to register land holding in the names of their Nisei children, who were American citizens. Another was to place controlling interest of their property in the hands of American friends. Perhaps a more important aid, though, than these legal but evasive tactics was that the outbreak of World War I sharply increased the need for agricultural workers. The continued arrival of the Japanese immigrants who were eligible under the Gentlemen's Agreement, combined with the movement of the Japanese out of the cities, created an available work force that suddenly was in high demand. Moreover, after the United States entered the war, Japan became an ally, and the official ties between the two countries were strengthened. As a result, until the end of World War I, overt anti-Japanese sentiment in California was noticeably reduced.

When the war ended, the demand for agricultural products went down, and thousands of veterans came home looking for work. By then, too, it was obvious that the Gentlemen's Agreement had not stopped the growth of the Japanese population and that the Alien Land Law had not prevented the Japanese from increasing their land holdings. Hence, the agitation against the Japanese (whether Issei or Nisei) began to increase as the war approached an end.[7] A major effort of those who wished to exclude the Japanese and their children from America went into revising California's Alien Land Law. In 1920, an amended Alien Land Law was passed. This law attempted to close the loopholes of the earlier law. It even included a provision that prohibited the Issei from acquiring control of land by placing it in the names of their children. Since the Nisei were citizens of the United States, however, this provision was soon declared unconstitutional.

Exclusion

The Alien Land Law of 1920 represented the last major effort of the exclusionists to achieve their objective by working primarily at the state level. Their attention increasingly was centered on the idea of immigration restriction (or, if possible, exclusion) at the national level. And as mentioned in our discussion of racism in chapter 3, the time was ripe for a national approach. The doctrine of white supremacy had become increasingly popular throughout the United States, as had the demand that the United States be protected against "the rising tide of color" through some form of federal restriction on immigration. Thus, the "California position" on the question of restriction had finally captured the sympathies of a national following.

The main thrust of the national movement was in the direction of some type of quota system rather than toward a system of exclusion. The Immigration Restriction Law of 1921, for example, established a quota system for many countries but recognized the validity of the Gentlemen's Agreement. In this way, the Japanese were exempted from the quota system. Nevertheless, in May 1924, a new Immigration Act was passed that not only repudiated the Gentlemen's Agreement but also denied Japan an immigration quota. At last, the dream of the exclusionists had been realized. Immigration from Japan had been stopped. This result is especially amazing when we consider that the number of Japanese who would have been eligible for admission each year under the quota system was 146!

Why did the United States accept the principle of exclusion for the Japanese (and thereby single Japan out for international humiliation) when the quota system would have reduced the number of Japanese immigrants to almost nothing? Surely what may be called the "racist climate of opinion" had something to do with it. Even some Americans who vigorously opposed a quota system for other nations were in favor of excluding the Japanese. Still, most leaders apparently favored a continuation of the Gentlemen's Agreement with the addition of a quota for Japan. The government of Japan apparently was ready to accept this new form of restriction since it applied to many other nations as well.

The crucial scene in this international tragedy was played primarily by Secretary of State Charles Evans Hughes, Ambassador Masanao Hanihara, and U.S. Senator Henry Cabot Lodge. At Hughes' suggestion, Ambassador Hanihara prepared a letter to Hughes that summarized the understandings of the Gentlemen's Agreement, expressed the Japanese government's willingness to modify the agreement if that pleased the United States, and briefly commented on the immigration bill then under consideration by Congress. The ambassador's comments concerning the immigration bill were guarded and very proper. He assured Secretary Hughes that the Japanese government did in no way contest the right of the United States to regulate immigration but, in fact, wished to cooperate with the United States in doing so. He also emphasized that Japan did not wish for its citizens to go where they were not wanted. He did urge, though, that no discriminatory legislation be passed. Exclusion from the United States, he said, would be "mortifying . . . to the Government and people of Japan" (Daniels, 1969:101). Hanihara's closing remarks, however, stated that exclusion of the Japanese would have "grave consequences." This letter was given by Secretary Hughes to the U.S. Senate in the hope that it would clarify for the Senate the terms of the Gentlemen's Agreement. Instead, it led Senator Lodge to speak in favor of Japanese exclusion on the ground that the phrase "grave consequences" was a "veiled threat" against the United States. Lodge's stand destroyed the support for a quota system for Japan and led fairly directly to an exclusion provision in the new immigration law.

As Ambassador Hanihara had warned, the Japanese were very angry and resentful. The United States had, in their view, violated its own principles of equality and justice as well as the Gentlemen's Agreement. The primary issue was whether Japan was to be treated as an equal among nations. While it is impossible to weigh fully the consequences of these events, it is almost certain that the long-range relations between the two countries were damaged by them. Indeed, some scholars have suggested that it was an important link in the chain of events leading to the Japanese attack on Pearl Harbor in 1941 (Kitano, 1969:28).

The Second-Generation Period

The cessation of Japanese immigration to the United States in 1924 and the continuing status of the Issei as ineligible to become citizens left them in a very strange position. Like most other immigrant groups, they had come to America, established homes, started families, and filled various niches in the American economy. Indeed, in the latter respect, they had made quite a name for themselves. They were extremely industrious (to a fault, the natives thought), and by transferring many old-country skills, they had become prominent in such fields as agriculture and landscape gardening. But despite the obvious ability of the Issei to adapt to American conditions, even in the face of the exaggerated hostility of the natives, their standing in this country at the end of the 1907–1924 "settlement period" was anything but secure.[8] To a considerable extent, the claims of the Japanese community to fair treatment in this country rested on the fact that the Nisei were American citizens. This second generation of Japanese in America, then, represented an even bigger "bet" on the future than is normally the case. This generation would assure the continuation of the Japanese community in America after the Issei were gone. The second-generation period, therefore, was one in which the Issei continued to build on the economic and community foundations established during the frontier and settlement periods. Their goal was to assist the Nisei in achieving the standing in American society to which their citizenship entitled them, while at the same time they continued to hope that their children would adopt and exemplify the traditional virtues of Japanese society.

As mentioned previously, the second-generation members of ethnic groups in America typically experience certain stresses and strains. They are "marginal," standing on the edge of two different cultures and societies. They are neither one nor the other, neither fully alien nor fully American. As the Nisei grew, they, too, encountered problems of this type. The ideas and ways of the Issei began to seem old-fashioned and inappropriate to American conditions. The children frequently were embarrassed that their parents could not speak fluent English and were often ashamed of their own Japanese appearance and manners. They, of course, resented being teased by other American children about their physical features and were hurt and angered when they were called "Japs." As the Nisei became aware that their parents were not and could not become citizens, they sometimes used this point to emphasize the difference between themselves and their parents (Ichihashi, 1932:350).

The Issei did many things to aid the Nisei in bridging the gap between Japanese and American culture. They strongly approved of the Nisei attendance at public schools and constantly urged the children to study hard and bring honor to the family name. The Nisei were encouraged to participate in American-style youth organizations through the formation of Japanese Boy and Girl Scout troops, YMCAs and YWCAs, and all-Japanese baseball and basketball leagues. Also, as the Issei themselves underwent some degree of cultural assimilation, American ways of doing things were introduced into the home, the *kenjinkai,* and the Buddhist church.

As the Nisei began to reach adulthood, many of them felt that the older organizations established by the Issei did not meet their special needs. Even though they were Americans, they faced the same sort of prejudice and discrimination that was directed against their parents. Many natives, indeed, made no distinction between the two generations. They "all looked alike" to many natives and were considered to be aliens like their parents. Job discrimination was a particularly galling source of worry and frustration. The Nisei often asked themselves the questions "What good is our American citizenship?" and "What can we do to claim our rightful place in this our native land?" (Hosokawa, 1960:191, 489).

During the 1920s, some young Nisei began to establish protective groups similar to the Japanese associations founded by the Issei. At first, these were local "loyalty leagues" or "citizen's leagues"; by 1930, however, an umbrella organization of Nisei—the Japanese American Citizen's League (JACL)— was formed (Hosokawa, 1969:194). The JACL made its appeal to all Nisei regardless of *ken,* religion, or political persuasion. The JACL represented the Nisei's ambition and determination to rise in American society and be accepted as equals.

Although the JACL was originally formed to combat anti-Japanese activities, the organization quickly moved to adopt the forms of accepted American political organizations and to build an image of loyalty to America (Hosokawa, 1969:197). They began to give attention to such conventional matters as getting out the Nisei vote, electing Japanese Americans to public office, and working to gain citizenship rights for the Issei (Hosokawa, 1969: 200). But these efforts were not terribly effective. Among other things, the program of the JACL was hampered by the fact that the nation was in the midst of the Great Depression. For most Nisei, therefore, participation in the JACL was mainly social. Whatever the JACL's formal success during this period, however, it did accelerate the cultural assimilation of the Nisei (Kitano, 1969:82).

By 1941, the Japanese American community had been developing for about fifty years. The Issei had been notably successful economically and in raising their families, though they had experienced special hardships with the cessation of immigration and the denial of citizenship. The Nisei had undergone a high degree of cultural assimilation and were striving for secondary structural assimilation. Some members of the third generation, the Sansei, were now on the scene. It is true that anti-Japanese activities continued to exist, especially during election years. But neither these hostile activities nor any of those prior to this period may easily be compared to the events in the months following December 7, 1941.

War, Evacuation, and Relocation

The aerial attack on Pearl Harbor led to a declaration of war against Japan, to the establishment of martial law in Hawaii, and to the quick arrest of over 12,000 German, Italian, and Japanese aliens. It also provoked a renewed attack in many newspapers against all of the Japanese, aliens and citizens alike. Many of the old hate slogans were revived and elaborated—"once a Jap, always a Jap"; "all Japanese are loyal to the Emperor"; "the Japanese race is a treacherous race"—and there were rumors that the Japanese were planning extensive sabotage. Once again, it was charged that the language schools had indoctrinated the Nisei in favor of Japan and that the other Japanese community organizations were fronts for Japanese patriotic fanaticism (tenBroek, Barnhart, and Matson, 1954:93–94).[9] In the face of the growing fears of an invasion of the West Coast, of espionage, and of sabotage, Pres. Franklin Roosevelt issued, on February 19, 1942, an executive order (No. 9066) authorizing the military authorities as a national-defense measure to prescribe military areas and to impose restrictions on the movements of all persons within those areas. Under this authority (supported by an act of Congress in March), Lt. Gen. John L. DeWitt, the commander of the Western Defense Command, issued a long series of public proclamations and civilian exclusion orders beginning on March 2, 1942.[10] General DeWitt argued that the entire Pacific Coast was particularly vlunerable to attack, invasion, espionage, and sabotage; that, for this reason, certain groups of people would be excluded from some designated military areas as a matter of "military necessity." Under these orders, all people of Japanese ancestry, whether aliens or citizens, were required to leave the prohibited areas.

The first destination of the evacuees was a group of fifteen temporary "assembly centers." From the assembly centers, the evacuees were transferred to ten permanent "relocation centers." This movement was started in March 1942 and was completed in November. In the process, more than 110,000 people of Japanese ancestry—over 70,000 of whom were American citizens—had been forced from their homes and imprisoned without warrants or indictments.[11] All of this presumably was required by "military necessity." The individuals involved were not accused of any specific acts of disloyalty, and they were not tried for any crime in a court of law! Why, then, was the mass evacuation and internment of the Japanese and Japanese Americans a "military necessity"?

One of the most revealing commentaries on this subject is contained in General DeWitt's explanation of the decision to evacuate. The general wrote as follows:

> In the war in which we are now engaged racial affinities are not severed by migration. *The Japanese race is an enemy race* and while many second and third generation Japanese born on United States soil, possessed of United States citizenship have become "Americanized," *the racial strains are undiluted.* . . . It therefore allows that along the vital Pacific Coast over 112,000 potential enemies, of Japanese extraction, are at large today. There are disturbing indications that these are organized and ready for concerted action at a favorable opportunity. *The very fact that no sabotage has taken place to date is a disturbing and confirming indication that such action will be taken* (quoted by Rostow, 1945:140; italics mine).

Thus, it seems that a very large group of people—most of whom were citizens of the United States—were arrested and imprisoned without trials purely and simply because of their race. It was assumed that while people from other nations may become Americans by birth, those of Japanese ancestry remain forever Japanese. And the "military necessity" for the evacuation and internment presumably was demonstrated by the fact that not one of the people so treated had actually engaged in sabotage!

The national security questions raised here are complex. As we have seen, the Issei and Nisei *were* a highly organized, "clannish" group. They did work hard to maintain the Japanese language and traditional forms of family and community life. And since the Issei were ineligible for American citizenship, their ties with Japan frequently were quite strong. Consequently, one may agree, as several justices of the U.S. Supreme Court have, that the military threat to the West Coast in 1942 was real and that reason and prudence required that those of Japanese ancestry should be regarded in a special light. However, even if one were to agree that considerations of this type are reasonable, does it follow that the evacuation and relocation program was a suitable response?

Consider, for instance, the situation in Hawaii. There the Japanese population comprised over 30 percent of the total, as compared to less than 2 percent of the population of the West Coast. Moreover, since Hawaii had been attacked once already, there was at least as much reason to believe that a planned invasion would strike there as at the West Coast. Hawaii, as mentioned above, was placed under martial law; and after a period of investigation, approximately 1,800 Issei and Nisei were sent to the mainland for internment. Of great significance, however, is that those taken into custody in Hawaii were arrested on the basis of individual actions and charges. There was no program to take people into custody on the basis of their racial or ethnic identity.

Consider, too, the way the problem of "presumed sympathy" was handled among the more than 1 million enemy aliens of German and Italian descent. People included in this category had to abide by certain security regulations. They could not enter military areas, own or use firearms, travel without a permit, and so on. If German or Italian aliens were suspected of disloyal acts or were caught violating a regulation, they could be arrested, and if they were arrested, they were required to appear before an alien enemy hearing board. After hearing a case, the board could recommend internment, parole, or unconditional release. Here again, as in Hawaii, individual cases were treated individually. People were not arrested and interned simply because they were enemy aliens. Of even greater significance is that the security regulations cited above did not apply in any way to *citizens* of German and Italian descent. It is difficult to escape the conclusion that "the dominant element in the development of our relocation policy was race prejudice, not a military estimate of a military problem" (Rostow, 1945:142).

So far we have seen that over 110,000 people of Japanese ancestry were forced to leave their homes during 1942 and were placed in relocation centers on a plea of "military necessity." As will be shown later, the great majority of these people were still in the centers when the U.S. Supreme Court declared near the end of 1944 that the relocation program had been illegal. For several years, then, tens of thousands of people who were completely innocent had been placed illegally in prison camps. What were these camps like? How did they affect the lives of those who were forced into them?

The Relocation Program

Approximately ten weeks after the attack on Pearl Harbor, the evacuation of the Japanese and Japanese Americans from the West Coast began. Both before and after the evacuation orders, there was great confusion. Each day brought new rumors concerning what was to be done. In January, Attorney General

Biddle stated that there would be no "Wholesale internment, without hearing and irrespective of the merits of individual cases" (Leighton, 1946:17). Early in February, Biddle urged people not to persecute aliens, either economically or socially. He warned that such persecution could easily destroy the aliens' loyalty to the United States. But many people did not agree with Biddle. A few days after his warning, the mayor of Los Angeles called for the removal of the entire Japanese population to inland areas. In the following week, an opinion poll showed that there was a widespread sentiment on the Pacific Coast (especially in California) favoring the internment of all Japanese aliens. There was some sentiment favoring the internment of Japanese Americans as well (Leighton, 1946:21).

Throughout this period, numerous acts of hostility against the Japanese and Japanese Americans were reported: jobs were lost, credit was discontinued, signs appeared saying, "No Japs Allowed," Japanese girls were attacked by men pretending to be FBI agents, and so on. Despite these problems, however, the government apparently still did not intend to carry out a mass evacuation. Tom C. Clark (later a justice of the Supreme Court) was quoted by the *Los Angeles Times* as promising "that there would be no mass evacuation, no transfer of people by the scores of thousands" (Leighton, 1946:34). Even after the announcement of Public Proclamation No. 1, General DeWitt was quoted as saying that "no mass evacuation is planned for Japanese" (Leighton, 1946:34). Nevertheless, only a short time later, a mass evacuation was underway.

Understandably, many Japanese Americans could hardly believe it. Everything they had been taught about the American system of democracy argued against such a possibility. They understood that, ideally at least, individuals are judged by their own acts. Even if every member of a person's family were a convicted felon, the person in question still must be regarded as innocent until proven guilty. The strong belief in the American system and the disillusionment that accompanied the evacuation are reflected in the following comments by a small farmer's son, a social service student, and a Japanese American soldier, respectively (Leighton, 1946:27):

> I was very confident that there would be no evacuation on a major scale. . . . the American system of education . . . gave me faith that our government would not be moved by economic pressure and racial prejudice.

> It grieved me to think that evacuation had . . . set up a sharp line between a racial minority and the dominant group in a country which had spoken of equality of opportunity.

> They are evacuating all the Japanese from the Coast and even trying to take away our citizenship. I don't know why I am in the Army. I want to see democracy as it is supposed to be, but this is getting just as bad as Hitler.

The evacuation proceeded in two main stages spread over a period of approximately seven months. The first stage removed people from their homes to hastily prepared assembly centers in racetracks, fair grounds, and live-stock exhibition halls (tenBroek, Barnhart, and Matson, 1954:126). Japanese and Japanese Americans of both sexes, all ages, and various socioeconomic categories were required to leave behind everything they could not carry. Many people sold their homes, businesses, and other possessions at cut-rate or "panic sale" prices. Others stored their goods or simply left everything in locked houses hoping that they would be safe until their return. Many farmers were forced to leave fields in which their life's savings were invested. The economic cost alone to the Japanese and Japanese Americans was enormous. Of at least equal importance, however, were the incalculable costs in human misery and humiliation. Probably only those who have experienced it can appreciate fully the emotional impact that is created when proud families and individuals are suddenly imprisoned even though they have committed no crime. Men and women who, on one day, were leading productive lives and planning for their children's futures were, on the next, assigned identification numbers and placed in guarded barracks with hundreds of others.

Most of those detained in the assembly centers gradually were moved to one of the relocation centers. These centers were placed away from the coastal areas and, in most cases, in climates that were harsh. Two each were in California (Manzanar and Tule Lake), Arizona (Poston and Gila River), and Arkansas (Rohwer and Jerome); and one each were in Idaho (Minidoka), Wyoming (Heart Mountain), Colorado (Granada), and Utah (Topaz).

The task of getting the camps ready for occupancy was very large indeed, and those who were given the job encountered numerous difficulties. In the first place, the camps were supposed to be built very quickly, from the ground up, in difficult terrain that was "either too hot or too cold, too wet or too dry" (Hosokawa, 1969:352). This meant that men, supplies, and equipment had to be assembled in remote places; and there were shortages of all these during the early days of the war. But there were other problems, too. The lines of authority and responsibility were frequently confused. The army, of course, was partially in control of the program and held ultimate authority over the inmates; but the War Relocation Authority (WRA), the civilian contractors, and some other government agencies all had something to say about certain portions of the operation. The result was that the camps were not finished when the first evacuees began to arrive. The new residents, therefore, were generally faced with various kinds of shortages and physical discomforts. Indeed, they had to do a substantial share of the construction work needed to complete the camps.

We have noted that the Japanese and Japanese Americans were bewildered by the evacuation and relocation program and that they generally felt it to be unjustified and undemocratic. There was some concern within the government also that this program—even given a serious external threat—might not be defensible in the full light of American traditions of justice. Consequently, many officials were eager to distinguish the evacuation and relocation program from the concentration camp and forced labor programs of the Nazis. Much of the language and planning for the relocation program seemed to be designed to put the entire matter in a pleasant light. For instance, the presidential order creating the WRA also created a War Relocation Work Corps. The Japanese who were leaving the prohibited military areas were invited to enlist "voluntarily" in the corps, which most of them did. This "enlistment" obligated the individual until after the war ended as a contribution "to the needs of the nation and in order to earn a livelihood for myself and my dependents" (Leighton, 1946:64). The individual agreed also to accept whatever pay the WRA specified. The evacuees were referred to as "residents," and their barracks were called "apartments." Even the labels *assembly center* and *relocation center* might be called, as Justice Roberts stated later, "a euphemism for concentration camps" (Tussman, 1963:210).

Whether or not the relocation centers were, in fact, significantly better than the concentration camps of the Nazis, it does seem to be true that the WRA administrators generally wanted them to be better. This point may be illustrated through a brief description of the largest of the camps (Poston), which was located near Parker, Arizona.[12]

Poston consisted of three units of barracks and other facilities (such as recreation halls, latrines, laundries, hospitals, water towers, and so on). The three units of the camp were intended to house approximately 20,000 people. The administrators of the camp were acutely aware that an effort should be made to organize the camps as democratically as possible under the circumstances. Their plan to achieve this goal was based on the idea that the camp should be modeled along the lines of a typical, self-governing, American community. This approach offered several possible advantages. First, it was hoped that a high degree of self-government would reassure the friendly aliens and, especially, the loyal citizens that the U.S. government recognized their rights and was concerned about their welfare. This may be viewed as a part of an effort to persuade the Japanese to accept the "fact" that the evacuation was a military necessity. It also became, as time passed, a part of an effort to show that the evacuation was a form of "protective custody." Second, if self-government were successful, then a much smaller force of outside guards and service workers would be needed. Third, it was hoped that the Poston community would soon be able to support itself through irrigation and farming the arid land of the Parker Valley. Not only would this decrease the government's expenses, but also it presumably would assist the Japanese in regaining their sense of independence and to feel that they were contributing to the war effort. Moreover, the reclamation of the desert would create a national asset that would endure beyond the war's end. Finally, if the administration's plan worked, the relocation centers might serve as an example of the differences between authoritarian and democratic responses to internal and external threats.

The first Japanese to arrive at Poston were volunteers; for the most part, they were Nisei who had decided to try to make the best of a bad situation.

They responded favorably to the administration's plan to build Poston as a model community, and they provided numerous services for the thousands of evacuees who soon began to arrive. They registered the new arrivals, explained to them the camp's regulations, and acted as guides. They also worked in the hospital, established a community store, and assisted with the necessary clerical work involved in organizing the project.

Most of the evacuees were not as willing as the early volunteers to accept the administration's plan to develop a "pioneering community." Many were understandably suspicious of the administration's motives. Many, also—especially among the Issei—questioned the motives of the volunteers and resented having such young people in positions of authority. The volunteers were often suspected of being "big shots" who had rushed to Poston first in order to "get in" with the administration. In addition, the evacuees faced numerous problems relating to housing, water, food, and other necessary things, which seemed all the more to call into question the sincerity of the administration's claims.

Consider, for example, the evacuees' living quarters. The barracks were flimsily constructed. Sometimes as many as eight people lived in one room. Mattresses were made by stuffing cloth bags with straw. There was hardly any furniture. The heat was intense in the summer, and the minimum temperatures during the winter occasionally fell below the freezing mark. And then there was the barbed wire and the guards. It is little wonder that some people felt betrayed at having been sent to such a place and either actively resisted or failed to cooperate fully with the administration's plans.[13] Nevertheless, block by block, the camp haltingly moved toward the administration's goal. A newspaper, police force, and fire department were established. A temporary community council was elected. Less than two months after Poston was opened, an irrigation canal was completed. People planted vegetable gardens and trees. Various kinds of social and recreational activities were organized. Schools were planned. By the end of August 1942, when Poston's population reached its peak of 17,867, the emergency phase of organization seemed past. The more optimistic members of the administration hoped that Poston would soon be a well-rounded and, in the main, typically American community.

There were still many underlying problems, however, that severely damaged the administration's program. For example, there were internal divisions within both the administrative group and the evacuee group that served to undermine morale. Some officials felt that the efforts to encourage participation in the government of the camp might lead to a loss of control over the camp. Moreover, among the evacuees, there existed a strong difference of opinion concerning the desirability of cooperating with the administration. The conservatives, most of whom were Issei, did not trust the administration and were not sure that they wished to assist its program. Many of them were not even sure it would be good for them if America won the war. The liberals, most of whom were Nisei, were impatient with those who did not try to prove their Americanism. Many in this group were enjoying the new responsibilities and experiences camp life had made possible. They wished to work toward full acceptance as Americans.

As community morale sagged, there was an increase in stealing, name calling, and violence. Some evacuees believed there were FBI informers among them, and some of the suspected informers were assaulted. By the middle of November 1942, distrust and anger were widespread among the residents of Poston.

The dissatisfaction of the residents cluminated in a demonstration and general strike in Unit I. The event that triggered the disorders was the arrest of two evacuees, who were accused of having participated in a gang attack on a fellow resident. While the two arrested men were being held and investigated, their families and friends began working to have them released. A delegation of Issei visited the project director to offer evidence that the suspects were innocent, but they were turned away by the FBI investigators. The next day, a few hundred demonstrators gathered at the jail and soon announced there would be a general strike. The remainder of the day was marked by demonstrations, protest meetings, and attempts to negotiate. Early the next morning, the evacuees selected a group of twelve men—eleven of whom were Issei—to act as an Emergency Executive Council. By now it was clear that real leadership within the camp had passed to the Issei. For the next five days, the Emergency Executive Council was the governing body among the Japanese in the unit.

As the general strike developed, some members of the administration urged that the army be asked to take charge and bring their troops inside Poston's boundaries. Some members suggested that the strike was a pro-Japanese plot and illustrated the need to show the "Japs" their place. This suggestion was repeated in the camp of the military police, resulting in some wild talk about attacking and shooting "the Japs." The ranking project administrator did not, however, turn matters over to the army. He chose, rather, to negotiate with the Emergency Executive Council and to follow through on the official policy of encouraging self-government in the project. The following day, there was a meeting of the assistant project director and the leaders of the strike at which the administration announced that one of the two prisoners would be released. The other prisoner, however, was to be brought to trial in an Arizona court. From this point on, the evacuees' efforts focused on the release of the remaining prisoner. After several days of negotiation, an agreement was reached. The Emergency Executive Council agreed to assume full responsibility to bring an end to the strike and to restore order and cooperation within Poston. In return, the remaining prisoner was released.

Although the strike in Poston ended on a cooperative note and without the use of military force, the form of self-government that emerged was not the one that had been planned originally by the WRA. Many officials were discouraged by the course of events in Poston and in most of the other relocation centers as well. For example, several weeks after the Poston strike, a "riot" at the Manzanar Relocation Center resulted in the killing and wounding of some of the evacuees. Consequently, the WRA abandoned the idea of developing the relocation centers as model communities. The decision was made, rather, that the best policy would be to "resettle" all loyal evacuees outside the centers as soon as possible. This new plan was strengthened when the War Department reversed an earlier stand regarding military service for the Nisei by announcing its intention to form an all-Nisei combat team. Eventually, over 20,000 Japanese and Japanese American men were inducted following this change of policy. More than 6,000 Nisei served in the Pacific theater, primarily as interpreters and translators. Most of the rest served in the 100th Battalion and the 442nd Regimental Combat Team. These units compiled an outstanding battle record in the European theater.[14] The decisions to resettle the evacuees and to enlist the Nisei for military duty led to a program of clearance and recruitment. Each evacuee was asked to answer a questionnaire concerning his or her background and loyalty to the United States. The registration program came as a surprise to the evacuees and resulted in anxiety, confusion, and resistance throughout the relocation centers.

The focus of controversy—around which several important issues revolved—was question 28: "Will you swear unqualified allegiance to the United States of America and . . . foreswear any form of allegiance to the Japanese emperor?" (Thomas and Nishimoto, 1946:47).[15] A "yes" answer to this question was almost impossible for most Issei. They were, after all, ineligible for citizenship in the United States. If they now disclaimed allegiance to Japan, they would be "men without a country." Four days after the first questionnaire was tried, question 28 was revised as follows: "Will you swear to abide by the laws of the United States and to take no action which would in any way interfere with the war effort of the United States?" (Broom and Kitsuse, 1956:28). Although the revised question was acceptable to most Issei, the loyalty registration crisis was not settled.

Consider some of the undercurrents. As may well be imagined, many of the evacuees were extremely bitter and disillusioned by everything that had happened to them during the preceding year. Now, suddenly, they were asked to declare unswerving loyalty to the United States. Additionally, they correctly assumed that a "yes" answer to question 28 might mean they or some member of their family would be drafted into military service (or be pressured to "volunteer"). Many also had accepted the government's argument that they had been interned, at least in part, for their own safety; so they now feared that they would be forced to leave the relocation centers to be resettled in some place where hostility toward them would make life uncomfortable or, possibly, unsafe. Furthermore, some of the evacuees believed that they could gain time to think the matter over by refusing to answer or by answering "no." On the other hand, a "no" or a refusal to answer certainly involved some risks. Would a "no" interfere with the individual's efforts to recover property that had been lost in the evacuation? Would a presumably disloyal person be sent to a special prison camp? What effect would a declaration of disloyalty have on a person's job or educational opportunities following the war? The cross-pressures on the evacuees meant that a simple yes or no answer to question number 28 could not easily be interpreted. It also meant that the existing intergenerational conflict between the Issei and Nisei was sharpened, adding to the general turbulence in the centers.

These complications interfered with the WRA's plan to grant leave clearances to the "loyal" Japanese (i.e., those who answered "yes") and to segregate the "disloyal" Japanese in a special camp (the Tule Lake Relocation Center). By November 1943—less than a year after the Poston strike—over 18,000 people had been segregated at Tule Lake.[16] However, as noted earlier, there was ample reason to believe that many of those at Tule Lake were not really disloyal. After further checking, in fact, over 8,500 of the segregants eventually were cleared.

The most surprising evidence of the deep-seated confusion among the Japanese was revealed by the effort to resettle those who were regarded as loyal. At first, the resettlement program seemed very effective. By the end of 1943, more than 17,000 people—most of whom were Nisei—had been cleared and released from the centers. As time passed, though, decreasing numbers of cleared residents chose to leave the confines of the camps. Despite an active effort on the part of the WRA to make resettlement attractive to the evacuees, nearly 80,000 people remained in the centers at the beginning of 1945. Approximately half that number were still in the centers as the WRA moved to close them in the summer of 1945. It seems reasonable to conclude, as the WRA itself did, that the treatment of the Japanese in the United States during World War II had tended "to disintegrate the fiber of a people who had previous to evacuation, been unusually self-reliant, sturdy, and independent" (War Relocation Authority, 1946).[17]

Legal Issues

The primary legal issues raised by the evacuation and relocation program were addressed by the U.S. Supreme Court in three different cases. The first of these *(Hirabayashi* v. *United States)* reached the court in June 1943, over two years after the relocation program had been set into motion. By this time, the situation that had led to the creation of the program had been altered markedly. Various categories of people already had been released from the relocation centers. Most of these were Nisei students who were attending school in the Midwest and East. But as a result of the army's new recruitment effort among the Nisei, many of those who were released were servicemen or their wives. Nevertheless, most of the aliens and citizens of Japanese ancestry were still being held in the relocation centers, and those who had been released could not return to their homes. Moreover, it still was to be decided whether the government's treatment of the Japanese and Japanese Americans had been constitutional.

Gordon Hirabayashi was arrested, convicted, and jailed for violating two of General DeWitt's orders. He violated a curfew order by failing to stay in his place of residence between the hours of eight P.M. and six A.M. He also did not report as ordered to register for evacuation. Hirabayashi's appeal to the Supreme Court maintained that the curfew and evacuation orders represented an unconstitutional delegation of congressional authority to the military and that the curfew should have applied not only to citizens of Japanese ancestry but to all citizens within the military areas.

In a unanimous opinion, the court stated: "Distinctions between citizens solely because of their ancestry are by their very nature odious to a free people" (Tussman, 1963:190) but ruled nevertheless that the facts supported the military commander's judgment that there had been a danger of espionage and sabotage and that the curfew order had been appropriate (Tussman, 1963:192). Among the "facts" accepted by the court was the idea that those having ethnic affiliations with an enemy nation may be more dangerous to national security than other Americans (Tussman, 1963:191).

Although the opinion upholding the curfew order was unanimous, three justices expressed reservations. Justice Douglas, for example, agreed that "where the peril is great and time is short" (Tussman, 1963:194), it may be necessary to make group distinctions; but he emphasized that the basic issue was loyalty not ancestry. Justice Murphy emphasized even more strongly that "distinctions based on color and ancestry are utterly inconsistent with our traditions and ideals" (Tussman, 1963:197). He added that the restrictions on the Japanese Americans "bears a melancholy resemblance to the treatment accorded to members of the Jewish race in Germany" (Tussman, 1963:197). Justice Rutledge was concerned that the case might weaken the court's power to review military decisions. But even with these reservations, the court gave the appearance of agreeing with some of the charges (e.g., "a Jap is a Jap") that had long been the stock in trade of the most vocal anti-Japanese groups.

The second of the three court cases under review here, *Korematsu* v. *United States,* concerned primarily the constitutionality of the evacuation of the Japanese Americans from the West Coast. Fred Korematsu had been born in the United States, had never been out of the country, did not speak Japanese, and was not suspected of disloyalty. He had attempted to avoid the order to leave his home and had been convicted and given a suspended sentence. The Supreme Court upheld Korematsu's conviction. Unlike in *Hirabayashi,* however, the decision was not unanimous. Justice Roberts argued that Korematsu's constitutional rights had been violated. Justice Murphy stated that the exclusion resulted not from military necessity but from the mistaken ideas people had about the Japanese and that the episode "falls into the ugly abyss of racism" (Tussman, 1963:213). Justice Jackson refused to accept the idea that a given act (in this case, refusing to leave home) could be a crime if committed by a citizen of one race but not by a citizen of another.

The reservations and disagreements that plagued the court's members in their deliberations concerning the curfew and the evacuation reached full force in their consideration of *Endo* v. *United States*. Like Fred Korematsu, Mitsuye Endo had been born in the United States, did not speak Japanese, and had committed no specific act of disloyalty. Endo challenged the right of the WRA to imprison her and other loyal Japanese Americans; on this, all of the justices agreed. The court ordered that Ms. Endo and all other loyal Americans be set free unconditionally. Justice Murphy, who had only reluctantly agreed to the curfew and had rejected the evacuation, stated that the entire evacuation program had been discriminatory and was "utterly foreign to the ideals and traditions of the American people" (Petersen, 1971:90). In one critic's opinion, "One hundred thousand persons were sent to concentration camps on a record which wouldn't support a conviction for stealing a dog" (Rostow, 1945:146).

The full effects on the Japanese and Japanese Americans of the devastating experience of evacuation, relocation, and resettlement are beyond exact calculation. The dollar losses alone have been estimated to be around 400 million dollars in 1942 dollars (Hosokawa, 1969:440). Approximately one-tenth of this amount (also in 1942 dollars!) eventually was recovered in damages after the war (Petersen, 1971:107). Of course, no meaningful estimate may be made of the emotional costs that were suffered by the thousands of people who saw their hopes and aspirations destroyed and their families broken. What is plain in all of this is that the Japanese have been subjected in America to a level of discrimination similar to that encountered by the largest nonwhite minorities in the United States.

At the end of the second-generation period, the Japanese Americans had generally accepted the desirability of cultural and secondary structural assimilation. Many of them embraced the goal of primary structural and, perhaps, marital assimilation as well. What were the effects of the catastrophic events of World War II on their adjustment to American society?

Japanese American Assimilation

Cultural Assimilation

Our previous reasoning about rates of assimilation has shown that it is necessary to think in terms of several subprocesses such as cultural assimilation, secondary structural assimilation, and so on. We have seen also the necessity to take into account certain important factors that usually influence the course of assimilation, such as the size of the immigrant group, the social distance between the immigrants and the host society, whether the group entered voluntarily, the timing of the immigration, and the goals of the immigrants. In the case of the Japanese in America, the factor of intergenerational differences also has assumed an unusual importance. The Issei have been even more "clannish" than most first-generation groups, and their level of cultural assimilation was generally low. The desire of the Issei to maintain their own heritage, coupled with their resistance to adopting American ways, created barriers to the cultural assimilation of the Nisei. The Japanese language schools, as mentioned earlier, were designed to assist the Issei in transmitting their language and heritage and to prevent the development of a wide cultural gap between the generations. However, also as noted previously, the schools were not really very successful in this. Although the Nisei were restrained and "Japanesey" in the home, they apparently moved rapidly toward the American pattern of behavior in school and other public settings. The opposition between the Issei and Nisei also, as has been shown, was increased by the evacuation and relocation experience. The effect of this increased intergenerational friction, though, may have differed among the older and younger Nisei. Those who were adolescents and young adults may have been propelled toward Anglo conformity by the evacuation and relocation.[18] However, since the contacts of the children with Anglo-Americans were reduced during this period and their contacts with other Japanese were increased, they may have become more Japanese in culture and thought than otherwise would have been the case (Broom and Kitsuse, 1956:25).

Little has been said so far concerning the Sansei. But this third generation is of special importance in any effort to assess the rate of assimilation among Japanese Americans. According to the ideas of Park, the Sansei should be more assimilated than the Nisei. Their degree of cultural assimilation, in particular, should approach that of the Anglo-American majority.

The facts concerning cultural assimilation are far from complete and must be pieced together from several different sources. The evidence is generally based on studies of small samples, although some results from a national sample of Japanese Americans are also available. The findings of these studies are not totally consistent, but they strongly suggest that the Sansei have assimilated culturally more than the Nisei, who, in turn, have assimilated culturally more than the Issei. Kitano (1969:156–157), for instance, has examined differences in the way the members of the three generations respond to certain statements regarding traditional beliefs and attitudes. The expected pattern of intergenerational differences emerged clearly on matters of ethnic identity (e.g., "Once a Japanese, always a Japanese"), individual-group orientation (e.g., "A person who raises too many questions interferes with the progress of a group"), and realistic expectations (e.g., "Even if one had talent and ability, it does not mean that he will get ahead"). The pattern was either weak or not present, however, in regard to the respondents' views on means and ends, masculinity and responsibility, and passivity. For instance, although the Nisei and Sansei differed from the Issei on some points, they did not differ significantly from one another. In regard to some other views, the Issei and Nisei were more nearly in agreement, and the Sansei were different.

Some of the inconsistencies found by Kitano may have been due to the small size of the sample, the geographical location represented, problems with the wording of the questionnaire, and so on, rather than to any real departure from the expected pattern of cultural assimilation. This interpretation has been strengthened in general by the results from four other studies. For example, Connor (1974:161) found that the Issei in his study were most likely to agree with statements reflecting traditional child-rearing ideas (e.g., "Parents can never be repaid for what they have done for their children"), the Sansei were least likely to agree, and the Nisei were intermediate in agreement. In a comparison of Nisei and Sansei, Feagin and Fujitaki (1972: 18) have found that although an individual's religious affiliation is a complicating factor, with Buddhism serving to support the traditional culture, some clear differences in cultural assimilation exist between the Nisei and Sansei. To illustrate, the Nisei were more likely to be comfortable speaking Japanese and to do so regularly in the home than were the Sansei. They also felt more strongly than the Sansei the importance of maintaining Japanese customs and traditions.

Some pertinent results have been presented by Matsumoto, Meredith, and Masuda (1973) in a study of sex and generation differences in ethnic identification among Japanese Americans in Honolulu and Seattle. Once again, the general pattern of increasing cultural assimilation by generation was discovered. The results of the latter study must be viewed with some caution, however, because there were some important differences between the Honolulu and Seattle findings. In Seattle, the Japanese identification of the Sansei was significantly lower than among the Nisei; in Honolulu, however, this difference was not significant. Even more important is that the fifty-item measure of ethnic identification used in this study included a broad range of topics that touch on several aspects of the process of assimilation. It is possible, therefore, that a more detailed analysis might lead to somewhat different results. Finally, using the national sample (excluding Hawaii) of UCLA's Japanese American Research Project, Woodrum (1978: 80) found that in terms of English proficiency and religious affiliation, the Nisei were more culturally assimilated than the Issei. In terms of religious affiliation alone, the Sansei were more culturally assimilated than the Issei.

With the evidence at hand, it seems reasonable to conclude that, as a rule, the Sansei are more assimilated culturally than the Nisei and that the Issei are less assimilated culturally than either of the other two generations.

Our interest so far has centered on the generational differences in cultural assimilation within the Japanese American group. The problem now to be considered concerns the extent to which the Sansei have become assimilated culturally in comparison to Anglo-Americans. Connor reports that the Issei and Nisei in his study believed the Sansei are "completely Americanized." Are they?

Only two of the studies cited above contain pertinent information. For example, although Connor found much less acceptance of traditional Japanese ideas among the Sansei than among the members of the other two generations, he nevertheless found more acceptance of these ideas among the Sansei than among a sample of Anglo-Americans. Kitano also found noticeable differences between the Sansei and the Anglo-Americans in regard to certain beliefs and attitudes. In particular, the Sansei were between the Nisei and the Anglo-Americans in their beliefs about masculinity and responsibility and in their beliefs about passivity.

In addition to the findings of specific studies, however, there is ample impressionistic evidence that many Sansei are very much aware of and interested in their Japanese heritage. As one would expect on the basis of Hansen's thesis (mentioned in chapter 1), many third-generation Japanese Americans are caught up in a revival of cultural nationalism. A major theme of this revival is that Japanese Americans should reject the Anglo conformity of the Nisei and actively promote some form of cultural pluralism in which the valued traditions of Japan, as modified by the American experience, may be sustained and elaborated. The participants in this movement are extremely critical of the older generation's willingness to "make the most of a bad situation and push ahead" (Fujimoto, 1971:207) or, even worse, to focus attention on the presumably "beneficial" effects of the wartime relocation. They view the historical experience of the Japanese minority in America as being essentially like that of the Chinese, Koreans, and Filipinos and quite similar to that of the blacks, Chicanos, and Indians. As Ichioka (1971:222) has stated in a critical review of Hosokawa's book *Nisei: The Quiet Americans,* "In this time of political, social, and moral crisis in America, old and new problems demand radical approaches, not tired orations. . . . We bid the old guard to retire as 'quiet Americans.' "

On the basis of these observations, we may offer another generalization concerning the Sansei: although their level of cultural assimilation is higher than that of the two preceding generations, they still exhibit some elements of the traditional culture of Japan and are, in many cases, actively attempting to renew their ancient heritage.

Given the comparatively high degree of cultural assimilation among the Nisei and Sansei, how far have these groups moved toward the American pattern in terms of the other main subprocesses of assimilation? We have seen already that the Japanese Americans have attained in some respects a high degree of secondary structural assimilation (e.g., education and occupation) but have not yet reached the income level of the dominant group. Let us turn now to the available evidence on the remaining subprocesses of assimilation.

Secondary Structural Assimilation

In addition to education, occupational attainment, and income, the main types of secondary structural assimilation are membership in nonethnic formal organizations and movement into desegregated neighborhoods. In a study of a small number of Nisei and Sansei in Los Angeles, Kagiwada (1972) showed that fewer than one-half of either generation participated regularly or occasionally in the activities of Japanese organizations.[19] The individual's attachment to the Japanese community in this respect was somewhat weaker among the Sansei. Although these findings do not show that the Nisei and Sansei are participating in Anglo-American organizations, they do suggest that such a shift may be in progress. This interpretation is supported to some extent by the finding of Feagin and Fujitaki (1972:23) that the Christians among their sample of Japanese Americans belonged to proportionately few organizations comprised entirely of Japanese. They also found, however, that the Buddhists of both generations were more strongly connected to the Japanese community than were the Christians. Interestingly, they found, too—and this point is consistent with Hansen's thesis—that the Sansei within each religious group were slightly more traditional than the Nisei. And, finally, Woodrum (1978:80) found that the organizational affiliations of the Sansei indicate that those over twenty-four years of age have experienced slightly less secondary structural assimilation than those under twenty-four.

Kagiwada's findings in regard to neighborhoods also suggest the occurrence of a substantial degree of secondary structural assimilation. Fewer than one-half of either generation claimed to live in a neighborhood in which more than 10 percent of their neighbors were Japanese. In contrast, more than half of the study participants indicated that at least 50 percent of their neighbors were white. In this case, though—and again consistent with Hansen's thesis—the Nisei appeared to be somewhat more assimilated than the Sansei. However, the view that the Japanese Americans increasingly are moving into predominantly non-Japanese neighborhoods is supported by Kitano's (1969:161) observations. In his opinion, the Japanese Americans are substantially assimilated in regard to housing in Hawaii, New York, New England, and Chicago; and they are partly assimilated in California and other parts of the West Coast.

Primary Structural Assimilation

If the Japanese Americans are participating less in all-Japanese organizations and are participating more in "mixed" organizations (including schools and businesses), then presumably some foundation has been laid for the more "social" activities that indicate the occurrence of primary structural assimilation. Very little evidence exists on this point. However, one finding by Feagin and Fujitaki supporting this presumption is that more than two-thirds of their respondents—Buddhists as well as Christians—did not wish their children to associate mainly with members of the Japanese community. Moreover, among the Christian Sansei, the majority of those who were engaged, "going steady," or dating had a non-Japanese companion. Even among the more traditional Buddhist Sansei, over one-fourth reported having a non-Japanese companion. In a similar vein, Kagiwada (1972) has reported that one-third of the Nisei and Sansei respondents in his study had a comparatively large number (25 percent or more) of close friends who were white, although less than one-third of the sample members indicated that more than 90 percent of their friends were Japanese. The finding of increasing primary structural assimilation finds some support also in Woodrum's analysis of some data from the national sample of the Japanese American Research Project. The Sansei report having many more non-Japanese friends than the Nisei, who, in turn, have more non-Japanese friends than the Issei.

Marital Assimilation

Marital assimilation represents the end point among the subprocesses of assimilation we are studying. Trends in mixed ethnic marriages, therefore, are of special importance. However, even though intermarriage is considered to be "the surest means of assimilation" (Kennedy, 1944:331), the interpretation of statistics on intermarriage requires caution. For example, when a marriage occurs between a member of the dominant group and a member of a subordinate group, we ordinarily consider this to be evidence of marital assimilation by the partner from the subordinate group; however, if the friends of the married couple are drawn mainly from the subordinate group, if the couple lives in a neighborhood composed primarily of others in the subordinate group, and if the children of the marriage are raised in the religion and culture of the subordinate group, are we still to call this assimilation? Consider, also, this situation: minority-group members who marry "out" frequently select partners from other minority groups. Does this represent assimilation? With these questions in mind, let us examine some of the results of the available studies on intermarriage among the Japanese.[20]

Except in Hawaii, interracial marriages of all kinds in the United States have been low. This is due in large part, of course, to the fact that such marriages frequently have been illegal. Burma (1963) has studied all forms of interethnic marriage in Los Angeles between 1948 and 1959 by analyzing information gathered from marriage licenses. The period studied by Burma was chosen because before 1948 the laws of California prohibited intermarriages of whites with members of another race, and during 1959 it became illegal to require a marriage license to show an applicant's race. The data of the study, therefore, reflect what was happening during a crucial time span in an area possessing a comparatively large Japanese American population. Over 375,000 marriage applications were counted for the eleven-year period. More than 3000 of these involved some form of racial mixing, and 600 of the racially mixed applicants were Japanese (Burma, 1963:163). Burma calculated that by 1959 interracial marriages among all groups in Los Angeles County had become more than three times as frequent as in

1948. His data also show that out-marriages involving Japanese Americans rose from approximately 11 percent of all out-marriages in 1949 to nearly 23 percent of the cases in 1959.[21]

A subsequent study of Japanese out-marriage by Kikumura and Kitano (1973) draws together the findings of several reports, including their own results from Los Angeles County during 1971 and 1972. Based on studies in Fresno and San Francisco, reported by Tinker (1973), the trend in inter-marriages between white Americans and Japanese Americans noted by Burma apparently has continued, especially among the Sansei. Tinker found that in Fresno in 1969–1971 half of all marriages involving Japanese Americans were out-marriages. A similar level of out-marriage also was discovered by Kikumura and Kitano in Hawaii for 1970 and in Los Angeles during 1971 and 1972. The latter authors conclude that the various reports strongly suggest that out-marriages have become so frequent among Japanese Americans that the Sansei are approximately as likely to marry outside the group as within it.[22] Finally, Parkman and Sawyer (1967:597) have compared inter-marriage rates during the years 1928–1934 with those of 1948–1953 and have found that the rate of Japanese out-marriage roughly tripled between the two periods.

The trend toward increasing marital assimilation among the Japanese Americans found in these geographically limited studies is generally confirmed by two more broadly based studies. On the basis of the national sample of the Japanese American Research Project, Woodrum (1978:80) found a steady increase in marital assimilation not only among the three generations under discussion but within the younger and older members of the Nisei and Sansei groups as well. Younger Nisei and Sansei are more likely to have married out than the older members of their generations, while the younger Nisei are less likely to have married out than the older Sansei. Similarly, on the basis of a national public use sample prepared by the U.S. Bureau of the Census, Gurak and Kritz (1978:38) have analyzed intermarriage statistics for 35 ethnic groups and have found that the Nisei marry out more frequently than the Issei. This intergenerational trend should not be exaggerated, however. Gurak and Kritz have found also that 31 of the 35 groups in the analysis have higher out-marriage rates than do the Nisei. Moreover, the Nisei who marry out are less likely to marry a member of the Anglo-American core group than were the Issei.

Though the case is far from proven, it seems reasonable to say that the Japanese Americans have been moving rapidly in the direction of complete assimilation in regard to each of the four subprocesses we have examined. However, it is unclear that the *amount* of assimilation in regard to each sub-process is what would be expected on the basis of Park's and Gordon's ideas. For instance, although it does seem that the Japanese Americans are more assimilated culturally than either structurally or maritally, it is not clear that all types of structural assimilation are more nearly complete than marital assimilation. On the other hand, the assimilation sequence suggested by

Gordon's work—cultural, secondary structural, primary structural, and marital —has not been disproven either. Finally, some of the evidence examined here indicates that the Sansei may have stopped moving toward the acceptance of certain aspects of American culture and are engaged, rather, in a revitalization of their ethnic subculture. It is not clear, however, whether this revitalization is to be interpreted simply as an example of the workings of Hansen's "law." The movement appears to involve an effort to construct a new ethnic identity that relates Japanese Americans to all other Asians and to all other colored minorities as well as to their Japanese forebears. We will have more to say on this in chapter 8.

Our findings, then, are complicated and not entirely consistent. Despite the number of important questions that are still unanswered, though, it is easy to see why the Japanese Americans frequently are mentioned as evidence that any group—regardless of their race, culture, or history of oppression— can move fully into the mainstream of American life, usually within three generations. It also is easy to see why controversy continues over the final outcome of this drama of association between two such apparently different groups. Much of the evidence seems to suggest that Park's and Gordon's analyses are correct and that complete or practically complete assimilation awaits the Japanese Americans. But some of the evidence does not fit this interpretation, and it may be, as Petersen (1971:208) states, "a false prognosis."

Japanese American "Success"

The success of the Japanese in American society, especially in terms of education and occupation, has raised the following question in the minds of many people: how have the Japanese Americans been able to overcome the stigma of a nonwhite identity and to do so in a comparatively short time against such great odds? Two explanations of this phenomenon are the value-compatibility theory and the community-cohesion theory.

Value Compatibility

As a part of the program to release the Japanese and Japanese Americans from the relocation centers, some 20,000 Issei and Nisei were resettled in Chicago. This large-scale resettlement created an opportunity for social scientists to observe and attempt to understand the impact of such a change on the culture and personalities of the evacuees. A three-year study was conducted in which several hundred families participated. The study showed that the Japanese, as a group, first settled in slum housing and accepted menial, unskilled, and poorly paid jobs. For the Issei, this situation did not change very rapidly. The Nisei, however, quickly took advantage of their high education, youth, and cultural assimilation to move into semiskilled, service, and managerial jobs. They also moved out of the undesirable residential districts and into more expensive housing. Not only were the Nisei accepted by employers, landlords, and neighbors, they generally were praised because they were well groomed, courteous, and showed respect for authority. Under these conditions, the Nisei were able to accomplish in less than five years a measure of secondary structural assimilation greater than that of several other ethnic groups that had been in Chicago for a much longer time. They had become, to a large extent, a middle-class group.

To explain this rapid transformation, Caudill and DeVos (1956) have stressed three factors. First, the Japanese did not encounter in Chicago the intense prejudice and discrimination that had hampered them on the West Coast. Second, as a result of the relocation experience, the Nisei were now much less under the control of the Issei and were much freer to abandon Japanese ways. Third, the wartime labor shortage opened employment opportunities to these diligent and well-educated people. While the effects of these factors help us to understand why the Issei and Nisei found opportunities in the economy of Chicago, they do not explain very well why they succeeded in their jobs after they got them. To explain this surprising fact, Caudill and DeVos (1956:1107) have suggested that there is "a significant compatibility (but by no means identity) between the value systems found in the culture of Japan and the value systems in American middle class culture." The argument here is not that the Japanese and American middle-class cultures are similar in general. It is, rather, that certain key values are common to these otherwise quite different cultures. As noted earlier, both the Japanese and the middle-class Americans stress the importance of politeness, respect for authority and parental wishes, duty to the community, hard work, cleanliness, neatness, education, occupational success, the pursuit of long-range goals, and building a good reputation. On the basis of his separate studies, Kitano (1969:76) has expressed the point as follows: "All in all, Japanese reverence for hard work, achievement, self-control, dependability, manners, thrift, and diligence were entirely congruent with American middle-class perceptions."

The value-compatibility theory, then, suggests that the worldly success of the Japanese in America has occurred because the two cultures "mesh" in certain significant ways. From this viewpoint, Japanese American children are taught in the home to give a high priority to certain goals and purposes. As they pursue these goals, their behavior is generally of a type that conforms closely to the ideal model accepted by the dominant group. Even when some of the goals set by Japanese culture are at odds with those of American culture and may, therefore, lead to inner conflict for the Japanese American, the total external result may be even greater approval by the members of the dominant group. For example, although Americans generally are presumed to think individualism is superior to group conformity, this evaluation is limited to those who already are considered American! Consequently, the traditional Japanese emphasis on the importance of conformity may become an asset to a person who wishes to join the dominant group.

Community Cohesion

The primary focus of the community-cohesion theory differs from that of the value-compatibility theory. The question in this case is not "Do the Japanese Americans possess certain values that promote success in the American setting?" The question is, instead, "How have the traditional success values of Japan been preserved and transmitted to the younger generations?" The social institutions that usually are regarded to be of central importance in the transmission of social values are the family and the church. The family, of course, is normally the group that plays the largest role in teaching the child the language, ideas, and customs of the society, while the church plays a more formal role in teaching the child the basic values of the society. Presumably, therefore, if the Nisei typically have possessed the success values learned by the Issei in Japan, and if the Sansei also have possessed these same values, then a study of the Japanese family and religions might explain how these values have been handed down so effectively from generation to generation.

In the minds of some scholars, this idea is useful but is only a part of the story. A too narrow focus on the family and the church reveals some contradictory tendencies. In many ways, as we have seen, the Japanese family has been strong and close knit; nevertheless, the generation gap between the Issei and Nisei was much larger in a number of important respects than has been true within most other ethnic groups in America. The average age of the Issei, to repeat, was higher than has generally been true for first-generation parents. And the Nisei rapidly turned to Christianity, while the Issei, in general, remained Buddhists. Petersen (1971:202–207) contends that the differences between the Issei and Nisei have led, in fact, to a high degree of intergenerational conflict over things such as dating, courtship, marriage, and politics. He emphasizes, though, that the various forms of adolescent rebellion of the Nisei were not translated into the kind of general social rebellion that frequently has occurred among second-generation immigrants. Instead of high rates of delinquency, gang violence, and truancy, the Nisei have usually been considered to be "good" boys and girls by their teachers, law enforcement officers, and social-welfare officials. Nevertheless, the intergenerational conflict that did exist was sufficiently serious to make us wonder how the Issei were able to perform the task of value transmission.

A similar argument may be constructed in regard to the Buddhist-Shinto-Confucian religious tradition within the Japanese churches. Although this tradition is too complex to be outlined here, we may note at least that it is intimately entwined in all of Japanese civilization and culture. The moral and ethical concerns of the Japanese family, mentioned above, have themselves been shaped by the ideas of the Japanese religions. Such crucial elements of Japanese morality as devotion to duty are stressed by the family and by the churches. Once again, we might easily conclude that the Japanese churches have played the decisive role in the transmission of traditional values to the Japanese Americans.

If the Nisei and Sansei have received substantially intact the moral values of traditional Japan, and if this cultural miracle is only partly to be explained as the work of the family or the church, then how is it to be explained? Miyamoto (1939; 1972) and Petersen (1971) have argued strongly that the transmission of the traditional values to the Nisei and Sansei has been accomplished by the entire Japanese community. According to Miyamoto (1972:218), "the Japanese minority maintained a high degree of family and community organization in America, and these organizations enforced value conformity and created conditions and means for status achievement." From this standpoint, both the family and the church have been embedded within a strong, cohesive community, a community that has enabled these institutions to function effectively in the face of certain internal weaknesses.

Consider again our earlier finding that the traditional Japanese family was not thought of as a union of two people who were in love but as a union of two families. The extended family unit thus created was, in turn, connected in numerous ways through other marriages to the larger community. An important effect of this pattern of interrelationships is that everyone in the community has important obligations to many others within the community. The other side of the coin is that the family may call on the larger community for assistance and support. It also may rely on many other individuals to exert pressure on youngsters to behave in ways that will bring honor to the family and community rather than shame and trouble. If a child's parents have emphasized the importance of being polite and diligent, they may be assured that many other people will be watching to see that the child obeys the parents' instructions. When children deviate from the expected pattern of behavior, other adults are likely to admonish them or, at the very least, to report misbehavior to the parents. In this way, the child grows up in a close-knit, supportive community even when the generation gap within the immediate family is quite wide. The efforts of the parents to influence their children are paralleled by the agreements that exist within the broader community, and children have difficulty finding adult allies to support their efforts to "go against" their parents. The highly cohesive Japanese community typically has left little room for the argument that "all the other kids are doing it!" The community also has left little room for individuals to seek their private goals at the expense of the ethnic group. Children have learned instead that they should avoid at all cost any behavior that might bring dishonor to the ethnic group.

Please notice that, as presented, the community-cohesion theory implies that Japanese solidarity in America was a continuation of the traditional solidarity of Japan. It is quite possible, however, that at least some of this community's internal strength may be traced to its economic position in America. To a greater extent than has been typical, the Japanese initially did not intend to settle permanently in America; they were "birds of passage" or "sojourners" who maintained a very strong attachment to their homeland. The condition of sojourning, according to Bonacich (1973:585–588) is a necessary ingredient in the development of a specific economic status known as the "middleman minority." Such minorities, which have appeared throughout the world at different times in history, are referred to as "middlemen" because "they occupy an intermediate rather than low-status position" (Bonacich, 1973:583). Such groups typically concentrate in commerce and trade. (The Jews of Europe afford a very good example.) But of special importance in the present context is that sojourning minorities typically reveal a high level of group solidarity. Since sojourners do not plan to remain in the new society, they are strongly motivated to cultivate their ties with other members of their own ethnic group and to avoid strong ties with those in the host group. The resulting high level of ethnic solidarity is, as we have seen, an invaluable shield against the hostility of the dominant group. The individual in such a community gains support from the community. In return, the individual exhibits loyalty to the group and pride in it. A community that contains a high proportion of proud and loyal members does not easily lose its confidence in the face of defeat. It is more likely, rather, to redouble its efforts to succeed.

A Comparison of Success Theories

The community-cohesion explanation of the worldly success of the Japanese Americans is not totally opposed to the value compatibility explanation. Both theories stress the importance of the possession of cultural values that relate to successful action. They do differ, however, in two important respects. The value-compatibility theory implies that the success of the Japanese Americans rests mainly on the "good fit" between the behavior flowing from Japanese values and the expectations of the host group. The community-cohesion theory, though, implies that values such as diligence and long-range planning would promote achievement under a variety of circumstances, perhaps even in the face of a "bad fit" between the values of the minority and the expectations of the majority. The latter interpretation has received some support from the fact that Japanese immigrants to some other countries have been notably successful.

The community-cohesion idea, though, adds a new and important emphasis. From this perspective, the success of the Japanese Americans has depended on the *way* their values have been transmitted. The entire ethnic group has been involved in the transmission process. Each child has been taught that the family's values are the community's values. And each child, consequently, has received general approval for "correct" behavior and general disapproval for "incorrect" behavior. The highly cohesive ethnic group has set the standards of behavior for the individual and has assisted the individual in adhering to these standards even in times of adversity.

The community-cohesion explanation of the success of the Japanese Americans appears to be stronger than either the value-compatibility explanation or cohesion theories which emphasize singly the role of the family or the church. It helps us especially to understand why the exceptionally wide generation gap among the Japanese has not resulted in the large amount of problem behavior that frequently has occurred among second-generation immigrants.

The community-cohesion explanation also affords a more satisfactory framework for exploring how an ethnic group's success values (among others) have been carried over into the actions of the group's members. For instance, with only minor changes, several of the adjectives we have presented to describe Issei parents may be used to describe the parents of many other ethnic groups. It really has not been unusual for immigrant parents to make a determined effort to teach their children obedience, respect for authority, and the desirability of "getting ahead" in life. The really unusual thing about the Issei is that their efforts were more frequently rewarded than generally has been true. An emphasis on the role of community cohesion in the transmission of values directs our attention to the high frequency with which other people in the Japanese community have supported the parents' efforts.

Kitano (1969:68) illustrates this point in a story of a Nisei child who broke his arm in an athletic contest. The child was told by a series of Japanese adults, including his scoutmaster, his parents, his doctor, and his schoolteacher that "Japanese boys don't cry"; and he was praised when he did not cry. In this way, the child was consistently rewarded in a wide range of social settings for not doing something that might bring shame to his ethnic group as well as to his family. Incidents of this sort were a daily reminder to the Nisei that they were Japanese and that the entire community expected them to behave as their parents had instructed them. More important, such incidents served to assure children that they would almost surely be rewarded for "good" behavior and punished for "bad" behavior.

Neither of the types of theories under discussion, however, offer much reliable advice to the person who wishes to learn from the case of the Japanese Americans how to accelerate or retard the assimilation of a particular ethnic group. Suppose, for example, that the strongly cohesive Japanese community has indeed been the secret of Japanese American success. What assurance is there that same formula may be applied in the case of a different ethnic group that possessed a markedly different background and history? Just how, exactly, does one proceed to construct the equivalent of the community cohesion that has developed among the Japanese in an unplanned way over a period of many centuries? While these questions definitely should quash the easy assumption that the lessons of the Japanese American experience may be applied directly to the solution of the problems of other racial minorities within the United States, they do nothing to diminish the value of these ideas as they apply to the Japanese Americans. Nor should they discourage us from further explorations based on the clues that have been discovered. For example, the pattern of "enhanced striving" under adverse conditions that we have found among the Japanese has been noted also within some other ethnic groups that typically are high in community cohesion.[23]

A more stinging set of criticisms of all success theories, including the two we have considered, has been presented by some Asian American militants. Among the many points they make, three especially should be noted. First, it is argued that the success story of the Japanese and other Asian American groups is a myth or stereotype; it is only one, exaggerated side of the tale. As Okimoto (1971:14) states, "to dwell exclusively on our accomplishments is to present an incomplete picture" that overlooks the sacrifices that were made "in our pilgrimage into the Land of Milk and Honey." Second, the success stereotype serves the majority as a "put-down" for other minorities, especially the other colored minorities. The majority readily points to the Japanese and other successful Asian Americans and says, "They have made it; why can't you?" Third, the Asian American militants criticize the human meaning of the success values themselves. Is the material success that has always lain at the center of the values of the Anglo-American majority really a worthwhile goal for human beings? Is this not a "culture-bound definition of success?" (Takagi, 1973:151). In the view of some Asian Americans, the answer to the latter question is a resounding "yes!" Okimoto (1971:17) puts it this way: "I doubt whether we have succeeded in any but the narrowest materialist definition of the word. For in a broader spiritual and humanistic sense we have failed abysmally, not only as a minority group but as compassionate human beings as well."

Evidently, these questions and observations plunge us headlong into the arena of conflicting value premises, about which something was said in chapter 1. They also illustrate in concrete terms the conflict between the ideology of Anglo conformity and such alternatives as cultural pluralism and separatism. Whether one prefers or rejects Anglo conformity, however, it is generally agreed that the experience of the Japanese Americans confirms the rule that nonwhite groups are especially subject to severe discrimination in the United States. It seems uncontested, too, that the Japanese Americans have been exceptional in the extent to which they have undergone cultural and secondary structural assimilation. The evidence on primary structural and marital assimilation is less clear-cut. There is ample reason to believe that both of these subprocesses are underway; however, there is also good reason to believe that the contemporary revitalization of ethnic consciousness among the younger Japanese Americans is no passing fad. The assessment of Levine and Montero (1973:33) seems justified: "There is little evidence that the subculture will soon wither away." Hence, it appears that many Japanese Americans are reexamining the options open to their group and are casting a more suspicious eye on the ideals of Anglo conformity. Some form of pluralism, which previously was most popular among the Issei, has found new adherents among the Sansei and Yonsei.

Let us now pursue some of these issues further through a consideration of the experience of the Mexican Americans.

KEY IDEAS

1. Even though they have experienced exceptionally high levels of prejudice and discrimination, the Japanese Americans are an exception to the generalization (a) that nonwhite minorities in the United States have not attained high levels of education and occupation and (b) that second-generation immigrants exhibit high levels of social deviance.
2. An analysis of a group that has not responded to prejudice and discrimination in the usual ways may afford clues concerning why the usual responses arise and how they may be prevented.
3. The Japanese family and community in America have been highly cohesive.
4. When Japanese nationals within the United States experienced discrimination, they could—and often did—turn to the Japanese government for assistance.
5. The Japanese generations in America have been unusually distinctive. This distinctiveness is largely due to the interference with immigration, beginning with the Gentlemen's Agreement and the cessation of immigration by the Exclusion Act of 1924.
6. The evacuation and relocation program during World War II resulted in the imprisonment of over 70,000 citizens of the United States without any charges or criminal convictions.
7. An effort was made to organize the relocation centers along the lines of a typical American community. This largely unsuccessful attempt widened further the gap between the Issei and Nisei.
8. Cultural assimilation has been comparatively low among the Issei and comparatively high among the Nisei and Sansei.
9. The Sansei are not completely assimilated culturally, and some evidence supports the idea that pluralism is gaining in popularity among them. More frequently than the Nisei, the Sansei have openly raised questions concerning the human costs of the worldly success of their group.
10. The Nisei and Sansei have moved substantially in the direction of secondary structural, primary structural, and marital assimilation.
11. It is not established that the *amount* of assimilation that has occurred in regard to each of the four main subprocesses of assimilation is consistent with Gordon's theory.
12. The history of the Japanese Americans generally supports the idea that disadvantages based on racial distinctiveness are not necessarily permanent in American society.

13. One explanation of the achievement of the Japanese Americans is that there is a significant compatibility between certain key values in traditional Japanese and American middle-class cultures.

14. Another explanation of Japanese achievement in America is that the success values of Japan have been transmitted from the Issei to the Nisei and from the Nisei to the Sansei. Although the exact way this transmission has been achieved is unclear, it seems likely that the highly cohesive Japanese community in America has played a central role.

NOTES

1. The "yellow peril" was the central element in the stereotype of the Chinese. It signified their presumed hatred of America and their intention physically to conquer the United States following a period of "peaceful invasion." For a discussion of these points, see tenBroek, Barnhart, and Matson, *Prejudice, War and the Constitution,* pp. 19–29.

2. A small but famous group of so-called First Year Men did go to Hawaii in 1868—the year of the restoration of imperial rule. For an account of this immigration see Marumoto, " 'First Year' Immigrants to Hawaii & Eugene Van Reed," *East Across the Pacific,* pp. 5–39.

3. This doctrine was put into effect in the historic U.S. Supreme Court case *Plessy* v. *Ferguson,* 1896, which is discussed in chapter 7.

4. A full description of this event has been presented by Howard H. Sugimoto, "The Vancouver Riots of 1907," *East Across the Pacific,* pp. 92–126.

5. The terms *Issei, Nisei,* and *Sansei* mean literally the first, second, and third generation. Two other frequently used generational terms are Yonsei and Kibei. The Yonsei are the fourth generation. The Kibei are Nisei who were sent to Japan as children in order to receive a traditional Japanese upbringing.

6. We should note again that the Little Tokyo and Little Japan communities established by the Issei, like those of many other ethnic groups, were not simply replicas of those in the old country. The Issei adapted a number of American styles, implements, and manners to the Japanese setting. This is another instance of the process of ethnogenesis whereby new ethnic communities are created.

7. The well-known exclusionist Sen. J. D. Phelan, for instance, stated that "the native Japanese are as undesirable as the imported" (Daniels, *The Politics of Prejudice,* p. 83).

8. The names *settlement period* and *second-generation period* are used by Miyamoto (Miyamoto, "An Immigrant Community in America," *East Across the Pacific,* pp. 220–221.

9. The Nisei were especially vulnerable to the charge of loyalty to Japan because of the difference between American and Japanese laws concerning citizenship. The United States is one among several nations that grant citizenship to those born within the country (the principle of *jus soli*), while Japan is among the several nations that grant citizenship on the basis of

kinship (the principle of *jus sanguinis*). The Nisei, therefore, were citizens of both the United States and Japan.

10. For two excellent presentations of the details of these events, see tenBroek, Barnhart, and Matson, *Prejudice, War and the Constitution,* pp. 99–184, and Thomas and Nishimoto, *The Spoilage,* pp. 1–52.

11. In 1940, there were about 127,000 Japanese and Japanese Americans in the United States. Of these, 47,000 were aliens, and 80,000 were American citizens. Approximately 90 percent of these 127,000 people lived in California, Arizona, Oregon, and Washington (Thomas, *The Salvage,* p. 3).

12. The following discussion of life in the Poston Relocation Center is based on the excellent study by Leighton, *The Governing of Men.*

13. For a further analysis of this point, see the stimulating discussion by Grodzins, "Making Un-Americans," pp. 105–131.

14. For a full discussion of the role of Japanese Americans in World War II, see Hosokawa, *Nisei,* pp. 393–422.

15. Question 27 also concerned the individual's loyalty and was prominent in the controversy. It read: "Are you willing to serve in the armed forces of the United States on combat duty, wherever ordered?" On the basis of their answers to questions 27 and 28, the evacuees became divided into "yes-yes" and "no-no" groups.

16. For a full analysis of the registration and segregation programs, see Thomas and Nishimoto, *The Spoilage,* pp. 53–361.

17. Quoted by Broom and Kitsuse, *The Managed Casualty,* p. 32.

18. For a discussion of this point, see Kitano, *Japanese Americans,* p. 28.

19. Since the publication of these findings, Kagiwada has criticized his study, among others, for having been conducted within an assimilationist framework. He has concluded that "a more realistic framework would view these pluralistically oriented groups as struggling to maintain their religio-cultural integrity against the tremendous odds of assimilationist forces within our society" (Kagiwada, "Confessions of a Misguided Sociologist," p. 163). This criticism, however, appears to be directed toward the scope and interpretation of the findings reported here and not at their accuracy.

20. Problems of interpretation sometimes arise also from the way intermarriage rates are reported. Rodman gives this example. Suppose there are six marriages in which both partners are Catholic and four marriages in which only one partner is Catholic. Since, in this case, four of the ten marriages are mixed, we may say the rate *for marriages* is 40 percent; however, since there are sixteen Catholics in all, only four of whom are in a mixed marriage, we may say with equal logic that the rate *for individuals* is 25 percent. Either rate may be used, but confusion occurs when one is mistaken for the other (Rodman, "Technical Note on Two Rates of Mixed Marriage," pp. 776–778).

21. Calculated from Table 6 in John H. Burma, "Interethnic Marriage in Los Angeles," p. 163.

22. There is some evidence that this generalization may be less applicable to those who have a religious affiliation. In a study of 141 Buddhist and Christian Japanese Americans, Feagin and Fujitaki did not find a single instance of outmarriage (Feagin and Fujitaki, "On the Assimilation of the Japanese Americans," p. 28). It also is possible that the extent of marriage

across racial lines overstates the degree to which Japanese Americans are pulling away from their ethnic group. Petersen argues that in Hawaii the children of white-Japanese couples generally are identified as white or Japanese but not both and that, therefore, the Japanese group is maintaining its distinctiveness (Petersen, *Japanese Americans,* p. 224).

23. For an analysis of this pattern among the Jews and Chinese, see Eitzen, "Two Minorities," pp. 221–240.

Six

The Chicanos

Despite great obstacles, this population as a whole is clearly moving further away from lower-class Mexican traditional culture and toward Anglo-American middle-class culture. . . .

Fernando Penalosa (1970:43)

The North American culture is not worth copying: it is destructive of personal dignity; it is callous, vindictive, arrogant, militaristic, self-deceiving, and greedy . . . it is a cultural cesspool and a social and spiritual vacuum for the Chicano.

Armando B. Rendon (1973:354)

The preceding chapters have highlighted the point that the population of the United States has to a large extent been built up by successive waves of immigrants from various parts of the world and that these immigrants, broadly speaking, entered this society voluntarily. In the case of the Chicanos, however, we confront a second kind of situation. Like the black and Indian Americans, the Chicanos did not originally become a part of American society through voluntary immigration. The southwestern or "borderlands" region of what is now the United States, in which the Chicano population is concentrated, was settled by people of Spanish-Mexican-Indian ancestry long before it was settled by Anglo-Americans. Consequently, as Sanchez has stated, "the Spanish Mexicans of the Southwest are not truly an immigrant group, for they are in their traditional home."[2] Except for the Indian Americans, the Chicanos have been the only American ethnic minority to enter the society through the direct conquest of their homelands. Some students believe this is a fact of overriding importance, a fact that makes totally inapplicable to the Chicanos the assimilationist ideas we have explored thus far. Unlike the Irish, Germans, Italians, Jews, Japanese, and all other groups we have discussed except the Indians, the Chicanos have not become "newcomers" to American society by leaving the old country and crossing oceans. In a very important sense, as noted in chapter 1, they have not migrated to American society at all. American society has "migrated" to them. From this standpoint, the expectation that the experience of the Chicanos can be analyzed properly in terms of any or all of the three main ideologies of assimilation discussed previously is considered to be a serious mistake. It is argued, rather, that to understand the Chicano experience we must employ an anti-assimilationist ideology and framework. What basis is there for such a claim? What ideas might such a view contain?

The Colonial Analogy

The principal reasons to assume that something is wrong with a conventional assimilationist interpretation of the Chicano experience may be most easily appreciated by considering again the predictions one would make on the basis of Park's race cycle theory. The Chicano group has now been in existence since 1848, quite long enough to have passed through the conflict and accommodation stages and to be well into the final stage of complete assimilation. In terms of our modification to Gordon's concepts, we should by now have witnessed a high degree of cultural and secondary structural assimilation and a substantial degree of primary and marital assimilation. In fact, however, the relations between the Chicanos and Anglos in the borderlands have been marked by repeated instances of "falling back" into the conflict stage of Park's cycle. Considering the length of time having elapsed since 1848, the levels of most forms of assimilation strike many observers as unexpectedly low.

We have seen that different ethnic groups have tried, with varying success, to preserve their cultures and have been, in varying degrees, the objects of prejudice and discrimination. We have seen, too, that there are good reasons to question whether immigrant minorities have ever been assimilated in precisely the way Park's ideas would suggest. Nevertheless, we also have seen that as a guide to an understanding of the experience of many European groups in the United States—especially those from northern, western, and central Europe—the ideas of assimilationist theory are of considerable value. People of different heritages have been incorporated solidly into the society of the United States and have for many purposes come to view themselves mainly, if not exclusively, as Americans.

But how well would these ideas serve us if we wished to understand, say, interethnic relations in Africa? The colonized minorities of Africa generally have been in a very different situation than the immigrant minorities of the United States. In contrast to the more or less voluntary movement of the immigrant minorities to America, the colonized minorities of Africa generally were indigenous to the areas in which they became minorities and were forced to "join" the society of the colonizers. Furthermore, the colonized minorities of Africa typically were not numerical minorities. They were inferior in power, of course, which is why we call them minorities, but by sheer weight of numbers, if nothing else, they have been in a better position than immigrant minorities to maintain their cultures in the face of the dominant group's efforts to establish its own culture as the only acceptable one (Blauner, 1972:53).

The economic situation of the colonized minorities of Africa also has differed noticeably from that of the immigrant minorities in America. Although the American immigrant minorities usually have had to take whatever kind of work they could get—at least initially—they frequently have been able to move on to something more desirable after a while and to exercise some degree of choice in what they would accept. As we have seen, even their first jobs were likely to be ones that some Anglo-Americans were doing or had done recently. The complaint that "they" are undercutting us economically and are taking "our" jobs away has been heard monotonously in America. But this kind of labor difficulty did not arise in the African colonies. There the indigenous populations usually were required to engage in only the hardest, most menial kinds of tasks. The better jobs were reserved for members of the dominant group. Ordinarily, the opportunity to move around and compete freely with the members of the dominant group did not exist or was very limited (Blauner, 1972:55).

Under these conditions, the colonized minorities in Africa have not usually come to think of themselves as French or Dutch or English, and they have not typically moved into the mainstream of the dominant group's social life. The colonized minorities of Africa, instead, have looked forward to the day when the European invaders could be forced to leave and return to their own countries. The cycle of race relations here has not been characterized by a steady movement forward out of the stage of accommodation into the final stages of assimilation. Rather, it has been primarily a "back-and-forth" movement between the stage of accommodation and the prior stage of conflict.[3] In its main or "classical" form, which has been witnessed repeatedly in Africa since World War II, this oscillation has continued until the dominant white group has, in many instances, been thrown out of power and the previously colonized minority has become the majority. In many of these cases, of course, large numbers of the dominant white group have fled or been driven out of the country. The final stage of relations between the dominant Europeans and colonized Africans, then, appears to be a conflict (usually violent) followed by separation rather than an accommodation followed by assimilation.

Several observers have suggested that the kind of race relations existing between the invaders and natives in much of Africa affords a much more understandable picture of the relations between Anglos and Chicanos than do the ideas of assimilationist theory. Moore (1970:464) states that the concept of colonialism "describes and categorizes" the initial contacts of the Mexicans and the Americans. Similarly, Blauner (1972:119) argues that "the conquest and absorption of the Mexican population is an example of classical colonialism," while Acuña (1972:3) states that "the conquest of the Southwest created a colonial situation in the traditional sense." In fact, the

Chicanos may be viewed as a people who have undergone classical colonialism not once but twice. The Indians of Mexico were first subdued by the Spaniards. Then, after Mexico became an independent nation, a portion of her population was subjugated by another migrant group. As in the case of African colonialism, one group (first the Spaniards and then the Anglo-Americans) invaded and occupied the territory of another group (the Mexicans). The invaders have regulated closely the position of the conquered people within their society, particularly the kinds of work that were deemed suitable for members of the minority. For most of the period since the borderlands became a part of the United States, the Chicanos have been expected to perform mainly hard, menial, or "stoop" labor. Thus, the original Mexican American population—what Alvarez (1973:924) has called "the Creation Generation"—has long been thought to have been in a fundamentally different position than the Irish, German, or other ethnic minorities that were immigrating to America during the same period. Although the European groups definitely have displayed certain antiassimilationist sentiments, as seen in cultural pluralism, the clannishness of the Chicanos has generally been more troublesome for the dominant group. Consequently, the reactions of the Anglo-Americans—particularly in Texas—appears to have involved more force, more overt coercion, and a generally higher level of ethnic discrimination than usually has been true for the European minorities. From this perspective, one should not expect them to move into the mainstream of American life or to cease their existence as a profoundly distinctive group. One should expect, instead, that there will be constant tension in the direction of separation or even secession.

Although the colonialist perspective as we have discussed it has existed and been applied to the Chicano experience for many years, the frequent and explicit application of this view may be traced to the decade of the 1960s (Cuéllar, 1970:149). As the protest activities of the black Americans during this period gathered momentum, spokesmen for the Chicanos became both more numerous and more visible. Many intellectuals within the group were critical in speeches and in print of the usual assimilationist interpretations of the condition of the Chicanos put forward by (mainly) Anglo-American scholars. An important result of these efforts has been the emergence and diffusion of an antiassimilationist interpretation of the Chicano experience called *Chicanismo*. Although Chicanismo is not a unitary, systematic philosophy—it is still being sharpened, debated, and modified—some version of the colonialist perspective is a central element within it. Chicanismo usually emphasizes not only the unity of the Chicano people but also their relationship to the much larger Spanish-Indian peoples of Mexico and Central and South America. This much larger population—*La Raza*—is seen as sharing a very ancient and complicated heritage stemming not only from Spanish culture but also from the Aztec, Inca, Maya, and Toltec cultures. The Chicano heritage, therefore, is a rich mixture of Indian and Spanish civilizations. Its heroes include such courageous fighters against Anglo imperialism as Joaquin Murieta and Juan Cortina and also the illustrious Montezuma and the scholars and scientists of the Indian high civilizations (Murguía, 1975:9). Chicanismo thus affords not only an interpretation of how the Chicano population came into being but also emphasizes the antiquity and grandeur of Chicano history. It serves to explain the troubles of the Chicanos and to increase their awareness of themselves as members of a distinctive and oppressed group. The members of the Chicano movement see themselves both as a unique product of New World colonialism and as, in some ways, sharing the fate of other colonized minorities within the United States and throughout the world (Cuéllar, 1970:151). They tend to reject "the cold and materialist Anglo culture" and to prefer, instead, the "family warmth and solidarity" (Murguía, 1975:9) of Chicano culture.

We now have considered some of the ways that an antiassimilationist perspective may differ from the more common assimilationist views, including cultural pluralism. Specifically, we have considered that three of America's minorities—Indian Americans, Chicanos, and black Americans—have been forced to join American society and that two of these groups—the Indians and Chicanos—have been conquered on their own land and have undergone a process of colonization quite similar to that experienced by the native populations of Africa.[4] We have seen that in the case of the Chicanos, some version of the colonialist interpretation has for some time been preferred by many members of the group itself and that, more recently, the colonialist interpretation has afforded a focal point around which the ideology of Chicanismo has been organized. Those who support the Chicano movement, therefore, frequently suggest that the most desirable solutions to the problems of the Chicano group lie in the direction of separation or secession. More often, however, the main aim is to combat Anglo conformity and to promote cultural pluralism.

To assess the competing claims of the assimilationist and antiassimilationist interpretations of the Chicano experience, let us begin with the landings of the Spaniards in Mexico during the second decade of the sixteenth century. Here, as in the case of the landings of the English in Virginia and Massachusetts approximately one hundred years later, a conquering European, Christian group established itself on lands previously occupied by native American groups. In both instances, the dominant migrant group gradually expanded its frontiers to create an increasingly large colonial territory. The expansion of the English frontier toward the west and of the Spaniards toward the north were the processes that would one day bring these two enormous colonial developments together.

The specific course of colonial development in the English and Spanish territories differed in a number of significant respects. For one thing, the two powers' entire approach to colonization were different. We have described in chapter 2 the heavy reliance of the English on a private, profit-sharing method to promote exploration and colonization. The exploration and colonization of the Spanish territories, however, relied more strongly on the initiatives of the crown and the church. The Spanish monarchs were interested primarily in acquiring lands and precious metals, while the Roman Catholic church wished to save the souls of the "heathens." The English, too, were interested at first in these very same things. But after a while it became clear that there was no gold and silver treasure on the Atlantic coast, and the efforts of the English to Christianize the Indians proved to be largely futile.

These differences in colonization methods and experiences had one consequence of special importance for us: the relations between the conquering Europeans and the conquered Indians developed along significantly different paths in the two cases. As noted in chapter 2, the relations between the English and the Indians became predominantly hostile and were interspersed with warfare. Unlike the Dutch, Irish, or Germans, the Indians soon were considered to be permanently outside of the developing Anglo-American society. The policy of the Anglo-Americans toward the Indians became one of exclusion and extermination. By and large, the Indians moved west as the Anglo-American frontier advanced.

The relations between the Spaniards and the Indians in Mexico also were frequently hostile, but the Spaniards were much more successful than the Anglo-Americans in the matter of converting the Indians to Christianity, at least to many of its outward forms. Consequently, even though the Spanish also took an enormous toll in human lives and misery, the cross as well as the sword marked the advance of the northern frontier of Mexico. The policy of the Spaniards was to bring Christianized Indians into the colonial society they were building—peacefully if possible but by force if necessary. The "place" of the Indians in Mexican society, to be sure, was at the very bottom. They provided most of the manual labor that was needed to construct and maintain the *haciendas* and to exploit the riches of the earth. They were the *peons,* who were bound to the Spanish masters and the land in a form of human slavery. But they also were human beings and Christians, and they were accepted as an integral, if lowly, part of Mexican society.

The Spaniards' policy of counting the Indians "in" rather than "out" led, during a period of three centuries, to a much higher degree of marital (and other forms of) assimilation of the Indians with the dominant Europeans than was true on the eastern seaboard. Although the exact nature of this assimilation process lies beyond our scope, two things should be noted. First, just as the English subscribed generally to the Anglo-conformity ideology of assimilation, the Spaniards adhered generally to what we may call the Hispano-conformity ideology. The Indians were expected to do their very best to move toward a mastery of Spanish culture and ways of acting. Nevertheless—and this is the second point—by the time Mexico achieved independence in 1821, the culture and population of Mexico had become very much more "Indianized" than had the culture and population of the

United States. Whatever may have been the intentions of the dominant Spaniards, the melting-pot process of assimilation was more significant in Mexico than in the United States.

The Hispano-Indian society of Mexico and the Anglo-American society of the United States came into direct and continuous contact after the Louisiana Purchase in 1803. The line of contact between these groups was exceptionally long and blurred. It stretched in a poorly defined way from a point west of New Orleans, through Texas to the Rocky Mountains, north along the Rockies, and then west to the Pacific. The treaty through which the United States secured Louisiana from France did not give a detailed description of the boundaries of the territory. This fact helped to create and maintain an almost constant state of tension along the frontier, first between Spain and the United States and then, later, between Mexico and the United States. Many Americans, including such illustrious figures as Thomas Jefferson and John Quincy Adams, seemed to believe that Texas definitely had been included in the purchase, but the Spanish and Mexican governments disagreed. Many other Americans believed that it was the "Manifest Destiny" of their country to span the continent and that the frontier should be extended to the Pacific, by force if necessary. In this way, a struggle began that led, by 1848, to the transfer of the entire American southwest from Mexico to the United States and to the creation of the Chicano minority group.

The process through which the Chicano group has emerged may be visualized more clearly by a consideration of some of the events that occurred in Texas after 1803. Spain's claim to the eastern portion of Texas was disputed openly by the United States until 1819. However, two events placed matters on a different footing. First, Spain and the United States completed a treaty through which the United States acquired Florida but gave up all claims to Texas. This treaty established the Sabine River as the boundary between Louisiana and Texas. Second, in 1821, Mexico's long struggle to gain independence from Spain was successful. As a result, all of Spain's remaining North American territories came under the control of the new nation of Mexico, and all of the subsequent efforts of the Americans to push their frontier westward involved conflicts with Mexico.

The Mexican government was worried from the beginning that it might be unable to secure its long, sparsely populated northern frontier from the encroachments of the Americans. Many people in the United States did not accept the treaty agreements that had been concluded with Spain. Many southerners, in particular, were eager to expand the cotton industry into the rich lands of east Texas. Furthermore, the United States had recently been flexing its muscles in international affairs (e.g., the Monroe Doctrine) and was clearly in a stronger military position than the young Mexican nation. Also, the Americans generally did not hide the fact that they regarded themselves to be racially superior to the heterogeneous population of Mexico. The majority of Mexico's citizens were either Indians or Spanish Indians *(mestizos)*. And the heritage of the "pure" Spaniards was itself suspect in the Americans' minds because of the centuries of interaction between the Spaniards and various African populations (e.g., the Moors).

The Mexicans had some reason for optimism, however. Since they had established a democratic form of government based on a constitution similar to that of the United States, they hoped their northern neighbor would extend a helping hand. Presumably, the United States would have a greater respect for the territorial integrity of a constitutional government than it had had for that of imperial Spain. Beyond this vague hope, however, was something more concrete. Shortly after Mexican independence, Moses Austin, an American citizen, obtained permission from the Mexican government to bring a group of American settlers into Texas. In one sense, the agreement to colonize Texas with Anglo-Americans would merely promote their dominance in the area, but the Mexican strategy was based on a deeper consideration. All of the Anglo-American settlers were expected to qualify as colonists by becoming citizens of Mexico and members of the Roman Catholic church. In this way, the Mexican officials hoped to decrease the American pressure along the frontier. They would permit certain Americans into Texas, but they would select the colonists to be admitted and would maintain control over them. At the same time, they would build up the population of the province as a buffer between the two nations. Hopefully, border relations would be improved, and Texas would become a less tempting target for a forcible invasion.

This strategy ultimately failed. Less than fifteen years after Mexico gained her independence from Spain, Texas broke away from Mexico to establish still another independent republic. Some observers have argued that an armed conflict in Texas was the predictable—even inevitable—result of the confrontation of rival and clashing cultures. But this argument ignores a very important point: to a considerable extent, the main cleavage in Texas during the colonial period was not between Mexican natives and Anglo-American immigrants. It was, rather, between those who favored a strong central government and those who preferred greater provincial autonomy. It is true that the Anglo-Americans were overwhelmingly in the latter category; but it also is true that a large proportion of the native Mexicans joined them in opposing the central government.

A basis for native Mexican and Anglo-American immigrant cooperation was created and maintained by able leaders from both sides. Stephen Fuller Austin, the leader of the first group of Anglo-American immigrants to Texas, was enthusiastic about the prospect of an independent Mexico and the development of Texas within it. He was sincere in his acceptance of Mexican citizenship and was a respected link between the native and immigrant groups. From the native Mexican side, such men as Ramón Músquiz and José Antonio Navarro worked energetically to assist the assimilation of the Anglo-Americans into Mexican society. But the goodwill and substantially mutual interests of the native and immigrant leadership in Texas did not extend to Mexico City. In a way, the central authorities fell a victim to their own plan. The colonization program was so successful that by 1835 the Anglo-American immigrants outnumbered the native Mexicans in Texas by about five to one. Hence, as the talk of revolution spread, most of those who favored it were, simply as a matter of numbers, Anglo-Americans; when the revolution erupted, the Texan armies were comprised mainly of Anglo-Americans. Nevertheless, a large proportion of the native Mexicans in Texas believed that various actions of the central government had been unjustified. Kibbe (1946:33) has estimated that as many as one-third of those who opposed the government of Santa Anna were native Mexicans, and several all-native units participated in the actual fighting during the Texas revolution (Barker, 1943:333).

After the defeat of Santa Anna in 1836, Texas was established as an independent nation. The conflict between Texas and Mexico did not stop, however. Most of the Texans believed the boundary between the two countries was the Rio Grande, while still others thought Texas extended beyond the river to the Sierra Madre mountains. The Mexican government, on the other hand, did not officially concede that Texas was lost to them. Even those in Mexico who did recognize that Texas was now independent believed the boundary was the Nueces River. As a result, the large tract of land between the Rio Grande and the Nueces River continued to be an active battleground. Although the native Mexicans of Texas—the *Tejanos*—were a numerical minority, they were not yet treated systematically as an ethnic minority. An ethnic line of distinction existed, of course, but it was a blurred rather than a sharp line. Taylor (1934:21) has described the situation as follows: "During the period of confusion some Texans were fighting with Mexicans . . . other Texans were committing depredations against both Texans and Mexicans, while Mexicans could be found on both sides." Gradually, however, friendships between the *Tejanos* and the Anglo-American Texans became more difficult to maintain, and the relations between the groups gradually became more strained. Anglo-American Texans, in particular, increasingly failed to distinguish the *Tejanos* from Mexican nationals and came to regard the conflict in Texas as one of "Mexicans" versus "Americans."

Many of the Anglo-American Texans did, in fact, still regard themselves as Americans. Individuals of this persuasion frequently were eager to have Texas join the United States. Since this goal was shared by many people within the United States, allies were not hard to find. As early as 1820, while Mexico was still a Spanish colony, Thomas Jefferson had expressed the opinion that "Texas, in our hands, would be the richest state in the Union" (Rives, 1913:23). Consequently, it is hardly surprising that after only some ten years of independence, Texas agreed to become a part of the United States.

The annexation of Texas aggravated rather than ended the hostilities in the borderlands. President Santa Anna had warned, in 1843, that "the Mexican government will consider equivalent to a declaration of war against the Mexican Republic the passage of an act for the incorporation of Texas with the territory of the United States" (Faulkner, 1948:324). After the annexation, diplomatic relations between the two governments were broken, and both sides prepared for war. Since the United States accepted Texas' claims concerning the boundary between the two nations, President Polk ordered General Taylor to occupy the land between the Nueces and the Rio Grande. The Mexicans, of course, considered this an invasion of their territory; in April 1846, a battle between Mexican and American troops occurred north of the Rio Grande. In May, President Polk asked Congress for a declaration of war against Mexico, claiming that Mexico "has invaded our territory and shed American blood on American soil" (Faulkner, 1948: 325). Abraham Lincoln was among those who did not agree with this explanation of the situation. His own view was that the war was "unnecessarily and unconstitutionally commenced by the President" (Faulkner, 1948: 325).

Constitutional or not, a war was underway. The conflict involved not only the disputed territory between Texas and Mexico but all of Mexico. General Taylor moved south of the Rio Grande to Monterrey; Colonel Kearny directed the conquest of California; General Scott invaded at Vera Cruz and captured Mexico City. In February 1848, Mexico surrendered under the terms of the Treaty of Guadalupe Hidalgo.

The treaty ceded to the United States over one-half of the territory of Mexico. The Rio Grande was established as the boundary of Texas, and the great bulk of the land that now comprises the southwestern region of the United States was acquired. The Manifest Destiny of the United States to stretch from the Atlantic to the Pacific had now been achieved. The Spanish-Mexican-Indian group that was left behind as Mexico's northern frontier receded were now a conquered group. As individuals, they had the right either to "retain the title and rights of Mexican citizens, or acquire those of citizens of the United States" (Moquin and Van Doren, 1971:246). Those who did not declare their intention to remain Mexicans automatically became citizens of the United States after one year. At this point, they were entitled legally to enjoy the same rights and privileges as all other U.S. citizens. In practice, however, they generally were viewed as a defeated and inferior people whose rights did not need to be taken too seriously. Politically speaking, therefore, the Mexican American or Chicano minority became a distinguishable group as a result of the conquest of Mexico by the United States. Their entry into the society, to repeat, was quite different from that of the Irish and Germans, who were arriving in the United States in large numbers during this very same period. The Chicanos had not decided to leave their native land and go to the United States. They simply discovered one day that by a mutual agreement of Mexico and the United States, the places where they lived were no longer in Mexico. In fact, to continue being Mexicans, they had either to leave their homes and move south of the new border established by the treaty or declare officially their intention to remain Mexican nationals within the United States.

　　The Treaty of Guadelupe Hidalgo did not end the physical violence between the Anglos and Chicanos within the borderlands. Although there exists no accurate tabulation of the violent interethnic encounters that have taken place between individuals and groups, it has been reported that the number of Chicanos killed in the Southwest during the years 1850–1930 was greater than the number of lynchings of black Americans during that same period (Moquin and Van Doren, 1971:253). In Moore's (1976:36) opinion, "No other part of the United States saw such prolonged intergroup violence as did the Border States from 1848 to 1925."

　　But if the treaty did not end the violence, it did mark the point beyond which those of Mexican descent were subordinated to the Anglo-Americans. A system of ethnic domination and subordination had been given birth. An important explanation of how such systems arise has been presented by Noel (1968). Noel argues that a system of ethnic stratification invariably results from contacts between ethnic groups if (1) one group has greater power than the other, (2) there is competition between the groups over scarce resources, and (3) ethnocentrism is present. Our description of contacts between Mexicans and Americans in the borderlands strongly suggests that all three of these essential ingredients were present. The superior power of the Anglo-Americans was demonstrated, of course, by the outcome of the war with Mexico. The desire of the Anglo-Americans for the land, as we have noted, was apparent for decades prior to the war. Though ethnocentrism was most conspicuous from the Anglo-Americans, feelings of superiority existed on both sides. Hence, the Americans had ample incentives to compete with the Mexicans for Texas; they had the power to seize it if necessary, and they typically had a low regard for the Mexican people.[5] The combination of these ingredients created a highly unstable situation along all of Mexico's northern frontier, especially in the area of Texas.[6]

　　The strip of land between the Nueces River and the Rio Grande was the scene or staging area for many of the most spectacular conflicts. Numerous so-called filibustering expeditions were launched by Americans in an attempt to extend U.S. territory even more deeply into Mexico. There were, in fact, so many of these collective acts of plunder and brutality that one author has referred to the period 1848–1878 as "The Golden Age of Anglo-American filibustering" (Taylor, 1934:29). The traffic, however, was not entirely one way. Between 1859 and 1873, the flamboyant Mexican leader Juan N. Cortina initiated a series of deadly raids along the Texas border. Cortina, who was born near Brownsville, Texas, developed a deep hatred of *"gringos"* during the Mexican and American war. Throughout most of the 1850s, he lived on the Texas side of the river, gathered about him a band of roguish *vaqueros,* and was indicted for theft and murder (Lea, 1957:159–160). He came prominently to attention in July 1859 in the first of a series of "Cortina wars." After rescuing a former servant from the Anglo-American marshal in Brownsville and wounding the marshal, Cortina brought together his men and captured Brownsville in an early-morning raid. For the next two months,

Cortina's force remained in the area between Brownsville and Rio Grande City, burning, looting, and killing. During the following years, Cortina's daring exploits won him labels ranging from "cattle thief" to "champion of his race" (Lea, 1957:159). They also provoked continuous, bitter conflicts with military and law-enforcement authorities on both sides of the Rio Grande.

The Cortina wars fanned the flames of ethnic hatred in Texas, and untold numbers of innocent people were their victims. The Anglo-Americans became increasingly suspicious of all "Mexicans" and were quick to punish anyone suspected of aiding Cortina. Similarly, Cortina did not waste time dealing with Chicanos who were suspected as informers. Obviously, the Chicanos were caught in the middle. Although some of them undoubtedly aided the Mexican raiders, a large majority were loyal to the United States. Many of them, in fact, were active in the fight against Cortina. Nevertheless, the mutual hatred of many of the Anglo-Americans and "Mexicans" became so intense that many on both sides of the ethnic line began to consider killing a representative of the other side to be a source of pride rather than a crime.

The interethnic violence in Texas reached a peak during the early 1870s. In response to a raid by "heavily armed Mexicans" on the village of Nuecestown, Texas, a group of Anglo-Americans organized "brutal outrages, murdering peaceful Mexican farmers and stockmen who had lived all their lives in Texas" (Taylor, 1934:55). By the end of 1875, however, the worst of the disorders was over. The combined actions of the authorities on both sides of the Rio Grande led to a reduction of border raiding. Cortina was commissioned as a general in the Mexican army and was stationed far from the border in Mexico City. By 1878, after more than forty years of almost continuous friction and warfare, the Anglo-Americans had established an uneasy control over the land between the Nueces River and the Rio Grande and over the Chicano people who lived there.

The next three decades were relatively quiet along the Rio Grande. But if this period seemed to be one of accommodation, the hatreds and antagonisms smoldered at its very surface. Violent group conflict was always a possibility and was frequently a reality. Various incidents—shootings, lynchings, beatings, and so on—continued. Each incident usually led to some form of retaliation from the injured side, which, of course, aggravated the matter still further. Relations between the Chicanos and the Texas Rangers, in particular, were very poor. In the years to come, the rangers increasingly were viewed by Chicanos as an official expression of hatred against them.

The period of relative quiet was brought to an end by political and economic troubles. As we discuss later, employment opportunities for the ordinary Mexican citizen were declining in Mexico and increasing in the United States during the first decade of the twentieth century. At the same time, there was mounting opposition to the repressive regime of the dictator Porfírio Díaz. These factors encouraged the successful overthrow of Díaz by liberal revolutionaries in 1911. The new government was short-lived, however. The following period of conflict kept the border in a state of agitation.

When Francisco "Pancho" Villa crossed the border into New Mexico, raided Columbus, and killed a number of Americans, President Wilson sent Gen. John J. "Blackjack" Pershing into Mexico to capture Villa. Pershing searched for Villa for nine months but returned home emptyhanded. The years of revolution in Mexico and the border crossings by Villa and Pershing severely damaged the relations between Mexico and the United States, but they also fanned the flames of distrust and hatred that had existed for so long between the Chicanos and Anglos. As a result, an unknown number of innocent civilians—possibly as many as five thousand—were killed during this time (McWilliams, 1973:111).

Quite clearly, the period of apparent accommodation between Chicanos and Anglos while Díaz was in power in Mexico had ended. It ended not only in open conflict between Mexico and the United States but also between the two ethnic groups within the United States. This "reversion" to an earlier stage in Park's race cycle is a dramatic illustration of the point that the experience of the Chicanos has differed fundamentally from that of the European minorities. The periodic eruption of organized conflict between Chicanos and Anglos poses a serious challenge to the central ideas of the assimilationist perspective and suggests that a perspective that includes the colonialist view may be necessary for this analysis.

The claims of the colonialist theorists have not gone unchallenged. Probably the most frequent objection to the unqualified application of the colonial analogy to the Chicano experience concerns the question of *when* the analysis should actually begin. While it is undeniable that the Chicanos had first arrived in the borderlands over three centuries before this territory was annexed by the United States, the critics of colonialist theory are more impressed by a series of events that coincided with the peak of the new immigration from Europe. These events laid the groundwork for arguing that the Chicanos, though Americans through conquest, are nevertheless similar in most essential respects to the Europeans of the new immigration. Let us turn to the basic ideas of this contention.

The Immigrant Analogy

How can a comparison of the Chicanos to the new immigrants possibly be valid? The basic reason offered is this: although the Chicanos occupied the Southwest long before the Anglos, comparatively few of them resided on the American side of the border prior to 1900. For nearly fifty years after the signing of the Treaty of Guadalupe Hidalgo, relatively few Mexican nationals moved to the United States with the intention of becoming permanent residents. An unknown but probably large number of people did move back and forth across the border in search of work. At this time, however, such movements were mainly informal; little was kept in the way of records. For one period, in fact, between 1886 and 1893, there are no official records of immigration from Mexico into the United States.

In a way, this is not so strange. Please recall that until 1875 the United States had no federal laws restricting immigration. America's policy was to have an "open door" to the world, to encourage people to move to the United States and share the labors (and rewards) of developing the continent. Even when the attention of the nation did turn to immigration, the main focus of debate was the new immigration from Europe and the yellow peril from the Orient. After the Chinese Exclusion Act was passed and the Gentlemen's Agreement was put into effect, there still was little concern about the immigration of Mexicans. Our policy toward Mexico remained unrestrictive. The border patrol did not begin operations until 1904, and its first efforts to control immigration from Mexico, strange to say, seem to have been directed primarily against the Chinese (Grebler, Moore, and Guzman, 1970:519). Mexicans continued to cross into the United States legally and with ease. Some effort was made to prevent people who were poverty-stricken or socially undesirable from entering the country. For most practical purposes, however, a Mexican national could enter the United States legally (at a small fee) simply by obtaining permission at a border station. Still, as had been true since the end of the Mexican and American war, the flow of legal immigrants was only a trickle. Less than 17,000 entrants were counted during the entire last half of the nineteenth century. Not until 1904 did the number of legal immigrants from Mexico in one year exceed 1,000 (U.S. Bureau of the Census, *Historical Statistics,* 1960:58–59). Beginning with that year, however, the number of entrants from Mexico began to rise substantially. The official count of immigrants for the decade 1900–1909 was over 31,000. But this figure appears greatly to understate the extent of the actual rate at which Mexicans were entering, and remaining in, the United States. One official report estimated that "at least 50,000 'nonstatistical' aliens" arrived in "normal" years (Gómez-Quiñones, 1974:84). Another estimate suggested that the figure may have reached 100,000 (Bryan, 1972:334). No one can be sure, of course, how many of those who entered in a nonimmigrant status then became permanent residents of the United States, but it seems certain that a great many did.

The sudden sizable flow of immigrants from Mexico during the first decade of the twentieth century was greatly exceeded during the second decade, but a still greater wave of Mexican immigrants came during the period 1920–1929. Altogether, more than 700,000 legal immigrants entered during the entire thirty-year period. From a purely official and numerical standpoint, then, the great period of Mexican immigration had hardly commenced when the peak of the new immigration had been reached, and it did not reach its crest until the new immigration had dwindled noticeably.

During this period, the composition of the Chicano population was transformed. Before 1900, most Chicanos either had been among those conquered in the Mexican and American war or were their descendants. From this standpoint, the Mexican immigrants of the period after 1900 were in many respects the first generation—entering more or less voluntarily and with the intention to become residents of the United States—of what has become our nation's second-largest minority. From this standpoint, also, barely enough time has passed really to test the three-generations hypothesis. The modern Chicanos are predominantly Mexican nationals who have entered the United States since 1900 or are their descendants. From an assimilationist perspective, therefore, they are, in the main, even "newer" than most of the new immigrants. They have seemed slow to assimilate—so this argument goes—because they are actually recent immigrants. They are not, strictly speaking, people who "got here first"; and they have not really had as long to adopt the American "way" as those who arrived in the United States before 1910. In short, the immigrant analogy downgrades the significance for the process of assimilation of the "historical primacy" of the Chicanos.

From the colonialist viewpoint, of course, the immigrant analogy misses the mark entirely. Even though, technically, the large population movement from Mexico to the United States since 1900 is an example of "immigration," is it really reasonable to call people who move from one side of a politically arbitrary (and mostly imaginary) border to the other "immigrants?" Is it reasonable to do this, in particular, when the "immigrants" are moving into a territory that previously had been a part of their homeland, with which they have maintained continuous contact, and in which their native culture still flourishes? (Blauner, 1972:55). Aren't such people more nearly "home-comers" than "newcomers?"

Alvarez (1973) believes it is more accurate to consider the people in this movement simply to be migrants rather than immigrants. In the first place, there is an obvious geographical difference between the immigration of the Irish or the Russian Jews and the immigration of the Mexicans. The latter could cross the border that separates the two countries so much more easily than the European immigrants could cross the Atlantic Ocean that the comparison of the effects of the two types of movement may seem a bit farfetched. It is hard to believe that the psychological impact or meaning of moving across the border would be very similar to that of leaving Europe for America. In most instances, the European immigrants realized that they were leaving the old country for a long time, possibly for good; that they would arrive in a very different and strange land; and that their children would grow up under conditions differing radically from those they had experienced as children. Can the same things be said in general of the Mexican "immigrant?" Physically speaking, the territory of the United States and Mexico is continuous, and the land surrounding both banks of the Rio Grande is very similar. Along most of the border, there is no geographical line to separate the two countries. As noted previously, Mexican workers had frequently moved back and forth across the border prior to 1900 in search of work. Crossing the border was a familiar and fairly unimportant act. There is little reason to suppose that most of these who participated in the "im-migration" from Mexico during the early part of the twentieth century

thought of themselves as moving irrevocably from an old, familiar environment into a new and alien one.

There is another reason, closely related to the first, for rejecting the
idea that Chicanos may be analyzed adequately as a fairly recent immigrant
group. Not only are Mexico and the United States physically continuous,
they are culturally overlapping. As we have seen, the Anglo-Americans
established numerical and cultural dominance, as well as political and economic dominance, in much of the Southwest during the nineteenth century.
However, in some parts of the Southwest, the Chicano population has remained larger than the Anglo-American population; throughout the borderlands, the Chicanos have retained a strong and distinctive culture. This has
been especially true in those cities, towns, and counties that are adjacent to
the border, but it also has been true in many areas that are far removed
from the border. Even at considerable distances from the border, Spanish has
continued to be the primary spoken language of many, if not most, Chicanos.
Hundreds of Spanish place names dot the map of the American Southwest,
and numerous Spanish words and terms have found their way into the
vocabularies of the Anglo-Americans. In short, important elements of
Mexican culture have been sustained within the United States. The presence
of these familiar cultural elements almost surely has served further to modify
the Mexican's "immigration" experience. It seems unlikely that the Mexicans
have felt unalterably separated from their native land, as have so many other
immigrants, or have felt so strange within the host country. It seems much
more likely, rather, that many Mexicans have felt right at home in the
Southwest and have not felt too strongly the usual pressure that is placed
on immigrants to become "Americans."[7] Even if the pressure was felt, it
certainly could be more easily resisted than is ordinarily possible.

The final reason to be considered here for regarding those who moved
from Mexico to the United States after 1900 as migrants rather than immigrants stems directly from the colonialist perspective itself. Whatever one
may conclude concerning the attitudes and reactions of the post-1900
Mexican newcomers, the relationship of this group to the host society was
still strongly influenced by the fact that the Mexicans who had been "left
behind" by the Treaty of Guadalupe Hidalgo were a conquered people in
their own land. Even if we assume that the Mexicans who came to the
United States after 1900 did regard the change as large and permanent, and
even if they did feel that they were foreigners in the United States, they still
could not assume the "normal" status of immigrants. The problem, according
to this argument, is that the members of the host society did not distinguish
between the "colonized" Mexicans and the "immigrant" Mexicans. The latter
group could not function as immigrants because the host group did not
recognize them as such. They were forced into the same kinds of jobs, housing,
and subservience as the former. As Alvarez (1973:930) has stated, "Socio-
psychologically, the migrants, too, were a conquered people." From this
perspective, Mexicans who have come to the United States since the Anglo-

American conquest—even those who have come since 1900—have merely joined the ranks of the existing colonized Chicano minority. Assimilation theorists may regard the large population movements of this century as "immigration" if they wish, but the similarities between the Mexican "immigration" and European immigration are, from this standpoint, largely superficial.

The above comparison of the immigrant and colonial analogies shows that each emphasizes different aspects of the history of Chicano and Anglo-American relations. Many of the most important facts are not themselves in question. It is true, as is stressed in the colonialist account, that the Mexicans occupied the borderlands hundreds of years before the Anglo-Americans arrived and, thus, may claim historical primacy; that the Anglo-Americans, through the annexation of Texas and the Mexican and American war, forced Mexico to cede the Spanish Southwest; that the relations between the Chicanos and Anglos in the borderlands have been even more filled with conflict and tension than usually has been the case for immigrant minorities; and that the processes of assimilation have not produced as much change among the Chicanos as one would expect to occur in an immigrant population in over 140 years. But it is also true that the great majority of the Chicano population is comprised of people who have entered the United States from Mexico since 1900 and their descendants. It may be possible, therefore, that if one starts the analysis with the "migrant generation" (Alvarez, 1973:926) of the early 1900s, the processes of assimilation may be operating among the Chicanos in a fairly "normal" way. To help evaluate these clashing interpretations, we now turn to some of the main features of the Chicano experience since 1900.

Mexican Immigration and Native Reaction

We have seen that a combination of social turmoil in Mexico and economic opportunities in the United States led to a sharp rise in Mexican immigration during the first decade of the twentieth century. The Mexicans' opportunities for work, however, were mainly in the hard, dirty, and poorly paid jobs in railroading, mining, and agriculture. The conditions of work experienced by large numbers of Mexicans and Mexican Americans in these three industries during the early portions of this century has had a lasting effect on the Chicano community. Railroad work, which was the main kind at first, assisted to take significant numbers of Mexicans out of the Southwest into other parts of the United States. In many instances, railroad crews completed their jobs far from the border area and were forced to accept other jobs wherever they happened to be. Many Chicano communities outside the Southwest were started in this way (Gómez-Quiñones, 1974:88). Even more important in its effects has been the way the Mexican labor force generally has been organized. In each of these main industries, the work force was organized in gangs; frequently, the work gangs included all of the members of a family. This meant that entire families were intermittently on the move, living in temporary and frequently unsanitary housing. It means also that the children of such families were frequently engaged in unsafe, backbreaking labor and did not receive adequate schooling or health care. Additionally, migratory agricultural labor, which gradually became the primary source of employment for Mexican labor, is seasonal. Employers generally assumed and expected that the migratory Mexican workers would go "home" to Mexico when the work ran out.

The movement of Mexican labor into agricultural work was greatly facilitated by America's entry into World War I. In California, the demand for workers in the citrus, melon, tomato, and other industries increased sharply, encouraging Mexicans to come across the border to perform these necessary tasks. The other southwestern states were similarly affected. Workers were needed in Texas to tend the cotton, spinach, and onion crops. While in Arizona, New Mexico, and Colorado, there was a shortage of workers to raise vegetables, forage crops, and sugar beets. From the beginning, these forms of labor were "seasonal, migratory, and on a contract basis" (Gómez-Quiñones, 1974:89). To meet this increased demand for "stoop" labor, the Commissioner of Immigration and Naturalization approved, in 1917, some special regulations to permit Mexican farm workers to enter the United States in large numbers. Although the regulations soon were modified to permit temporary workers from Mexico also to fill jobs in railroad maintenance and mining, the "invasion" of agricultural work by both temporary and permanent immigrants from Mexico was the most prominent result. Indeed, the events of this period served to stamp into the public's mind a stereotype of the Mexicans and Mexican Americans as agricultural workers.

As noted previously, the increasingly large migration of Mexicans to the United States during this time was not a topic of general concern or debate. Even though the Mexican migration reached its peak in 1924—the same year in which the Immigration Act established the quota restrictions on European immigration and excluded the Japanese—the "open door" policy remained in effect for Mexicans. The new law, in fact, contained provisions that made it possible for a Mexican immigrant to work on the American side of the border during the day but to stay at his residence in Mexico during the night (Moore, 1976:48). Moreover, as the open door began to close on people of many other nationalities, cheap labor from Mexico became even more attractive to employers in the United States. Consequently, Mexican immigration jumped sharply during the 1920s both in absolute numbers and as a proportion of the total of all immigration to this country (Grebler, Moore, and Guzman, 1970:64).

The mutual attraction of Mexican labor and American employers, however, began to subside shortly after the immigration restrictions on other nationalities had gone into effect. Both because the Mexican immigration had become so large and the agricultural sector of the American economy had gone into a downturn, Mexican immigration now became a subject of national controversy. Predictably, the demand now arose that the quota system established in 1924 be extended to cover Mexicans. To support this demand, some of the restrictionists claimed that the Mexicans were socially undesirable. A Texas congressman referred to them as "illiterate, unclean, peonized masses" who are a "mixture of Mediterranean-blooded Spanish peasants with low grade Indians" (Moore, 1976:47). As things developed, however, no extension of the restrictive legislation was needed. The flow of Mexican immigration was dampened, first, by certain changes in the procedures for admitting immigrants and then by the onset of the Great Depression of the 1930s.

The main change in the admission procedure was this: in the late 1920s, the United States discontinued the practice of issuing permanent visas at the border stations. Instead, those who wished to immigrate from Mexico were now required to file an application at an American consulate. This change greatly increased the costs and inconvenience connected with a legal entry into the United States and made a permanent change of residence less attractive to Mexicans. It also decreased the chance that a permanent visa would be granted even if a person made the effort to obtain one. The consular officers began to apply strict standards to determine whether an applicant for a visa was likely to become a public charge in the United States (Moore, 1976:47). To prove that they would not become public charges, the applicants were required to show that some citizen or resident of the United States would support them if necessary (Grebler, Moore, and Guzman, 1970:78). Under these circumstances, many people preferred to cross the border illegally. Illegal immigrants—the so-called wetbacks—could avoid the cost of waiting at the border as well as the possibility that they would not be admitted. Of course, once the illegal immigrants reached the United States, they were fugitives and were in no position to insist on ethical treatment or to stand upon legal rights. As a result, the wetbacks frequently fell prey to the unscrupulous and discriminatory acts of labor contractors, employers, and underworld businesses. These conditions helped to make the life of the migratory or contract laborers even harsher. They also frequently were regarded with special hostility and suspicion by Mexican Americans, who have often feared that the uncontrolled entrance of Mexican laborers to the United States would depress working conditions for them.

Although Mexican immigration appeared to be tapering off in the face of these control measures, a dramatic reduction in the flow followed the great financial crisis of 1929. The immediate and primary cause of this decline, of course, was the great reduction in employment opportunities. The prospects were so unattractive, indeed, that the Mexican immigration of 1931 fell below 4,000 for the first time since 1907. The annual number of new arrivals fell even further in the subsequent years of the 1930s and did not begin to recover noticeably until the beginning of World War II.

In addition to the fact that the Great Depression made the United States a less attractive destination for migrants, there was another development of special importance. Many groups and officials within the United States sought to decrease unemployment and the costs of government welfare by deporting Mexican aliens. Some aliens, of course, as in the previous periods, had returned voluntarily to Mexico when their jobs dried up. But many did not; and the border patrol increased its efforts to locate and deport people who had become public charges or were in the United States illegally. At the same time, the authorities in many American cities found that it was much less expensive to pay the transportation and other costs of sending people to Mexico than it was to maintain them on welfare rolls. These combined national and local efforts to save money by "sending the Mexicans home" were in some ways a preview of the evacuation of the Japanese and Japanese Americans nearly a decade later. As in the case of the later "round-up" of the Japanese, little attention was paid either to the preferences of the evacuees or to their legal status (Grebler, Moore, and Guzman, 1970:524). Mexicans who were naturalized citizens frequently were "repatriated" along with Mexican nationals. Many native Americans of Mexican ancestry were scrutinized closely and were intimidated by the prospect of "repatriation." In some cases, families were broken apart when the Mexican father was sent "home," while his American-born children remained behind. The entire "repatriation" program emphasized to the Mexican American community just how vulnerable they were to the actions, sometimes whimsical, of government officials. In some instances, the deportations spread panic within the *barrios*. People became afraid that if they applied for relief, they would be sent to Mexico. As a result, it is quite possible that many people who were eligible for relief did not apply. Many others, apparently, concluded that they might be better off in Mexico than in the United States and voluntarily left the country. Whether willingly or not, uncounted thousands of U.S. residents of Mexican heritage were literally "shipped" to Mexico. McWilliams (1972: 386) indicates that over 200,000 Mexicans left the United States during a twelve-month period of 1931–1932 alone. The total impact of the repatriation program was probably much larger. Grebler, Moore, and Guzman (1970:526) state that the Mexican-born population of the United States declined during the 1930s from 639,000 to around 377,000. More important, though, than the sheer numbers of people who were forced or encouraged to leave the United States as a part of the "charity deportations" is that American citizens of Mexican heritage were shown dramatically that they were not necessarily considered to be full-fledged citizens. As long as there was a shortage of cheap labor, the "Mexicans" were welcomed and praised as cooperative, uncomplaining workers, but when economic times were bad, "American" officials wanted the "Mexicans" to go "home."

There was little need for additional cheap farm labor in the United States until World War II created a new manpower emergency. This time, however, the "cooperative" Mexican labor force was not so easily pulled across the border. For one thing, the war had created a labor shortage in Mexico, also; for another, Mexico's government was no longer so easily persuaded that the United States was a "good neighbor." So instead of permitting an unrestricted out-migration of workers, Mexico agreed to allow *braceros* (farmhands) to enter the United States on certain conditions: the *braceros* were to receive free transportation and food; they were not to be given jobs presently held by American residents; they were to receive guarantees concerning wages, working conditions, and living quarters; and only a limited number of workers could be employed within a given year (McWilliams, 1973:266). It was agreed, too, that specified Mexican officials could make inspections and investigate any complaints that might arise. With these guarantees and protections, Mexican workers flocked to the *bracero* program. Between 1942 and 1945, over 167,000 agricultural workers were recruited under the plan.[8]

The *bracero* program is of special interest for two reasons. First, it provided some experience for both Mexico and the United States concerning the problems of planning and regulating the back-and-forth movement of temporary workers between the two countries. At the very least, the results of the program have shown how difficult the task is. For example, as World War II progressed, the employment opportunities for Mexican workers increased in the United States, and as they did, the flow of illegal temporary workers also increased. Many Mexican workers found it to be much more convenient and less expensive to be illegal aliens than *braceros*. And the American employers—chiefly the growers and ranchers—also found that they could save time and money (and avoid "red tape") by hiring illegal aliens. Consequently, in many cases, the illegal aliens and the *braceros* were receiving different wages and benefits while working together in the same fields (Grebler, Moore, and Guzman, 1970:67). Needless to say, this situation produced many confusions and contradictions. It also produced an increase in the border patrol's efforts to locate, arrest, and deport illegal migratory workers. This effort reached its pinnacle during 1954–1955 in a highly publicized roundup called "Operation Wetback."

Even though hundreds of thousands of illegal workers (and an untold number of legal entrants and American citizens) were returned to Mexico, many of them quickly came back to the United States either legally or, again, illegally. The existence of a mixture of legal and illegal temporary workers of Mexican descent has continued to raise questions about the status of the Chicanos in our society. The dominant group's frequent failure to distinguish the Mexican Americans from the Mexican nationals has been made easier by the presence of so many of the latter. Both groups are easily considered by many members of the dominant group to be especially suited for hard manual labor and to be unsuited to possess all of the rights and privileges of American citizens. The idea also has been encouraged that Mexican Americans as well as Mexican nationals are "really" foreigners who may go "home" if they do not like conditions in the United States.

To complicate the picture still further, many members of the Chicano community also have been ambivalent about the presence of many new arrivals from Mexico. On the one hand, the newcomers are often welcomed because they serve in important ways to replenish and strengthen the prized and distinctive culture of the Chicanos. But, at the same time, they constitute a deep pool of reserve laborers who may be called on by employers to keep wages low or to resist the efforts of American citizens to form strong and effective labor unions. They also afford a continuous excuse for the border patrol and many other official agencies to pry into the private lives of those who "look Mexican." For this reason, as in the days of the welfare repatriations, Chicanos still are much more exposed than most other Americans to the threat and the actuality of being deported illegally.

The *bracero* program is of special interest for another reason. As McWilliams (1973:269) has suggested, it gave the Mexican government a firm basis on which to protest acts of discrimination against not only their citizens in the United States but also against Chicanos. For example, in October 1943, the Mexican government issued a formal protest "against the segregation of children of Mexican descent in certain Texas schools." The Mexican government also was aware of many other incidents of discrimination, particularly in Texas. One of these occurred when Sergeant Macario Garcia, a winner of the Congressional Medal of Honor, ordered a cup of coffee in a café in Sugarland, Texas, and was refused service. A fight developed, and Sergeant Garcia was arrested on a charge of aggravated assault (McWilliams, 1973:261). In another incident, a Chicano PTA group in Melvin, Texas, was refused a permit to use a community-center building. These and many other cases of overt or probable discrimination against Chicanos, as well as Mexicans, led the Mexican government in 1943 to halt the *bracero* program in Texas. This action led Gov. Coke Stevenson of Texas to make a goodwill tour of Mexico, proclaim a good neighbor policy for Texas, and to appoint a Good Neighbor Commission (McWilliams, 1973: 270). But these efforts, as well as some others on the local level, failed to satisfy the Mexican government, and the *bracero* program was not resumed in Texas during World War II.

The problem of discrimination against Chicanos during World War II, however, was by no means restricted to Texas. Certain events that took place in the Los Angeles, California, area during this period were at least equally alarming and may have had a greater, more lasting effect on the relations of Anglos and Chicanos. At about the same time the Japanese were being evacuated and interned, a number of incidents involving Chicanos—primarily young males—were given wide publicity in the Los Angeles newspapers. Many, perhaps most, Chicano youths living in the so-called Flats of East Los Angeles and Boyle Heights belonged to or were associated with various juvenile "gangs." There was nothing unusual about this. Beginning with the 1880s, the Flats had been occupied successively by Irish, Armenian, Russian Molokan, Slav, Jewish, and finally, Mexican immigrant groups (Dworkin,

1973:410). The Mexican juvenile gangs—like those that had been prominent within the preceding ethnic groups—varied in their size, chief interest, age composition, and so on. Many of these Chicano "gangs," however, were especially cohesive and troublesome to people in positions of authority. Whenever they were not actually engaged in "delinquent" behavior, they talked as if they soon would be. Probably of greater importance, though, they flaunted their distinctiveness and pride in their Mexican heritage. They called themselves *pachucos* and dressed in a manner that most members of the dominant group considered "outlandish."

The most admired appearance among the *pachucos* required one to have a duck-tail haircut and to be dressed in a striking costume called a "zoot suit." The zoot suit was distinguished by the trousers and the jacket. The trousers were tight at the ankles and the waist extended up over the chest. The main part of the trouser legs was very full. The jacket was long, full, and very broad in the shoulders. All of these features combined made the *pachuco* gang or the zoot-suit gang very visible to other members of the community. They also served as a focus of criticism and ridicule by members of the dominant group.

The summers of 1942 and 1943 witnessed two particularly notable events involving *pachuco* "gangsters." The first of these centered on the mysterious death of a young Chicano, José Díaz, following a fight between two rival gangs near an East Los Angeles swimming hole. Díaz's skull had been fractured, apparently in a fight, but an autopsy showed that he probably had been drunk when he died and that his injuries could have occurred in an automobile accident. The press coverage of this event has been described by McWilliams (1973:229) as "an enormous web of melodramatic fancy." The gravel pit near which the "gang" fight occurred was referred to as "The Sleepy Lagoon," and it was emphasized in the newspapers that the case involved Chicanos. Twenty-four young men were arrested. Following a trial that lasted several months, nine of these young men were convicted of second-degree murder, and eight others were convicted of lesser offenses. The convictions were appealed on the grounds that the trial had been conducted in a biased and improper way, in an atmosphere of sensationalism. The prosecution had played upon the fact that the defendants were of Mexican heritage, had duck-tail haircuts, and wore zoot suits. These improper tactics were criticized by the appeals court, which overturned the lower court's decision. After nearly two years of imprisonment, the case was dismissed "for lack of evidence" (McWilliams, 1973:231). While this outcome was viewed as a great victory for justice and the Chicano community, the fact still remains that seventeen young men served prison sentences for a crime they were not proven to have committed. Their crime, it seems, was that they were Chicanos.

The Sleepy Lagoon trial, conducted as it was during the period of the Japanese internment and with generous press coverage, strengthened the impression held by many people that the Chicanos were "just naturally" criminals. The supposed natural link between Mexicanness and criminality seemed to receive official support shortly after the arrest of the Sleepy Lagoon defendants. Capt. E. D. Ayres of the Los Angeles sheriff's office presented to the grand jury a report of the results of his investigation of what was considered to be the "problem of Mexican delinquency." Captain Ayres' suppositions, conclusions, and chain of reasoning sounded much like those presented by General DeWitt to justify the wartime treatment of the Japanese. In Captain Ayres' view, those of Mexican ancestry are more likely to engage in violent crimes than are those of Anglo-Saxon heritage because such behavior is an "inborn characteristic." Anglo-Saxon youths, said Captain Ayres, may use their fists or kick when they fight, but the "Mexican element" feels "a desire to use a knife or some lethal weapon . . . his desire is to kill, or at least let blood" (McWilliams, 1973:234). Such opinions, presented by a police official during these tense days, could hardly have increased the dominant group's understanding of the underlying causes of the behavior of the *pachucos*. The answer lay in an entirely different direction. As noted by Sanchez (1972:410), the *pachuco* movement grew not out of the violent nature of the Spanish-speaking people but from the discriminatory social and economic situation in which the Chicanos lived. Nevertheless, the stereotype of the naturally violent *pachuco* gangster was apparently widely believed.

The publicity surrounding the Sleepy Lagoon trial, the presentation of the Ayres report, and numerous contacts between the police and *pachuco* fighting "gangs" prepared the way for a second major series of incidents focusing primarily on the Chicanos. For approximately one week, from June 3 through June 10, 1943, the city of Los Angeles was rocked by what have come to be known as the "Zoot-Suit Race Riots." These disorders may be described as a series of mob attacks by off-duty policemen, U.S. sailors, and other servicemen directed mainly at Chicanos and people who wore zoot suits. The zoot suits, particularly when worn by those of Mexican descent, had gradually come to symbolize for many members of the dominant group an open defiance of constituted authority and moral degradation. Consequently, those who wore them appeared to many to be enemies of the state who needed to be "taught a lesson."

The violence between the servicemen and the "zooters" began when a group of sailors were beaten up—allegedly by a gang of Chicanos—while they were walking through a slum area of the city. On the following night, about 200 sailors "invaded" the east side of Los Angeles in a caravan of some twenty taxicabs. On their way, they stopped several times to beat severely at least four Chicano youths wearing zoot suits. In the following days, the local newspapers featured reports concerning violence (and threats of violence) between servicemen and "zooters." By June seventh, the numbers of people engaged in the disorders had swelled into the thousands. Throughout all of this, the Los Angeles police department reportedly took few steps to curb the activities of the servicemen and, for the most part, seemed to avoid the areas in which violence was occurring until after the conflict was over. The police in some cases simply followed along behind the servicemen to arrest the Chicanos who had been attacked! The disorders were not brought under control until after the military authorities intervened. Servicemen were ordered to stay out of downtown Los Angeles, and the order was enforced by the shore patrol and military police.

There can be little doubt that many members of the Anglo-American group subscribed to the theory of innate criminality among Chicanos and more or less openly approved of the efforts of the servicemen to "clean out" the "zooters." It seems clear, too, that the zoot suit itself became a hated symbol of Chicano solidarity and defiance. In a large number of instances, the servicemen stripped the suits from their victims and ripped them apart. An official view of all this was illustrated dramatically when the Los Angeles City Council declared that it was a misdemeanor to wear a zoot suit (McWilliams, 1973:245–250).

The repercussions of the Sleepy Lagoon trial and the zoot-suit riots were felt throughout the United States as well as abroad. The disorders were headline news in newspapers all over the United States. Zoot-suit and other race-related conflicts broke out in several other cities across the United States following the Los Angeles disorders. And just as the incidents of discrimination against Chicanos in Texas had led the government of Mexico to end the *bracero* program, the ambassador from Mexico asked for an official explanation of the zoot-suit riots. The explanation—that there was no prejudice or discrimination against people of Mexican ancestry—was hardly convincing. The war effort of the United States had been damaged; the allies of the United States had been given yet another reason to wonder about the strength of this country's commitment to racial and ethnic equality; and the enemies of the United States had been given a powerful weapon of propaganda that they did not hesitate to employ.

During all this time, of course, Chicano youths (and even some non-citizen aliens) were subject to the wartime military draft in the United States (Scott, 1974:134). Considering the level of discrimination against these young men at the time, they seemed more eager to serve and fight for the United States than might have been expected. As in the case of the Nisei, the displacements and humiliations experienced by the Chicanos during the early war years appeared generally to heighten their desire to prove their loyalty and worth rather than the reverse. As a result, a disproportionately high number of Chicanos served in the armed forces; also, like the Nisei, they comprised a disproportionately high share of the casualty lists and were frequently cited for their outstanding fighting qualities and contributions to the war effort. The first Congressional Medal of Honor awarded to a drafted enlisted man during World War II went to José P. Martínez. Altogether, thirty-nine Chicanos received the Congressional Medal of Honor (Scott, 1974:140). The valor of the Chicano fighting men earned the general respect and approval of their Anglo-American comrades-in-arms. Whereas in the early days of the war they frequently had been shunned or harassed by other servicemen as disloyal, undisciplined *pachucos,* they now generally were accepted on equal terms.

On this basis, they fully expected their position in civilian life after the war to be far better than it had been before the war. Their return to civilian life, however, was marked by bitter disappointment. They found mainly that the prejudices and the various forms of discrimination they had encountered before the war still remained. They still might be refused service in a restaurant; they still had difficulty obtaining work outside of the occupations that traditionally had been assigned to them; and they still saw that the young people of *La Raza* typically attended segregated schools (Scott, 1974:141). The reality of the continuation of prejudice and discrimination against them came as a severe shock to many returning veterans. Despite their loyal and costly services to the country, they still were second-class citizens. This discovery jolted not only the Chicano veterans but their friends and families as well. The entire Chicano community was affected, and an increased awareness of their collective problem as a minority group was stimulated. Hence, the period since World War II—and especially the 1960s—has been described by many observers as an "awakening" of the Chicanos. This awakening has been marked by a sharp increase in organized political and protest activities by Chicanos in all of the main sectors of American life.

For roughly seventy-five years after the end of the war between Mexico and the United States, Chicanos in the Southwest typically did not engage actively in politics. Since the armed conflicts between Anglo-Americans and those of Mexican descent had continued to erupt during this period, any effort on the part of Chicanos to assert themselves was viewed with great suspicion by the members of the dominant group. Consequently, the first organizations that may be considered "political" in nature were very careful to adopt objectives that were likely to meet with the approval of Anglo-American leaders. For example, the most famous and successful organization of Chicanos—the League of United Latin-American Citizens (LULAC) —was comprised mainly of people who emphasized assimilation into American society and felt it was their duty to develop "true and loyal" citizens of the United States (Cuéllar, 1970:143). We should not be surprised to learn, however, that even this presumably uncontroversial goal aroused the fear in some Anglo-Americans that the "Mexicans" were forgetting "their place."

The years of World War II, however, brought significant changes in the Chicano community. In the first place, as noted above, a large number of Chicanos served in the armed forces. This experience permitted them to work side by side with Americans from different regions of the country and from different socioeconomic origins. In the process, they learned a great deal about the opportunities and privileges that most American citizens took for granted. They came to expect, also, that as equals in battle they were entitled to equal opportunities when they returned to civilian life. Many of these men felt "completely American." As such, they were unwilling to think of themselves as "Mexican" or to accept the inferior status generally accorded Mexicans. As expressed by Alvarez (1973:932), they were more likely to argue, "I am an 'American' who happens to be of Mexican descent. I am going to participate fully in this society because, like descendants of people from so many other lands, I was born here." In short, they accepted the immigrant analogy.

The war years did more than solidify the servicemen's acceptance of American identity, however. The events of the war accelerated the movement of Chicanos into the cities. As a result, this traditionally rural population was brought into a more extensive and intimate contact with the Anglo-Americans. Large numbers of these migrants were exposed to even more overt forms of discrimination than they had learned was customary—for example, the zoot-suit riots. They learned in this way that the opportunities of the city, attractive though they were in many cases, were nonetheless severely limited for "Mexicans."

The combination of continued, and even increased, discrimination against Chicanos on the home front and the new expectations of the returning servicemen set the stage for the emergence of some new, more aggressive, political and social organizations following the war. In the immediate postwar years, one such organization, the Community Service Organization (CSO), was formed in California; another, the G.I. Forum, was formed in Texas. Both of these groups have sought to represent the interests of Chicanos on a wide social, economic, and political front (Cuéllar, 1970:145–147). As the decade of the 1950s drew to a close, however, some Chicanos came to feel that organizations like LULAC, CSO, and the G.I. Forum were not pressing vigorously enough for equal rights. They thought, too, that the established organizations were not pursuing the correct strategy in the political arena. For these reasons, the Mexican American Political Association (MAPA), the Mexican American Youth Organization (MAYO), and the Political Association of Spanish-speaking Organizations (PASO) were formed in California and Texas, respectively, with the intention to put direct pressure on the major political parties, including the nomination or appointment of their members to public office. A spectacular example of the success of this approach may be seen in the election of Chicanos to various offices in Crystal City, Texas.[9]

We may summarize by saying that the prominent early Chicano organizations moved in a gingerly way into the political arena. They took great pains to reassure the Anglo-Americans that they did not intend to create a disturbance but only to make themselves and their ethnic brethren into "better" (i.e., more Anglicized) citizens. As time passed, however, different organizations were formed for the purpose of placing greater pressure on the dominant society in an effort to gain more nearly equal treatment. In this way, a renewed emphasis on cultural nationalism emerged as a central feature of the Chicano movement beginning in the 1960s.

This emphasis on cultural nationalism has brought into sharp relief many of the issues that are of greatest interest to us here. What are the goals of the Chicanos within American life? How important is it to Chicanos that their culture be strengthened and developed? To what extent are the processes of assimilation affecting the distinctiveness and solidarity of the Chicanos? The answers to these and other similar questions help to answer the larger question "How useful are the colonial and immigrant analogies when applied to the Chicano experience?"

Generation and Assimilation

Our previous discussions of immigrant ethnic groups have emphasized the importance of differences among the generations. Chapter 5, concerning the Japanese and Japanese Americans, in particular, showed that the generations were sufficiently distinct to bear different names. This distinctiveness was caused mainly by the immigration pattern experienced by this group. Most of the Japanese immigrants came during a period of roughly three decades (1890–1920). Thereafter, the Japanese population of the United States grew almost totally by natural increase until after World War II. For the most part, Issei males had married only Issei females. The Nisei children, therefore, were overwhelmingly native Americans born of foreign parents. It was very unusual for a Nisei to have only one parent who had been born in Japan. This pattern, of course, has been common among nearly all immigrant groups to America, at least in the beginning. But among most other groups, the stream of foreign immigrants generally has continued in a fluctuating manner far beyond the original point of primary immigration. In this way, the foreign-born and native generations have continued to be mixed. An important result of this process is that many native-born Americans have had one parent who is an immigrant and one who is a native American. Obviously, whether one has two foreign-born parents, one foreign-born parent, or two native-born parents may have a significant effect on the type and extent of one's own assimilation in America. Also, the proportional size of these different groups within an ethnic group surely is a significant matter.

Both of these factors—the number of children of foreign, mixed, or native parentage and the proportion of the group that is foreign-born, mixed, or native—have played an especially important role in the Chicano experience. The reason for this is fairly apparent. The nativity and parentage categories are unusually mixed for this ethnic group. In fact, no other American ethnic group presents such a variegated picture of nativity and foreignness.

Consider, again, the main features of the situation of the Chicanos. The original Chicanos were natives, but they were viewed by the invading Anglo-Americans as aliens. Immigration to establish permanent residence during the latter half of the nineteenth century was relatively low, but the movement of Mexican nationals back and forth across the border was nevertheless continuous. Then, when the great immigration of the period 1900–1930 took place, the native Chicanos—most of whom were the children or grand-children of natives—became a numerical minority within the Chicano group. Most Chicanos during this period were foreign-born. The restriction of Mexican immigration and the welfare repatriations of the thirties, as we have seen, decreased the proportion of the Chicano population that was foreign-born. At the same time, an increasing proportion of the population was comprised of children of native or mixed parentage. For example, between 1950 and 1960, both the foreign-born and the natives of foreign or mixed parentage declined as a proportion of the total Chicano population (Browning and McLemore, 1964:5).

The pattern through which the Chicano population has developed affects the study of intergenerational differences in important ways. For example, among all ethnic groups in America, the category "natives of native parentage" includes the third and subsequent generations. But since among the Chicanos this category includes the descendants of the original settlers as well as those who have migrated to the United States since 1900, it is a more diverse category for this group than for the others we have studied. Nevertheless, since the Mexican immigration of the twentieth century (including the illegal immigration) has continued at a high level, a large majority of the natives of native parentage are the descendants of relatively recent migrants. Consider, too, that the closeness of the mother country and the frequent movements back and forth across the border by some members of *each* of the nativity and parentage groups call into question the easy assumption that each generation should be more assimilated than the preceding one. In fact, this is one reason why those who regard the Chicanos to be a colonized minority believe that the intergenerational differences within their group will remain smaller than would be true for an immigrant minority. The crucial questions for us in this regard include "Is the Chicano culture being renewed and invigorated among the third and subsequent generations? Do the natives of native parentage exhibit levels of cultural assimilation that are consistent with the predictions flowing from the immigrant analogy? Or is some new, distinctive hybrid culture being formed?"

As was true in our discussion of the Japanese Americans, the data needed to determine whether or in what ways the Chicanos are assimilating are far from complete. Although many different sources are of value, an indispensable body of information concerning this ethnic group has been compiled and tabulated by the U.S. Bureau of the Census. It is appropriate to consider at this point certain problems in the use of these data as well as some of the major things they reveal.

The Census Reports

So far, we have referred to the Chicanos or to those of Mexican ancestry without attempting to define exactly *who* the members of this group are. Because the Chicanos are dispersed over a large geographical area, because they have come into American society both through conquest and through immigration, because their immigration has been heaviest during the twentieth century, and because legal immigration has been greatly exceeded by illegal immigration (Frisbie, 1975:4–5), they are an extremely heterogeneous group and present some special problems to anyone who wishes to make accurate general statements about them. The difficulties may be illustrated by considering the efforts of the U.S. Bureau of the Census to identify the members of this group.

The Census Bureau first attempted to count this population in 1930. The census enumerators were asked to classify people as "Mexican," whether they were foreign or native born, on the basis of their "racial" characteristics. This approach was found to be deficient; so, in the 1940 census, a question on mother tongue was presented to a 5 percent sample of the entire population. On the basis of the answers to this question, the Census Bureau was able to count the number of people in the sample who listed Spanish as their mother tongue. Although the effort to identify the Chicano population in terms of the mother-tongue criterion was discontinued after 1940, this approach did enable the investigators to divide the group into three nativity and parentage categories. These are the foreign-born, the natives of foreign or mixed parentage, and the natives of native parentage. This method of classification, of course, "lumps together" the foreign-born persons who have been in the United States for many years and those who have arrived only recently, and it does not distinguish the native whose grandparents were immigrants from the native whose ancestors settled in the United States during the sixteenth century. Nevertheless, it affords a crucial tool for the study of intergenerational differences.

In the 1950, 1960, and 1970 population censuses, the Bureau of the Census approached the identification of the Chicanos in still another way. In these years, lists of Spanish surnames were drawn up, and the Chicanos were identified among those who were "white persons of Spanish surname." The use of Spanish surnames as a way to identify Chicanos is also subject to certain criticisms. For example, many people who have Spanish surnames are neither from Mexico nor are the descendants of Mexicans. Also, some people of Mexican descent have changed their names through marriage or as a matter of convenience. Despite these and some other imperfections, this method of counting and classifying the Mexican American population has proven to be extremely useful.[10] On this basis, it has become possible to conduct a number of highly informative (if not completely exact) analyses concerning the ethnic group of interest to us here. For instance, we may now examine the changes that are occurring through time in the occupations, incomes, and levels of education of the Spanish surname population, and we may compare these changes to those that are occurring within the Anglo-American population. In this way, we may determine in a broad way whether, or in what ways, the two populations are becoming more or less similar. The census tabulations also assist us in gaining an appreciation of some of the changes that are occurring from generation to generation within this ethnic group. Such comparisons assist us in estimating the level of secondary structural assimilation at various points in time and at various locations throughout the United States. Useful as these comparisons are, though, they do not reflect completely some of the kinds of diversity that exist among the Chicanos. For this reason, we rely also on a number of other sources of information.

Let us first consider some basic points about this large ethnic group. Although substantial Chicano groups are to be found in several states outside the Southwest—mainly in Illinois, Indiana, New York, Michigan, and Washington—in 1970, approximately 87 percent of the members of this group (about 4.7 million people) lived in the five southwestern states of Arizona, California, Colorado, New Mexico, and Texas. Hence, the special reports of the Bureau of the Census focus entirely on these latter states. The reports show that the Spanish surname population has increased at each census period both in absolute size and as a proportion of the total population. During the decade 1950–1960, California surpassed Texas as the state having the largest *number* of Chicano residents, while New Mexico has remained the state with the largest *proportion* of people of Spanish surname within its borders.

But let us look further into the matter of where the Spanish surname population is located. It is widely known that the Chicano population was for many years concentrated in various farm and rural areas. It may be something of a surprise, therefore, to discover that during the last several decades the Spanish surname population has rapidly become predominantly urban. For example, in 1970, over 85 percent of the Spanish surname population of the Southwest lived in urban areas, while less than 13 percent were classified as rural nonfarm and less than 2 percent lived in rural farm areas (U.S. Bureau of the Census, *Persons of Spanish Surname,* 1973:16). We should note, however, that there are some substantial differences among the southwestern states in this respect. For instance, in California, nearly 91 percent of the Spanish surname population lives in urban areas, while the urban percentage in New Mexico is about 65 percent. Still, even in New Mexico, a large majority of those who live in rural areas do not live on farms.

In addition to the differences among the southwestern states in the proportion of Spanish surname persons who live in the cities and rural nonfarm areas, the cities themselves differ in the absolute and relative sizes of the Spanish surname population. For example, in terms of absolute size, the most "Mexican" metropolitan areas in the United States are Los Angeles-Long Beach (over 910,000); San Antonio (over 314,000); and San Francisco-Oakland (over 216,000). Since there are large differences in the total populations of the cities of the Southwest, however, some smaller metropolitan areas have a decidedly visible Chicano population and "atmosphere." Especially notable among these are El Paso, Brownsville-Harlingen-San Benito, Laredo, San Bernardino-Riverside, Ontario, McAllen-Pharr-Edinburg, Corpus Christi, Albuquerque, and Phoenix (U.S. Bureau of the Census, *Persons of*

Spanish Surname, 1973:87–89). Clearly, in most of these cases the very names of the cities suggest their Spanish heritage and alert one to the presence of their Spanish surname residents.

Now we are almost ready to discuss the various subprocesses of assimilation. Before doing so, though, a bit more information is needed concerning the size and distribution of the nativity and parentage groups among persons of Spanish surname. Let us note again that even though the Chicano group has been present in the Southwest for over 130 years, those of foreign or mixed parentage have outnumbered the natives of native parentage during most of the twentieth century. Indeed, given that probably more than 4 million illegal immigrants have arrived since World War II (Frisbie, 1975:5) and that many of these immigrants have remained in the United States but do not participate in the censuses, it is possible that the natives of native parents still are not a majority of the Chicano group. If the census figures are taken at face value, however, by 1960, the natives of native parents again became a majority of the Spanish surname persons in the Southwest.[11] But as before, what is true for the Southwest is not necessarily true for the separate states in the region. In New Mexico and Colorado, for example, a large majority of the Spanish surname population have always been natives of native parents; in California, however, this segment of the population comprised only 44 percent of the Spanish-surname population in 1970. These facts highlight from a different perspective what we observed previously: the migration of foreign-born Spanish surname people to California has continued at a high level, and they suggest again a basic fact about the Chicano group: it is very heterogeneous; therefore, our generalizations about them must be even more tentative than for most other American ethnic groups. With these limitations in mind, we turn to a brief consideration of the main subprocesses of assimilation.

Chicano Assimilation

Cultural Assimilation

We have seen that the ethnic groups in America—whether immigrant or colonized—typically have tried to maintain their cultural heritages. The degree to which this has been true, however—as well as the group's success in doing so—has varied among the ethnic groups. In regard to success (and possibly effort as well), the Chicanos have been one of the leading ethnic groups in America. Consider again, for instance, what usually has happened in the important matter of language use. Despite a great number of exceptions and local variations, the general pattern among American ethnic groups has been for the use of the ancestral tongue to diminish noticeably across the generations and for English to become the usual language among those in the third and subsequent generations. We should restate perhaps that this decline of the mother tongue sometimes has been hastened by a rush to embrace the American way and sometimes has been due to the fact that a particular group was too small or too scattered to resist outside pressures effectively. The Chicanos afford a marked contrast to the usual pattern. Even though it is not possible to state even roughly what proportion of the Chicano population has, over the years, preferred to maintain their native culture, it seems quite likely that the proportion has been high in comparison to most other American ethnic minorities. But whether this is true or not, it is clear that they have been the primary contributors to the maintenance of the Spanish language in the United States over a comparatively long period of time. For this reason, Spanish is more likely to survive in the United States than is any other foreign language.

Grebler, Moore, and Guzman (1970:424) have studied the extent to which Chicanos have retained the Spanish language. Their samples contained people from different income groups and different areas of residence within Los Angeles and San Antonio. Several findings are of special interest. First, the researchers found that a majority of the people they interviewed (55 percent in San Antonio and 56 percent in Los Angeles) were bilingual. However, whether they were bilingual or not, a large majority (91 percent in San Antonio and 84 percent in Los Angeles) were more comfortable in Spanish than in English. Second, the extent to which the sample members were fluent in Spanish also depended on their income levels and on the con-centration of other Chicanos within their neighborhoods. The higher-income participants were more likely to be fluent in English than those with lower incomes, and those who live in neighborhoods containing a high proportion of Chicanos were more likely to use Spanish frequently than those who live in less "Mexicanized" neighborhoods. Finally, these same factors apparently affect the extent to which Chicanos prefer to use Spanish in conversations with their children. In both San Antonio and Los Angeles, between 33 and 73 percent of the parents in the low-income groups reported that they use Spanish with their children all or most of the time. Although parents in the highest income groups were more likely to use English than Spanish with their children, between 10 and 22 percent of these parents also reported a preference for Spanish as the language of the home.

How have the Chicanos succeeded in maintaining the Spanish language in the face of dominant-group pressures to adopt English? In general, of course, the answer to this question is to be found in the fact that this group is concentrated heavily in the borderlands near Mexico. The sustaining in-fluence of Mexico, however, is frequently indirect. Grebler, Moore, and Guzman (1970:429) note in this respect that Spanish-language radio stations located in the United States play an important role in assisting the individual in maintaining both his language and his ethnic identity. In the mainly Chicano neighborhoods of San Antonio and Los Angeles, for instance, the Spanish-language radio stations are more popular than those using English. Even among those living in predominantly Anglo-American neighborhoods, between 18 and 25 percent of the Chicanos report that they prefer the Spanish-language radio stations.

Spanish-language television stations, too, play a part in assisting the Chicano community in retaining and strengthening its ethnic distinctiveness, especially among those of low income in predominantly Chicano neighborhoods. It cannot be determined exactly whether the present influence of the Spanish-language media is greater or less than that ever attained by any other foreign-language group. For one thing, many other groups were much more active in the publication and circulation of newspapers. It seems clear, nevertheless, that the Spanish-language media are very influential among the Chicanos, and it is possible that this influence may well increase. For example, in 1960, over one-half of all foreign-language radio broadcasting in the United States was conducted in Spanish. No other foreign language is used exclusively by any station. Also, there is evidence that many commercial advertisers have learned that the large Chicano market may be approached profitably through Spanish-language radio and TV broadcasts. The high concentration of Mexican Americans at various points throughout the borderlands, the closeness of Mexico, and the success of the Spanish-language radio and TV stations all help to explain the preference for and frequent use of Spanish by most Chicanos. This preference and usage, in turn, afford strong evidence that cultural assimilation is not occurring among the Chicanos in the same way as it typically has among the European minorities. It is true, of course, that the older members of the group and those who are foreign-born probably rely most heavily on Spanish, and it is true that this pattern has been common among many other ethnic groups. Nevertheless, the proportion of children in the group who learn Spanish as their first language and in whose homes Spanish is the preferred language continues to be amazingly high.

The persistence of the Spanish language among Chicanos and the high degree of bilingualism even among natives of native parents raises a technical issue not considered so far. Without saying so, our previous discussions of cultural assimilation have implied that as the members of a given ethnic group adopt English as their main or preferred language, they simultaneously and in the same degree give up their native language and substitute English for it. This implication has seemed reasonable as we have discussed the various European groups. Even the Japanese Americans have seemed generally to conform to this idea. The Issei tried very hard, both in the home and through the Japanese language schools, to teach the Nisei fluency in the Japanese language. But, as we have seen, this effort was not very successful. The case of the Chicanos, though, has shown that given the right combination of circumstances, an American ethnic group may be (and perhaps remain) substantially bilingual. Unquestionably, the acquisition and maintenance of fluency in two languages is not easy. In many cases, the individuals who are involved in this process wind up speaking a hybrid tongue that is ridiculed and despised by the language purists on both sides.[12] Indeed, the observation frequently has been made that Chicanos are "illiterate in two languages." Whether such an assertion is true, or is even testable, goes beyond our present discussion. We may note in passing, though, that Grebler, Moore, and Guzman (1970:424) found that only a very small fraction of their respondents in San Antonio and Los Angeles were unable to converse comfortably in either language. In many instances, of course, individual Chicanos have followed the traditional route to cultural assimilation and have given up the Spanish language entirely. But the more common pattern among the members of this group thus far has been to *add* English to their language repertoire. Increasingly, especially among those who prefer the label Chicano, the effort is made to cultivate one's language skills in both Spanish and English. Hence, the kind of cultural assimilation we might expect on the basis of Park's or Gordon's theories—the substitution of Anglo for Chicano culture—seems remote. However, if the ideas of assimilationist theories seem inadequate to explain what is occurring among the Chicanos, the ideas of colonialist theory also fall short. Although they are critical of many facets of Anglo-American culture, most Chicanos are "learning the rules" of Anglo culture. They are in many cases adding the new to the old. Moreover, they appear in general to accept the necessity, if not the desirability, of secondary structural assimilation, that is, "integration." Let us examine some facts in this regard.

Secondary Structural Assimilation

Our examination of secondary structural assimilation among the Chicanos focuses on their occupational distribution, incomes, educational attainments, and residential location.

As noted previously, the Chicanos have from the beginning played a distinctive role in the American labor force. By 1920, Chicano workers were much more likely to be employed as farming, mining, or railroad laborers than in any other capacity. And they were far more likely to be found in these occupational pursuits than were Anglo-American workers. This concentration in certain types of work has not, of course, been complete. And, especially since the beginning of World War II, Chicanos have been moving out of "their" customary occupations and into many different jobs that pay more and carry with them a higher level of social prestige. This trend may be visualized by a consideration of the changes in the proportion of Chicano males who have been represented within a few key occupational categories at the time of several censuses of the U.S. population. The occupational categories selected form a rough hierarchy of social prestige, with the professional, technical, and kindred category standing at the top.

An inspection of Table 6.1 shows that since 1950 Chicanos have been shifting steadily out of the lowest-prestige occupational category and into the three higher-prestige categories. In 1950, for instance, the category "farm

TABLE 6.1
Percentage of Chicano and Anglo Workers in Selected
Occupational Categories, 1950, 1960, and 1970

Occupational Category	1950 Chicano	1950 Anglo[a]	1960 Chicano	1960 Anglo[a]	1970 Chicano	1970 Anglo[b]
Professional, technical, and kindred workers	2.1[c]	7.9	3.9	11.1	6.3	14.8
Craftsmen, foremen, and kindred workers	12.9	19.8	15.8	20.6	20.6	19.5
Operatives, including transport	18.8	20.0	22.9	19.5	25.1	11.5
Farm laborers and foremen	23.4	4.0	16.0	2.0	8.0	1.3

Sources: U.S. Bureau of the Census. *Characteristics of the Population* (1953:276–278); U.S. Bureau of the Census. *Characteristics of the Population* (1964:217); U.S. Bureau of the Census. *Characteristics of the Population* (1973:761–765); U.S. Bureau of the Census. *Persons of Spanish Surname* (1953:23–42); U.S. Bureau of the Census. *Persons of Spanish Surname* (1963:38); U.S. Bureau of the Census. *Persons of Spanish Surname* (1973: 60).

[a] Anglo = white — Spanish surname
[b] Anglo = total — Negro — Spanish heritage
[c] Totals do not add to 100 because some occupational categories are not shown.

laborers" included the largest proportion of workers, but, by 1970, this category was only about one-third of its previous size. During this same period, the "professional" group tripled in relative size.

Before we conclude that Chicanos are moving rapidly toward occupational assimilation, several cautions are in order. Perhaps the most important is that although the rate of increase in the professional category is faster among the Chicanos than the Anglos, the actual gap between the two groups has widened. For example, the rate of change for Chicanos between 1960 and 1970 was 54 percent in comparison to 33 percent for the Anglos; however, during that same period, the gap between the two groups increased from 7.2 percent to 8.5 percent.

At least two other points concerning Table 6.1 should be noted. First, the broad occupational categories used in the table do not reveal where the Chicanos are within the groups listed. Even when Chicanos gain access to the more "desirable" occupations, they frequently are in the lower-paid positions. Second, the table does not reveal the substantial variations that exist among the five southwestern states and the relative sizes of these categories. For instance, a higher proportion of Chicano professionals are to be found in California and New Mexico than in the remaining three states.

The occupational disadvantage of Chicanos is revealed starkly by a glance at some of the figures concerning income within the group. As in the case of their occupational distribution, the Chicanos showed a steady improvement during the period 1950–1970. For example, in 1950, the annual average (median) income of Chicanos fourteen years and over ranged from $980 in Texas to $1,628 in California. The annual median income for Anglo males fourteen and over in the United States at that time was $2,751. In 1960, the average income among Chicanos had risen markedly, ranging from $2,029 in Texas to $3,849 in California, for an overall average of $2,804. During the same time, the average for white males had risen to $4,337. This means that despite the absolute increase in Chicano incomes, the ratio of Chicano to Anglo incomes was only .65. Then, from 1960 to 1970, the median Chicano income for all states rose to $4,445. By this time, however, the comparable median for Anglos was $6,772—a Chicano to Anglo ratio of .66. In short, even though Chicano incomes have risen steadily, the average gap between their incomes and those of the Anglos has hardly narrowed.[13]

Whether people find it to be possible to move out of low-prestige, poorly paid jobs into jobs that are generally thought to be more desirable depends to a considerable extent on the educational levels of the people involved. It is of special importance, therefore, to know if the educational level of the Chicano population has been increasing over time and across the generations. Such increases would be expected if this ethnic group has been moving in the direction of secondary structural assimilation. Some pertinent information is presented in Table 6.2.

Four aspects of Table 6.2 support the view that the Chicanos are becoming more assimilated in regard to education. First, those born in the United States have reached a noticeably higher level of education than those born in Mexico. Second, the level of education has increased for each of the nativity groups at each succeeding census. Third, with only one exception, those who may be termed loosely the third generation (i.e., the natives of native parentage) have received more education than those in the second generation. Finally, the gap between the second and third generations is slowly widening. It should be noted, however, that the distance between the second and third generations has never been large and that, in 1970, the

TABLE 6.2

Median Years of Schooling of the Chicano Population by Year, Nativity, and Sex

Nativity	1950		1960		1970	
	Male	*Female*	*Male*	*Female*	*Male*	*Female*
Born in Mexico	3.7	3.8	4.1	4.4	6.2	5.9
Natives of Mexican parentage	7.1	7.1	8.4	8.2	9.7	9.1
Natives of Native parentage	7.0	7.2	8.6	8.8	10.4	10.4

Sources: U.S. Bureau of the Census. *Persons of Spanish Surname* (1953:23–42); U.S. Bureau of the Census. *Persons of Spanish Surname* (1963:14–23); U.S. Bureau of the Census. *Persons of Spanish Surname* (1973:24–41).

third-generation Chicanos still remained below the Anglo-American average (12.1 years). These latter points indicate that educational assimilation is not yet complete among the Chicanos and that the third generation is only slowly moving away from the second.

Another important measure of the extent to which secondary structural assimilation is occurring for a given ethnic minority is the degree to which the group lives in segregated residential areas. Although prior to the onset of the Great Depression, the Chicanos were mainly a rural people engaged in agricultural labor, they have subsequently moved rapidly into the metropolitan areas. By 1950, some 66 percent of the Chicanos lived in urban areas; by 1960, this figure had climbed to 79 percent; and, in 1970, over 85 percent of the members of this ethnic group were urban dwellers.

While these figures show that the Chicano population is now preponderantly urban, they do not tell us how the Chicanos are distributed within the various cities. It is obvious, of course, that there is a substantial amount of ethnic residential segregation within nearly all cities of the United States. We have emphasized previously that American ethnic groups always have tended to congregate, as well as be segregated, in certain areas and that these frequently have become known as "their" parts of town. This observation applies also to the residential patterns of Chicanos. In most cities of the Southwest, the Chicanos long have been, and still are, noticeably segregated from both the Anglos and blacks. The extent of this segregation, however, varies greatly among the cities, reflecting the many factors that affect residential assimilation.

The extent to which the Chicanos and the Anglos are segregated residentially may also be changing over time; if so, this would be a very important social change. If the level of residential segregation has remained unchanged for several decades or has increased, this would indicate strongly that a full merger of the ethnic groups was hardly just over the horizon.

Despite the importance of this topic, little is known about it. The best information presently available is based on data gathered on southwestern cities during the decennial census of 1960. For each of thirty-five cities, Grebler, Moore, and Guzman (1970:275) have calculated an index number to represent the level of Chicano-Anglo residential segregation. The type of index chosen by these authors (called an index of dissimilarity) is one of several that sociologists have used to measure the extent of segregation. The basic idea of the index of dissimilarity is this: if people were to move into neighborhoods without regard to their ethnicity, then people of different groups within a city would live in every neighborhood, and the proportion of each group living in each neighborhood would be the same as their share of their city's total population (Taeuber and Taeuber, 1964:29). For instance, if half the people in a given city were Chicanos, and if ethnicity had nothing to do with selecting a residence, then half the people in each part of the city would be Chicanos; and there would be no segregation. On the other hand, if all of the city's Chicanos lived together, and there were no other ethnic groups represented among them, then there would be complete segregation. The index of residential segregation, therefore, ranges from a low of zero (no segregation) to a high of 100 (complete segregation). Although this way of estimating residential segregation has faults, it is extremely useful and easy to understand.

As mentioned above, the residential segregation of the Chicanos in southwestern cities varies widely. Just how widely may be seen in the following: the lowest levels of Chicano-Anglo residential segregation in 1960 were found in Sacramento, California (29.7), and Galveston, Texas (33.3), while the highest levels were found in Odessa (75.8) and Corpus Christi, Texas (72.2), (Grebler, Moore, and Guzman, 1970:275). The residential segregation indexes for most of the cities, however, lay nearer the high end of the range than the low end. Hence, although there are large and important differences among southwestern cities, the typical situation is a fairly high degree of Chicano-Anglo residential segregation.

To interpret these facts, it is helpful to have a standard of comparison. Although the extent of black-white residential segregation will be discussed more fully in chapter 7, we may note here that in none of the thirty-five southwestern cities was the black-white index lower than the Chicano-Anglo index. For instance, in Sacramento, the black-white residential segregation index was 61.9; in Odessa, it was 90.5. Moreover, in most of the cities, the level of residential segregation existing among the Chicanos and blacks was higher than that between the Chicanos and Anglos. Stated differently, although Chicanos are highly segregated from Anglos, they are even more highly segregated from blacks.

But what were the levels of residential segregation before 1960? And how have they changed since then? The evidence concerning changes in the residential segregation of blacks is good and will be reviewed in chapter 7. For the Chicanos, however, there is practically no information. One suggestive comparison has been made for Chicago (Taeuber and Taeuber, 1964). During the thirty-year period from 1930 to 1960, the Chicano-Anglo residential segregation index declined from 71 to 54. Although a decline of 17 points in thirty years certainly does not suggest the rapid and complete residential assimilation of the Chicanos, this change gains significance when it is compared to the comparable figures for blacks. During the same interval, the residential segregation index for blacks and whites changed from 85 to 83 (Taeuber and Taeuber, 1964:377). If this were only an isolated case, we might dismiss it. But it is not. It is unlikely that any city in America experienced a 17-point decline in the residential segregation of blacks during the same period.[14] Nevertheless, we cannot generalize with complete confidence from the experience of a single city. At the present, we can only repeat that the average levels of residential segregation for Chicanos, though high, are substantially lower than for blacks.

One other comparison may assist us in evaluating the extent of Anglo-Chicano residential segregation. Since most other ethnic groups have tended to cluster together, we may ask whether the ethnic neighborhoods of the old immigrants have disappeared. The example of the Chicano is instructive here, also. In 1960, when the residential segregation index stood at 54 for Chicanos in Chicago and at 83 for blacks, the indexes for the Irish, Norwegians, and Swedes were, respectively, 31, 37, and 30. We see, therefore, that the levels of residential segregation for Chicanos in 1960 in some American cities (e.g., Sacramento and Galveston) were actually quite similar to those of some old immigrant groups in Chicago. This comparison shows that it is at least possible for Chicano-Anglo residential segregation to decline to comparatively low levels.

Primary Structural Assimilation

The evidence reviewed above shows that, in general, Chicanos have been moving out of rural areas and into the cities and that within the cities they are less segregated from Anglos than are blacks. It shows, too, that Chicanos who are natives of native parentage more nearly approximate the educational level of the Anglo-Americans than do Chicanos of mixed or foreign parentage and that Chicanos are more likely now to be working in jobs that previously were almost exclusively held by Anglo-Americans. Each of these forms of secondary structural assimilation favors an increase in the amount of equal-status interaction that will occur between Chicanos and Anglos and thereby raises the probability that friendships will develop across the ethnic line. We would expect, therefore, an increase in the number of Anglo-Chicano friendships on the job, in the neighborhood, and among those of similar education and income. We also would expect more friendships to form between Anglos and Chicanos of native parentage than between Anglos and Chicanos of mixed or foreign parentage.

Although little is known concerning the trends in Chicano-Anglo friendship formation, some valuable evidence has been provided by the work of researchers in UCLA's Mexican American Study Project (Grebler, Moore, and Guzman, 1970). The researchers gathered information on the friendships of Chicanos in three large cities during various periods of the respondents' lives. The study participants in Albuquerque, Los Angeles, and San Antonio were asked about the ethnicity of their friends when they were children, about the ethnicity of their present friends, and about the ethnicity of their children's friends. In this way, each person was asked to report on three generations of experience. In all three cities, the participants reported that the extent of out-group friendship relations had increased through time (Moore, 1970:134).

For example, while 45 percent of the participants in Albuquerque said that all of their childhood friends had been Chicanos, only 22 percent of them said this was still true. And only 12 percent of these same participants said that all of their children's friends were Chicano. In other words, the extent of friendly relations with non-Chicanos appears to have increased markedly for these people and for their children. The same pattern of increasing out-group friendships was found also in Los Angeles and San Antonio. In Los Angeles, those claiming exclusively Chicano friends for themselves as children and for their own children fell from 52 percent to 18 percent; in San Antonio, the decline was from 70 percent to 39 percent.

As expected, this overall pattern differed for those who lived in more or less desegregated neighborhoods, and it also varied by income levels. For example, in Los Angeles and San Antonio, the Chicanos who lived in neighborhoods having relatively few Chicanos ("frontier" or desegregated areas) were more likely to have predominantly Anglo friends than were those living in neighborhoods having a relatively large number of Chicanos ("colony" or segregated areas). And, for the most part, those of higher income who lived in frontier areas were more likely to have predominantly Anglo friends than were those of lower income (Grebler, Moore, and Guzman, 1970:397). The income differences discovered within the desegregated neighborhoods, however, did not hold up within the segregated areas. People of higher income within the colony areas were hardly more likely to report a predominance of Anglo friends than were those of lower income in those areas.

Taken together, these findings from three of the main centers of Chicano culture suggest that with the passage of time Chicanos decreasingly have only Chicano friends. Although this generational trend is much more pronounced among those living in desegregated neighborhoods and among those of higher income, it suggests that if the occupational, educational, and residential assimilation of Chicanos continues, primary structural assimilation also will increase.

We have emphasized that when a dominant and subordinate group are brought together by conquest, the groups frequently react to one another with greater mutual hatred and rejection than if the minority had arisen through immigration. For this reason, the Chicanos frequently have been described as having a low assimilative potential. Despite the forces working toward ethnic separateness, however, we have seen that the Chicanos and Anglos are in some respects coming closer together. Let us turn now to that "most infallible index" of assimilation, intermarriage (Kennedy, 1944:331).

Marital Assimilation

Several studies of Chicano intermarriage have been conducted, with the majority of them focusing on Los Angeles, Albuquerque, and San Antonio. Three main findings stand out. First, the occurrence of out-marriage among the Chicanos is much lower in some places than in others. For instance, in the early 1960s, the rate of out-marriage for marriages was 20 percent in San Antonio (Alvírez and Bean, 1976:285), 33 percent in Albuquerque, and 5 percent in Edinburg, Texas (Murguía and Frisbie, 1977:384). Second, in no study has a very high rate of out-marriage been discovered. The highest out-marriage rate reported for marriages was 48 percent in Albuquerque in 1967. Nevertheless, and third, most of the data show there has been a gradual increase in the rate of out-marriage.

In a study comparing rates of out-marriage in San Antonio, Bradshaw and Bean (1970:393) demonstrated that the rate for marriages in 1850 was about 10 percent. One hundred years later, the rate had approximately doubled. Since then, the rate of out-marriage in San Antonio has increased more rapidly, rising by 1973 to 27 percent (Murguía and Frisbie, 1977:384). Changes in the same direction have been noted in some other studies. In Los Angeles, for instance, the rate of out-marriage for individuals has risen from 9 percent during the 1920s to 25 percent in 1963. And, in Edinburg, Texas, the rate has risen from 5 percent in 1961 to 9 percent in the early 1970s. However, not all of the studies indicate a rise in out-marriages. In Corpus Christi, for instance, the rate hardly changed between the early 1960s and 1970s, going from 15 percent to 16 percent (Alvírez and Bean, 1976:383). And, in Albuquerque, a rapid rise from 33 percent in 1964 to 48 percent in 1967 was followed by a sharp decline to 39 percent in 1971 (Murguía and Frisbie, 1977:384).

The weight of the above evidence suggests that out-marriage among Chicanos is very gradually increasing. The main counterevidence is the recent decline in Albuquerque. Even here, though, the rate in 1971 (39 percent) was over two and a half times as high as in the period 1929–1940 (Murguía and Frisbie, 1977:384). Although the decline in the late 1960s may represent a reversal of the long-term trend, the best assumption seems to be that the change will be temporary.

Evidence from a different kind of analysis also supports this conclusion. Mittlebach and Moore (1968) have examined out-marriages in Los Angeles during 1963 to see whether there is a difference among the several Chicano generations. In line with the idea that succeeding generations will show higher levels of marital assimilation, these researchers found that the rates were lowest for those born in Mexico and highest for natives of native parentage. In other words, whether one examines the overall out-marriage rates at different points in time or the rates for those in different generations, the main finding is the same: Chicanos are moving slowly toward marital assimilation.

Some writers believe the evidence on out-marriage supports the immigrant analogy. Mittlebach and Moore (1968:53) state that in Los Angeles, at least, the rate of Chicano out-marriage "is roughly that of the Italian and Polish ethnic populations in Buffalo, New York, a generation ago." Similarly, Penalosa (1970:50) concludes that many contemporary changes among the Chicanos suggest they are coming to resemble "a European immigrant group of a generation ago."

Chicano "Success"

What does the evidence on the various forms of assimilation among the Chicanos tell us about the success with which they have adapted to American life? How, for instance, do they compare with the Japanese Americans? Although the Chicanos have been moving toward the American mainstream, from the perspective of Anglo conformity, they have not been as "successful" as the Japanese Americans. In nearly every—if not every—aspect of assimilation, the Chicanos less nearly approximate the Anglo-American ideal than do the Japanese Americans. They have not relinquished their culture as rapidly; they have not attained equal levels of occupation, education, and income; and they appear to be more segregated in their friendship and marital patterns. Why is this true?

This question lies at the very heart of the ideological issues we have discussed throughout this book. In some respects, the comparative "failure" of the Chicanos in terms of Anglo conformity may with equal force be seen as "success" from the perspective of cultural pluralism. The Chicanos have been more successful than the Japanese Americans in their efforts to maintain and develop their own distinctive heritage, the desirability of which seems clearly to be acknowledged by many Japanese Americans, particularly among the Sansei and Yonsei. Please recall, though, that ideal cultural pluralism (as sketched in chapter 3) calls for a high level of secondary structural assimilation, just as does Anglo conformity. Hence, in this regard, the Chicanos still have not reached the goal of ideal pluralism. The trick, of course, is to be successful in worldly ways without failing in the cultural, social, and marital spheres of group life.

But what if worldly success can be purchased only at the price of cultural failure? What if the maintenance of the culture is itself an obstacle to the attainment of worldly success? These explosive questions have been in the forefront of the frequently bitter debate concerning public policies relating to the Chicanos.

Consider again, for example, the question of the use of Spanish in the schools. The dominant group insisted until the latter part of the 1960s that only English was the legal and proper language of instruction in the schools. Chicano children have been said to suffer from a language "barrier" that must be "surmounted." From this point of view, teaching the children in Spanish only retards their assimilation into the mainstream of American life. Even when the desirability of bilingual education has been acknowledged, the curriculum usually has been designed to "phase out" Spanish as early as possible.

The assumption underlying this stand is that the possession of a Mexican heritage is a handicap in the modern world. From the Chicano point of view, however, this assumption is simply a part of a broader struggle between the Chicano and Anglo cultures. A frequent observation concerning classical colonialism is that oppressor groups not only conquer the territories of the groups they subordinate but also attempt to destroy the native cultures. Thus, Chicanos consider the insistence that they give up Spanish and undergo full cultural assimilation to be an example of "cultural imperialism." The complexity of the disagreement between those who insist that Mexican culture retards secondary structural assimilation (i.e., achievement and success) and those who oppose this view may be illustrated by a very brief consideration of some studies of Chicano culture that have been conducted by Anglo-American social scientists.

Two early studies on this subject have been very influential. Beginning in the 1940s, Florence Kluckhohn, an anthropologist, initiated a series of studies of the Spanish Americans (Hispanos) of northern New Mexico. Her fundamental idea was that all human cultures contain values that specify the approved solutions to five inevitable human problems. For instance, in Kluckhohn's (1956:346) view, each culture will tend to emphasize the importance of the past, the present, or the future. Consequently, one may say that the members of a given society tend to share a past, present, or future "orientation." Kluckhohn argued that we may compare different societies (or groups within a given society) in regard to various value orientations. She believed that the dominant value concerning time in American society is an orientation toward the future. Members of the dominant group place a high value on such things as planning for the future and saving "for a rainy day." In contrast, Kluckhohn believes, the Spanish Americans of northern New Mexico emphasize the present. In her view, "Planning for the future or hoping that the future will be better than either present or past simply is not their way of life" (1956:348). In a similar fashion, Kluckhohn compares the dominant American and subordinate Spanish American cultures in regard to each of the remaining four value orientations. The Anglo-American culture is found to stress (in addition to future orientation) individualism, accomplishment, mastery over nature, and the perfectibility of humans. The Spanish American culture, in contrast, stresses the present, collective goals or familism, being rather than doing, fatalism, and the imperfectibility of humans. Although Kluckhohn states that these cultural differences are not absolute, she argues that they are largely responsible for the slow rate and degree of assimilation of the Spanish Americans. The resemblance of this explanation for the "failure" of those of Spanish heritage to that of the value-compatibility explanation for the "success" of the Japanese Americans (discussed in chapter 5) is apparent.

The second influential early study of interest to us here was conducted by Saunders (1954). Like Kluckhohn, Saunders was interested in trying to discern the major features of the culture of the Spanish Americans and to show how these differed from the dominant culture of the Anglo-Americans. Unlike Kluckhohn, however, Saunders was specifically interested in the health and illness behavior of these two groups. Since the groups appeared to differ markedly in some aspects of their health behavior, Saunders suggested that these differences were produced by the underlying differences between the two patterns of culture. For instance, he noted that Spanish Americans are more likely to resist or refuse hospitalization than are Anglo-Americans, and he argued that this difference was due in some measure to the fact that placing people in the hospital when they are sick is contrary to the Spanish Americans' belief that a sick person should have his family near the bedside. According to Saunders, "Good medical care, from the Anglo point of view, requires hospitalization for many conditions. Good medical care, as defined in the culture of the Spanish Americans, requires that the patient be treated for almost any condition at home" (Saunders, 1954:166).

In addition to this presumed ethnic difference along the individualistic-familistic dimension, Saunders also indicated some other differences in the values and attitudes of the two groups that made hospitalization more objectionable to the Spanish Americans. Their emphasis on the present, for example, was seen to conflict with the desire of hospital personnel to schedule visits and treatments rigidly in advance. Also, the apparent faith of hospital personnel in an activistic, scientific approach to the curing of illness is vastly different from the presumably more passivistic, semireligious approach that has been traditional among some of the Spanish Americans. Among the people studied by Saunders, the belief was widespread that a number of common diseases such as *mal de ojo, susto,* and *empacho* could not be treated by the scientifically trained Anglo-American health personnel. Indeed, it was believed that these health practitioners in most cases did not even know of the existence of these diseases. Consequently, only a traditional healer such as a *curandero* could diagnose and treat them. Through comparisons of this type, Saunders hoped to explain to Anglo-American health practitioners why they frequently have difficulties in their relations with Spanish-speaking patients. He hoped, too, that an understanding of these apparent differences would assist the scientific healers in bridging the cultural gap that existed between them and their patients.

The studies of Kluckhohn and Saunders stimulated the interest of a number of other researchers in the question of the value differences between Anglos and Chicanos, particularly as these differences affected their health beliefs and practices.[15]

For some years, the scholarly comparisons showing that underlying differences in the value orientations of Chicanos and Anglos were responsible for the Chicano's distrust of scientific medicine went largely unchallenged. It is true that some students, including Saunders (1954:169) did suggest that at least some of the differences between the two ethnic groups might be a result of the fact that most Chicanos (especially those who had been studied) were below the socioeconomic average of most Anglo-Americans and that, therefore, the presumed value differences between the two groups might be differences in social-class values rather than cultural values as such. Still, the idea was widely accepted that it was useful to describe the Anglo and Chicano cultures by terms such as "activism" and "passivism." It was accepted, too—

as Saunders had assumed—that a practical result of such analyses might be that members of the dominant group would become more effective in dealing with members of the Chicano minority. They might, in fact, "assist" the minority-group members toward assimilation.

One manifestation of the rise of the Chicano movement has been a furious attack on the "cultural determinism" exemplified by Kluckhohn, Saunders, and their followers. Among the most vigorous and thought-provoking criticisms have been those of a group of Chicano scholars. Romano (1968), for example, has maintained that such concepts as "present orientation," "fatalism," and "familism" are viewed by Anglo-American scholars as elements of traditional culture and that the idea of traditional culture, in turn, is used to label Chicanos as passive recipients of whatever fate may thrust upon them. Such ideas, Romano contends, serve to add the weight of social-science opinion to the popular stereotypes that already exist concerning the Chicanos. These social-science stereotypes strengthen the notion that the Chicanos are unprogressive or are stagnant and fatalistic (Romano, 1968:24). Hence, the Chicanos are held to be largely responsible for their own unfortunate circumstances—a situation that can only be changed through full cultural assimilation. In a similar vein, Vaca (1970:26) argues that this view indicts Chicano culture as possessing values that prevent success in American life. For instance, if Chicanos are fatalistic, present oriented, and do not value achievement, then it is hardly surprising that they fail at school. From this standpoint, failure in school seems to refer not to whether the pupils learn the three R's but whether they "refuse" to adopt Anglo-American cultural values. In this way, success in school is equated with movement toward the cultural patterns of the dominant group. Both Romano and Vaca argue that this approach to an understanding of the cultural differences between Chicanos and Anglos is only a mask for the Anglo-conformity ideology and that it should be totally dropped. The conventional social-science analyses, from this point of view, present a "vicious," "misleading," and "degrading" picture of Chicano culture. It is a picture that distorts reality and implies that Chicano culture should not continue to exist within contemporary American society.

In keeping with this much more positive view of Chicano culture, several studies in the health field have failed to support the main implications of the value-orientations approach. To illustrate, in a study of the reliance of Chicanos on folk medicine, Karno and Edgerton (1970) found that Chicanos were more likely than Anglos to report having a family physician and to state that psychiatrists really help people who are mentally ill. Sheldon (1966) and McLemore (1963) have found evidence to suggest that when Anglos and Chicanos of similar social class levels are compared, the two groups are alike in certain important areas of health behavior. Weaver (1973:97) has discovered that in some respects—even when the social class levels are equal—the Chicanos show a greater acceptance than Anglos of certain aspects of scientific medicine. While Hoppe and Heller (1975) have found that even when Chicanos may be described as more "familistic" than Anglos, this difference may encourage rather than inhibit the use of certain kinds of preventive health facilities. Taken together, both the philosophical criticisms of scholars like Romano and Vaca and the factual criticisms of several researchers in the health field afford a sufficient foundation to question the usefulness of the value-orientations approach to an understanding of the place of Chicanos in American life. The value-orientations approach assumes that the culture of the Chicanos is defective and must be changed if Chicanos are to assimilate in the secondary structural sphere. Its advice to Chicanos is give up your heritage and move into the mainstream of American life. In this way, whatever problems the Chicanos may be having are held to be the fault of their culture, not of the society that surrounds them. In keeping with this verdict, many members of this ethnic group appear to have concluded that separation or secession may be the only solutions to the problem of cultural survival. Nevertheless, most Chicanos seem to be determined to find a middle way wherein the Spanish language and pride in *La Raza* will move side by side with increasing secondary structural assimilation. They have rejected the value-orientations analysis of their situation and are engaged in constructing a stronger, more cohesive community.

The evidence we have reviewed concerning the cultural, secondary structural, primary structural, and marital assimilation of the Chicanos may be interpreted to lend partial support to either the immigrant or the colonial analogies. Neither interpretation seems to fit all the facts. The Chicanos appear to be statistically, as they are in reality, both a conquered and an immigrant minority. We will return to this puzzle in chapter 8 after a consideration of the experience of black people in America.

KEY IDEAS

1. The relations between Chicanos and Anglos represent a second kind of intergroup contact. Like the Indian and black Americans, the Chicanos originally entered the United States through force rather than through voluntary immigration.
2. Some social analysts think a sequence of intergroup relations that is initiated through forced entry cannot be understood in terms of the theories of Anglo conformity, the melting pot, or cultural pluralism. They believe, instead, that a variation of colonialist theory (e.g., internal colonialism) affords a more accurate picture of the relations between Chicanos and Anglos.
3. Colonized minorities—in contrast to immigrant minorities—usually remain in their homeland, are especially committed to the preservation

of their native culture, and are prevented from moving about freely to compete for jobs with members of the dominant group. Under these conditions, the sequence of race relations does not move steadily "forward" toward full intergroup merger; it is characterized, rather, by a "back-and-forth" movement out of conflict into accommodation and back again into conflict. This sequence is interrupted by the expulsion or annihilation of one group or the other.

4. The Spanish approach to colonization differed from that of the English. A key difference was that the Spanish included the Indians in the developing colonial society, while the English excluded them. As a result, the Indians of Mexico have moved much further toward full assimilation than have the Indians of the United States.

5. The Chicano group emerged out of a long series of conflicts between the United States and Spain and between the United States and Mexico. Although the Texas revolution was not based on ethnic differences, the ethnic cleavage gradually deepened following Texas' independence. The Chicano group emerged as a distinct minority group at the end of the Mexican-American war.

6. The Treaty of Guadalupe Hidalgo did not end hostilities between the Chicanos and Anglos in the borderlands. Continuous struggle, marked by intermittent open conflict, was a conspicuous element of border life well into the twentieth century.

7. Although the Chicano group was created when the United States forcibly occupied the southwestern and western lands previously owned by Mexico, most of the present members of the group are not the descendants of that "creation generation." The Chicano population of the United States has grown overwhelmingly through immigration from Mexico since the beginning of the twentieth century.

8. Since Mexican immigration reached its peak later than the peak of the new immigration, many social analysts think of the Chicanos as being even "newer" to America than the new immigrants. Their apparent slowness to assimilate, therefore, may be due to their comparatively recent arrival in the United States.

9. Advocates of the colonial analogy dispute the claims of those who prefer the immigrant analogy. It is said that Mexicans who move to the United States are best thought of as migrants rather than immigrants. From this viewpoint, the movement of Mexicans across an arbitrary political boundary into an area that is both geographically and culturally similar to their homeland is not to be compared to movements of Europeans across oceans into a country with a much different culture. Moreover, when Mexican nationals have reached the United States, the members of the dominant group typically have greeted them with even higher levels of prejudice and discrimination than has usually been directed toward European immigrants.

10. Three widely publicized examples of dominant-group discrimination against Chicanos are the "charity deportations" in the 1930s, the "Zoot-Suit Race Riots" in the 1940s, and "Operation Wetback" in the 1950s. In each of these cases, some officials of the dominant group demonstrated that they made no real distinction between Chicano citizens and Mexican nationals. They also revealed their belief that all people of Mexican ancestry are innately inferior. As in the case of the evacuation and internment of Japanese Americans, many citizens were illegally punished, in this case through deportation, intimidation, and physical assault.

11. The *bracero* program illustrates how the relations of the dominant group in America to its minorities may be altered by international events.

12. World War II and the Chicanos' active participation in it increased the group's commitment to Anglo conformity and led many of its members to expect a sharp decline in prejudice and discrimination following the war. When the expected changes did not occur, the Chicano group commenced an "awakening" that has been expressed in a higher degree of formal social and political organization and in a sharp increase in interest in the goals of cultural pluralism. There also has been an increase in interest in separatism and secession.

13. Although the Chicanos, in general, show higher levels of cultural, secondary structural, primary structural, and marital assimilation than in 1950, it seems unlikely that the differences between Chicanos and Anglos will soon disappear. Assimilation in jobs and income, for example, is not occurring rapidly enough to noticeably reduce the gap between the two groups.

14. A popular explanation of the comparative lack of worldly success by the Chicanos has focused on the way their values differ from those of the Anglos. It has been claimed that such things as their "present orientation" and "familism" are obstacles to success. From this perspective, Chicanos must hasten to rid themselves of their culture if they wish to get ahead in American life.

15. This value-orientations approach has been vigorously attacked as a form of cultural imperialism that works in the service of the Anglo-conformity ideology. Chicanos do not believe that their heritage is defective or is a handicap to achievement. They believe, instead, that dominant-group discrimination is the biggest barrier to secondary structural assimilation. Perhaps greater group cohesion will assist the group in moving toward ideal cultural pluralism or, if that fails, toward a greater degree of separation from the dominant group.

16. Neither the colonial analogy nor the immigrant analogy fits all the facts of the Chicano experience. Their history includes both colonization and immigration, and an adequate account of their present and future social reality must reconcile these facts.

NOTES

1. As stated in chapter 1, the matter of an appropriate name for the ethnic group discussed in the present chapter is very controversial. Probably no other American ethnic group has been more absorbed by the questions "Who are we?" "Where do we belong?" "What shall we call ourselves?" Each term of group identification that has been adopted by certain segments of this population has been considered inaccurate or offensive by those in some other segment. Since the members of the group vary so widely in their specific histories, geographical locations, social characteristics, and aspirations, this state of affairs is not too surprising. In addition to Chicano, the terms *Mexican American, Latin American, Spanish American, Hispano, Spanish surname, La Raza,* and *Mexicano* have all been prominent as identifiers of this group, and each has a fairly specific connotation that sets it apart from the others. The term *Chicano,* for instance, frequently is preferred by the younger members of the group and by those who favor cultural pluralism, separatism, or secession as group goals. The term *Mexican American* usually is preferred by older group members and those who favor Anglo conformity, while the terms *Hispano* or *Spanish American* designate those in northern New Mexico and Colorado who trace their ancestry directly to the Spaniards. In this chapter, the term *Chicano* is used most frequently, and it is intended to designate all people who trace their ancestry to Mexico, either before or after the Spanish conquest. For a discussion of different terms of self-reference within this group, see Nostrand, " 'Mexican American' and 'Chicano,' " pp. 389–406.
2. George I. Sanchez, quoted by Grebler, Moore, and Guzman, *The Mexican-American People,* p. 545.
3. Lieberson shows that this pattern has been typical in situations in which the migrant group has been dominant (Lieberson, "A Societal Theory of Race and Ethnic Relations," p. 908.
4. The terms *internal colonialism* and *the third world perspective* often are used to emphasize that there are some differences between the experience of classical colonialism and that of nonwhite people in America (Blauner, *Racial Oppression in America,* pp. 54, 70).
5. For a discussion of the attitudes of Anglo-Americans toward Mexicans during the nineteenth century, see McLemore, "The Origins of Mexican American Subordination in Texas," pp. 660–663.
6. For an elaboration of this theory, see ibid., 656–670.
7. The rate of naturalization among Mexicans has been, in Moore's opinion, "extraordinarily slow" (Moore, *Mexican Americans,* 2nd ed., p. 49).
8. Calculated from Table 4–3 in Grebler, Moore, and Guzman, *Mexican-American People,* p. 68.
9. For accounts of the Chicano movement in Crystal City, see Camejo, "Texas Chicanos Forge Own Political Power," *Introduction to Chicano Studies,* and Gutierrez and Hirsch, "The Militant Challenge to the American Ethos."
10. The problems of using different identifiers have been discussed by Hernández, Estrada, and Alvírez, "Census Data and the Problem of Conceptually Defining the Mexican American Population."

11. Calculated from Table A, *U.S. Census of Population: 1960, Persons of Spanish Surname*, p. IX.

12. The Spanish-English language of the border has been called Pocho (Murguía, *Assimilation, Colonialism and the Mexican American People*, p. 93).

13. These figures are taken from the following sources: *U.S. Census of Population: 1950, Persons of Spanish Surname*, pp. 23–42; *U.S. Census of Population: 1960, Persons of Spanish Surname*, pp. 38–39; *U.S. Census of Population: 1970, Persons of Spanish Surname*, p. 42; *U.S. Census of Population: 1950, Characteristics of the Population*, p. 297; *U.S. Census of Population: 1960, Characteristics of the Population*, p. 578; and *U.S. Census of Population: 1970, Characteristics of the Population*, p. 833.

14. In the period 1940–1960, for example, the largest decline among 109 American cities was 13.9 in Sacramento, but nearly all of this change occurred between 1950 and 1960 (Taeuber and Taeuber, *Negroes in Cities*, pp. 39–41).

15. For a review of these studies, see Weaver, "Mexican American Health Care Behavior: A Critical Review of the Literature," pp. 85–102.

Seven

Black
Americans

The analysis of chapter 6 has revealed several important parallels between
the history of the Chicanos and the history of many colonized peoples
throughout the world. Chief among these is that, through conquest, the
Chicanos lost lands to which they had had a long-standing claim. Initially,
they did not enter the United States voluntarily. Consequently, many members
of this ethnic group have felt they are conquered people in their own land.

The Chicanos, of course, are not alone among American minorities in
this respect. The Indian Americans were undeniably natives in their own
land, and they most assuredly have not become a part of American society
either voluntarily or through immigration. Although the relations between
the various European colonial powers and the Indians often took the form of
treaties between nations in which the Indians sold or leased their lands, the
primary contacts between the two groups took place within a framework of
conflict. In the normal course of events, peace occasionally broke out amidst
the warfare. The Indians were more interested in repelling the invaders than

they were in becoming a part of their society, and the Anglo-Americans were more interested in expelling or annihilating the Indians than they were in assimilating them. The overall result was that the Indians were forced off nearly all of the lands that the Europeans considered desirable.

With these ideas and examples as a background, we turn to a consideration of America's largest, most conspicuous racial minority—the black Americans. Unlike the European minorities, black Americans did not migrate voluntarily, and unlike the Chicanos and Indian Americans, they were not present on American soil when the English arrived. Like the Chicano experience, therefore, the black experience does not fit neatly either the colonial or immigrant perspectives. As a result, both viewpoints have been prominent in the arguments concerning the place and future of black Americans in American life.

Servants and Slaves

Although black people were represented among the first groups to arrive in the New World, the first instance of black "immigration" to what is now the United States occurred in Virginia in 1619. It is recorded that the Virginia settlers bought "twenty Negers," who arrived on a Dutch warship (Frazier, 1957:3). Although not much is known concerning the treatment of these twenty people, one thing appears to be established: they were purchased as indentured or bonded servants rather than as absolute slaves. At this time, many of the white people who were a part of the English colony in Virginia had come there under a similar arrangement. Englishmen who were impoverished or had been convicted of a crime were sometimes sold into bondage for different periods of years. Even free men who had not run afoul of the law were sometimes willing to accept a period of servitude in return for their passage to the New World. This system was recognized in England as legal and profitable to all parties, and the servants under this arrangement were sometimes referred to as slaves (Handlin, 1957:7–9). Through such contracts England profited by reducing the number of people who were public charges; the purchaser of the servants profited by having cheap "slave" labor available for a fixed period; and the servants profited by the opportunity to escape their unpleasant circumstances at home and to get a new start in life.

The condition of bonded servitude was certainly far different from freedom, but it was one that might end after a specified number of years and, perhaps, might lay the foundation for a new and better life. Even during the period of indenture, the slave had certain rights and was, therefore, legally protected from excessive harshness by the master. Initially, these protections apparently applied to the black bonded servants as well as to the white. English law during this period stated that "a slave who had been baptized became 'infranchised'" (Frazier, 1957:23). Those who were so treated might then become free. Although it is probable that black servants were not treated in exactly the same way as white servants, even in the early years, much evidence favors the view that the laws regulating the rights and obligations of servitude applied to the members of both races and all nations.[1]

The main issues that provoked racially discriminatory legislation were the question of the length of the term of service, the problem of the standing of Christianized slaves, and the legal position of the children of slaves. For at least twenty years after black servants were introduced into Virginia, many employers had a definite preference for white laborers and, also, were unwilling to commit themselves for long periods to the support of servants. As time passed, however, the profitability of black labor increased, and so, understandably, did the masters' desire for it. Hence, by the 1660s, both Maryland and Virginia had taken legal steps to make the attainment of freedom more difficult for black slaves. For example, in 1664, Maryland's legislature passed an act that required all non-Christian slaves, especially "Negroes," to serve *durante vita* (for life) (Frazier, 1957:25). The law also decreed that a free woman who married a slave also became a slave for the life of her husband and that all of her children would be slaves like the father (Frazier, 1957:27–28). This particular law was later repealed to prevent unscrupulous masters from marrying their white female servants to black male servants in order to force the women into longer periods of servitude and to gain possession of their children. In the meantime, however, the noose around the freedom of black people was permanently tightened. Since the law of 1664 had left open the possibility that Christianized blacks might someday become free, a new law was passed stating that baptism did not amount to manumission(i.e., being freed).

A similar process of legalizing lifetime slavery for blacks, even those who were Christians, occurred in Virginia. In 1661, a law imposing penalties on runaway slaves distinguished clearly between black and white runaways and implied that the period of indenture for at least some blacks was forever (Handlin, 1957:13). Another law passed in the same year made this racial distinction hereditary. The ability of any black person to gain freedom in Virginia seems to have ended by 1682. In that year, a law was passed establishing black slavery for life, whether an individual had been baptized or not. In hardly more than sixty years, then, the black people who had entered the colonies of Maryland and Virginia were removed from a legal position similar to that of the indentured servants from other nations and were downgraded to a status of lifelong bondage. But the gap in status was not yet absolute. The terms *servant* and *slave* were still sometimes used interchangeably, and the conclusion had not yet been reached that to be a slave *meant* that one was black.

The continuing possibility that at least some white people also might be reduced to the type of slavery that by now had been forced on the blacks had an understandable effect on the immigration of whites to Maryland and Virginia. The white servants in these colonies sometimes wrote letters to their relatives and friends back home warning them not to come to these colonies. Travelers also told of the harshness of white servitude. Such places as Pennsylvania and New York, therefore, frequently were more attractive to freeborn immigrants who feared they might be bound over as servants if they went to Maryland or Virginia. The desire of the masters in the latter colonies to encourage the immigration of white settlers and an increasing preference for black labor on the plantations led to a gradual strengthening of the position of the white slaves (Handlin, 1957:15). The blacks, who had come to the colonies involuntarily and who did not write horror stories to those back home, were unable to benefit from this small source of protection. Neither were they able at this point to become enfranchised through baptism and, thus, claim the protection of the laws of England. In this way, the condition of the white servants gradually improved while the condition of the black slaves slowly became worse.

The spread of the plantation system of agriculture increased the width of the status gap between black and white servants. Black laborers could not desert the plantation and disappear among the citizenry nearly so easily as could white laborers. Therefore, the masters' investment in black laborers was protected. Furthermore, black women and children could be used in the fields along with the men, thus decreasing the number of unproductive hands at the masters' disposal (Frazier, 1957:29–30).

As the plantation economy developed throughout the South, it was obvious to the members of the planter class that the fewer rights laborers had and the harder they could be required to work, the lower would be the cost of their labor and the larger would be the planters' profits. Thus, the planters encouraged measures that moved the blacks further from the status of human beings and toward the status of mere property. Under these conditions, the blacks had descended by the beginning of the eighteenth century into a state of complete, abject, legally defenseless bondage. The term *slave* became unambiguous. It now came to mean a subhuman being whose legal rights were hardly more than those of cattle. The Negroid features, and particularly the black skin, had become its symbols. The equation of blackness and the slave status became fixed, making it impossible even for "free" blacks to enjoy the rights that legally were theirs.

The descent of the black slaves to the status of property to be used as the masters saw fit even when the slaves were Christians did create some new problems for the whites. In the first place, the importation of slaves increased so rapidly that in some places the planters became alarmed by the possibility that the slaves would become too numerous to control. Georgia, for example, attempted at first to prevent the importation of black slaves entirely so that rebellions would be less likely to occur and the colony would be easier to defend. In South Carolina, the number of black slaves had become so large by 1700 that the planters were permitted to have no more than six adult black males for each white servant (Frazier, 1957:32).

A second problem created by black chattel slavery concerned its morality. How could supposedly Christian people hold other people in such an oppressive bondage? How could they do so especially if the oppressed people also were Christians? This dilemma was the source of the spectacular controversy regarding the abolition of slavery. Those opposing slavery and favoring its abolition argued fiercely that slavery was morally wrong. Those favoring slavery and opposing its abolition defended it as morally justified.[2]

The picture painted by the abolitionists emphasized the degrading and inhuman aspects of slavery. Since the slaves had no legal standing, they could be bought and sold at will. Families could be, and were, broken apart and separated forever. Moreover, countless numbers of slaves were brutally beaten, maimed, or killed by ruthless masters or, more often, plantation overseers. The slaves simply had no control over their own lives. Slaves had, as the Supreme Court stated in the decisive Dred Scott case in 1857, "no rights that a white man need respect." One may well wonder how, in a presumably democratic, God-fearing land, such a system of bondage could have been defended. As Handlin (1957:32) has asked, "How did bondage square with freedom?"

Two main and related questions occupied the attention of the combatants. First, is it morally wrong to enslave other people? Second, whether or not the system of black slavery in America was morally wrong, what were its effects on the slaves? Stripped to its essentials, the main line of reasoning employed by the defenders of slavery's morality is this: the blacks are innately inferior; they need the aid of the whites to "progress" from a savage to a civilized condition; therefore, slavery is morally right. This formula was designed in Handlin's (1957:33) words "to purge the guilt of men who believed in liberty but were the masters of slaves." Note that this defense of slavery does not claim the system might not be abused by certain individual masters who, as individuals, were morally reprehensible. The apologists for slavery emphasized the close, companionable, and affectionate relations that frequently existed between the planter class and their lovable "darkies." If the system was totalitarian, it was claimed that for the most part it was benevolently so. It was viewed, in effect, as a complete and admirable system of social welfare. Although the slaves worked hard and for long hours, every basic need was provided by the masters so that the slaves could live happy and carefree lives.

The evidence presented on the question of the essential brutality or benevolence of American slavery is immense. Large numbers of eyewitness and first-person accounts have been gathered to "prove" each point of view. For every story illustrating the injustices heaped on the slaves, one may find another to illustrate that the masters and slaves generally held a deep affection for one another. While many slaves ran away from their masters, many others remained with them even after they had been given their freedom.

The weight of scholarly opinion on this vexing issue has waxed and waned. As recently as the first quarter of the twentieth century, Phillips convinced many of his fellow historians that the accusations of those who had opposed slavery before the Civil War were exaggerated and distorted. Through a painstaking study of plantation records, Phillips found evidence that the relations between the races typically were friendly, kind, and gentle. He acknowledged that there were many instances of injustice and brutality, but he thought these were no more common than anywhere else in the world. Phillips thought that "on the whole the plantations were the best schools yet invented for the mass training of . . . the American Negroes."[3] From this viewpoint, despite slavery's obvious faults, it appeared to Phillips to be basically a humane system.

Since the 1940s, however, the antislavery viewpoint has gradually undermined the work of Phillips and his followers. By 1959, the finest available scholarship had, in Elkins' (1968:20) words, "overwhelmingly reversed" Phillips' moral position and had established that American slavery was (as the abolitionists had always claimed) a generally vicious, unjust, and brutal system.

Many types of evidence have been used to discredit the view that the black slaves were usually happy, contented people—what we may call the *"Gone With the Wind"* version of slavery (Jacobs and Landau, 1971:100). Some of the most controversial evidence, however, concerns various forms of resistance to slavery. Many people have asked, "If slavery were so intolerable, why didn't the slaves rebel?" To those who have believed that the slave system was essentially just, the answer has seemed obvious. On the whole, the blacks were satisfied with slavery! According to one writer, black people have a naturally cheerful disposition and, provided they are well fed, are "easily made happy."[4] Aside from the fact that we now recognize such thinking to be stereotyped and superficial, a closer inspection of the historical record does not bear out the nonresistance thesis. At the time of their capture (primarily in the valleys of the Gambia, Niger, and Congo rivers), many blacks vigorously resisted enslavement. And as they were being transported through the infamous "Middle Passage" to the New World, many incidents occurred aboard ship. There were instances in which the slaves overcame the crews and captured the ships on which they were imprisoned. These revolts were so common that "they were considered one of the principal hazards of the slave trade" (Frazier, 1957:85). Moreover, when escape or attack seemed impossible, many slaves jumped overboard to their deaths.

The resistance to slavery by no means ended after the slaves arrived in America. Throughout the nearly two and one-half centuries of American slavery, most of the main forms of overt and covert resistance known to mankind were employed. From the beginning, individual slaves revolted against the system by running away, and considering the difficulties of all other forms of resistance, this may have been the most effective way to strike back. In many cases, fugitive slaves banded together into outlaw groups, establishing so-called maroon communities in various inaccessible places. The likelihood of escape by running away, however, was dramatically improved near the beginning of the nineteenth century. At this time, the existing arrangements for assisting fugitive slaves, primarily those in the northern states, were enlarged and made more efficient. A complicated network of people and facilities known as the Underground Railroad gradually took form. Several "tracks," including one to Florida, developed. However, during the decades immediately preceding the Civil War, the center of the railroad's activities was Ohio. Hundreds of "stations" and "operators" assisted the fugitives in their long journey to havens in the North and in Canada.

Many free black people participated actively in the abolitionist movement and in the work of the Underground Railroad. Men like David Walker, Martin Delany, and Frederick Douglass issued ringing denunciations of slavery and encouraged black slaves to resist and, if possible, escape. Women such as Sojourner Truth and Harriet Tubman also became famous as abolitionists. Tubman, "The Moses of Her People," is reported to have made nineteen trips to the south and to have assisted 300 slaves in escaping (Frazier, 1957:98). Since the operations of the railroad were conducted with the utmost secrecy, the exact number of slaves whose escape was aided is unknown. Estimates have been constructed, however, and some authorities believe that the South, between 1810 and 1860, may have lost as many as 100,000 slaves in this way (Davie, 1949:45). It is certain that the number had swelled during those years to such proportions that southern politicians demanded strong federal legislation to help stem the flow. In 1850, a strict Fugitive Slave Law was passed as a part of a larger congressional compromise concerning slavery. This law required citizens of the northern states to return fugitive slaves to their owners. It also placed many free blacks in the North in danger of being kidnapped or falsely accused as runaways.

Individual forms of resistance to slavery were supplemented by organized resistance. As noted previously the leaders of the Georgia Colony recognized slave insurrections to be a distinct possibility and tried, therefore, to prevent the importation of slaves. The same fear existed in the other colonies, and many precautions were taken to prevent uprisings. Efforts were made to keep the ratio of black slaves to whites below a certain level. Slaves of the same tribe frequently were separated or forbidden to speak to each other. Most slaves were not permitted to speak their native tongues or to retain their African names. They were permitted to travel only for short distances and under careful surveillance. White slave patrols were used extensively to police the activities of blacks and to interfere with any disapproved organizational efforts. In most places, it was illegal for a slave to learn to read or write or for anyone to teach a slave these skills. News of slave unrest was suppressed to diminish the possibility that such news might generate or strengthen resistance in other places. In brief, the masters took great pains to keep the slaves in a state of ignorance and to disrupt communications among them. Under such circumstances, planning and executing a revolt was no easy matter.

Despite these efforts and the often cruel punishment of those involved in such plots, at least 200 insurrections, and possibly as many as 1,200, were planned between 1664 and 1860 (Jacobs and Landau, 1971:100), and at least fifteen were actually carried into effect (Davie, 1949:44). At least fourteen others were on the verge of erupting at the time they were discovered, although none of the revolts was very large or successful.

Three uprisings during the nineteenth century attracted widespread attention. The first of these was led in 1800 by a slave named Gabriel Prosser, who worked as a blacksmith in the vicinity of Richmond. This man apparently used biblical quotations to persuade other slaves that their situation was similar to that of the Israelites under the pharoahs and that God would help them to gain their freedom (Bardolph, 1961:35). Although many slaves were involved in Gabriel's insurrection plan, a torrential rain and the betrayal of the conspiracy by two slaves brought the effort to a quick end. Gabriel was captured and hanged.

A second notable slave insurrection was organized in 1822 by Denmark Vesey in Charleston, South Carolina. Vesey had been permitted to purchase his freedom in 1800 and, therefore, had had the opportunity to move about and to gain a knowledge of current events. For instance, he apparently knew something about the French Revolution and the successful slave revolt in Haiti. He used this information to inspire the slaves he contacted to organize and rebel. Whenever he observed slaves behaving subserviently toward whites, he would chide them. Vesey's conspiracy was revealed by a loyal house slave, and the authorities arrested over seventy of its leaders. Vesey and thirty-four others were hanged; the remainder were deported from the United States.

The most famous uprising was led by Nat Turner in 1831 in Virginia. Unlike Vesey, Turner was not free, nor was he a careful planner. His approach to insurrection was mystical. He claimed to hear voices from heaven and to be "called" to free his people. The revolt began when Turner and a handful of followers killed all the whites in his master's household. After that, the group moved from place to place, killing a total of fifty-five white men, women, and children. Local whites and the state militia quickly scattered Turner's band. After a six-week search, he was captured and later hanged.

In addition to the well-known uprisings noted so far, one other deserves mention. This revolt occurred in Louisiana during 1811 and was the largest slave insurrection ever to take place in the United States. According to Genovese (1974:592), "between 300 and 500 slaves, armed with pikes, hoes, and axes but few firearms, marched on New Orleans with flags flying and drums beating." The rebels were engaged by a force of militia and regular troops, and were rapidly defeated. Although this uprising was well organized and much larger than those led by Prosser, Vesey, and Turner, it occurred so far away from the older, more settled regions of the south that it did not receive the same kind of attention or arouse too much concern.

The willingness of slaves to protest their treatment increased with the onset of the Civil War. White southerners became ever more fearful that the slaves, especially the field hands, would rebel. A number of additional steps were taken to control them. For instance, the patrol laws were strengthened, slave rations and supplies were increased, and picket lines were doubled to discourage escape tries. But as the Union Army invaded various portions of the Confederacy, and as the prospects increased that the slaves in those areas would soon be freed, many of them were encouraged to raise objections to the way they were treated. According to Davie (1949:45), many slaves refused to accept punishment, were insolent to their masters, frequently assaulted whites, informed for the Union armies, and joined the Union armies as recruits. Frazier (1957:108) states that half of the 186,000 black Union Army troops were from the South.

As the plantation system approached its zenith, the masters' control methods were "fine tuned." On the legal side, the system became more precise and rigid than ever before; on the interpersonal side, the masters may well have exhibited more of the legendary paternal concern than in previous periods. Even though individual flight and organized rebellion among the slaves increased during this time, many observers have felt that the slaves' response was slight in relation to the oppressiveness of the regime. Even if one accepts the highest estimates of the numbers of runaways and insurrections, one may still wonder why the numbers were not much larger.

The interest surrounding this question has generated a wide-ranging and complex modern debate concerning slavery, a debate that is of interest not only to scholars but to anyone who searches for solutions to the contemporary social problems of black Americans. Though it involves oversimplification, we may gain some appreciation of the relationship between the various interpretations of slavery and the efforts to solve modern problems by considering very briefly three leading points of view. Each of these viewpoints, we should emphasize, is opposed to the proslavery interpretation of Phillips mentioned earlier.

The first interpretation to be considered has been forcefully presented by Elkins (1968). In Elkins' view, the resistance of the black slaves in the United States was less than one would have expected because the slave system here was even more oppressive than slave systems usually are. Elkins (1968: 52–80) has compared American and Latin American slavery and believes there were some important differences between them. In the United States, slavery gradually became much more precise, definite, all-inclusive, and severe than in Latin America. In the United States, black people were presumed to be slaves unless proved otherwise, and, as we have seen, the term of servitude was for life. Also, in the United States, marriages between slaves, even when conducted by ministers, were not legally binding. Furthermore, in the United States, slave masters had the power of life and death over slaves. None of this is meant to suggest that a slave's life in Latin America was easy. Elkins does argue, though, that slaves in Latin America could more easily become free and, once free, were more easily accepted into the dominant society. Social distinctions based on color did not become so sharp as in the United States.

Elkins maintains that the differences between American and Latin American slavery arose because the quest for profit in the latter was restrained by the power of the church and the state. This restraint enabled the black slaves of Latin America to maintain an essentially human status. In the United States, the slave experience was so shocking, so total, so brutal, that it stripped away not only traditions but also reduced the slaves personally as well as legally to a subhuman condition.

Elkins pursues this thesis in a fascinating way. He suggests that the American system of slave control resembled the total control of the twentieth-century concentration camp. Just as prisoners who are exposed to absolute power in concentration camps become psychologically debilitated, docile, and childlike, black American slaves also experienced profound personality disintegration. The psychological effects of slavery, indeed, afford a realistic underpinning for the so-called Sambo stereotype of the slave. This image of the typical personality of the black slave assumes he "was docile but irresponsible, loyal but lazy, humble but chronically given to lying and stealing" (Elkins, 1968:82).

This explanation not only appears to account for many of the facts of black American slavery but (as we note again later), it also is congruent with some arguments stating that many of the modern problems of black Americans may be traced to the direct effects of slavery. It is not settled, however, that black American slaves were as genuinely submissive as Elkins suggests nor that black slavery in America was worse than any other kind. Mintz (1969:30–31), for instance, points out that during its earliest and latest periods, Spanish slavery in the West Indies was at least as bad as American slavery. Patterson (1977:415) also considers it an error to believe that American slavery was especially pernicious. He argues, too, that the "Sambo" personality type may be found among slaves of any time or place.[5]

Probably the most startling and controversial attack on Elkins' thesis has been presented by Fogel and Engerman (1974). The analysis of these authors has, so to speak, stood Elkins on his head. Instead of viewing the slave system as purely repressive and psychologically destructive, Fogel and Engerman have assembled evidence to show that the masters used the carrot as well as the stick, that they made many efforts to reward the slaves whose personal and family behavior followed the dominant pattern and who worked diligently to help make the farm or plantation prosper. The result of the masters' efforts to motivate the slaves more by rewards than by punishments, claim Fogel and Engerman, was that the typical slave was a vigorous and productive worker. He was not at all the "Sambo" portrayed by traditional historians and folklore, a person who would lie, steal, feign illness, behave childishly, and shirk his duties (Fogel and Engerman, 1974:231). Rather, because the masters gave careful attention to such matters as slave management, diet, family stability, bonuses, and promotions, the slaves were much more efficient workers than either northern farm workers or free southern laborers (Fogel and Engerman, 1974:192–209). Instead of being "Sambo," the slave laborer became the type of well-motivated worker portrayed by Horatio Alger (Gutman, 1975:165). From this perspective, the modern problems experienced by black Americans cannot be explained as a continuation of the damage done to the personalities and families of blacks during the ordeal of slavery.

Even though the interpretations of Elkins and Fogel and Engerman reach opposing conclusions concerning the effects of slavery on the motives and actions of the slaves, both interpretations have been attacked by advocates of a third interpretation. In the opinion of Gutman (1975), for example, despite their many differences, both of the above approaches share a common flaw. Both see the slaves essentially as passive beings who can only have been what the master class wanted them to be. As Gutman (1975:166) states:

> Sambo and the slave Horatio Alger are very different men. But the model which has created the archetypal enslaved Afro-American remains the same. In both models, the enslaved are "made over" by their owners.

In contrast to these views, which portray the beliefs and behaviors of slaves purely as reactions to the requirements of the masters, Gutman stresses the active role played by the slaves in charting their own course despite the heavy restrictions placed on them by the masters. Ellison (1964:316) has encapsulated this view as follows:

> Are American Negroes simply the creation of white men, or have they at least helped to create themselves out of what they found around them? Men have made a way of life in caves and upon cliffs, why cannot Negroes have made a life upon the horns of the white men's dilemma?[6]

The simplified description we have presented of differing interpretations of black slavery has focused only on the central thrust of the system for the subordinated group. In fact, however, the system had many different effects, and the debate concerning it has ranged over a very broad spectrum of issues. Of special importance has been the analysis of the effects of slavery on the black family, to which we return later in the chapter.

Immigrant or Colonized Minority?

The experience of black people in America up to the time of the Civil War resembled in some respects that of both an immigrant and a colonized minority. They were an "immigrant" minority in the sense that they had been removed from their native lands and had entered the host American society as a subordinate group; unlike European immigrants, however, their subordinate position was not regarded as something temporary, something to be left behind as the process of assimilation worked its magic. The blacks also resembled a "colonized" minority in the sense that they had been physically "conquered" and, subsequently, had not been accepted as suitable candidates for full membership in the society of the conquerors. But they were not a conquered people in their own land. Thus, the very structure of the relations between the native, dominant whites and the "immigrant" but enslaved blacks was such that neither the immigrant nor the colonial perspectives seem completely applicable.

Although some black people became highly assimilated culturally, they were very unusual. The majority of the blacks, and especially the black slaves, were deliberately kept from learning any more of the white man's ways than was absolutely necessary. At the same time, and partly as a result, little structural assimilation occurred during the long ordeal of the slave period. Even the free blacks were subject to a high degree of discrimination and were not readily accepted into the mainstream of American institutional life.[7] On the other hand, the classical solution of the colonized minority's dilemma—throwing the invaders out—was hardly possible. However, the goal of ending the domination of the whites by leaving the United States and, perhaps, returning to Africa was the subject of serious discussion and concrete actions.

The most notable example of a secessionist solution to the "Negro problem" during this period began in 1816 when an organization called the American Colonization Society was founded. This organization was founded primarily to assist free blacks in leaving the United States. It was supported by some blacks and by many whites who feared the free blacks would spread unrest among the slaves. In 1822, the American Colonization Society established a colony for free blacks on the West Coast of Africa. In 1824, the colony was named Liberia, and the main settlement, Munrovia, was established. The colony grew slowly during the next twenty-five years and, in 1847, was declared a republic.

Although Liberia still exists today as the second oldest black republic (after Haiti) in the world, the return of black Americans to this African state was not successful as a solution to American race problems. In the first place, fewer than 3,000 colonists from America were present in the colony at the time it became a republic. In the second place, some influential black leaders in America—even some, like Delany, who favored some kind of separatist solution—did not support the Liberian experiment.

While neither an assimilationist nor a colonialist interpretation seems truly congruent with the situation of the blacks in America before the Civil War, it seems clear that the essential character of the relations between the races during that period is most nearly captured by the colonialist view. For example, even if it were granted that the relations between blacks and whites in most instances were basically humane and mutually considerate, it still is true that the blacks (whether slave or free) were not on the road to full assimilation. Among the slaves whose ancestors had arrived during the colonial period, many more than three generations had passed, but the black experience up to the Civil War was in no important respect comparable to that of the colonial Dutch, Irish, or Germans. On the other hand, one can find significant parallels between the condition of the blacks and the Indians.

Both peoples had been subjected to a tremendous cultural shock. Their customary ways of living had been shattered. Their primary choices in life were reduced to extreme subordination, annihilation, or flight. As Blauner (1972:54) asserts, "Whether oppression takes place at home in the oppressed's native land or in the heart of the colonizer's mother country, colonization remains colonization."[8]

The relative superiority of the colonialist interpretation of the ante-bellum period does not assure us, however, that it is the proper tool for analyzing events in the twentieth century. That question must wait until we have reviewed the major features of the black experience in America since the Civil War.

Emancipation and Reconstruction

As the Civil War approached, the popularity of abolishing slavery waned. Lincoln himself favored deportation as a solution to the "Negro problem," and even after the war was underway, he stated clearly that his main purpose in fighting it was to save the Union rather than to affect the status of slavery. Some time passed before he was convinced that freeing the slaves was essential if the southern rebellion was to be crushed. Moreover, many people in the North shared the opinion of white southerners that black people were naturally suited to servitude and should not be encouraged to seek equality. This opinion was sufficiently common during the early years of the war that northern officers were generally unwilling to accept blacks as soldiers. There were even reports of northern officers who returned runaway slaves to their southern masters! This situation was altered, however, when Lincoln issued the Emancipation Proclamation on January 1, 1863. Among other things, the order proclaimed the southern slaves to be free and authorized the armed forces of the United States to enlist freedmen. Black regiments from Massachusetts, New York, and Pennsylvania were soon organized, and when the North began to draft military recruits, blacks were included. But, as usual, the inclusion of the blacks did not mean they were treated equally. They did not at first receive the same pay as the white troops, and white officers were embarrassed to be assigned to command them.

By the end of the war a Freedmen's Bureau had been established to assist all former slaves to assume their new status as free people (Frazier, 1957:115–116). There were between 3.5 and 4 million freedmen, and most of them had no way to earn a living (Davie, 1949:21). In addition to the sheer size of the task, the bureau labored under constant criticism. Nevertheless, until it expired in 1872, the bureau made a substantial contribution to the welfare of the former slaves.

The task of providing for the freedmen, however, was only a part of the broader task of rebuilding or reconstructing the economic and political systems of the South. The outcome of the war had determined that the federal government was supreme, but it had not determined what the status of the now-defeated Confederate states would be. In President Lincoln's view, the southern states had never really left the Union; therefore, they continued to exist as states and the job of reintegrating them did not require a massive reorganization. His Proclamation of Amnesty and Reconstruction in 1863 offered a pardon to nearly all southerners who would pledge allegiance to the United States and agree to support the abolition of slavery.

Lincoln's ideas concerning Reconstruction were bitterly opposed by a group of Republican leaders in Congress, the so-called Radical Republicans. This group disagreed with Lincoln's view concerning the status of the seceded states. They argued that the southern states had committed suicide, so to speak, and that they should be forced to meet stiff requirements in order to be readmitted to the Union on an equal footing with the loyal states. They also argued that the seceded states should have the status of a conquered province and should come under the jurisdiction of Congress rather than the president.

After the assassination of President Lincoln in the spring of 1865, Pres. Andrew Johnson adopted a Reconstruction plan similar to Lincoln's. On the basis of this plan, Johnson quickly recognized the governments of Louisiana, Arkansas, Tennessee, and Virginia. By the end of 1865, the Thirteenth Amendment had been ratified, all of the Confederate states had been recognized by the president, and all except Texas had held conventions and elected representatives and senators to Congress. In only a few months, President Johnson apparently had achieved the political restoration of the South.

This result did not please the Radical Republicans. For one thing, the South already was taking steps to deny equal rights to blacks. Some new southern laws, called "Black Codes," gave the Radical Republicans the political leverage they needed to fight the president's program.[9] They led the fight to pass the Civil Rights Act of 1866. This act, based on the Thirteenth Amendment and passed over Johnson's veto, declared blacks to be citizens of the United States, gave them equal civil rights, and gave the federal courts jurisdiction over cases arising under the act (Faulkner, 1948:401). Soon after this, Congress approved the Fourteenth Amendment and four sweeping Reconstruction bills. The governments of the South were declared illegal, and the states themselves were divided into five military districts. The general in charge of each district was ordered to hold new elections in which the freedmen could participate equally. The new state legislatures created by these elections were to write new constitutions to assure all citizens the right to vote. An acceptable constitution and the approval of the Fourteenth Amendment were required for the readmission of a state to the union. By 1870, these conditions had been met by all eleven former Confederate states, and they were again represented in Congress.

Congressional Reconstruction infuriated the members of the old planter class and nurtured a hatred that has been slow to die. In the elections creating the Reconstruction legislatures, 703,400 black and 660,000 white voters were registered (Franklin, 1961:80); for the first time, black legislators were elected to public office. Among the whites, many who were elected were "carpetbaggers" from the North and "scalawags" (union loyalists) from the South. The composition of these conventions and the widespread bribery, fraud, and theft that became common in the governments established by them led quickly to charges that "Negro-carpetbag-scalawag" rule was the result of a "conspiracy to degrade and destroy the Southern way of life" (Franklin, 1961:103). Such charges ignore certain pertinent facts. In regard to composition, only in South Carolina did black legislators outnumber whites; only in Mississippi and Virginia did Northern whites outnumber Southern whites (Franklin, 1961:102). In regard to honesty, the graft and corruption emerging within the Southern Reconstruction governments was often small by comparison with that occurring in the North during this same period. In Franklin's (1961:151) opinion, "the tragedy of public immorality in the Southern states was only part of a national tragedy." It should be said also that despite the unfavorable conditions under which they labored, the Reconstruction governments succeeded to some extent in placing political power in the hands of the common people. For the first time, many poor whites were able to vote and to participate directly in the affairs of government.

Many blacks soon began to express the new freedoms granted by Emancipation, the Civil Rights Act, and the Reconstruction acts. The assertion of their rights violated the traditional "etiquette" of race relations that symbolized and helped to maintain the whites' position of dominance. Whites were further provoked to untold instances of retaliation against blacks by the fact that blacks were now competing directly with them for jobs.

The whites also developed direct, organized, secret methods to intimidate and punish blacks who attempted to exercise their new rights. The most spectacular of the organizations attempting to force the blacks back into their traditional servile position and, simultaneously, to restore political power to the whites was the Ku Klux Klan, formed in 1866.[10] The initial purpose of this organization was to provide amusement to white gentlemen, but it was soon discovered that the Klan's peculiar costume and symbols could be used to frighten many of the blacks. Accordingly, the Klan's purpose soon became the destruction of the Reconstruction governments and the return of black people to their traditional subordinate status. The main tactics of the Klan involved mysterious incantations, cross burnings, and somber warnings delivered in full costume at night. But when these methods seemed insufficient, house burnings, floggings, and murder were added. The Klan quickly became a convenient "cover" for anyone (whether members or not) who wished to punish or intimidate black people. Such tactics were so effective that black people soon found it expedient to show no interest whatever in political matters. They found it was safer to proclaim that politics was "white man's business." This protective reaction, adopted during the Reconstruction period, was to last for many decades.

As the Klan's campaign against blacks became increasingly terroristic, some states and the federal government passed anti-Klan laws. Even some members deplored the violence and felt that things had gotten out of hand. But the efforts to control the violence against blacks and to prevent intimidation were not successful.

These repressive methods became somewhat less common as the whites found other ways to regain control of the state governments. For example, with the closing of the Freedmen's Bureau, the blacks lost an important source of economic aid and, thereby, became more dependent on the local landowners for assistance. When political privileges were restored to the Confederate veterans, and the Supreme Court struck down some portions of the laws designed to enforce congressional Reconstruction, the whites were aided in reestablishing political control. The Democratic Party became the main instrument for the "redemption" of the South, ensuring for decades that the southern states would vote "solidly" in that party's column. The disputed presidential election of 1876 led to the complete withdrawal of federal troops and the end of Reconstruction.

The Restoration of White Supremacy

Race relations in the South had been dramatically and irrevocably altered by war, emancipation, defeat, and Reconstruction. The successful campaign of the old planter class, with the aid of the poor whites and many business people, to end Radical Republican Reconstruction and recapture political control of the South did not put everything back into its prewar place. It is true that in many cases the freed slaves returned to their original plantations as laborers or tenants. In such cases, the old master-slave relation was hardly altered. Even in such cases, though, neither whites nor blacks could forget that the latter had openly challenged white dominance during the Reconstruction years. Neither could they ignore the fact that blacks were now free to move about and, where possible, to sell their labor in the open market. Having succeeded in recapturing the state governments and bringing about the withdrawal of federal troops, the whites wished fully to reestablish their dominance over the blacks; as a part of this effort, they insisted the racial problem was a southern problem that should be resolved by southerners without "interference." The northerners, in turn, had been left in a state of exhaustion by all the efforts that had gone into assuring the freedom and civil rights of blacks. Their general response to the white southerner's demands to be given a free hand, therefore, was to "wink and look the other way."

The economic and legal weapons used by the whites to return the blacks as nearly as possible to a condition of slavery are of considerable interest. On the economic side, there developed a new system of agricultural production that reduced many blacks to a state resembling slavery. On the legal side, the folkways of southern race relations were extended and enforced by law to include almost every aspect of race relations.

The planters still retained most of the productive land. But they generally were bankrupt. They had lost their slaves without compensation and generally were unable to pay wages for labor. These circumstances gave rise to a new system of agriculture to replace the old plantation system. The new system worked in the following way: banks and other lenders advanced money to the planters for a certain (usually large) share of the planter's next crop. The planters, in turn, advanced money and supplies to tenants for a certain share (also usually large) of their portion of the next crop. This system of crop sharing by tenants and landowners had a number of consequences. While it did permit the South's agricultural economy to resume production, it created a vicious circle of borrowing and indebtedness. Because cotton was the cash crop in greatest demand, this method of financing also led to the overproduction of cotton and the rapid depletion of the soil's nutrients. Each of these elements helped to drive large numbers of landowners out of business. Large numbers of tenants and owners no longer could earn a living in agriculture and were, thereby, forced to migrate to the cities (Davie, 1949:63–67).

The tenancy and "sharecropping" system worked to the disadvantage of practically everyone but the lenders. But it worked to the greatest disadvantage of the black tenants. Many white landowners did not make public the exact records of the amounts they received for their crops or of the amounts of credit they had extended to their tenants for food, clothing, and supplies during a given year. Since many tenants could neither read nor write, they had no effective way to challenge the owner's statement of what they were entitled to from the sale of the crop or what they owed the owner for supplies. Moreover, black tenants soon learned they were in no position to insist that they be given an accurate statement of their earnings and debts. For a black person even to hint that he was being cheated by a white was regarded by the whites as the height of insolence and was sure to be punished. Consequently, the tenants could do little or nothing when they learned after the sale of the crops that their backbreaking labor was to be rewarded by an increase in their debt. The tenants, especially the black tenants, were kept by these devices in a condition of peonage hardly better than the slavery from which they presumably had recently escaped.

The process of lowering the social standing of the blacks from the pinnacle reached during Reconstruction involved legal as well as economic weapons. The primary areas of conflict for many years were the right to vote and segregation in public transportation. Following the Civil War, many railroad and steamship lines refused to permit blacks to purchase first-class accommodations. And as a part of the Black Codes regulating the movements and privileges of the freedmen, Mississippi, Florida, and Texas each passed laws restricting the use of first-class railroad cars by blacks (Woodward, 1957:xiv–xv). The laws were the first of many so-called Jim Crow laws passed by southern legislatures to segregate the blacks from the whites.[11] When the Lincoln-Johnson governments in the South were overturned, and the congressional reconstruction governments were established, these first Jim Crow laws were repealed. But as the quest to reestablish white supremacy grew, Jim Crow legislation began to reappear. At first, only the right to vote and to use public transportation were very much affected. In time, however, every aspect of life—schooling, housing, religion, jobs, the courts, recreation, health care, and so on—was included.

The repeal of the first Jim Crow laws did not reflect the sentiment of most southern whites and did not mean that they were ready to accept racial equality in "social" matters. Even before the end of the Reconstruction period, in fact, both the churches and the schools had become almost completely segregated without any legislation whatever. Although the whites gave indications they intended to keep the races largely apart, the end of Reconstruction did not herald an all-out legislative campaign to reenslave the blacks. Numerous observers of the situation in the South during the years immediately following the end of Reconstruction were surprised to see many instances in which black people received equal treatment in public places (Woodward, 1957:16–26). Nevertheless, the influence of those who favored the complete segregation of blacks in every sphere of life increased with each year. Interracial violence was extremely common. And, increasingly, the whites—especially those of the lower or "cracker" class—sought to prevent blacks from participating in elections. Also, during this period, the rate at which blacks were being lynched by whites began to rise dramatically (Frazier, 1957:160).

Gradually, the pressure mounted to separate the races in every way, to disfranchise the blacks, and to place them in a position of complete subordination. The campaign to bring these results about generally centered on the right of blacks to vote and on segregation in public transportation. In order to prevent blacks from voting, it was necessary to devise a scheme that would circumvent the Fifteenth Amendment. In 1890, Mississippi set the trend by enacting provisions in its constitution creating certain requirements for voters. During the succeeding twenty-five years, all of the old Confederate states changed their constitutions or their laws in order to reduce the number of blacks who voted. The methods employed relied on three main ideas, usually used in combination.

In some states, voters were required to be able to pass "literacy" tests or to be property holders. In some states, the voters were required to pay a poll tax, usually months in advance of an election. And, in some states, the procedure for nominating people to office was restricted to whites (the white primary) on the ground that the nominations were not elections and were, therefore, a "private" matter. These qualifications also had a deterrent effect on many white voters. However, several loopholes in the laws were created to decrease their effects on whites. For instance, in order to meet the literacy test, a person might be required to show an "understanding" of some portion of the federal or state constitution. Since white officials were in charge of these "tests" and decided who had passed, only black people were ever found to be "illiterate" and to be unqualified to vote.

Another technique to permit whites only to evade the other voter qualifications was the notorious "grandfather clause." Under one type of grandfather clause, people could qualify as voters only if their ancestors had been eligible to vote in 1860 (Frazier, 1957:157). Since practically no southern blacks could meet this type of test, and many whites could, a grandfather clause disqualified many more blacks than whites. Some idea of the efficiency of these methods may be seen from the records in Louisiana. In 1896, there were over 130,000 black voters in that state; in 1904, there were less than 1,400 (Woodward, 1957:68).

The other main focus of the segregationists' efforts—public transportation—led to a momentous decision by the U.S. Supreme Court affecting the civil rights of all Americans. In 1890, Louisiana passed a law requiring separate rail-car facilities for whites and blacks. The law stated that "all railway companies carrying passengers . . . in this state shall provide equal but separate accommodations for the white and colored races" (Tussman, 1963:65). Under the law, whites and blacks were not permitted to sit together in a coach or a section of a coach. Criminal charges could be filed for a violation of the law.

In 1896, this law was challenged in the Supreme Court in the famous "separate but equal" case *Plessy* v. *Ferguson*. Plessy, who was stated to be "seven-eighths caucasian," had been ordered to leave a coach assigned to members of the white race and had refused to comply. He had been arrested and jailed for violating the law. The main legal point in Plessy's case was that he had been deprived of his rights under the Fourteenth Amendment to the Constitution. The majority of the court argued that even though the amendment was intended to achieve the absolute equality of the races, neither the amendment nor any other law could abolish social distinctions based on color.

The majority's opinion was eloquently challenged by Justice Harlan. Justice Harlan argued there were two main reasons for declaring the Louisiana law unconstitutional. First, in his opinion, it violated the personal freedoms of all of the people of Louisiana. It was the purpose of the Thirteenth, Fourteenth, and Fifteenth amendments to make the Constitution color blind and to remove the race line from our system of government. But if the logic of the court's majority were accepted, the possibility would be opened for the states to regulate the relations of the races far beyond the sphere of public transportation. For example, if a state may prescribe separate railway coaches, then it may also insist that whites and blacks must walk on opposite sides of the street or sit on opposite sides of the courtroom or be segregated in public meetings. By this reasoning, Harlan pointed out, the state could require the separation in railway coaches of Protestant and Catholic passengers or of native and naturalized citizens.

Justice Harlan also believed that in the long run the decision would stimulate racial resentment and hatred. The real meaning of the Louisiana law, he argued, is that whites consider blacks to be so inferior that it is degrading to mingle with them in any way. The statute was not intended to guarantee that blacks would not be forced to associate with whites but that whites would not be forced to associate with blacks. Such an approach to race relations is a serious mistake, Harlan believed. "The destinies of the two races in this country," he wrote, "are indissolubly linked together, and the interests of both require that the common government of all shall not permit the seeds of race hate to be planted under the sanction of law" (Tussman, 1963:81). The result of attempting to segregate the races by law would be to assure that racial conflict would continue and be a threat to the security of both races.

Harlan's fear that the result of *Plessy* would be the extension of racial segregation not only in railroad coaches but in many other spheres of life was clearly justified. Within three years, every southern state had adopted a law segregating the races aboard trains. By 1910, most of these same states had extended segregation to include the waiting rooms in railway stations; by 1920, racial segregation in the South (and a few adjoining states) had become the normal practice in almost every public matter. In time, signs proclaiming "whites only" or "colored" were displayed at drinking fountains, rest rooms, theaters, swimming pools, libraries, public telephones, bathing beaches, hospital entrances, restaurants, and so on. In many instances, the laws regulating the permissible behavior of the members of the two races states exactly, in feet and inches, how far apart their separate entrances into public buildings or places of amusement must be and how close together they were allowed to sit or stand. Of course, in all of these situations, the separate facilities for blacks were supposed to be equal to those for the whites. In fact, this was almost never the case. In only a few short years, the white southerners had succeeded by law in creating a caste system similar to the one in India. All black people, regardless of their attainments or personal qualities, were beneath all white people. Once again, as in the period of slavery, the black people had no rights the white people were bound to respect.

In some ways, the Jim Crow system that emerged after 1890 was an even more efficient instrument of subordination than slavery had been. It is true that the blacks under Jim Crow were no longer legally the property of the whites, but then it is also true that the whites no longer had as strong an incentive to be concerned about the welfare of blacks. Under slavery, at least some of the blacks were in close daily contact with some of the whites, and those contacts were frequently friendly and compassionate (though it is easy to exaggerate this). The Jim Crow system made many forms of friendly and understanding contacts between the races practically impossible. Residential segregation *increased* as the Jim Crow system became more pervasive. Blacks increasingly were pressured into slum "darktown" or ghetto areas that were occupied solely by blacks.

The system of enforced racial segregation also may have been in some ways as difficult to bear psychologically as slavery had been. During the period of slavery, a major source of emotional sustenance for blacks was the hope, however faint, that someday they might be free, that laws would be enacted to release them from bondage, to give them full legal standing and civil rights. Emancipation, the Thirteenth, Fourteenth, and Fifteenth amendments, and Reconstruction all seemed to fulfill this dim and ancient hope. For nearly three decades, there was some reason to believe that these legal changes were going to be substantially effective. Black people voted, were elected to office, moved about fairly freely, mingled with whites in public places, and owned property. Interracial conflicts and violence were present throughout the period to be sure, but formal slavery had been irrevocably abolished. It did not seem that most of the whites actually wished to re-establish white supremacy or that they would be able to do so if they tried. Gradually, however, the majority of the whites, north as well as south of the Mason-Dixon line, lost interest in the struggle to assure that the changes effected by the Civil War would be thoroughgoing and permanent. The Supreme Court's decision in *Plessy* cleared the way for the rise of Jim Crowism and the virtual reenslavement of black people in many southern and adjoining states. Although under the Jim Crow system black people still retained significant freedoms such as the right to attend schools (albeit inferior ones) and to own property, the laws permitted under *Plessy* had practically neutralized the *intent* of the post-Civil War amendments to the Constitution.

We should note in passing that although legal segregation was established only in the southern and some bordering states, many forms of racial discrimination, including some segregation, occurred in other parts of the country. Even in states that had enacted special civil rights laws attempting to guarantee the rights contained in the federal constitution, many discriminatory practices existed. For example, hotels were suddenly "filled" when black guests tried to register, or theaters were "sold out" when black patrons arrived. Cases have been reported in which blacks have been served "doctored" foods in restaurants to discourage them from returning (Davie, 1949:290). Moreover, socially enforced residential segregation has been the rule throughout the United States. Nevertheless, the Jim Crow laws of the southern states helped create and strengthen a system of racial discrimination that went far beyond the extralegal discrimination that has been prevalent in many parts of the United States.

Migration, Urbanization, and Employment

Some black people began immediately after the Civil War to exercise their new freedom to move about. At first, this movement took place almost entirely within the South and consisted primarily of migration from the rural areas into the cities. During the decade 1861–1870, for instance, the black population of fourteen southern cities increased by roughly 90 percent (Frazier, 1957:190). Many social and economic forces favoring migration out of the South were at work, however. In the rural South, crop failures, the boll weevil, and soil depletion were crippling the cotton industry. In the cities, many jobs that traditionally had been "Negro jobs" were either being displaced by machines or were being taken over by whites. At the same time, these "push" factors were operating in the South, many "pull" factors were arising in the North. The latter were sharply increased by the outbreak of World

War I. Suddenly, the supply of cheap labor that had been provided by European immigration was halted, and it was stopped just at a time when the demand for labor to produce war materials was rising. Northern employers looked to the South for a new supply of cheap labor; starting in 1915, a large contingent of blacks headed north. This movement is of special interest not only because it was the largest mass migration of blacks from the South up to that time, but also because it originated mainly in the Deep South rather than in the border states. Most of the migrants sought jobs in New York, Chicago, Philadelphia, and Detroit. The black population of these cities increased during the decade by nearly 750,000 (Frazier, 1957:191). The newcomers found jobs in iron and steel mills, automobile construction, chemicals, and other industrial settings. They received much higher wages than they were accustomed to in the South, and northern employers, for the most part, found them to be competent and easier to work with than immigrant laborers from foreign countries.

Just as the great migration of Mexicans into the United States in this century has caused many observers to believe the immigrant analogy applies to them, the great migration of black Americans to the North also has been compared to the European immigrations. From this perspective, although black Americans have been physically present within the United States for centuries, their entry into the American industrial economy as "immigrants" actually has been underway for less than three generations. Hence, even though their experience up to the time of World War I may properly be characterized as colonial, their experience since that time increasingly has been that of recent immigrants (Kristol, 1972). We examine this contention more fully later.

The end of World War I and the onset of the Depression years of the early 1920s and the entire decade of the 1930s greatly reduced the migration of southern blacks to the North and West, but the movement was by no means stopped. The black population of these regions continued to rise throughout the period and at a much faster rate than in the South.

The next great surge of black migration accompanied World War II. As in the case of World War I, many blacks moved to the war plants in the cities of the North and West. Again, Chicago, Detroit, New York, and Philadelphia received large numbers of these migrants. However, by this time, the South also had become far more industrialized than previously, so many migrating blacks moved to southern cities such as Birmingham, Houston, Norfolk, and New Orleans. And for the first time, western cities such as Los Angeles, Portland, and San Diego drew sizable numbers of blacks out of the South.

The favorite single destination for migrants was Harlem in New York City. This black community grew during the period under discussion into the largest urban black population in the world (Davie, 1949:100). Although Jim Crow laws continued to dominate the lives of black southerners, many of their brothers had escaped to other regions of the country, had learned to live in cities, and were working in industrial occupations. These migrants were still subjected to many types of informal, extralegal discrimination. Nevertheless, northern blacks enjoyed a greater degree of formal and legal equality, and this legal advantage afforded a basis from which to launch an energetic, if painfully slow, judicial and legislative offensive against all forms of discrimination affecting blacks and—by extension—all other minority groups in America. This offensive, generally referred to as the Civil Rights Movement, may be dated from the period in which Jim Crowism was becoming established in America.

The Civil Rights Movement

The Supreme Court's decision in *Plessy* v. *Ferguson* marks the point at which black people in the South officially had lost the battle to retain most of the advantages won in the Civil War. As we have noted, however, the decision in *Plessy* was not only a signal to the South that it might go ahead on a state-by-state basis to reduce blacks to the position of second-class citizens; it also was a ratification of many changes that already had occurred in the relations between the races. The level of white violence against blacks had risen sharply, the doctrine of innate black inferiority was gaining in strength (as discussed in chapter 3), and many blacks feared that to continue open resistance to white supremacy was foolhardy. Even before *Plessy* made it official, therefore, black people already had been forced into an inferior status, and some black leaders had concluded the wisest course of action was to accept the fact that whites were not going to permit black equality, at least not in the short run. A better course of action, many believed, was to declare publicly the willingness of blacks to stay in their place, to attempt to "measure up" to white standards, and perhaps thereby to "win" white approval and acceptance.

The most influential statement of the view that blacks should accept a new accommodation with whites on the white's terms was voiced by the black leader Booker T. Washington. Washington, the founder and principal of Tuskegee Institute, voiced his opinion on this subject in a speech at the Atlanta exposition of 1895. Washington's famous "Atlanta Compromise" was carefully designed to assure white people that blacks were ready to accept their inferior status in the political arena. He stated: "In all things that are purely social, we can be as separate as the fingers yet one as the hand in all things essential to mutual progress" (Washington, 1959:156). He argued further that blacks were still too recently removed from slavery to take their place as equals among the whites. He emphasized that blacks must adopt an economic program of manual labor and self-help as the best means to win their full rights as citizens rather than engaging in political action. They must be content, he thought, with the gradual achievement of recognition. The Atlanta speech implied that the "deficiencies" of black people, rather than the discrimination of whites, was responsible for the generally deplorable conditions among blacks. Washington advocated agricultural and industrial training rather than higher education for blacks. Needless to say, these views were very flattering to the whites and were immediately praised by them. It has been reported that many of the white people who heard Washington's speech leaped to their feet in a standing ovation, while many blacks in the audience sat silently weeping. Washington became a celebrity almost overnight. Until his death twenty years later, he was the most influential and powerful spokesman for black America. His views on race relations were central to the so-called Tuskeegee point of view, which stressed appeasement of the whites, segregation, and the importance of self-help.

Washington's approach to the race question was widely accepted among blacks as well as whites. But its acceptance was not universal. For example, in 1902, Monroe Trotter (1971:35) attacked Washington as a "Benedict Arnold of the Negro race." In 1903, W. E. B. DuBois established himself as Washington's leading critic. DuBois, the holder of a Ph.D. degree from Harvard University, called Washington's teachings propaganda that was helping to speed the construction of a racial caste system. In 1905, a small group of black "radicals" under the leadership of DuBois formed the Niagara Movement to express opposition to Washington's program. They disagreed with him emphatically on many major issues. Their "Declaration of Principles" stated that black people should protest the curtailment of their political and civil rights. They pointed out that the denial of opportunities to blacks in the South amounted to "virtual slavery." And they proclaimed their refusal to accept the impression left by Washington and his followers "that the Negro American assents to inferiority, is submissive under oppression, and apologetic before insults." In contrast to Washington's strategy of submission, the members of the Niagara Movement insisted that agitation and complaint is the best way for blacks to escape the "barbarian" practices of discrimination based on race (Meier, Rudwick, and Broderick, 1971:58–62).

Given the time at which it was made, the Niagara declaration seemed very "radical." Jim Crowism was reaching full fruition. In the minds of most people, blacks as well as whites, the segregation of the races in the South would remain the "solution" to the race problem until the blacks were able to "live up" to white standards and "earn" gradual acceptance as equals. It should be observed, though, that for all their differences the Washington "conservatives" and the DuBois "radicals" agreed that blacks should strive to establish economic independence; that they should join together to attempt to solve their problems; and that the ultimate goal of any strategy should be the full acceptance of black Americans as first-class citizens of the United States (Meier, Rudwick, and Broderick, 1971:xxvi, xxvii). They disagreed sharply on whether the proper means to the attainment of their ends should be humility, subservience, and patience or an aggressive, indignant demand for the immediate recognition of their rights.

The Niagara group was not large or immediately very influential. But their declaration revealed dramatically that not all blacks accepted Washington's policy of submission. More important, however, is that, in 1909, most of the Niagara group's members merged with a group of white liberals to form the National Association for the Advancement of Colored People (NAACP). The NAACP was, in the words of a later report, "the spiritual descendant of the Abolitionist Movement" (Meier, Rudwick, and Broderick, 1971:178). The leaders of the NAACP opposed "the ever-growing oppression," "the systematic persecution," and the disfranchisement of black people. They demanded that everyone, including blacks, be given free public schooling that would focus on professional education for the most gifted—what DuBois had earlier called "the talented tenth"—as well as industrial training for all who wished it. However, this goal could not be achieved unless blacks received equal treatment under the law. Consequently, the NAACP adopted a legal and legislative strategy. It called on Congress and the executive to enforce strictly the Constitution's provisions on civil rights and the right to vote, and it urged that educational expenditures for black children be made equal to those for whites (Meier, Rudwick, and Broderick, 1971:65–66).[12]

The NAACP soon began to make its presence felt. As editor of the organization's official magazine, *The Crisis,* DuBois was able to place his ideas before a large audience; in 1915, the organization's legal efforts assisted to bring about a Supreme Court decision declaring the "grandfather clause" unconstitutional. After Booker T. Washington died later in that same year, the NAACP became the leading organization devoted to the civil rights of black Americans.

The acceptance of the NAACP by blacks, however, was never total. At the very time of its inception, in fact, certain events were forcing many blacks to conclude that no amount of legal action could guarantee them first-class citizenship. Although the recent black migrants to the cities were finding many new lines of work and receiving better pay than ever before, they soon discovered that the cities—even the northern cities—were not the promised land. In the North, there was competition between the races for jobs, housing, and the use of public recreational facilities. In the South, the blacks were hemmed in on every side by Jim Crow restrictions. As a result of these conditions, many cities became powderkegs of racial resentment and unrest.

Three types of interracial violence were prominent during this period. Lynchings, especially of blacks by whites, were a source of great concern. Although the actual number of lynchings was somewhat lower between 1910 and 1920 than in the two previous decades, the circumstances under which they occurred and the publicity they received led to more open and angry denunciations by black spokesmen than in the past. Many lynchings were conducted in an especially sadistic way and in a carnival atmosphere. Some victims were tortured and burned; some newspapers issued invitations to whites to come to witness a lynching or a burning; and some militant black leaders advocated armed resistance as a solution to these problems (Meier, Rudwick, and Broderick, 1971:96–98).

Another main form of violence during these years consisted of mob attacks by whites on the property of black people and on the people themselves. This type of violence was most common in the cities of the South. For the most part, in these outbreaks, blacks were unorganized and defenseless. They tended to remain fairly passive in the face of the white attacks. The situation was different in the North, however. In several outbreaks in the northern cities, the blacks organized and retaliated against the whites. These latter conflicts were of the type usually described as race "riots."

The summer following the end of World War I was filled with such a large number of mob attacks by whites and by race riots that James Weldon Johnson (1971:304), head of the NAACP, referred to it as "the Red Summer." Approximately two dozen outbreaks occurred in American cities in the summer of 1919. Fourteen blacks were publicly burned, eleven of them alive (Lincoln, 1961:56).

Two other points were of special significance at this time. First, the rise of white nativist sentiment was expressed in a revival of the Ku Klux Klan after a "slumber of half a century" (Osofsky, 1968:314). Second, all of these things—lynchings, burnings, mob attacks by whites, race riots, and the Klan revival—had occurred during or immediately following a great war "to make the world safe for democracy." Between 350,000 and 400,000 black Americans had served during World War I. The inconsistency between the nation's lofty international ideals and the actual conditions at home was not lost on many blacks.

All of these elements combined following the war to give a large number of blacks a new sense of their racial identity, and this new awareness was accompanied by an upsurge in expressions of black pride. This "Black Renaissance" was visibly furthered by a group of writers and artists located in Harlem. At the same time, many blacks were more convinced than ever before that the prospects of black people in America were very poor. Under these conditions, the legalistic approach of the NAACP did not seem sufficiently direct or vigorous to many blacks. The situation seemed to call for statements, plans, and actions that would effectively express the deeply felt anger of the black community and mobilize the community's efforts in relation to a common goal. In the minds of hundreds of thousands of black Americans, the program offered by a new leader, Marcus Garvey, seemed the answer to a prayer.

Garvey, a dark-skinned man, was born in Jamaica in 1887. He came to the United States during World War I and organized the Universal Negro Improvement Association (UNIA). The association's major long-range goal was to enable black Americans to leave the United States and settle in an independent nation in Africa. As Baker (1970:8) has said, "Garvey's UNIA was an effort to have Black Americans vote with their feet."

Somewhat ironically, Garvey's colonization program had been inspired by a reading of the "conservative" Booker T. Washington's *Up From Slavery*. Garvey admired Washington's emphasis on racial separation and self-help.

His ideas concerning the eventual solution of America's racial problem, though, were radically different from Washington's. While Washington saw separation as a tool to be used to gain eventual acceptance by white Americans, Garvey visualized the renunciation of American citizenship and the permanent separation of the two races.

The idea of recolonization, of course, was not at all new. But Garvey's "back to Africa" movement represented the first time a black man had attempted to organize such a venture. Moreover, the effort came at a time when large masses of black Americans were congregated in urban ghettos and were ready to listen. Garvey (1970:25) lashed out at most black leaders for "aping white people" and for exhibiting "the slave spirit of dependence." These so-called leaders, he said, were "Uncle Toms" who could not be trusted. He argued that the time had come for blacks to be self-reliant, to have a country of their own in Africa. The purpose of the UNIA was to inspire "an unfortunate race with pride in self and with the determination" to take its place as an equal among races (Garvey, 1968a:295).

The philosophy of independence preached by Garvey fired the imagination of black people not only in America but throughout the world. In America, his message appealed mainly to the lower-class, urban masses. Middle-class or professional and business people were offended by his attacks on them and their acceptance of white standards. They were offended, too, by his contempt for those, like DuBois, who were of mixed ancestry and had light-colored skin. Garvey's heroes were men like Denmark Vesey, Gabriel Prosser, and Nat Turner.

In August 1920, the First International Convention of the UNIA met in New York. Twenty-five thousand delegates from all over the world—including an African Prince and several tribal chiefs—gathered to hear Garvey's opening address (Cronon, 1968:64). The convention drafted a "Declaration of Rights of the Negro Peoples of the World," containing twelve major complaints and fifty-four demands (Garvey, 1968b:296–302). The declaration protested lynchings, burnings, Jim Crow laws and practices, inferior schools, exclusion from labor unions, exclusion from elective offices, discrimination in wages, unfair treatment in the courts, and so on. Among the demands cited in the declaration were the insistence that blacks be given the right to be governed by people of their own race and the right to repossess Africa. The convention elected Garvey as the provisional president of the African republic. It also declared the colors red (for the blood shed by black people), black (to symbolize their racial pride), and green (for the fresh hope of a new life) to be the colors of the black race. Finally, they adopted an international anthem (Cronon, 1968:67–68).

Under Garvey's leadership, the UNIA established a number of black-run business enterprises, including the Black Star Steamship Line. This line was intended to link black people throughout the world and to provide the transportation they would need to return "home." The UNIA also established the Universal African Legion, the Black Eagle Flying Corps, the Universal

Black Cross Nurses, and some other organizations designed to promote self-reliance and black pride. These organizations—with their members dressed in smart uniforms—dramatized Garvey's ideas and attracted widespread attention and admiration.

Garvey's tactics also earned him the enmity of most other influential black leaders in America and of various governments at home and abroad. For example, the U.S. Department of Justice and a committee representing the state of New York attempted to prove that Garvey was a radical agitator and a threat to the government. The governments of Britain and France attempted to force the Republic of Liberia in Africa to cancel its plans to permit the UNIA to send colonists there.

Garvey's numerous enemies slowly closed in on him. Both the NAACP, which by comparison seemed "conservative," and the socialists, under A. Philip Randolph, agreed that Garvey must be stopped. They were assisted in their efforts by Garvey's own shortcomings as an administrator. In 1922, Garvey's black opponents assisted in having him indicted for mail fraud; in 1923, he was convicted and imprisoned in the federal penitentiary in Atlanta. Although his sentence was commuted in 1927, he was deported to Jamaica as an undesirable alien. After his deportation, the UNIA no longer had an inspiring leader, and the influence of the largest mass movement among black Americans to that date waned. The scandal and suspicion created by the trial, imprisonment, and deportation of Garvey discredited the idea of recolonization for some time to come and led to a rapid decline of the UNIA. The organization did not disappear entirely, though, and its nationalistic message has had an enduring influence among black Americans.

Two direct descendants of the UNIA have been very prominent. The first of these—the Lost Nation of Islam—came into existence less than five years after Garvey's deportation. The second—to which we turn later—did not arise until the mid-1960s.

The Lost Nation of Islam (or Black Muslim) group was launched by two inspiring leaders. The first of these, W. D. Fard, was a man of mystery. Little is known about him. He appeared in the black community of Detroit in 1930 and then mysteriously disappeared just four years later. His primary doctrine was that the white race was the devil on earth; that black Americans were the lost tribe of Shebazz; and that the salvation of blacks lay not in the white man's religion, Christianity, but in the black's true religion, Mohammedanism (Lincoln, 1961:72–80). Fard founded the Temple of Islam and assembled a devoted following. Chief among his disciples was Elijah Poole, who became known as Elijah Muhammad. After Fard's sudden disappearance in 1934, Elijah Muhammad assumed the leadership of the movement and took the title "Messenger of Allah" (Lincoln, 1961:15–16).

The teachings of Elijah Muhammad, like those of Marcus Garvey, advocated race pride, self-help, and the separation of the races. However, his views differed from Garvey's in at least two important respects. First, although Garvey stated that Jesus had been black and that black people should renounce Christianity and its white symbolism, religion had been secondary to politics in the UNIA. Among the Black Muslims, however, religion has been the dominant element. They have developed an extremely demanding moral code that is quite puritanical. It forbids the use of tobacco or drugs. It also forbids extramarital sexual relations, racial intermarriage, dancing, attendance at movies, participation in sports, laziness, lying, and a host of other things.

Second, the political goals of the Black Muslim movement also differ from those of the UNIA. Garvey's main goals were to return black people to Africa and Africa to black people. Elijah Muhammad, however, was neither so explicit about his political objectives nor so determined to leave the United States. The Muslims have called at various times for a separate nation right here in the United States and have suggested that several states should be set aside for this purpose.

The most important difference between the Garvey movement and the Black Muslim movement, however, is that the latter has gradually gained in strength and influence over the years. The number of people who are officially members of the Black Muslim organization is unknown, though it may not exceed 200,000, but the effect of the movement extends far beyond its membership. Certainly, the teachings of Elijah Muhammad and his famous convert Malcolm X have been widely circulated within the United States and overseas. Many people who do not belong to the Muslim church or subscribe to all of its teachings nevertheless have developed respect for the Muslims' high standards and strict discipline. They have developed respect, too, for the effects the standards and discipline have had on the lives of their members. The Muslims have been notably successful in the rehabilitation of ex-convicts and drug addicts, and they have been successful in their efforts to build a strong economic base. The strict moral code and philosophy of economic independence have had an especially powerful appeal to the many helpless and victimized black people who reside in the urban ghettos of America. It has played a significant role in "revitalizing" the lives of many people who previously had given up in the face of seemingly overwhelming difficulties.

The importance of the Black Muslim movement cannot be measured solely in terms of its official size. After the collapse of the Garvey movement, it served as a valuable repository of black separatist philosophy and as a continuing reminder to black Americans that there was a genuine alternative to the goal of "integration." Nevertheless, Garvey's imprisonment and deportation effectively halted large-scale nationalistic activities among blacks for over three decades.

The NAACP, of course, had maintained its legal warfare against discrimination throughout the period under discussion. But with the onset of the Great Depression in 1929, the association was increasingly criticized for its relative inactivity in economic matters. The Depression struck hard at all American workers, to be sure, but its effects on black workers were particularly devastating. They had been systematically excluded from most units of the leading labor organization, the American Federation of Labor (AFL). And, as usual, they were "the last hired and the first fired."

These circumstances led to some significant developments in the strategy and tactics of black Americans. We have noted already, for example, the rise of the Black Muslims. By the mid-thirties, the NAACP felt compelled to announce some changes in its economic policies. Also, during this time of economic catastrophe, the Socialist and Communist parties were actively trying to recruit blacks into their ranks, though with little success. Of special interest, though, was the organization of a number of new protest groups whose main objective was more and better jobs for black people. These organizations were part of a widespread effort to persuade black Americans to use their substantial economic power as a lever to improve conditions. The common slogan of these organizations, "Don't Buy Where You Can't Work," emphasized that their primary weapon was the economic boycott. The boycott was supplemented by another of organized labor's standard weapons, the picket line.

One of the new organizations to employ this direct-action approach was the New Negro Alliance, Inc. The alliance grew out of a spontaneous protest occurring at a hamburger grill in Washington, D.C. (Bunche, 1940:122). This grill was located in a black residential area and depended entirely on black customers. Early in 1933, the black workers at the grill were fired, and white workers were hired to replace them. Several onlookers were outraged by this act of blatant discrimination and formed a picket line at the grill. This tactic quickly led to the reinstatement of the black workers and to the establishment of the alliance. This form of protest was so successful that many other groups, including the NAACP, adopted it. The NAACP's new willingness to address the economic problems of black people, however, continued to be a secondary aspect of its program. Its legal approach was still primary. Increasingly, the NAACP's main efforts focused on the issue of school segregation.

The beginning of World War II signaled the close of the Great Depression. The demand for labor rapidly increased as armament production rose. The boom spread to construction, service industries, transportation, and other sectors of the economy, but the sudden increase in the demand for labor served mainly to put the huge force of unemployed whites back to work. Before the United States entered the war, blacks were practically excluded from government-funded war production. The main jobs that opened up for blacks were as service workers and farm laborers (Myrdal, 1964: 409–412).

The continuation of conspicuous discrimination in the midst of still another global war "to make the world safe for democracy" enraged many black Americans. Two forms of discrimination were particularly galling, discrimination in war production and in the armed forces. Both of these areas involved federal dollars and, therefore, seemed to represent national policy. One leader, A. Philip Randolph, established, in 1942, the March on Washington Movement, which sought to organize millions of black people "so that they may be summoned to action over night and thrown into physical motion." He argued that "mass power" used in an orderly and lawful way was "the most effective weapon a minority people can wield" (Randolph, 1971a:230). Although the United States still had not entered the war at the time Randolph issued his first call to march, President Roosevelt was eager to prevent any large demonstration of unrest. In June 1941, the president issued an executive order (No. 8802) prohibiting racial discrimination in defense industries, in government, and in defense training programs. The order also established a Fair Employment Practices Committee (FEPC) to investigate possible violations of the order.

The principle of nonviolent direct action had a broad appeal. Some leaders, however, felt that the March on Washington Movement's application of the principle left much to be desired. Specifically, they objected to the exclusion of whites from participation in the movement and to the absence of a program to prevent mass protest from becoming violent. Consequently, still another new protest organization, the Congress of Racial Equality (CORE), was formed to further the use of nonviolent direct action. CORE leaders were afraid that many embittered black Americans were ready to employ violence in a desperate attempt to force the dominant group to grant them civil and social equality. Bayard Rustin observed, in 1942, that some blacks had concluded it would be better to die to gain victory at home than to die on a foreign battlefield in defense of white Americans. He also reported that many blacks even hoped for a Japanese victory "since it don't matter who you're a slave for" (Rustin, 1971:236).

CORE's philosophy represented an attempt to apply the methods of Jesus and Gandhi to the race situation in America. It rested on the conviction that social conflicts cannot really be solved by violent methods, that violence simply breeds more violence, and that "turning the other cheek" has the power to shame the evildoer. This approach was later adopted and refined by Martin Luther King, Jr.

The practical expression of these beliefs involved a carefully graduated set of steps. In a conflict situation, the first step was patient negotiation. If this effort failed, the next step was to attempt to arouse public opinion against the opponent's discriminatory actions. Only after these remedies were exhausted did CORE advocate the use of boycotts, picket lines, and strikes.

In addition to patient negotiations, agitation, and the use of labor's protest methods, however, CORE developed a new technique of nonviolent direct action. The technique's first use appears to have occurred in 1942 following an incident of discrimination in a café against two CORE leaders, James R. Robinson and James Farmer. After nearly a month of negotiation, including several attempts to talk with the restaurant's managers by telephone and in person, the CORE leaders sent the last of several letters to the café's management saying that unless the management agreed to talk with them, they would be forced to take some other course of action. More than a week later, an interracial group of twenty-five people entered the restaurant and took seats. The white people among the group were served promptly, but the black people were not served at all. However, the white people did not eat. Instead, they told the manager that they did not wish to eat until their black friends also had been served. The manager angrily refused, so the group simply continued to occupy a large number of the restaurant's seats. When customers who were waiting to be served saw they would be unable to be seated, they left. After a period of fuming, the manager had all of the protesters served. Thus ended successfully the first "sit-in," a technique of protest that became increasingly popular during the next two decades (Farmer, 1971:243–246).

The protest tactics of organizations such as the March on Washington movement and CORE were only a part of the complicated interracial situation that existed in the United States during World War II. We have seen previously that the tense early years of the war were marked by numerous open confrontations and violence between ethnic groups. Chicano "zoot suiters," it will be recalled, had been attacked in Los Angeles and some other American cities; Chicanos in the armed forces had been discriminated against both inside and outside of the service. We have seen, too, that intense anti-Japanese sentiments supported the fateful evacuation and illegal internment of the Japanese from the West Coast. During this period, various forms of violence involving blacks and whites also erupted. Confrontations reminiscent of the "Red Summer" of 1919 occurred in Mobile, Alabama, in Beaumont and El Paso, Texas, in Philadelphia, Pennsylvania, and in Newark, New Jersey. The largest outburst took place in June 1943 in Detroit, Michigan. Racial tensions in Detroit had been building over a long period of time as both white and black southerners moved there to work in the automobile industry. According to one account, 25 blacks and 9 whites were killed, and over 700 other people were injured (Osofsky, 1968:420).

These confrontations and the memory of the interracial violence following World War I raised fears that a similar bloody period might follow World War II. Two prominent forces acted to reduce the likelihood of violence. The first of these was the decline of European colonialism. The Allies in World War II had fought not only against fascism but also, officially, against the doctrine of white supremacy as well. During the course of the war, large numbers of nonwhite peoples in the United States, including Chicanos, Japanese Americans, Indian Americans, Chinese Americans, and black Americans, became more aware of their kinship to the nonwhite peoples of the entire world. They also had become aware that many of these colored and oppressed peoples, like themselves, were fighting and dying to save the very nations that had been historically the main representatives of the white-supremacy theory. Certainly, the experiences of many men and women in uniform emphasized the disparity between the official principles of the United States and the actual practices within it. The way the military services were organized supplied daily examples of the discrepancy. Throughout the military services, Jim Crow practices were common. And since many military training camps were in the South, black servicemen faced segregation when they left the camps. They were frequently in danger of physical assault not only by local citizens but by officers of the law as well. For instance, a black soldier was shot in Little Rock, Arkansas, because he would not tip his hat and say "sir" to a policeman. Another black soldier was shot by two police officers because he had taken a bus seat reserved for a white in Beaumont, Texas (Rustin, 1971:235). In Centerville, Mississippi, a sheriff obligingly shot a black soldier in the chest merely because a white MP asked him to (Milner, 1968:419).

As the old colonial empires were dissolved following the war, and as new independent nations arose in their place, incidents such as those described above became increasingly embarrassing to American leaders. How could the United States explain to the peoples of other nations the discrepancy between its ringing declarations of human rights and the treatment of its own minority groups at home?

The external pressures on the American government were accompanied by a series of important changes in its official domestic policies. The patient legal work of the NAACP and the direct-action methods of the March on Washington Movement and CORE had begun to show some dramatic results. For example, in 1948, as President Truman and Congress considered the advisability of instituting a peacetime military draft, the leader of the March on Washington movement, A. Philip Randolph, took a strong stand against segregation in the armed forces. Randolph stated that unless the military services were desegregated, he would lead a nationwide campaign to encourage young people to disobey the law. He stated further, "I personally will advise Negroes to refuse to fight as slaves for a democracy they cannot possess and cannot enjoy" (Randolph, 1971b:278). Later that year, President Truman acted to end all segregation in the armed forces of the United States. (See Osofsky, 1968:465.)

The NAACP's battle to end segregation in public education had gradually gained strength through an impressive series of court victories. As early as 1938, the Supreme Court ruled that the State University of Missouri was required to admit a black applicant to its law school. Similar rulings were handed down in cases affecting the law school of the University of Oklahoma (1948), the law school of the University of Texas (1950), and the graduate school of the University of Oklahoma (1950). These rulings led to an all-out effort by the officials of segregated school systems to improve the facilities for black students and, if possible, to make them physically equal to those for whites. These victories also laid the groundwork in 1954 for one of the most important court cases in the history of the United States: *Brown* v. *Board of Education of Topeka*.

The *Brown* case differed from the other cases just mentioned in a very important respect. The earlier cases had not called into question the "separate but equal doctrine" approved in the court's *Plessy* decision in 1896.

Now, however, the court brought this doctrine directly under review. The question of central importance was this: even if the separate educational facilities for the minority group are equal in buildings, libraries, teacher qualifications, and the like, do these "equal" facilities provide educationally equal opportunities? The court ruled that they do not. Chief Justice Warren, speaking for the court, argued that to separate children

> from others of similar age and qualifications solely because of their race generates a feeling of inferiority as to their status in the community that may affect their hearts and minds in a way unlikely ever to be undone. . . . We conclude that in the field of public education the doctrine of "separate but equal" has no place. Separate educational facilities are inherently unequal (Clark, 1963:159).

Segregation in public schools was unanimously held to violate the "equal protection" clause of the Fourteenth Amendment and was, therefore, declared unconstitutional. In a separate ruling on the same day, the court also declared segregated schools to be a violation of the "due process" clause of the Fifth Amendment.

In its *Brown* ruling in May 1954, the Supreme Court recognized the difficulties that would be encountered in the effort to desegregate public schools. Consequently, the court issued a second *Brown* decision in 1955 on the question of *how* the transition from segregation to desegregation was to be achieved. The court emphasized that variations in local conditions had to be taken into account in planning for the change and that the primary responsibility for the implementation of the 1954 ruling rested with local authorities and the lower courts. The court insisted, however, that local school systems must "make a prompt and reasonable start toward full compliance" with its decision and racial discrimination in school admissions must be halted "with all deliberate speed" (Tussman, 1963:45–46).

The *Brown* rulings ushered in a new era of hope among blacks and of heightened resistance to "integration" among whites. White citizens councils, described by some blacks as "the Klan in gray flannel suits" (Osofsky, 1968: 479), were formed throughout the South to find ways to prevent school desegregation. The KKK itself underwent another revival. All of the old charges of the white supremacists were again brought forward. And many southern politicians searched frantically for the legal grounds needed to overturn the court's school desegregation decisions. Although school desegregation was initiated promptly and successfully in many southern communities, the general intensity of white reactions to desegregation efforts began to make clear to black Americans that change "with all deliberate speed" might, in fact, be very slow. The growing pessimism among blacks was fueled by numerous incidents of intimidation and violence throughout the South.

An important episode in the struggle to desegregate the schools occurred in Little Rock, Arkansas, during the 1957–1958 school year. The Little

Rock school board had gone to work on a school desegregation plan in 1954 almost immediately after the first *Brown* decision. While the board was developing its plan, the state officials of Arkansas were attempting to "nullify" the *Brown* decisions. The central feature of the Arkansas nullification plan was an amendment to the state constitution declaring the *Brown* decisions to be unconstitutional. Despite the state of Arkansas' stand, the school officials of Little Rock moved ahead to desegregate. Nine black school children were selected to attend Central High School beginning in September 1957. On the day before school opened, the governor of Arkansas, without notifying the school officials, assigned units of the Arkansas National Guard to Central High School and declared the school "off limits" to black children. When the nine black students attempted to enter school the next day, the national guardsmen, on the governor's orders, prevented them from entering. Each day for the next three weeks, this performance was repeated. At the end of this time, President Eisenhower sent regular federal troops to Central High, and the students at last were admitted. Federal troops remained at the school for the rest of the school year, a year filled with tension and disturbances. The threat to law and order was so serious that by the end of the year the school board begged the courts to permit them to discontinue their plan.

These events raised some very serious questions. Could a state nullify a Supreme Court decision? Who was responsible for the chaos surrounding the effort to desegregate Central High? Should a desegregation effort be discontinued or delayed if it threatens to lead to racial conflict? The court's rulings on these questions were unanimous. No state can nullify a decision of the court. The state of Arkansas, therefore, acted unconstitutionally in preventing black children from attending Central High. Moreover, the actions of the governor and other officials of the state of Arkansas had been, in the court's view, largely responsible for all of the turmoil surrounding the desegregation effort. The governor's actions had increased opposition to the desegregation plan and encouraged people to oppose it. Finally, the court refused to accept the idea that desegregation attempts should be carried out only if no violence or disorder were threatened. The importance of public peace was recognized, of course, but black children's rights to an equal education were not to be sacrificed in the name of law and order.

Despite the court's unwavering stand on the correctness of its *Brown* decisions, it could not arrest the declining faith of many black people in the law's unaided power to bring about a swift end to the many forms of racial discrimination they faced (of which school segregation was only one). Of particular importance was a sharp increase in unemployment among blacks. The serious, visible decline in their economic circumstances at the very time when their complete legal liberation seemed to be at hand produced renewed bitterness.

Something more specific, however, served to precipitate a new phase in the effort to assure the civil rights of black Americans. On December 1, 1955, in Montgomery, Alabama, Mrs. Rosa Parks refused to yield her bus seat to a white person and was arrested. As the news of Mrs. Parks' arrest spread, black people in the city began to call for a boycott of the local buses. In less than a week, nearly all of the more than 40,000 black citizens of Montgomery had rallied around a dynamic new leader, Martin Luther King, Jr., in a massive boycott of the buses. At first, the boycott was intended to last only one day, but various incidents of harassment and intimidation by whites led to a decision to continue the boycott indefinitely. This decision was followed by further, more violent, acts of intimidation. For instance, on January 30, 1956, King's home was bombed; two days later, the home of another protest leader, E. D. Nixon, also was bombed. On February 22, twenty-four black ministers and fifty-five others were arrested for nonviolent protesting (King, 1971a:297).

The confrontation between blacks and whites over segregation in Montgomery ended in the desegregation of the buses more than a year later. During that time, the bus boycott became a symbol of nonviolent resistance throughout the South and the entire world. Martin Luther King, Jr., became the leading spokesman for the philosophy of nonviolent protest and the most prominent figure in what rapidly became a new phase of the relations between whites and blacks in America. The events in Montgomery and Little Rock contributed to a growing conviction among black Americans that, in King's (1968:523) words, "Privileged groups rarely give up their privileges without strong resistance." To promote the philosophy and practices of nonviolent protest, King founded the Southern Christian Leadership Conference (SCLC) in January 1957.

The decade following the Montgomery bus boycott was filled with many new and dramatic developments in American race relations. Although the legal approach continued to play an indispensable role, direct action became a far more popular tactic, especially among young people. A sit-in by college students at a Woolworth store lunch counter in Greensboro, North Carolina, in February 1960, set off a veritable chain reaction of student sit-ins throughout the South and of white reactions to them. These events led rapidly to the formation of yet another organization devoted to nonviolent direct action, the Student Nonviolent Coordinating Committee (SNCC). Although the members of the new organization accepted the philosophy of nonviolence espoused by CORE and SCLC and were clearly inspired by Martin Luther King, Jr., they believed their goals could not be pursued vigorously enough within any of the existing organizations. The many lines of cleavage within the black community became prominent once again, though in a more complicated way than ever before. The older organizations, such as the once "radical" NAACP, were now regarded by many as "too conservative." Simultaneously, however, the older organizations were endorsing and adopting the "radical" tactics of direct action. Amidst charges of excessive "conservatism" and "radicalism," nearly all of the main black protest groups adopted some combination of legal and direct-action methods. In this process, the entire Civil Rights Movement became more militant. It also became increasingly critical of white liberals, who seemed too quick to counsel delay and patience in the face of injustice. The battle cry "Freedom Now!" gradually gained acceptance even among many black "conservatives." The NAACP, for example, sponsored many demonstrations during this period, and CORE pioneered still another new protest tactic by conducting an interracial "Freedom Ride" on a bus headed for New Orleans. Here, for the first time, white people joined in the protest. This ride ended when the bus was fire bombed in Alabama, but many others were to follow (Burns, 1963:55). The representatives of the different protest organizations found that whatever their legal rights were supposed to be, sit-ins, kneel-ins, lie-ins, boycotts, picket lines, and freedom rides might each be met by mob violence, tear gas, police dogs, arrests, jail terms, and, in some cases, by death.

The tempo of direct action increased during the spring of 1963. The number of demonstrations in the South reached a new high, and the non-violent technique was frequently used in the North as well. Two events of 1963 merit special attention.

The first of these took place in Birmingham, Alabama. Birmingham at this time was a symbol of southern white resistance to desegregation; its commissioner of Public Safety, Eugene "Bull" Connor, was an open and committed opponent of any form of interracial compromise. In this setting, black people still lived in almost total segregation, and the safety of their property and persons was uncertain. In the spring of 1963, a coalition of black leaders, under the direction of Martin Luther King, Jr., decided to join in and expand an ongoing nonviolent protest campaign in Birmingham. The protests began mildly early in April 1963, with well-organized demonstrators going to jail for conducting sit-ins at lunch counters (King, 1964:60). But before the protest campaign ended over a month later, thousands of demonstrators had been jailed and physically assaulted by police. On April 12, Good Friday, two of the protest leaders—King and Abernathy—were placed in jail, where they remained for eight days. After their release, the tempo of protest increased. Hundreds of young people were recruited and trained in nonviolent protest methods. On May 2, more than a thousand of them went to jail (King, 1964:99). Bull Connor and his police met the next day's marchers with clubs, high-pressure water hoses, cattle prods, and police dogs. The spectacle of unarmed, unresisting men, women, and children aroused enormous national and international sympathy and support. One week later, a formal truce was reached with a committee of Birmingham's business leaders. It was agreed, among other things, that lunch counters, rest rooms, and so on would be desegregated and that immediate efforts would commence to improve the employment opportunities of Negroes. The Birmingham protests had demonstrated dramatically that, in King's (1964:46) words, "the theory of nonviolent direct action was a fact."

The second event was the huge (approximately 250,000 people) March on Washington. Reviving the technique he had pioneered during the early years of World War II, A. Philip Randolph called for a massive protest march on the nation's capital to dramatize the problem of unemployment. The march, in August 1963, captured the attention of the entire country. For millions of people, Martin Luther King's famous "I Have a Dream" speech encapsulated the aspirations of the Civil Rights Movement. The march showed that the movement was beginning to look beyond direct-action protest toward a new focus on political action, beyond civil rights to a heightened concern for economic opportunity, and beyond appeals to the conscience of white people to a demand for equality.

The effects of the direct-action protests between 1956 and 1964 were mixed. In most states of the South, nonviolent direct action had achieved rapid changes in desegregating restaurants, theaters, buses, hotels, and so on. Even the old etiquette of race relations was crumbling. Black men and women increasingly could expect to be addressed by titles of respect and to be served courteously. The protests had been far less successful, however, in states such as Alabama and Mississippi. They were less successful, too, in bringing about changes in segregated schooling, poor housing, and discrimination in law enforcement in both the North and the South. Moreover, throughout 1964, instances of white violence against demonstrators increased. This escalation of violence by whites (especially when it involved white policemen) led to a gradual weakening of the allegiance of many blacks to the philosophy of nonviolent resistance. Increasingly, blacks fought back (National Advisory Commission, 1968:230–231). As these limitations of direct action became apparent, black leaders began to turn in different directions. The political pressure mounted by the March on Washington was increased through voter registration and "get out the vote" drives. With the strong support of President Johnson, President Kennedy's civil rights program was passed as the Civil Rights Act of 1964. This legislation prohibits discrimination in voting, public accommodations and facilities, schools, courts, and employment. However, official violations of the voting rights section of the law (Title I) occurred in the South soon after the law had been passed. Opposition to these violations was expressed in a nonviolent demonstration in Selma, Alabama, led by Martin Luther King, Jr. Shortly thereafter, Congress passed the Voting Rights Act of 1965. This new law suspends all literacy tests for voters and permits the federal government to station poll watchers in all of the states of the South (Osofsky, 1968:570–581).

In a formal sense, the major goals of the civil rights "revolution" had been reached. The legislation of 1964 and 1965 marked the end of official segregation in America. Yet something was clearly wrong. The laws had not, in fact, ended all forms of discrimination, and, like the direct-action demonstrations that preceded them, they had had little visible effect on conditions in the black ghettos of the cities. After a decade of notable victories, most of the black Americans' basic problems still remained. In addition to pervasive unemployment, underemployment, and poverty, the black ghetto was characterized by high "street" crime, poor health and sanitation, poor housing, inferior schools, poor city services, high divorce and separation rates, low access to "city hall," demeaning and inadequate welfare services, and high prices for inferior goods and services. What now was to be done? Should the Civil Rights Movement continue to rely mainly on nonviolent protest and the power of the ballot in the fight for equality? An answer from the past attained renewed popularity.

Black Power

We have mentioned that the *Brown* decisions encouraged most black Americans to believe the end of school segregation and other forms of inequality were near. We have seen, however, that these "rising expectations" were soon dampened by the strong evidence—as in Montgomery, Little Rock, and Birmingham—that many whites intended to resist the court's rulings in every way possible, including the use of violence. The primary reaction among blacks to the massive resistance of the whites, as noted above, was non-violent protest. This was not the only reaction among blacks, however. Not since the days of Marcus Garvey had so many black Americans appeared to be ready to listen to those who doubted the possibility or desirability of "integration" and who urged, instead, some form of separation. The organization that was best able to capitalize on this renewed interest in a separatist solution was the Lost Nation of Islam (the Black Muslims).

The Black Muslims, please recall, had been led since the mid-1930s by Elijah Muhammad. The Muslims had been hard at work during the intervening years but had not been able to attract many converts. However, during the late 1950s and early 1960s, the Muslims began to attract many more converts and a great deal of attention from the mass media of communication. A new and dynamic Muslim leader, Malcolm X, was a particularly effective advocate of the black nationalist philosophy.

Malcolm, who substituted "X" for the surname his grandparents had received from their slave master (Little), became the minister of the large Muslim temple in Harlem. Like his teacher, Elijah Muhammad, Malcolm X emphasized that black people must organize to regain their self-respect and to assert their collective power. Consequently, he and his followers sought some form of separation from white America. If the U.S. government would not pay the costs of sending blacks to Africa, then, Malcolm X argued, the United States should set aside some territory within its borders so black Americans could move away from the whites. Malcolm believed that such a separate territory should be given as payment for the long period during which black slaves worked without pay to help build America. Malcolm X also emphasized that he was not in favor of separation for its own sake but as the only way for black Americans to gain freedom, justice, and equality (Malcolm X, 1971b:390). He stated that integration was unacceptable only because freedom, justice, and equality could not be obtained in this way. Perhaps tokens of equality could be achieved through this method (e.g., "an integrated cup of coffee") but not true equality.

Malcolm X's view of the race problem took into account conditions throughout the world. He was very interested in Africa and believed strongly that black people throughout the world were interdependent and shared a similar destiny. In time, Malcolm and Elijah Muhammad came into conflict over various matters; in March 1964, Malcolm left the Black Muslim organization. He founded a rival group, the Organization of Afro-American Unity. This organization stressed the unity of all people of African descent throughout the Western Hemisphere and in Africa. Although all people of African descent were eligible for membership, its main purpose was to unify black America. The organization's charter emphasized the right of Afro-Americans to defend themselves against violence in any way necessary. Non-violent protest could succeed, Malcolm argued, only when the oppressors were basically moral, and in the United States, they are not (Malcolm X, 1971a).

Malcolm X was by no means the only black American who contended during the early 1960s that violence should be met with violence. As the violent reactions of whites to nonviolent protest became widespread, many blacks came to feel that violence was, in some cases, necessary. In addition to this "defensive" use of violence, however, some black Americans began to think in terms of attack. The most militant members of the group began to use the word "revolution" as more than a metaphor.

The clearest evidence of a shift among some blacks away from the acceptance of only "defensive" violence and toward the acceptance of "offensive" violence began to appear in 1964. For example, on July 16, an off-duty New York City police lieutenant intervened in a dispute between some black youths and a white man. When one of the youths attacked with a knife, the officer shot and killed him. Two days later, a rally called by CORE to protest the lynchings of civil rights workers in Mississippi led to a clash with police in which one person was killed. In the following days, police talked with mobs in the Harlem and Bedford-Stuyvesant areas of New York. The crowd attacked with Molotov cocktails, bricks, and bottles; the police responded with gunfire (National Advisory Commission, 1968:36).

The change in the mood of black Americans was unmistakable by the following summer. On a hot evening in August 1965, a California motorcycle patrol officer stopped a young black man for speeding near the Watts area of Los Angeles. After the driver failed a sobriety test, he was arrested. The officer radioed for assistance while a crowd of people began to gather. Within ten minutes, the crowd numbered more than 250 people. At this point, the prisoner's brother and mother arrived and began to struggle with the police. They, too, were arrested. By now, the crowd had more than tripled in size and had become very angry. As the police were leaving, they arrested a young woman whom they mistakenly believed had spat on them. This arrest angered the bystanders even more; and as the police left, the crowd threw stones at the police car (McCone, 1965:608).

Rumors concerning these arrests spread throughout the area. People were told the police had beaten the intoxicated driver, his family, and a pregnant woman. For several hours after the arrests, groups of black people stoned and overturned some passing automobiles, beat up some white motorists, and harassed the police (National Advisory Commission, 1968: 37).

Thursday, August 12, was fairly quiet. However, early in the evening, a large crowd gathered at the scene of the preceding evening's arrests. Three cars were overturned and set on fire. When firemen arrived, the crowd threw rocks. Also, snipers shot at them. Soon afterward, the rioters began burning stores and buildings owned by whites. Looting also began.

On Friday, August 13, the burning, looting, and sniping spread into the Watts area. During the afternoon, two city blocks on 103rd Street were burned out, while firemen were held off by sniper fire (McCone, 1965:615). Late in the afternoon, the governor of California ordered nearly 14,000 national guardsmen into the area to restore peace. Burning and looting spread into other parts of southeast Los Angeles, and the fighting between rioters, police, and guardsmen continued throughout Friday night and Saturday. Major fires and sporadic fighting continued throughout Sunday.

The Watts area rioting was the worst in America since the 1943 outbreak in Detroit. Thirty-four people were killed; over 1,000 were injured, 118 with gunshot wounds, and more than 600 buildings were damaged or totally destroyed. Estimates of the property damage ranged from 35 to over 40 million dollars. The pattern of burning and looting strongly suggested that the black rioters had intentionally focused their attacks on food, liquor, furniture, clothing, and department stores owned by white people.

The Watts area rioting sent shock waves throughout the nation. To many, perhaps most, white Americans, the violence seemed incomprehensible. After all, the preceding decade had been marked by momentous court decisions and legislative victories, and the Jim Crow system had been undermined by legal and nonviolent protest actions. Adding to the irony of the situation was the further fact that among the nation's black urban ghettos, Watts was a relatively attractive and pleasant place to live. The Watts explosion, coming when and where it did, intensified public discussion of the question "Why are black Americans rioting now, just when things are getting better?"

This fascinating question has given rise to several interesting theories of collective violence. One of the most popular ideas is that people become dissatisfied as they compare their present circumstances with some possible or anticipated future condition. Geschwender (1968) identifies three different theories based on this idea. The first (to which we have alluded) is called the rising-expectations hypothesis. According to this view, as conditions begin to improve, people begin to believe that real change is possible, and their hopes rise; however, since actual social changes may well occur more slowly than people desire or expect, they begin to perceive a gap between what they believe is possible and what actually exists. The presence of this ideal-real discrepancy produces discontent and is likely to generate collective action to speed change. The relative-deprivation hypothesis is closely related to the sequence just described. It differs, however, in specifying the way people determine whether change is occurring rapidly enough. Suppose, for instance, that black Americans during the early 1960s were experiencing rising hopes and that, in fact, social changes were proceeding so rapidly that the gap between hopes and reality was small. Discontent might still be generated, however, if blacks compared their progress not with some absolute objective but with the progress of whites. If the situation of whites was also improving at about the same rate as for blacks, then the gap between blacks and whites would not be narrowing. In this case, even though conditions were objectively improving for blacks, their subjective experience might be one of "no progress." Hence, in the face of real improvement, blacks might still feel relatively deprived.

The final theory of this type considered by Geschwender is called the rise-and-drop hypothesis. This view, proposed by Davies, strives to combine the insights of Marx and Engels, on the one hand, with those of de Tocqueville, on the other. The former writers argued (at least most often) that revolution should occur when people's life circumstances become so deplorable that they can't take it anymore. De Tocqueville, in contrast, proposes an early form of the rising-expectations view. Davies joins these ideas by suggesting that "revolutions are most likely to occur when a prolonged period of objective economic and social improvement is followed by a short period of sharp reversal" (quoted by Geschwender, 1968:7). When a period of improvement is followed by a sudden decline, even if the individual is still better off than previously, the expectations that were aroused during the former period now turn to frustration and anger. Such a state of mind may easily lead to violent outbursts.

Whatever the reason, the level of black protest increased during 1966. According to the National Advisory Commission (1968:40) forty-three major and "minor disorders and riots" occurred during that year, including a new outburst in Watts. Two of the major disorders, in Chicago and the Hough section of Cleveland, involved extensive looting, rock throwing, fire bombing, and shooting at the police. In each case, the disorders and riots were preceded by a history of dissatisfaction among blacks in regard to police practices, unemployment, inadequate housing, inadequate education, and many other things (National Advisory Commission, 1968:143–144), and they were usually precipitated by some seemingly minor incident, frequently involving the police. For example, in Chicago, the rioting commenced after police arrested a black youth who had illegally opened a fire hydrant in order to cool off with water.

Shortly after the Chicago violence had subsided, another event served to dramatize the heightened militance of many black Americans and their impatience with the rate of social change. The event was a speech delivered by Stokely Carmichael (1966), the chairman of SNCC, late in July. Like many black leaders before him, Carmichael urged black people to "get together," to organize in their own behalf. He rejected the idea that black

Americans could "get ahead" through individual ambition and hard work. What was needed, he said, was "Black Power." Carmichael argued that black people had to recognize that they were not the inferior beings whites had portrayed them to be. Black people are able to take care of their own business. Furthermore, as the Muslims have taught, black people must take pride in their black skins and physical features. They must learn that black is beautiful. The slogan "Black Power" was not completely new. Neither were the ideas of race pride and self-help suggested by it. However, the use of this phrase at this particular time took on special significance. The phrase was vague enough to encompass a wide range of perspectives. It symbolized the frustration of many integrationists as well as black nationalists. In the minds of many white people, though, the slogan was identified primarily with black revolutionaries and separatist organizations such as the Lowndes County Freedom Organization (the so-called Black Panther Party).

The increasing willingness of black Americans, especially the young adults, to demand an immediate end to racial inequalities and to back their demands with violence, if necessary, ushered in still another new phase in black-white relations. Just as the legal approach had been made secondary by the advent of widespread nonviolent protests, the use of violent methods now moved to the fore. As in the earlier shift, organizations, leaders, and methods that had at first seemed "radical" now seemed "conservative" by comparison. The level of violence was escalated again during the year 1967, with most of the disorders occurring in July. According to the National Advisory Commission (1968:112), there were between 51 and 217 disorders during the first nine months of the year, depending on one's definition of a "disorder." The commission focused on 164 disorders in 128 cities, 8 of which were judged to be "major" and 33 of which were judged to be "serious." The major disorders involved a combination of four factors: (1) many fires, looting, and reports of sniping; (2) more than two days of violence; (3) large crowds; and (4) the use of National Guard and federal forces along with local law-enforcement agencies. Among the eight cities having major disorders, those in Detroit and Newark were the largest and most damaging. The fighting in some cities included the use of tanks and machine guns. In Detroit alone, there were forty-three deaths, and property damage exceeded 40 million dollars. Also, significant damage occurred to residences, leaving many people without places to live (National Advisory Commission, 1968:107–116).

Many people believe that the "long hot summers" began to "cool" in 1968 and that 1967, therefore, was the peak year of violent protest. This conclusion has been challenged by Feagin and Hahn (1973). In an analysis of the information available on the years 1968–1971, these authors conclude that "serious ghetto rioting continued well into the 1970s." In 1968, for example, in the one-month period following the assassination of Martin Luther King, Jr., at least 172 cities experienced 202 race-related riots. This is a larger number of cities than reported ghetto violence during the entire year of 1967. An even larger number of riots (over 500) were reported for the year 1969. It is true that there were no major riots in 1969, but it is probable that there were more casualties and arrests than in some of the earlier, presumably "hotter" years (Feagin and Hahn, 1973:105–106).

Regardless of the actual numbers of riots and their distribution, however, the amount of public attention given to violent protests by black Americans began to decline after 1968. Many factors probably contributed to "taking the steam out" of the Black Power Movement. Such factors as the declining coverage by the media of mass communication and the changing tactics of law-enforcement agencies are frequently mentioned in this regard. Of probable importance, too, is that some of the most influential black leaders had never accepted the principles of separation or violent protest. For example, shortly before his assassination on April 4, 1968, Martin Luther King, Jr. (1971b:586), argued that "the time has come for a return to mass nonviolent protest." The continuation of violent tactics, he believed, would only stimulate increased white repression. Under these circumstances, it was foolhardy for blacks to continue such measures. Rather, in his view, nonviolence was more relevant as an effective device than ever before: "Violence is not only morally repugnant, it is pragmatically barren" (King, 1968:585). Apparently, most black Americans soon accepted this assessment. By 1973, legal and political approaches to the solution of the problem of racial inequality had once again become the primary weapons of the black Americans.

Our brief sketch has traced the slow and painful movement of black Americans out of slavery to citizenship and out of rigid segregation and the denial of equal rights toward an equalitarian, possibly "integrated" relationship with the dominant whites. We now turn, as we have previously in the cases of the Japanese Americans and Chicanos, to the question of the ways and the extent to which the movement toward intergroup merger (i.e., assimilation) has occurred.

Black American Assimilation

Cultural Assimilation

Each ethnic group we have considered so far has faced the question "As we adopt American culture, what shall become of our own culture?" We have seen that although there are important group differences in this respect, each group has made an effort to retain and transmit a portion of its heritage. The tendency of an ethnic group to attempt to retain its heritage has been shown to be intimately related, among other things, to whether a group has entered the country voluntarily. As a rule, groups that have come into the United States voluntarily have been more willing to undertake cultural assimilation than have the Chicanos and Indian Americans. From this perspective, we should expect that black Americans would have been very resistant to cultural assimilation. Even though black people were separated from their homelands—like many other immigrants—the separation was forced. It did not arise in any way from a dissatisfaction with life in the old country or the desire to start anew in another land. Thus, like the Chicanos and Indian Americans, black Americans initially did not wish to undertake cultural assimilation. Apparently, however, they had little choice in the matter. Those who survived the horrors of being captured and transported to America were in an extremely poor position to retain or transmit their heritage. The entire system of American slavery was constructed, in fact, to strip the slaves of their cultures and to replace these cultures with ways of thinking and acting that were deemed appropriate for slaves. People from many tribes and kingdoms, people who spoke different languages, and people with highly different levels of education were thrown together and treated as if they were alike. They were assigned new "American" names and were required to learn the rudiments of English. Every effort was made to force the slaves to discontinue their use of their own languages and customs. In this way, the link to the African past was severely disrupted. Frazier (1957:3–4), for instance, states that this process was so effective that significant elements of African culture have survived in only certain isolated areas. Myrdal (1964: 928) has put the matter in this way: "Negro institutions are . . . similar to those of the white man. They show little similarity to African institutions. In his cultural traits, the Negro is akin to other Americans." This view is not only defensible; it has seemed to many to be inescapable. Nevertheless, the question of the persistence and influence of the African heritage may not be dismissed so easily. Although it is generally agreed that the disruption of African culture was greater in the United States than any other part of the New World, it also is generally agreed that black Americans do possess some distinctive modes of speech, family life, religious observances, music, folklore, and so on. Myrdal (1964:930) concedes in this respect that black patterns of living do contain some "peculiarities" that may indicate the presence of a distinctive culture; but, to repeat, he denies that these differences may be traced to Africa.

A number of scholars have accepted both that there is a distinctive black American culture and that this culture is strongly related to the African traditions brought to America by the slaves. Consequently, they have sought to reveal the importance of African "survivals" to various aspects of black American life. In regard to language, for instance, Herskovits (1958:281–291) presents evidence showing that, in certain areas of the United States, many African words, names, and phrases that are used by blacks have been translated from African languages into English. Herskovits argues further that the high prevalence of common-law marriage among black Americans represents an adjustment of the polygynous family form to the American setting. And he suggests that mothers and grandmothers play an unusually important role in the families of black Americans, just as they did in the traditional life of West Africa. A similar argument pertains to certain religious rituals. Herskovits believes that the popularity of the Baptist church among black Americans is probably due to the similarity of its rituals to those of the river cults of West Africa.

Each of the above points is disputed by Frazier (1957). Although there is clear evidence of language survivals within a few isolated black American communities, such as the Gullah communities on the coasts of Georgia and South Carolina, such survivals do not seem to be widespread. Frazier argues also that the similarities between the family and religious lives of black Americans and those of West African tribes are more easily explained as having arisen within the United States than as being survivals of African customs. In general, Frazier (1957:7) holds that in the United States black slaves were so scattered throughout the South and were so thoroughly dominated on the plantations that they had little chance to preserve or transmit their African heritage.

The debate over black culture has continued to attract scholarly attention and, no doubt, the final word has not yet been spoken. An important, if unsurprising, result of the exchanges so far is that the terms of the inquiry have gradually been redefined. It has become increasingly accepted that a black American culture does exist, even though its main elements may not have been transmitted intact from their African origins. To illustrate, Levine (1977:6), in an analysis of slave songs, found that their "style . . . remained closer to the musical styles and performances of West Africa . . . than to the musical style of Western Europe." He found that a number of the characteristics of African cultures, such as the high praise given to verbal improvisation, have remained central features of black American songs. Levine argues that it is a mistake to assume that cultural elements must be unchanged in order to be "survivals" of African tradition. Such a view, he maintains, misinterprets the nature of culture itself. "Culture is not a fixed condition but a process. . . . The question is not one of survivals but of transformations" (Levine, 1977:5). Gutman (1976:212) expresses a supporting but somewhat more restrained view. He suggests that too little is presently known to allow one to trace important elements of black culture to their West African origins and that perhaps Herskovits did lay too much stress on the direct transmission of African traditions. Nonetheless, he believes Herskovits demonstrated some important continuities between the lives of the plantation slaves of the early nineteenth century and those of rural Mississippi blacks in the third decade of the twentieth century.

The above arguments are more than a mere academic exercise. As noted previously, the answers given to questions of this type are usually associated with some political position and imply a certain view of how the problems of black Americans should be solved. Myrdal (1964:928), for instance, not only argues that black American culture (to the extent it exists) does not derive appreciably from African traditions; he also states that blacks' distinctive traits are primarily the result of reactions to the discrimination of whites and the requirements of white society. Hence, the distinctive traits within black culture are "distorted" and "pathological" reflections of American culture. This view implies that such problems as poverty, high street crime rates, and unemployment result from improper and distorted cultural assimilation and will disappear as black Americans complete that process. What mainly is needed, from this perspective, is for black Americans to give up the remnants of their African heritage and adopt the standard American culture. An important implication of this suggested "solution" is that black Americans should not be proud of their distinctive characteristics and should strive to abandon all traces of Africa.

The idea that black culture is "pathological," that it has not served as a "positive" way to help black Americans to adapt to their environment, has enjoyed wide acceptance. A well-known version of this belief holds that the "deficiencies" of black culture may be seen in the "breakdown" of the Negro family. Although this view has been common at least since the influential work of Frazier (1939), its direct political impact is generally traced to an explosive document prepared by Moynihan (1965) to help shape the federal government's War on Poverty during the 1960s. This document, commonly called the Moynihan Report, was based on the assumption that "at the heart of the deterioration of the fabric of Negro society is the deterioration of the Negro family" (Moynihan, 1965:5). The "deterioration" of the Negro family was judged, in turn, to be the lasting result of the indescribable oppression experienced by black Americans during slavery. The inability of Negro slaves to contract legal marriages, the inability of the Negro male to act as breadwinner and family protector, and the frequent separation of family members at the auction block all led to the development of a matrifocal (mother-centered) family pattern. These conditions led also to a general acceptance among blacks of sexual promiscuity, plural "marriages," and illegitimacy. The main result of the general "weakness" of the black family in America is what Moynihan (1965:29–45) referred to as a "tangle of pathology" that may be seen in the "reversed roles of husband and wife," lowered levels of education and school attendance, lowered income, lowered IQs, and high rates of arrest, delinquency, unemployment, and narcotics use. The proper goal of government action, therefore, is to enhance "the stability and resources of the Negro American family" (Moynihan, 1965:48). Please notice that this analysis is consistent with Elkins' view, discussed earlier, that the modern problems of black Americans is a lingering consequence of the extraordinary harshness of the slavery period.

A storm of protest broke as the results of Moynihan's analysis became generally known. Although his description of the severity and immediate effects of the slavery period was generally accepted, his conclusions concerning their modern effects were not. Critics have attacked the idea that the problems of black Americans stem from the presumed weaknesses and failures of the black family. They have emphasized, instead, the many strengths, resources, and achievements of the black family (see, e.g., Billingsley, 1968; Rainwater and Yancey, 1967; Wilkinson, 1978). Hill

(1971), for instance, argues that within black families there are stronger kinship bonds than among whites, that there is a strong emphasis on work and ambition, and that there is an equalitarian (rather than a "matriarchal") authority pattern. The net result of many studies has been to cast grave doubts on Moynihan's thesis that there is a "tangle of pathology" within black families arising from a failure of black Americans to overcome the "disorganizing" effects of the slavery experience. Such a view, many critics have noted, emphasizes the effects of past discrimination but ignores or minimizes the effects of present discrimination. In this way, the modern social problems of blacks appear to result from failures within the black group to overcome the legacy of the past rather than from the contemporary actions of the dominant group, a view that, to many observers, seems to "blame the victim."

Although most of Moynihan's critics apparently accept his analysis of the historical effects of slavery on black family life while rejecting his "tangle of pathology" conclusion, some reject both his analysis and conclusion. For example, an important study by Gutman (1976) has unearthed considerable evidence showing that the inability of black Americans to form strong and lasting families during slavery has been greatly exaggerated. By studying the records of the Freedmen's Bureau, population censuses, marriage and birth registers, letters written by both blacks and whites, and so on, Gutman discovered that, despite the great hardships of enslavement, most slaves lived in households headed by men as well as women and that many slave couples had enduring relationships. Consequently, children frequently grew up in a home with two parents—parents who had gone through some accepted ceremony of marriage. The members of slave families were quite conscious of, and influenced by, their ties to kinfolks. For example, children usually were named for members of their blood kin group. Also, marriages to close blood relatives were discouraged. Although premarital intercourse was accepted, marriage was expected to follow if a pregnancy resulted. And, once married, the husband and wife were expected to remain faithful to one another. Gutman (1976:95–100) concludes from his analysis of slave marriages and families that despite the undeniable hardships and restrictions of slavery, black slaves were not simply disorganized, atomized individuals. Slavery surely narrowed the choice available to them, but slaves nonetheless were able to create a distinctive culture and social identity that was rooted in and transmitted by families. These families were struggling with discernible success to cope with the obstacles to family unity presented by the slave system. The presumption does not seem justified, therefore, that the contemporary problems of black Americans is mainly a reflection of their failure to develop a family pattern during slavery that was capable of transmitting "positive" values from one generation to the next.[14]

Let us now return to Ellison's (1964:316) question "Are American Negroes simply the creation of white men, or have they at least helped to create themselves out of what they found around them?" Whether we are examining the issue of cultural survivals or the issue of the strength of black families, the answer to this question appears to be that black Americans have for a very long time been in the process of constructing a distinctive new culture based on both the old and the new. We thus encounter again the process of ethnogenesis. The process of cultural assimilation involves not only the acceptance of a new culture and the rejection of an old one; it includes, also, the creation of a new culture.

We may acknowledge the reality of black culture and view its development as a positive thing, however, without claiming black Americans are low in cultural assimilation. Indeed, most students agree that blacks and whites of the same social-class levels are much more alike than different in their values and behavior (Gordon, 1964:173).[13] We conclude, therefore, that although black Americans are not simply and totally Americans in culture, their level of cultural assimilation is high.

Secondary Structural Assimilation

There can be no doubt that since emancipation black Americans have moved in many important ways toward full secondary structural assimilation. However, it is equally clear that a number of gaps still exist between the levels of whites and blacks in such significant matters as occupation, income, education, and housing. Moreover, as we shall see, if contemporary trends continue, the differences in these areas will not disappear soon.

Whites, of course, always have been more heavily concentrated than blacks in the higher-prestige, better-paying jobs, and they still are. Table 7.1 presents some information on the changes in the occupational distributions of black and white males between 1950 and 1970.

Several features of Table 7.1 are of interest. For example, although black males in professional and managerial work had more than tripled between 1950 and 1970, their proportion was still lower than that among white males in 1950. The proportion of black craftsmen increased during this time from 8 to 14 percent, while the proportion of white craftsmen remained almost the same. While both of these comparisons suggest that blacks are moving toward the white occupational pattern, the two distributions appear to be getting farther apart in some other respects. It is not easy to determine by inspection alone, therefore, whether the overall patterns are converging. The index of dissimilarity, which we first encountered in chapter 6, provides a convenient way to summarize these changes. According to Farley (1977: 197), the index of occupational dissimilarity for black and white males fell from 37 in 1950 to 26 in 1975, showing a movement in the direction of occupational assimilation. Although the figures are not shown in Table 7.1, an even greater change has occurred among females. The index of occupational dissimilarity for women declined from 53 in 1950 to 22 in 1975. This means that even though the occupational distributions of black and white women were further apart in 1950 than were the men's, by 1975, the women's distributions were closer together than were the men's. Of particular interest

TABLE 7.1

Percentage of White and Nonwhite Workers in Selected
Occupational Categories, 1950, 1960, and 1970

Occupational Category	Whites						Nonwhites					
	Males			Females			Males			Females		
	1950	1960	1970	1950	1960	1970	1950	1960	1970	1950	1960	1970
Professional, managerial	20[a]	23	30	18	19	20	4	5	13	7	9	13
Craftsmen	20	22	21	2	1	1	8	11	14	1	1	1
Operatives, service	25	26	25	32	30	29	36	43	41	34	36	44
Private household workers				4	4	4				42	39	18
Farmers, farm labor	7	6	6	3	2	2	24	12	6	9	4	1

Source: Adapted from Reynolds Farley and Albert Hermalin, "The 1960s: A Decade of Progress for Blacks?" Demography (August 1972):363, with permission of the Population Association of America.
[a] Totals do not add to 100 because some occupational categories are not shown.

here is a dramatic change in the proportion of black women working in private households. Over 40 percent of the employed black women in 1950 worked as household workers. By 1975, fewer than 10 percent of the employed black women held such jobs.

Although the occupational "upgrading" revealed by these statistics is encouraging for those who favor assimilation as a goal, they probably over-estimate the extent of occupational similarity between the races. Each of the occupational categories used in the comparison is quite broad. Within each of these categories, there is a substantial range of jobs of differing levels of prestige and pay; and blacks are more likely than whites to occupy the lower rungs within each of the broad occupational groups. Hence, even if the index of occupational dissimilarity were zero, occupational assimilation within the categories would probably still be incomplete.

The apparent reductions in occupational inequality also conceals another important source of real inequality. The figures cited are for blacks who are a part of the employed labor force. But large numbers of blacks are un-employed, underemployed, or are employed at substandard wages. For most of the years between 1955 and 1975, the unemployment rate for black males was roughly twice as high as for whites. Furthermore, during this time, un-employment among black teenagers was exceptionally high, rising in 1972 to over one-third of the entire sixteen to nineteen-year-old group (Darden, 1974:656–657). It appears, therefore, that while black males are now more likely to get jobs that previously were "reserved" for whites, they still are much less likely to get a job at all.

This pattern of a general movement toward assimilation may also be seen in figures concerning changes in black and white incomes. Between 1947 and 1975, there was an increase in the median incomes of both black and white families, and there was a rising standard of living for both groups. Also, during this twenty-eight-year period, the gap between the median incomes of blacks and whites declined noticeably. For example, in 1947, the average income of nonwhites was 51 percent of the white average; for blacks in 1960, it was 55 percent; in 1970, it was 64 percent; and, in 1975, it was 62 percent. From the beginning to the end of this period, the index of income dissimilarity dropped from just over 38 to just over 26 (Farley, 1977:198).

Since the most dramatic improvement in black incomes occurred during the period 1965–1970 (from 55 to 61 percent), following the main period of legislative changes and coinciding with the large-scale civil disorders, some observers believe that a historic shift has been started and that black incomes will continue to move rapidly toward catching up with whites (Wattenberg and Scammon, 1974:443–653). However, this dramatic movement toward closing the black-white income gap was actually reversed in the early years of the 1970s, falling to a ratio of 58 percent in 1973. Hence, although there has been considerable progress in black incomes since 1950, their average is still less than two-thirds that of white, and the overall gap is narrowing very slowly, if at all.

These general figures, of course, conceal many underlying differences of interest. For example, since women typically have lower incomes than men, and since more black than white families are headed by women, some of the income difference between the races reflects this difference in family form. Also, since whites on the average have a higher level of education and hold better-paying jobs, some of the difference in median incomes is due to these factors. And one study of black-white income changes has found that if full-time workers only are compared, the income gap is much smaller (about 77 percent versus 62 percent) than for all workers combined (Smith and Welch, 1978:3). It is accurate to say, therefore, that some of the income inequality between blacks and whites arises from differences in the social characteristics of the two groups. If there were no racial discrimination (by this reasoning), there should be no average income difference between blacks and whites whose social characteristics are the same. For instance, blacks and whites who work at the same jobs, are of the same age, and have the same levels of education and experience should, in the absence of discrimination, receive the same income.

Several studies have sought to determine the extent to which similar workers receive similar pay or, alternatively, what it "costs" to be black in America.[15] The methods used in these studies are too advanced for us to consider in detail. However, the underlying idea can be illustrated simply. In a study of family income, the U.S. Bureau of the Census presented incomes of family heads according to both their race and the number of years of school they had completed (Smythe, 1976b:215). This study showed that the median income for families whose head was black and had completed four or more years of college was at that time $14,158. However, the median income for whites of the same educational level was $18,479. Similarly, whites who had completed less than eight years of school earned more on the average ($6,689) than blacks who had attended high school for up to three years ($6,612). In other words, *so far as education alone* is concerned, it appears that blacks pay a price in the job market for being black. If nothing else were considered, this conclusion would be premature because factors other than education affect income. To illustrate, it is likely that the average age of blacks with college degrees is lower than for whites with a similar educational level. Since older people on the average have more job experience, some of the income difference we have noted may be due to experience differences between older white and younger black workers. Consequently, our comparison should be restricted at least to whites and blacks who have degrees and are of similar ages. By extending this approach, blacks and whites who resemble one another in many different social respects may be compared. When the groups have been "matched" in several important respects, it is reasonable to suppose that any remaining income differences are due largely to discrimination. By a similar method, Farley (1977:205) has shown that there is still a substantial difference in earnings between black and white males (over $2,000) that may be a result of discrimination. The results for females, however, contained a surprise. Although white females as a whole were slightly ahead of black females in income, the difference more than disappeared when a number of factors were considered. It appeared, indeed, that if black women were identical to white women in the respects considered in this study, they would earn around $760 per year *more* than white women. We may note in passing, though, that the average earnings of females are much lower than those of males within both races. For both sexes, however, educational gains (especially at the college level) make a substantial difference in the incomes they receive (Smith and Welch, 1978:vii). Therefore, estimates of black progress in the area of education usually focus on changes in the level of education and on changes in the pattern of schooling (i.e., desegregation).

Prior to emancipation, the vast majority of blacks were given no formal schooling. Consequently, changes in the level of education among black Americans since the Reconstruction period have been enormous. In 1870, 80 percent of black Americans were illiterate; in the same year, illiteracy among whites stood at 12 percent. By 1970, these levels had fallen to approximately 4 percent of all blacks over fourteen years old and to less than 1 percent for whites of the same age group (Goff, 1976:422). Also, by 1970, practically all children of both races between the ages of 7 and 13 were enrolled in school. Before the completion of high school and college, however, a larger proportion of blacks leave school, especially once the age of compulsory attendance has been passed. In 1970, among those eighteen to nineteen years old, 40 percent of blacks and 49 percent of whites were enrolled. These figures dropped further among those at ages twenty to twenty-four to 14 percent for blacks and 22 percent for whites (Taeuber and Taeuber, 1976: 195). By the early 1970s, the median level of education for all black and white adults had exceeded ten years and twelve years, respectively. As in the case of occupational and income trends, indexes of dissimilarity afford the best indication of the overall pattern of the relative educational changes occurring among blacks and whites. Between 1940 and 1975, for instance, the index of educational dissimilarity for black and white males twenty-five and over dropped from approximately 44 to 24 (Farley, 1977:191). Among females, the indexes declined from around 43 to 24. These findings show that the educational patterns of black and white Americans are moving in the direction of complete educational assimilation.

Not all of the evidence points in this direction, however. For instance, although the proportion of young black Americans who are enrolling in college has increased both absolutely and in relation to white Americans, white Americans are increasingly more likely to complete four or more years of college. Darden (1974:661) shows that among blacks between the ages of twenty-five and thirty-four the proportion who have completed college rose from 4.1 percent in 1960 to 7.9 percent in 1972, a gain of 3.8 percent. However, college completion among whites between the ages of twenty-five and thirty-four rose even more, from 11.9 percent in 1960 to 18.8 percent in 1972, a gain of 6.9 percent. Therefore, even though the rate of white increase was lower than the rate of black increase, the gap in total college completions actually widened from 7.8 percent to 10.9 percent during this period. As in the case of income gains, black progress, though real, is a part of a general increase within American society. Such an increase may or may not keep pace with that of the total population, and even when it does keep pace in a relative sense, the absolute differences may actually widen.

Educational levels, of course, reveal little concerning educational quality. But if, as the *Brown* decisions state, segregated schooling is damaging to those who are set apart, then the continuation of segregated schools reduces the quality of education for blacks. From this standpoint, educational assimilation is incomplete as long as the schools are segregated, even if the indexes of educational dissimilarity used so far were to reach zero.

The question to be answered here, then, is "To what extent have the nation's schools been desegregated?" and the answer to this question depends, further, on our answer to another: "When is a school *completely* desegregated?" Although several different answers may be given to this question, the principal one relies again on the main idea underlying the index of dissimilarity. When the black students are represented in every school in the same proportion as in the school district as a whole, then the desegregation of schools would be complete.[16] From this standpoint, the public schools of the South had, in 1954, an average index of segregation of 100.

Using this approach, Farley (1975:10) has shown that the average index of school segregation in fifty-eight southern urban school districts declined between 1967 and 1972 from 86 to 53. No other section of the country revealed such a low average index in 1972 (Pettigrew, 1974:55). The average index levels for urban districts in the other regions combined was 58. It is evident from these statistics that although many black children still attend schools that are totally or predominantly black, a substantial amount of desegregation of the public schools has taken place. It is also clear that most of this change has occurred since 1967, mainly as a result of court orders and busing (Farley, 1975:22).

Many questions concerning school desegregation still remain unanswered and are the subject of vigorous debate. It is still uncertain, for instance, whether relatively permanent desegregation can be achieved as long as residential segregation persists. For a long time now, whites have moved more rapidly to the suburbs than have blacks, and this trend has created many metropolitan districts that increasingly resemble white rings around a black core. The U.S. Supreme Court has ruled in the important case *Milliken* v. *Bradley* that it will not approve desegregation plans that attempt to cross school district lines to encompass an entire metropolitan area.[17] Hence, as long as the Court holds this view, it is possible that the large reductions in desegregation that have been achieved within many American cities may gradually be reversed by resegregation. Hence, the issue of housing segregation is intimately linked to school segregation.

In some areas of the South, housing patterns still reflect the effects of slavery and the plantation economy. In the ante-bellum South, the slaves and their family commonly lived in the backyards of the white masters (Taeuber and Taeuber, 1969:48). Consequently, the level of residential segregation in the South was typically less than it is in most parts of the United States today. Even when the Jim Crow system of deliberate, legal segregation came into being between 1890 and 1920, the southern pattern of interracial housing was not much affected. In the "Southern Plan" of segregation, it was unnecessary to force blacks into racially separate geographical areas. Both tradition and the Jim Crow system created such a vast social distance between the races that residential closeness did not threaten the respective social "places" of the two races. As black Americans began to stream out of the South during World War I, however, they entered northern states in which they were legally equal to the whites. Certain facts of northern life, however, prevented blacks from dispersing throughout all parts of the cities. There was, first of all, an economic barrier. Like the European immigrants before them, most blacks could afford to live only in the least expensive "slum" areas of the cities. But of great importance, also, was that black people faced an enormous amount of housing discrimination. Even when black people had the money to afford housing outside of the ghettos, they usually were unable to purchase it.[18] What Pettigrew (1975:36) refers to as the "Northern Plan" of segregation has relied on housing segregation rather than legal segregation. Interestingly, it appears that physical and social distance are to a degree interchangeable. As long as a dominant group's social position is unassailable, it may permit subordinates to be physically close. However, when the dominant group's efforts to maintain social distance begin to crumble, the group may erect physical barriers "as a second line of defense" (van den Berghe, 1967:30).

Comprehensive, detailed studies of trends in housing segregation in the United States prior to 1940 are unavailable. Some studies of selected cities have been conducted, however. These studies suggest that in northern and southern cities residential segregation increased gradually from emancipation to World War I and then accelerated sharply until 1930 (Taeuber and Taeuber, 1969:43–55).

Since 1940, the U.S. Bureau of the Census has published housing information on a large sample of American cities. Using this information, Taeuber and Taeuber (1969:32–41) have calculated residential segregation indexes for 207 American cities in 1960 and for 109 cities during 1940–1960. Their analysis establishes two important points. First, the average level of residential segregation of blacks and whites in American cities by 1940 was very high in every region of the country. No city in the Northeast, for instance, had a residential segregation index lower than 74.3, while most cities of this region had indexes between 80 and 89. One city (Atlantic City) had an index of 94.6. A similar pattern existed in the other regions, with the South having the highest average. Second, although there was a slight decline in residential segregation in most of the 109 cities studied between 1940 and 1960, the amounts were usually small, and the patterns within the cities were varied. For instance, some cities had an increase in residential segregation during one or both of the two decades studied. In any event, by 1960, the average level of residential segregation in American cities was still practically as high as it was in 1940. The national average in 1960 was 86.2, and the lowest regional average (for the Northeast) was 79.2. Indeed, the lowest single city (San Jose, California) registered the quite high segregation score of 60.4, while some cities (e.g., Orlando and Fort Lauderdale, Florida, and Odessa, Texas) approached complete residential segregation.

What has happened to residential segregation in U.S. cities since 1960? Because our cities have continued to grow and change, certain problems of comparison have arisen. As mentioned previously, blacks have continued to move into the central cities, and whites have continued to form suburban rings around them. To what extent, then, must the analysis of residential segregation focus on the metropolitan area rather than on the central city? Questions of this type have led to some controversy concerning the direction of residential segregation. For example, a study by Sørensen, Taeuber, and Hollingsworth (1975) extends the Taeubers' earlier study of 109 cities. This study finds a small average decrease in residential segregation in the United States between 1960 and 1970, bringing the average level below that of 1940. However, a different study by Van Valey, Roof, and Wilcox (1977:842), based on metropolitan-area as well as central-city comparisons, shows that the average level of residential segregation existing in 1970 was practically the same as in 1960. But whether residential segregation is remaining constant or is gradually declining, certain points seem to be beyond dispute. For one thing, it is clear that the occupational and income gains scored by blacks during the years since World War II are not being translated into residential assimilation. For another, it seems that efforts to promote full educational assimilation by desegregating the public schools will continue to require Americans to choose between neighborhood schools and desegregated housing.

What, then, are we to conclude concerning the secondary structural assimilation of black Americans? Our consideration of changes in occupational, income, and educational levels suggests that on the average black Americans are moving toward the pattern found among whites, that the black-white gap in each of these areas is declining. On the other hand, the changes in housing segregation have been unimpressive, and when compared to any ideal of perfect assimilation, all of the changes we have discussed are small. For this reason, most observers appear to agree with Farley (1977: 206) that "a continuation of the trends of the 1960s and 1970s offers no hope that racial differences will be eliminated soon."

This conclusion is by no means inescapable, however. In contrast to the view that racial discrimination will continue at a high level into the foreseeable future, Wilson (1978) has advanced the surprising and very controversial thesis that race itself is declining in significance as a factor affecting socioeconomic status. Stated very briefly, his reasoning is as follows: throughout the long years lying between the beginnings of black American slavery and the end of World War II, practically all blacks were members of an oppressed lower caste. Under these conditions, black people's racial affiliation rather than their economic circumstances determined their chances for occupational advancement; therefore, the inequalities between blacks and whites were, strictly speaking, *racial* in nature. Since World War II, however, the forces of industrialization (which we discussed in chapter 1) have led to the creation of a significant black middle class among whom occupational advancement depends more on class affiliation than on racial membership. Wilson (1978:3) argues that this "transition from racial inequalities to class inequalities" is revealed by the fact, presented above, that some black Americans seem to be gaining on whites in occupational status, income, and educational level at the same time that the economic conditions of many poor blacks are deteriorating even further. The results are a growing cleavage *within* the black community, an increase in the importance of socioeconomic class, and a decline in the importance of racial membership as such. As stated by Wilson (1978:152), "The recent mobility of blacks lends strong support to the view that economic class is clearly more important than race in predetermining job placement and occupational mobility." In short, well-educated blacks increasingly have the same opportunities for occupational advancement as whites while the uneducated members of all groups, including the whites, increasingly descend into a multiethnic "underclass." From this perspective, the object of modern programs to change the lives of poor blacks should focus specifically on those aspects of industrial life that create *class* inequalities. Such programs should not continue to operate on the assumption that racial oppression is still the paramount problem (Wilson, 1978:154).

Wilson's conclusions have stirred up a hornet's nest, so to speak. To mention only one prominent illustration, the Association of Black Sociologists (ABS) has published a denunciation of Wilson's book (*Footnotes,* December 1978:4). The ABS accuses Wilson of omitting significant facts "regarding the continuing discrimination against blacks at all class levels," of misinterpreting some of the facts presented, and of drawing unwarranted conclusions. The ABS states further that its members are "outraged over the misinterpretation of the black experience" and "extremely disturbed over the policy implications" of the book.

It is difficult to anticipate the full effects of this debate. Many of the central facts are not themselves a matter of dispute. Sampson (1978:4), for instance, has presented evidence that tends to support Wilson's view. Similarly, Featherman and Hauser (1978:381–382) note that "socioeconomic 'classes' are more visible among the black population than nearly a decade ago." Nevertheless, Featherman and Hauser also caution that outside of the occupational sphere the evidence is mixed. Wilson, of course, is aware that in such matters as public school education, residential segregation, and full political participation racial antagonism is still very much alive. His argument, however, is that the changes occurring in the economic prospects of black Americans at least assure that their very livelihood is not likely to be taken away as a result of racial discrimination. "At this point," Wilson (1978:153) thinks, "there is every reason to believe that talented and educated blacks, like talented and educated whites, will continue to enjoy the advantages and privileges of their class status."

The disagreement concerning Wilson's thesis should remind us that social scientific theories and evidence frequently suggest certain practical steps to be taken to solve social problems. It should remind us, too, that the interpretations offered by scholars inevitably have implications for various value systems.

Primary Structural Assimilation

The gains discussed above have increased the chance that blacks and whites will have social contacts in different situations. Desegregation in schools alone has brought hundreds of thousands of students, teachers, and parents together in new ways. And there is good evidence of an increase in cross-racial contacts in other settings, too. Between 1964 and 1974, researchers at the University of Michigan's Institute for Social Research have found an increase in contacts between blacks and whites in neighborhoods and on the job as well as in schools (*ISR Newsletter,* 1975:4).[19] Throughout this same time, too, as mentioned in chapter 4, the attitudes of white people became more favorable toward desegregation, a fact that presumably should have helped turn many of the personal contacts into friendships. The Michigan studies report, in fact, that this has happened. The proportion of whites who had no black friends declined from about 80 percent in 1964 to about 60 percent ten years later.

The extent to which whites have contacts with blacks, however, is not identical to the contacts of blacks with whites. Since there are so many more whites in America than blacks, blacks are much more likely to interact with whites than the other way around. For this reason (if no other) the amount of segregation may seem different to members of the two groups. An interesting illustration of this point is that more than 75 percent of the blacks included in the Michigan samples said they had some white friends.

We must observe, again, though, that important as these reported changes are, they are modest in relation to the ideal of complete primary structural assimilation. From this standpoint, whites and blacks are still mainly separated in their personal relations everywhere but in the schools. Even there, patterns of friendly association still tend to be largely with members of the same race. Everything considered, we must conclude that the level of primary structural assimilation among black Americans, though rising, is still low.

Marital Assimilation

The marriage of blacks outside their group—especially with whites—has long been a subject of interest.[20] An understanding of this process, though, has been complicated by laws in many states prohibiting black-white intermarriage, by differences in record-keeping procedures, and by a trend toward removing racial identifications from marriage records. In 1966, thirty-one states permitted interracial marriage; and, in 1967, when the Supreme Court ruled that such laws were unconstitutional, sixteen states still had them. At that time, too, only three states (Hawaii, Michigan, and Nebraska) published official records on interracial marriages (Heer, 1966:263). By 1976, the effort to remove racial identifications from marriage records had been successful in seven states and the District of Columbia (Monahan, 1976:224).

Despite the technical problems created by these conditions, some excellent studies have been conducted.[21] Three of the main findings of these studies are that (1) out-marriages among blacks have been much less common than out-marriages among other racial and ethnic groups, (2) the rate of black-white intermarriage went up rapidly during the 1960s in both the North and the South, and (3) the rate of black-white intermarriage is higher in the North than in the South.

Given the social and legal pressures opposing black-white marriages in the United States, the infrequency with which they occur is not surprising. In a study of interracial marriages in Los Angeles during the years 1948–1959, Burma (1963:160) found that black males were much less likely to marry out than were Japanese, Chinese, Filipino, or Indian males, and black females were even less likely to marry out than were black males. After all the turmoil and change of the 1960s, blacks were still found to be the least likely of thirty-five different American racial and ethnic groups to marry out (Gurak and Kritz, 1978:38). By comparison, the rates for the Japanese, Chinese, and Mexicans at this time were 24.4, 45.3, and 45.8, respectively.

Even though the level of black out-marriage is still extremely low when compared to other racial and ethnic groups, the rate of change has jumped noticeably since 1960. Monahan (1976) has conducted a nationwide survey of black-white intermarriage and found that the total proportion of mixed marriages rose from 1.4 in 1963 to 2.6 in 1970. Throughout this period, the proportion of black-white intermarriage was three to four times higher in the North than in the South, though the rate of increase appears to be much faster in the South than in the North.

It seems unlikely that the increasing rate of black-white intermarriage will soon produce a very large overall effect. In addition to the fact that the level of marital assimilation of blacks was extremely low to begin with and that the levels of primary structural assimilation of blacks are still low, there is the further fact that white opposition to marital assimilation is still noticeable. The fourth NORC survey on attitudes toward integration, for instance, found that in 1976 roughly 30 percent of the whites questioned still felt that intermarriages between blacks and whites should be outlawed (Taylor, Sheatsley, and Greeley, 1978:43). If that many whites still believe cross-racial marriages should be illegal then, presumably, a much higher proportion believes such marriages are not a good idea. These considerations all suggest that the level of marital assimilation among blacks in America will probably remain low for the foreseeable future.

Whether it is their intention or not, black Americans appear to be moving toward the goal of ideal pluralism. They appear simultaneously to be mastering Anglo-American culture and developing their own distinctive culture, and their level of secondary structural assimilation is generally rising. But while blacks and whites seem to be coming together in cultural and secondary structural ways, they appear to be remaining largely apart in their private relations. This broad assessment must not blind us to the continuing problems black Americans face in jobs, incomes, education, and housing. The remaining gaps in these areas do not assure us that the past separation of the races will not continue or deepen. On the other hand, for those who seek pluralism, there is no assurance, if secondary structural assimilation accelerates, that the culture of blacks and their separate social lives will survive the pressures of Anglo conformity.

Black American "Success"

One of the great questions of our time is "Why haven't black Americans been more 'successful'?" We have indicated already that in very broad terms a split has long existed between those who favor hereditarian and those who favor environmental answers to this question. With the general decline of the hereditarian position, however (discussed in chapter 4), public and scholarly debate increasingly occurred among various groups of environmentalists.[22] We actually have encountered this situation before in our discussions of the worldly success of the Japanese Americans and Chicanos. Please recall that in both of these instances an environmental explanation—value compatibility in the case of the Japanese Americans and value orientations in the case of the Chicanos—have been criticized by others mainly in environmental terms.

A similar situation has developed among environmentalists who are interested in the problems of black Americans. Earlier in this chapter, we discussed three different perspectives on black American slavery, none of which assumes black Americans to be inherently inferior to whites. We have observed, too, that the differing environmental perspectives on the effects of slavery are associated with differing interpretations of the experiences and strengths of the black slave family, and, taken together, we have seen that these perspectives have played a highly visible role in the analysis of the modern social problems of blacks.

During the 1960s, the view that blacks had been psychologically crushed under slavery (as expressed, for example, by Elkins) and the view that the black American family is a "distorted" and "pathological" remnant of the slave period (as expressed, for example, by Moynihan) were joined by a similar overlapping view designated by the term "the culture of poverty." This term, usually attributed to Lewis (1965), quickly became popular in discussions of poor people generally and of blacks in particular. The basic idea is that poor people develop a particular pattern of values and ways of coping with their difficulties and that this pattern is passed down essentially intact from one generation to the next. The children of the poor learn in their homes and neighborhoods ways of thinking and acting that middle-class people consider to be "deviant." Important among the values of the poor are an emphasis on the present that, when translated into behavior, results in an "inability to defer gratification." The poor live for the here and now, taking little thought for the future. Such values and behavior, according to the culture of poverty thesis, prevent poor people from taking school seriously or from working hard when they get a job. They do not succeed in these activities, therefore, and do not climb "the ladder of success." Since these "failure" responses are passed on to each succeeding generation, a vicious circle of poverty is created. The poverty of one generation breeds and ensures the poverty of its successor. Among black Americans, this poverty cycle may be traced back to the slavery period, as argued by Frazier, Elkins, Moynihan, and others. From this perspective, poor blacks live in families that are "culturally deprived" and are characterized by the "tangle of pathology" noted by Moynihan. Unless the poverty cycle is broken, the children of such families are destined to learn the same "defective" pattern of behavior exhibited by their elders and, inevitably, to remain as dependents on the welfare rolls. Black people, in this view, must be taught success values like those of the Japanese and Anglo-Americans.[23]

A heated controversy arose over this thesis. Indeed, the argument quickly overlapped and reinforced the existing cleavages concerning the effects of the slave experience on blacks and fed on the growing public interest in the Moynihan Report. Each of these foci of debate was strongly related to the federal government's policies in the War on Poverty. Millions of tax dollars were being committed to programs based on the assumption that the black family and culture were "defective" and must be replaced with the "healthy" or "normal" culture of the Anglo-Americans. Until this cultural transformation can be accomplished, it was said, poor blacks are doomed to go on perpetuating the culture of poverty and to remain trapped at the bottom of the socioeconomic ladder.

The culture of poverty debate has now filled the pages of numerous books, government publications, and scholarly articles, and it is much too far-reaching to be summarized here. We have seen already, though, that many observers doubt the black family, either now or during the slave period, is as weak or lacking in adaptive capacity as the culture of poverty thesis assumes. Moreover, most of the research conducted to determine whether poor people do, as claimed, possess a specific, distinctive culture has not supported this idea.[24] For example, the belief that poor black males do not take seriously the matter of getting and keeping jobs because they possess a "present orientation" (and are interested, therefore, only in the gratification of their many immediate desires) has been vigorously challenged by Liebow (1967). Instead of viewing the black worker as the carrier of "defective" values, Liebow (1967:64–65) maintains that what looks like a "present orientation" to the middle-class observer is, in fact, a "future orientation." The poor black worker is no less aware of the future than is his middle-class critic; but, says Liebow, these two people are looking at very different futures. The black worker is facing a future

> in which everything is uncertain except the ultimate destruction of his hopes and the eventual realization of his fears. . . . Thus, when Richard squanders a week's pay in two days it is not because, like an animal or a child, he is "present-time oriented," unaware or unconcerned with his future. He does so precisely because he is aware of the future and the hopelessness of it all (Liebow, 1967:66).

Many critics see in the culture of poverty thesis, as in the Moynihan thesis, an elaborate way to shift the responsibility for social change away from the majority and on to the shoulders of the minority. From this perspective, the culture of poverty thesis is just a "nice," "liberal" way of saying what the hereditarians have been saying all along—if they can't succeed, something must be wrong with *them*.[25] The implication of this thesis for public action is clear: we must assist them to change to become more like us. On a broader scale, this is the central argument of Anglo conformity.

We see in this conclusion a resemblance between the culture of poverty and Moynihan theses, on the one hand, and the immigrant analogy, on the other. The main thing poor blacks need is to give up their old culture, adopt that of the Anglo-Americans, and wait a few more years. Obviously, many people reject this analysis and feel that black Americans have waited long enough. From this vantage point, the worldly success of black Americans depends much more on the opportunities available to them than on changes in their culture. Once again, we see that the immigrant and colonial analogies and the various ideologies of group adjustment lie just beneath the surface of public debate over what should be done to promote secondary structural (and other forms of) assimilation among minority groups.

In the 1970s, Americans' interest in these and similar issues was quickened. In chapter 8, we explore the reactions of white Americans to the heightened protests of nonwhites during the 1960s, and we attempt to solve the puzzles that have arisen from our efforts to understand the differences in the patterns of group achievement in America.

KEY IDEAS

1. Like the Chicanos, black Americans appear to be in some ways a colonized and in some ways an immigrant minority. Up to the time of World War I, the black experience was so marked by oppression that the colonial analogy seems quite apt. The great northward "immigration" of World War I, however, laid a foundation for arguing that black Americans resemble a recent immigrant group.

2. Blacks in the English colonies did not at first occupy the status of chattel slaves. Their status was similar to that of the white bonded servants. In little more than half a century, however, their social position was that of mere property and slaves for life. Blackness had come to mean "slave."

3. The argument that the slaves were generally happy and contented ignores many facts. One of the most important of these is the large number of slave revolts that were planned and sometimes carried into effect. The revolts of Gabriel Prosser, Denmark Vesey, and Nat Turner are the most widely noted.

4. Some scholars have argued that the slave system of the United States was essentially different from and more oppressive than the slave systems of Latin America. A controversial argument favoring this thesis maintains that the "unbridled capitalism" of the United States turned plantations, in effect, into concentration camps. The result was the complete dehumanization of the slaves. Both the thesis of greater oppression and the thesis of complete personality destruction are still under review.

5. After the Civil War, southern whites were unwilling to accept the freed slaves as equals. The whites developed, therefore, a number of techniques to intimidate blacks and to restore control of the southern governments to the whites. There was not, however, an extensive system of laws regulating the relations of the races. The Jim Crow system of legal segregation developed mainly between 1890 and 1920—during the period of the new immigration. The development of the Jim Crow system was strongly encouraged by the Supreme Court's "separate but equal" doctrine in *Plessy* v. *Ferguson.*

6. As the Jim Crow system developed, black Americans were organizing to resist it and to claim their full rights as American citizens. The NAACP, the leading protest organization for decades to come, demanded full equality for blacks and launched a legal battle to attain it.

7. World War I was followed by numerous episodes of black-white conflict and the emergence of a mass secessionist movement under the leadership of Marcus Garvey. Garvey emphasized race pride, self-help, and the unity of black people everywhere.

8. During the Great Depression, black Americans began to adopt the boycott and other weapons of the labor movement as tactics to force equal treatment. The NAACP began to focus on the issue of school segregation.

9. The years during and immediately after World War II produced changes in federal policies aimed at reducing discrimination in employment, in schools, and in the armed forces.

10. In 1954, the Supreme Court ruled in *Brown* v. *Topeka Board of Education* that public school segregation was unconstitutional and was psychologically damaging to the segregated children. In the second *Brown*

decision, the court declared that desegregation should occur with "all deliberate speed."

11. Massive resistance by whites to the *Brown* decisions was met by a sharp increase in the use of nonviolent protest tactics by black Americans. Racial confrontations in southern cities such as Little Rock, Montgomery, Greensboro, and Birmingham crumbled the structure of Jim Crow segregation in public places and accommodations and paved the way for the passage of the Civil Rights Act of 1964 and the Voting Rights Act of 1965.

12. All of these changes assured the legal equality of black Americans. They did not, however, alter noticeably the living conditions of most blacks. During this period, many blacks, especially young blacks, turned away from nonviolent protest toward the use of violence. For several years, the cities of the United States were torn by racial violence.

13. Many observers have stated either that black Americans are culturally "nothing but" Americans or that their culture is a "distorted" variant of mainstream American culture. It seems more accurate to say that black Americans have developed and possess a distinctive culture of their own but that they, like the Chicanos, are moving toward an *additive* cultural assimilation.

14. Black Americans, especially females, appear to be moving toward secondary structural assimilation in jobs. There also has been secondary structural assimilation in incomes, again especially among females, but the trend among males slowed during the 1970s. The evidence on the education gap also is mixed, with the overall trend pointing toward educational assimilation (both in the years of schooling and in desegregated facilities); but there are several indications of slowed change in this respect. Finally, practically no change is occurring in the sphere of residential segregation.

15. While the rate of primary structural and marital assimilation has increased markedly, the total amount of these forms of assimilation is still very low, and the gap between blacks and whites will remain (at present rates of change) for a long time to come. The continued primary structural and marital separation of whites and blacks, along with the visible changes in cultural and secondary structural assimilation, suggests that blacks are moving toward the goal of cultural pluralism.

16. Although the "Jensen thesis" concerning black American achievement has revived the long-term dispute between hereditarians and environmentalists, public policy in the 1960s was more affected by a disagreement within the ranks of the environmentalists. Just as the comparatively high achievement of the Japanese Americans and the comparatively low achievement of the Chicanos have been interpreted by some to be a consequence of particular values found within their cultures, the culture of poverty thesis maintains that most blacks possess and transmit to

their children values that are obstacles to success. This thesis plays down the role of majority-group discrimination as a barrier to minority-group achievement.

NOTES

1. Jordan argues, in contrast, "that there is simply not enough evidence to indicate with any certainty whether Negroes were treated like white servants or not" (Jordan, "Modern Tensions and the Origins of African Slavery," *The Origins of American Slavery and Racism*, p. 86).
2. An interesting collection of views defending slavery has been assembled in McKitrick, ed., *Slavery Defended.*
3. Quoted in Elkins, *Slavery*, p. 11.
4. Sir Harry Johnston, quoted by Frazier, *The Negro in the United States*, p. 82.
5. Patterson (1977:416) notes, however, that even if Elkins is correct concerning the personality effects of slavery, it is not necessary to assume that these effects prevented slave revolts.
6. Quoted by John Horton, "Order and Conflict Theories of Social Problems as Competing Ideologies," p. 712.
7. Martin Delany described the situation in these words: "The slave is more secure than we; he knows who holds the heel upon his bosom—we know not the wretch who may grasp us by the throat." Quoted by Jacobs and Landau, eds., *To Serve the Devil*, p. 149.
8. The identification of colonization with extreme oppression, whether an actual colonial system is established or not, is explained by Wilson as follows: "Fundamental to the colonial model is the distinction between colonization as a process and colonialism as a social, political and economic system. It is the process of colonization that defines experiences which are common to many non-white people of the world, including black Americans" (Wilson, "Race Relations Models and Explanations of Ghetto Behavior," *Nation of Nations*, p. 262).
9. The Black Codes gave some recognition to the new status of blacks. In some states they could now acquire, own, and sell property; enter into contracts; and be legally married (Davie, *Negroes in American Society*, pp. 46–47). But some of the new laws restricted the freedom of blacks in so many ways that they could, in effect, be forced back into slavery.
10. The name is based on the Greek word for circle *(kyklos).*
11. The term *Jim Crow* apparently comes from a song and dance presented by Thomas D. Rice in the 1830s (Frazier, *Negro in the United States*, p. 157; C. Vann Woodward, *The Strange Career of Jim Crow*, p. 7).
12. Another important organization consisting of both blacks and whites was formed soon after the NAACP. The National Urban League, started in 1911, was an interracial effort to help blacks who were migrating to the cities to find jobs and get established. The Urban League has always been considered much more conservative than "protest" organizations like the NAACP.
13. From this perspective, the "peculiarities" of black social life are mainly reflections of social-class differences. Gordon agrees that lower-class blacks

are still not assimilated culturally but maintains this is not due to African cultural survivals (Gordon, *Assimilation in American Life,* p. 76).

14. Some subsequent results have not fully supported Gutman's view. See, for example, Agresti, "The First Decades of Freedom," pp. 697–706.

15. For illustrations, see Siegel, "On the Cost of Being a Negro," pp. 41–57, and U.S. Department of Health, Education, and Welfare, "Social Mobility in America," in *Readings in Sociology,* pp. 342–352.

16. Under these conditions of "complete" desegregation, of course, it would still be possible to have segregated classrooms *within* the schools.

17. For discussions of the implications of this important decision, see U.S. Commission on Civil Rights, Milliken v. Bradley.

18. The question frequently arises "Do blacks prefer to live in segregated housing?" A series of national polls shows that they do not and that their preference for desegregated housing is rising (Goldman, *Report From Black America,* p. 171).

19. For a full description of these surveys, see Schuman and Hatchett, *Black Racial Attitudes.*

20. Our interest here is limited to legally defined marriages. Over the centuries, of course, there has been a great deal of biological "mixing" or "miscegenation." According to Herskovits, only about 22 percent of black Americans are of unmixed African ancestry (Herskovits, *The American Negro*).

21. For references to this literature, see Monahan, "An Overview of Statistics on Interracial Marriage in the United States," pp. 223–231.

22. Jensen's article, of course, served to reinvigorate the hereditarian position (Jensen, "How Much Can We Boost IQ and Scholastic Achievement?," pp. 1–123).

23. Although some of the key elements of the culture of poverty are the same as those suggested by Kluckhohn as central to the value orientations of the Spanish Americans, there also are some differences (Kluckhohn, "Dominant and Variant Value Orientations," *Personality in Nature, Society, and Culture,* pp. 342–357). For a comparison of the two cultures, see Burma, "A Comparison of the Mexican American Subculture with the Oscar Lewis Culture of Poverty Model," *Mexican-Americans in the United States,* pp. 17–28.

24. See, for example, Coward, Williams, and Feagin, "The Culture of Poverty Debate," pp. 621–634, and Van Til and Van Til, "The Lower Class and the Future of Inequality," *Readings in Sociology,* pp. 313–321.

25. For a vigorous defense of this charge, see William Ryan, *Blaming the Victim.*

Eight

Ascending Pluralism

Ethnic diversity is an opportunity rather than a problem.

Andrew M. Greeley

Well, how *does* a nation of no one culture, no one language, no one race, no one history, no one ethnic stock continue to exist as one, while encouraging diversity?

Michael Novak

The American nationality is still forming: its processes are mysterious, and the final form, if there is ever to be a final form, is as yet unknown.

Nathan Glazer and Daniel P. Moynihan

The three preceding chapters have shown that the experiences of the Japanese Americans, Chicanos, and black Americans illustrate diverse problems in group adjustment. Some members of each group have adopted the Anglo-conformity ideology that is most approved by the dominant group. At the opposite pole, some secessionist sentiment is to be found among the black and Chicano groups. But many members of each of these groups exemplify, in preference as well as fact, some form of pluralism. In general, cultural pluralism is preferred; however, the more divisive pluralism we have labeled separatism (in chapter 3) is attractive to some members of these groups. Among black Americans, for example, 13 percent of a national sample contacted in 1969 said they thought Negroes would get ahead better if they controlled their own schools, ran their own businesses, and lived together in their own neighborhoods (Goldman, 1970:270).

Although cultural pluralism and, on a much smaller scale, separatism are very much alive among these nonwhite American minorities, one may reasonably wonder what general effect these ideologies are having on white Americans and on national policy. After all, the Japanese Americans, Chicanos, and black Americans combined represent less than one-seventh of the country's total population. Some crucial questions, therefore, are: what has happened to the descendants of the Italians, Jews, Poles, Hungarians,

Greeks, and others who came to America during the new immigration? Have they adopted Anglo conformity? Have they reached, or are they nearing, the goal of full merger with the dominant group?

These questions have received increasing attention since World War II. The war itself served to remind Americans that they were a nation of nations. German Americans, Italian Americans, and Japanese Americans were called on to fight against the home countries of their grandparents or parents. After the war, Americans of Hungarian, Czech, Lithuanian, Latvian, Estonian, Polish, and other eastern European ethnicities were torn as they watched the iron curtain of communism descend between them and many loved ones in their ancestral homelands.

Of considerable interest during this period was a new interpretation of assimilation in America proposed by Kennedy (1944). She had found in a study of intermarriage trends in New Haven, Connecticut, that the rate of out-marriage had steadily increased among seven ethnic groups. She concluded, therefore, that, as predicted by the Anglo-conformity theory, ethnic lines were indeed fading. However, her analysis revealed something else. The out-marriages were clustered along religious lines. When the members of three Protestant groups—the British, German, and Scandinavian Americans—married out, they were most likely to select partners from one of those same Protestant groups. The members of three Catholic groups—the Irish, Italians, and Poles—preferred Catholic partners if they chose to go outside their own ethnic group. Throughout the seventy-year period studied by Kennedy, Jewish exogamy remained low. Even when out-marriages crossed religious lines, Kennedy found religion was still an important consideration. Catholics, in particular, were unwilling to marry non-Catholics unless the wedding ceremony was Catholic. On the strength of these findings, Kennedy suggested that America's assimilation was occurring not in one but in three melting pots. Even though ethnic endogamy is loosening, "groups with the same religions tend to intermarry." Kennedy (1944:332) predicted, therefore, that "the future cleavages will be along religious lines." Kennedy's "triple melting-pot thesis" became the focal point of some subsequent analysis. Hollingshead (1950:624), for instance, concluded that "we are going to have three pots boiling merrily side by side with little fusion between them for an indefinite period."

Kennedy's findings were generally accepted, but her interpretation of them was questioned, notably by Herberg. In Herberg's (1960:34) view, "it would be misleading to conclude that the old ethnic lines had disappeared or were no longer significant." In the past, he argued, the nationality groups had considered religion to be a part of their ethnicity. But with the passage of time, religion has become the main instrument through which essentially ethnic concerns are preserved and expressed. The demands by the dominant group that minority groups conform to the Anglo-American pattern has focused more on language and general behavior than it has on religion. The three major religious groups, therefore, gradually have become equally "American" entities. As Herberg (1960:258) has expressed it, "To be a Protestant, a Catholic, or a Jew are the alternative ways of being an American." For this reason, people of Polish, Italian, or French-Canadian ancestry, for instance, find it much easier, and more American, to represent their ethnic concerns as Catholic concerns.

Glazer and Moynihan (1964:314) addressed the same issue in their influential analysis of ethnic groups in New York City and found, as Kennedy had, that the distinctions between the Irish, Italians, Poles, and German Catholics were being reduced by intermarriage. They agreed with Herberg, too, that as the specifically national aspect of ethnicity was declining, it was being replaced by religious affiliations and identities. Although these findings were not new, many Americans were surprised to learn that the religious distinctions that remained as ethnicity declined were themselves showing no signs of weakening. The groups that were forming along religious lines were, instead, continuing to nurture strong and enduring social differences.

Glazer and Moynihan also emphasized that the triple melting pot did not include blacks and Puerto Ricans.[1] Hence, despite the many changes in race relations that already had been effected by the Civil Rights Movement and the bright promise of further changes, the authors argued that the next stage of evolution in American society would maintain strong racial as well as religious distinctions. From this vantage point, the dramatic confrontations between whites and nonwhites that developed during the 1960s may seem understandable. This line of reasoning, however, did not alert Americans to another very surprising aspect of that turbulent period—a phenomenon referred to in such phrases as "the rise of the unmeltable ethnics" (Novak, 1971), "the new pluralism" (Feldstein and Costello, 1974:414), and "the resurgence of ethnicity" (Glazer and Moynihan, 1970:xxxi).

An Ethnic Revival

At just the moment when most social scientists were anticipating the rapid extinction of the remaining significant differences among white ethnic groups, these distinctions seemed suddenly to revive with startling intensity. At the end of the decade, in fact, Glazer and Moynihan (1970:xxxvi) noted that it no longer seemed true that religious identities were replacing ethnicity. Ethnicity was being reasserted in its own right by numerous white ethnic groups. New organizations were being formed by Polish Americans, Lithuanian Americans, Slovakian Americans, and many others. Television programs, shirt signs, and bumper stickers suddenly burst forth with commentaries announcing an awareness of, and pride in, an ethnic identification. But much more than pride was involved here. The new groups being revived (or formed) were very concerned about the rapid changes taking place in American life and the effects of these changes on their lives. This concern was particularly visible among white ethnics of lower-middle-class status, those who worked mainly in blue-collar jobs.

Most of the large-scale changes of the 1960s were perceived by working-class ethnic Americans as threatening to undermine their hard-won gains. Many white ethnics feared that the rules of "making it" in America had been changed. The War on Poverty, the apparent success of confrontation politics, and the growing opposition to the war in Vietnam all created the impression that hard work, obedience to the law, and patriotism were no longer highly valued in America. They felt betrayed and cheated.[2] When they protested the apparent abandonment of the traditional American virtues and insisted that *their* parents and grandparents had "made it" in America without a handout, they were described on television and in the newspapers as "flag wavers," "hard hats," and "pigs." They also were branded as racists.

The latter charge arose because many of the efforts to expand employment, housing, and educational opportunities for blacks, especially in the large urban centers of the north central and northeastern states, were openly and vocally opposed by working-class whites, many of whom were not Anglo-Americans. The resistance of white ethnics to public assistance for blacks aroused the belief that the so-called resurgence of ethnicity was really nothing but a "cover" for white racism.[3] But the interracial conflict was not simply a "white backlash." It had economic and political roots, and it involved the continued existence of many of the ethnic neighborhoods that had been created during the years of the new immigration.

Ethnic neighborhoods, as noted previously, were formed as places of refuge and protection in an alien world. The immigrants needed the support and assistance of others like themselves in order to establish a foothold in the new country. The ethnic neighborhood provided an economic base for the struggling newcomers. It also facilitated their efforts to organize and to participate collectively in the political system of America. In the neighborhood, they could exchange information concerning the location of jobs and the views of various candidates for political office. Through neighborhood organizations, they could combine their forces to combat discrimination in employment or to negotiate with "city hall." In the neighborhood, they could engage in deeply satisfying human relationships with others who shared their language, religion, cuisine, and memories of the old country. The ethnic American neighborhood, in short, has been a device to enable immigrants to come to grips with the new while preserving many of the psychological satisfactions of the old. Mikulski (1974:441) describes these neighborhoods as "genuine urban villages. Warmth, charm, and zesty communal spirit were their characteristics."

Viewed in this way, the ethnic neighborhood has many "positive," desirable features. It may, in fact, be cited as an excellent example of what is meant by cultural pluralism. However, ethnic neighborhoods, also, as described in chapter 3, have long been viewed with suspicion by native Americans. They are the "slums," the source of organized crime and many other social pathologies. The ethnic neighborhood is a living reminder that Anglo conformity has not been completely successful. Their continuance, especially into the third generation, strikes many people as "downright un-American." Certainly any effort to *strengthen* such neighborhoods in order to assure their continued existence flies in the face of the expectation that "the ethnics" will adopt full Anglo conformity and disperse into the broader society as quickly as possible. Consequently, efforts to reassert one's ethnicity are likely to be condemned or ridiculed. They are likely to be seen as an attempt to continue something "negative" and undesirable.

The rapid, large-scale social changes of the 1960s brought these "positive" and "negative" images of white ethnicity to the forefront of public discussion. Since in the large northern and eastern cities many white ethnic neighborhoods were close to black neighborhoods, the attempt to expand housing opportunities for blacks and to desegregate public schools had a large and immediate impact on the nearby white neighborhoods. When the residents protested that desegregation was being achieved at the expense of their distinctive traditions, their resistance was taken to be proof of white ethnic racism. The difficulty here, of course, is that one cannot easily tell how much of the resistance to desegregation is inspired by the desire to maintain valuable cultural heritages and how much is overt discrimination against blacks. As Glazer and Moynihan (1970:xxxix) have expressed it, "To emphasize the virtues of maintaining an ethnic neighborhood is different from emphasizing an exclusion of Negroes, in sense and logic, though the acts that serve one aim are hard to distinguish from the acts that serve the other."

Both private and governmental forces pressed against the white ethnic neighborhoods. These forces were closely related to the desegregation effort but went beyond it. On the private side, the "blockbusting" tactics of real-estate brokers and "redlining" policies of lending agencies each contributed directly to the disintegration of the neighborhoods. "Blockbusting" refers to the racially tinged methods used by real-estate dealers to frighten whites into selling their homes for less than the true value. Many whites fear that the movement of blacks into their neighborhoods spells doom not only for the area's ethnic integrity but for its economic value as well. Playing on these fears, real-estate brokers may arrange the sale of one home on a city block to a black family. Once the block has been penetrated, the "blockbuster" may buy a number of other homes cheaply from the remaining whites. The dealer then may turn a neat profit by selling the homes at much higher prices to middle-class blacks.

"Redlining" (or "blacklisting") does not necessarily lead to the replacement of white residents by blacks, but it does contribute to the deterioration of neighborhoods. As residential neighborhoods age, lenders at some point may become convinced that the housing there is no longer a safe investment. They may fear the area is on the verge of becoming a slum. When this happens, they may refuse to grant home-improvement loans to home owners, thus ensuring that the property will not be maintained and that the area will indeed become a slum.

The private pressures on the white ethnic neighborhoods have been multiplied by government policies. For example, the VA and the FHA frequently have followed the same policies as private lenders, refusing to make loans on old houses or houses in so-called marginal areas. Moreover, since World War II, the federal government has pursued a vigorous policy of urban renewal. This policy has required that dilapidated areas within cities be cleared to make room for public housing, highways, civic centers, and so on. The administrators and planners of urban renewal programs, of course, follow certain guidelines to determine which areas of the city are slums or are likely to become slums. Old and rundown houses, a high population density, and mixed land use are accepted as the most important signs that an area is "falling apart" and should be cleared for other purposes. These signs may be quite misleading, however. Many working-class white ethnic neighborhoods share these characteristics but are by no means "falling apart" (Krickus, 1974:434). Although they may appear to the casual eye to be decaying, they are many times places of hidden social strength (Kriegel, 1974: 419). Such neighborhoods are direct descendants of the "urban villages" created by the immigrants to meet life's challenges; for many people, they still serve this purpose.

The frequent inability of the white ethnics to prevent the physical destruction of their neighborhoods reflected some of the other problems that stimulated their resurgence as distinctive groups. In the first place, they had been subjected to a severe economic "squeeze." Many of them were struggling to make a living, keep their homes, pay their bills, and, perhaps, send a child to college. Although they were seriously pressed by inflation and unemployment, they were "too rich" to qualify for many of the governmental and private programs that had been established to assist poor people. As Mikulski (1974: 442) stated, "Colleges make practically no effort to provide scholarships for kids named Colstiani, Stukowski, or Klima."

Another important factor contributing to the growing anger of the white ethnics was a marked shift in the American political process. The formation of Franklin Roosevelt's New Deal during the Great Depression of the 1930s represented an alliance of labor, white ethnic groups, and liberal intellectuals. During the 1960s, labor and liberal leaders shifted their attention toward the nonwhite minorities, especially black Americans (Feldstein and Costello, 1974:417). The ability of white ethnics to be heard sympathetically in the halls of government was suddenly and sharply reduced. By the beginning of the 1970s, consequently, white ethnics increasingly were looking for ways to translate their many grievances into effective political action. They sought to ensure that government programs for the victims of discrimination did not ignore their needs and problems. They felt forced to compete with blacks, Chicanos, and Puerto Ricans for space, jobs, and federal dollars. At the national level, they supported strongly candidates such as Richard Nixon and

George Wallace; in local elections, candidates openly sought the "Polish vote" or the "Italian vote" in a way that had not been seen for many years. In this process, the white ethnics inevitably appeared to be opposed to progressive social change and to reducing discrimination against nonwhite Americans.

Some of those who have defended the demands of the white ethnics insist that their critics have failed to understand that the social changes of the 1960s were being accomplished disproportionately at the expense of the white ethnics who lived in the centers of the large cities. Novak (1971:14) observed that the white ethnics wished to know "why the gains of blacks should be solely at *their* expense. They themselves have so little and feel so constricted." Anglo-Americans who lived in the suburbs, worked in professional jobs, and sent their children to private schools were to a considerable extent insulated from the direct costs of desegregation programs and could afford, therefore, to see the resulting interracial conflict in purely moral terms. It was for them, to cite Novak (1971:14) again, "a moral gravy train."

But to interpret the resurgence of white ethnic awareness exclusively in terms of antiblack sentiment or the rational defense of group interest would be to miss another very important point. It seems almost certain that the white ethnics had never stopped being aware of their old-country identities. They had subdued regular displays of ethnic consciousness because, as Greeley (1971:18) has noted, "it was not considered good form in the larger society to talk about such subjects, save on approved days of the year like Columbus Day or St. Patrick's Day." But as black militance and consciousness grew stronger during the 1960s, and as American institutions began to recognize and accept the right of blacks to proclaim and celebrate their blackness, people of many other groups saw no reason to continue to hide their own ethnic pride. "What the Blacks have done," Greeley (1971:18) argues, "is to legitimate ethnic self-consciousness."

The ensuing debate over the future of racial and ethnic groups in America is still underway. Will the white ethnics follow the path of the colonial Scotch-Irish and Germans and for all practical purposes soon disappear into the American mainstream? Or will they persist as distinct groups? Will nonwhites follow the path of the colonial whites but at a slower rate? Or will they continue indefinitely as more or less separate groups? Will some form of pluralism be accepted by all groups—even the Anglo-Americans—thus encouraging many groups to maintain their distinctive heritages? Or will the Anglo-Americans insist on Anglo conformity? Finally, how likely is it that separation or secession will occur?

When Is Soon?

Any meaningful speculation about these important matters requires some further consideration of a prior question. When we say that an ethnic group will "persist" or that it will "soon disappear," what periods of time are involved? We have seen that the main point of reference in most discussions of group adjustment in America is the three-generations process. We have seen, too, that by this standard very few American groups have achieved full assimilation in the expected period of time. Even the colonial Scotch-Irish and Germans did not undergo primary structural and marital assimilation within three generations. The Germans, in particular, maintained their language and other cultural elements well beyond that time. (See chapter 2.) Indeed, it may still be possible in the last quarter of the twentieth century to find some distinctive patterns of behavior among the descendants of these colonial immigrants. In this sense, they may be said to "persist." Additionally, if the conditions were right, it is still possible that these faint traces of group identity could serve as the foundation for some sort of ethnic group revival. It is nonetheless true that the present levels of merger between these groups and the Anglo-American core are so high as to be virtually complete, and it is very likely that these levels of merger were reached before the end of the nineteenth century. Since the colonial Scotch-Irish and Germans began entering in force during the early part of the eighteenth century, we may say that the full Anglo-conformity assimilation of a northwestern or western European group in America may occur in less than 200 years, possibly in less than 150 years. Although this estimate extends the three-generations idea to as much as six or eight generations, it gives evidence that the full merger of some groups does occur, as Park said, "eventually." Moreover, if one adopts the cultural pluralists' definition of full assimilation, it is likely that the colonial immigrants approximated that goal in three or, at most, four generations.

Turning from the colonial immigrants to those who formed the old immigration, we find little to alter the conclusions just reached. Many of the old immigrants have been in this country for as long as six generations, and few have been here less than three. The level of cultural and secondary structural assimilation that has occurred between them and the Anglo-American core is high but not as high as that of the colonial immigrants. The old immigrant Irish and Germans in New York, for instance, are more distinguishable than their colonial counterparts (Glazer and Moynihan, 1964). While the present levels of old immigrant assimilation do not meet the strictest requirements of Anglo-conformity ideology, they certainly do qualify as cultural pluralism. Furthermore, there is no reason to suppose that the old immigrants are less assimilated at this point than the colonials were after a similar period of time. And there is every reason to suppose that with the further passage of time the old immigrants will move toward higher levels of Anglo conformity. Again, this judgment must be tempered with the realization that a number of events could revive and strengthen the ethnic bonds that still exist or that a new ethnic group might arise from the remnants of the old.

The status of the white ethnics of the new immigration is, as we have seen, a topic of contemporary debate. Why after two to three generations are these groups still so much in evidence? What is going to happen to them? Are the white ethnics "on the threshold of disappearance" (Dinnerstein and Reimers, 1975:140), or will they continue to play an important role in the future (Greeley, 1971:167)?

Such questions reveal clearly why it is essential to be specific about the time periods under discussion. Curiously, the prediction that the white ethnics will "soon disappear" is not necessarily inconsistent with the prediction that they will continue to be significant for some time to come. It all depends on what "soon disappear" and "some time to come" mean. In historical terms, "soon" may easily mean another generation or two. And "disappear" may mean a level of merger similar to that attained by the nineteenth-century Irish and Germans.

On the basis of these considerations, the following speculations seem reasonable. The white ethnics of the new immigration have not disappeared in three generations, but neither did the colonial or old immigrants.[4] While three generations is long enough to permit a high degree of cultural and secondary structural assimilation, the remaining forms of assimilation may take much longer. Even when the host and immigrant groups are similar in race and culture, full Anglo-conformity assimilation may require as much as eight generations. On the assumption that the new immigrants are moving toward a full merger with the dominant group, they should become decreasingly distinctive as time goes on. Within three more generations, they may be no more distinctive than the nineteenth-century Irish and Germans now are. Perhaps, given another two generations beyond that, they may be no more distinctive than the colonial Irish and Germans now are. In short, the sheer fact that the new immigrants have not disappeared within three generations is not really too surprising. The expectation that they would disappear has rested on a misunderstanding of the group adjustments that have occurred in the past. The speed of Anglo-conformity assimilation among the colonial and old immigrants has been much slower than is generally recognized; therefore, the belief that the merger of the new immigrants with the host group is unusually slow has not yet really been put to the test.

Nevertheless, even though the colonial and old immigrants resisted Anglo conformity and assimilation and frequently were successful in maintaining their identities well beyond three generations, the pluralist tendencies of the present period definitely seem to be stronger than at any previous time in our history. Not only are the minority groups themselves displaying a strong determination to protect and develop their heritages, but also the acceptance of cultural pluralism appears to be increasing among the members of the dominant group. Hence, it is by no means clear that the process of Anglo conformity, even if given sufficient time, will affect the new immigrants as much as it has the old. Cultural pluralism may be developing into the principal view of the way immigrants should become Americanized.

While this conclusion seems reasonable in regard to white ethnics, how well does it fit the situation of nonwhite Americans? Please recall that some observers have interpreted the conflict between the Anglo-Americans and the nonwhite American minorities in terms of the colonial analogy. Under this interpretation, the initial relations between the dominant group and the colonized minorities establishes a pattern that does not lead toward Anglo conformity. This pattern leads, rather, to an attempt by the minority to decolonize, perhaps through the establishment of separate nations, by over-throwing the invaders, or by leaving the territory altogether. The dominant group, for its part, prefers either that the nonwhites leave the territory or assimilate culturally while remaining apart and subordinate in all other ways. Since, in this view, both the dominant group and nonwhite minorities resist the full merger of the groups, one would expect the continuation of friction among them, resulting after a time in separation or secession.

The main criticisms of the colonial analogy rest on an effort to show that some nonwhite groups (e.g., the Japanese Americans) have achieved a high level of cultural and secondary structural assimilation and that the recent historical experiences of the Chicanos, blacks, and Indians resemble in essential ways those of the new immigrants from Europe. This argument—the immigrant analogy—does not claim that the immigration experience of the Japanese and the migration experiences of the other groups are identical to that of European immigrants. The nonwhite groups have faced, as Kristol (1972:205) concedes, "unique and peculiar dilemmas of their own." How-ever, as Glazer (1971:451) insists, "the differences are smaller and the similarities greater" than the colonial analogy suggests. From this standpoint, for instance, most blacks in the northern cities have not yet been there three generations, and while they have met less favorable conditions there than previous immigrants, their experiences have not been radically different from those of some of the white ethnics. The immigrant analogy does not deny the validity of the colonial analogy as an interpretation of some of the experiences of nonwhites in America (e.g., slavery, the conquest of the Indians and Chicanos, the relocation centers). It does assert, however, that in different ways the nonwhites are moving toward some form of assimilation, perhaps cultural pluralism, and are moving away from separation and secession. From the standpoint of national unity, the immigrant analogy is evidently more optimistic than the colonial analogy. Which, then, gives us the best basis for forecasting the probable course of race relations in the United States? As we have seen, the answer to this question is still a matter of keen debate. But it is possible, as frequently happens, that the wrong question has been asked. Since the history of black Americans, Chicanos, Japanese Americans, and Indian Americans contain certain elements that may justify either the colonial or the immigrant view, we may conclude (as people frequently do in such arguments) that both views are to some extent correct. Perhaps only time will tell which view most nearly describes the future. But this is really not a very satisfactory conclusion; so let us consider an alternative idea, proposed by Francis (1976), that may help to clarify the issue.

Primary and Secondary Ethnic Groups

We have stressed throughout that the conditions surrounding the initial contact between groups are extremely important in understanding the subsequent course of their relations. We have observed in general (1) that a conquered minority is likely to be hostile for a long period of time and to have separatist and secessionist tendencies and (2) that an immigrant minority is likely to exhibit hostility for a shorter period of time and to prefer assimilation. There is a substantial amount of evidence, drawn from racial and ethnic contact throughout the world, to support these generalizations. It is their strength, indeed, that sustains the debate over the colonial and immigrant analogies. For this reason, the alternative view we will consider does not question the accuracy of these generalizations. It attempts, instead, to explain why the conquest and immigration sequences usually, rather than always, result in tendencies toward secession and assimilation, respectively. In so doing, it may assist us to see the facts of conquest and assimilation in a new light.

As mentioned in chapter 2, Francis has suggested that in the modern world contacts between racial and ethnic groups lead to the formation of two main kinds of groups, which he calls simply *primary* and *secondary*.[5]

The members of primary ethnic groups enter a society as entire units: the members of secondary ethnic groups enter individually or in small bands. Since primary ethnic groups are complete social units at the outset, their relationship to the host society is mainly political. The group's members "remain firmly embedded . . . in a web of familiar relationships" (Francis, 1976:169). The primary ethnic group seems to be a "fragment" of its "parent" society. It is a "viable corporate unit" (Francis, 1976:397) that is able to "continue functioning in the host society in much the same way as . . . in the parent society" (Francis, 1976:170). The members do not wish equal treatment with the majority and wish to be a separate group. They, therefore, resist vigorously any efforts that the host society might make to bring about any aspect of assimilation.

The conditions leading to the formation of a secondary ethnic group are quite different. Its members are at the beginning completely dependent on the host society for the satisfaction of all their needs, economic as well as social. There are no established ethnic institutions; therefore, there is no web of familiar relationships. The ethnic group itself remains to be formed within the host society in response to the conditions there. The group's respective members possess little in the way of resources and cannot continue to function as they did in the parent society. The social pattern that the group develops represents a mixture of the cultures of the parent society and the host society. It is identical to neither but is in some sense a variety of each (Francis, 1976:223). The members of a secondary ethnic group desire equal treatment with the majority and are more willing to undergo assimilation than are those of a primary ethnic group (Francis, 1976:397).

This comparison of primary and secondary ethnic groups gives us an important clue concerning why colonized minorities are more likely to develop along nationalistic lines and to be more resistant to assimilation than are immigrant minorities. When minorities arise through conquest, they are more likely to form primary than secondary ethnic groups. When minorities arise through immigration, on the other hand, they are more likely to form secondary than primary ethnic groups. Since the primary ethnic group is a more nearly complete social unit from the beginning, an important objective is to hold what it has. Its relationship to the host society, therefore, is likely to be one of resistance to assimilation. The secondary ethnic group, in contrast, is formed in part as a response to discrimination by members of the host group. An important goal of the secondary ethnic group, therefore, is to ensure that its members are not objects of discrimination in such areas as jobs, education, and political participation.

Let us now apply the above reasoning to the debate over the colonial and immigrant analogies. Although colonized minorities are likely to form primary ethnic groups, and immigrant minorities are likely to form secondary ethnic groups, these outcomes are not inevitable. Primary ethnic groups may arise through migration, and secondary ethnic groups may arise through conquest. Knowing whether a group has entered the society by conquest or immigration enables a person to guess what type of ethnic group probably has been formed. But useful as this information is, it may lead us to miss a central point: regardless of whether a given ethnic group has been conquered or has come from elsewhere, the fundamental question is whether the group actually did become primary or secondary after coming into contact with the host society. It is the result of contact rather than the process leading to it that has the greatest effect on the subsequent relations of the dominant and subordinate groups.

The primary-secondary distinction clarifies another point that is hidden in the debate over the colonial and immigrant analogies. Whether the original contact between two groups leads to the formation of the primary or a secondary ethnic group, this situation is not fixed for all time. An ethnic group that initially becomes primary may at a later time be transformed into a secondary ethnic group and vice versa. This view of the outcome of contact between a dominant and a subordinate group, therefore, is much more dynamic than either the colonial or immigrant analogies.

The Future of Ethnicity in America

What does this alternative view tell us about the present and future relations of whites and nonwhites in America? Consider, for example, the Chicanos. As we have emphasized, this group clearly was created through conquest. The fact of conquest itself, however, is not so crucial for our understanding of the present and future condition of this dominated group as is the fact that following the Treaty of Guadalupe Hidalgo, the Chicanos became a primary ethnic group. They did not seek to enter the mainstream of the larger society and did not depend on its economy or other institutions for the satisfaction of life's needs. They maintained this position well into the twentieth century. Nevertheless, as the forces of industrialization and urbanization became strong in the Southwest, not only the Chicanos but Mexican nationals as well began to move into the American economy. The vast social changes accompanying the immigration of large numbers of Mexicans to the United States did not mean that the Chicanos had somehow stopped being a colonized minority or that the history of conquest between them and the dominant group could henceforth be disregarded (or rewritten to suit the purposes of assimilationists). These changes meant, rather, that the Chicano group was beginning the transformation from a primary to a secondary ethnic group. Despite the efforts of many, probably most, Chicanos to resist the transformation, this process has predominated throughout the present century. Since the end of World War II, the majority of Chicanos have moved into urban settings and have become dependent on the industrial economy for their livelihoods. At the same time, they increasingly have accepted their status as American citizens and have expected and demanded that they be accorded the rights and privileges of other Americans. In short, they have become predominantly a secondary ethnic group. It is this fact rather than the movement of large numbers of Mexicans to the United States since 1910 that justifies the expectation that the Chicanos now are moving toward the American mainstream. Most Chicanos appear to desire "the best of both worlds." While this formula for group adjustment is somewhat vague, the specific demands presented in behalf of the group (even by militants) generally imply an acceptance of cultural pluralism.[6] It seems likely that this perspective will continue to gain support in the years to come.

This judgment concerning the goals of the Chicanos must be accepted only tentatively. While the Chicanos are presently members of a secondary ethnic group and thus desire to be treated like other citizens, they may not remain so. The proximity to Mexico and the continuation of discrimination against them within the United States are forces that favor their possible retransformation into a primary ethnic group. Unless these citizens are permitted to advance (as compared to the dominant group) in income, education, political participation, health care, police protection, and housing, they may at some point reject pluralist goals and seek separatist or secessionist solutions instead. While such an occurrence is improbable, it certainly is not impossible. Even less likely, however, is the opposite possibility—that the Chicanos will soon embrace Anglo conformity. There is every reason to believe that the Chicanos will remain, and will wish to remain, a distinctive ethnic group within American life for many generations to come.[7]

A similar conclusion is appropriate for black Americans, though in this case our reasoning follows a different path. There can be no question that this group under slavery was cruelly treated and endured unbelievable suffering. These facts surely do suggest strong parallels between the experience of the black Americans and that of the Chicanos. We may, therefore, with considerable justification, view the blacks as a colonized minority. However, and this is crucial, *the blacks did not form a primary ethnic group.* How could they? They were not a fragment of a parent society. They represented many different nationalities and did not share a common culture. They were not independent of the host society. They were totally, unmercifully, dependent on it. Indeed, even the formation of a secondary ethnic group was greatly hindered by the slave system, with its vigilance and deliberate interference with the efforts of the slaves to communicate with one another and to organize. Only slowly, painfully, were the black slaves able to construct institutions of their own within the host society. They did this, however, and became in the process an integral element of American society—just as much a part of American history as the Anglo-Americans, the Scotch-Irish, or the Germans.

Our sketch of black American history in chapter 7 does not furnish the evidence needed to determine just how popular the various ideologies of group adjustment—ranging from Anglo conformity to secession—have been. We know only that their popularity has varied through time. But even without systematic evidence—and with all due respect to Garveyism—it seems safe to say that during most of the present century blacks have been mainly divided between cultural pluralism and Anglo conformity. The NAACP, the Urban League, CORE, the March on Washington movement, SCLC, and many other organizations have centered their efforts on improving jobs, education, income, housing, health care, and so on (i.e., on increasing secondary structural assimilation). Since these goals are common to both Anglo conformity and cultural pluralism, it is not clear which of these ideologies has been most favored.

The decade of the 1960s brought about noticeable changes in the perspectives of black Americans. They increasingly doubted that Anglo conformity was a desirable goal and that cultural pluralism was feasible; separatist ideas again gained a more sympathetic hearing. Whether this change in the mood of black America represents a long-term or short-term trend remains to be seen. However, one thing seems apparent. The continuation of discrimination against black Americans is sure to strengthen the hand of the separatist group, which may lead the black Americans toward the formation of a primary ethnic group. Either way, however, black Americans will continue to be a distinctive ethnic group within American society for many additional generations.

Given the above, the following tentative conclusions are offered. The main quarrel between the Anglo-Americans and white ethnics concerns cultural pluralism. The strength of Anglo conformity is greater among the former, while the strength of pluralism is greater among the latter. There is virtually no support within either group for separatism for whites or for secessionism.

The picture is different when whites are compared to nonwhites, but not drastically so. There is definitely some support within both sets of groups for separatism, with the strongest support being among the whites. For instance, many whites want blacks to be kept out of their neighborhoods and feel they have the right to keep them out (Taylor, Sheatsley, and Greeley, 1978:269). In both sets of groups, however, the predominant ideology in regard to the other set is cultural pluralism.

The increasing support for cultural pluralism among both whites and nonwhites suggests that a foundation is being constructed for a broad agreement on ethnic group goals. Although the popularity of separatism may not be ignored, pluralism has emerged as the chief alternative to Anglo conformity in American thought concerning racial and ethnic relations. This point is frequently obscured by criticisms of assimilationist theory. For example, many critics conclude their attacks on assimilationist theory by advocating cultural pluralism. Despite its rejection of full Anglo conformity, cultural pluralism (we have tried to show) is best understood as a form of assimilation.

To insist that Anglo conformity and cultural pluralism are both forms of assimilation, however, may obscure another important point. We must emphasize again that the differences between these two are by no means trivial. Quite different social policies and tactics of change are sometimes suggested by these two assimilationist ideologies. One of the clearest illustrations of this point is the example of bilingual-bicultural education presented in chapter 1. Most people who favor Anglo conformity are opposed to programs of bilingual-bicultural education. Although the opposition is strongest toward public school programs of this type, it extends also to private programs. We have seen, for example, that Anglo-Americans objected to the language schools of the Japanese. They also objected to the Talmud-Torah schools of the Jews, and, there has always been some suspicion that Catholic parochial instruction—even when conducted in English—is designed to maintain foreign ways in our midst. Nevertheless, the pursuit of Anglo conformity is not logically inconsistent with some versions of bilingual-bicultural education. For instance, some liberal Anglo conformists are willing to support bilingual-bicultural programs in the public schools for a comparatively short period of time. The aim of such a program is to act as a "bridge" between the culture of the home and the culture of the larger society. The expectation in this case is that minority children will be most successfully "weaned" from the parent culture if their primary instruction is conducted in the language of the home. As is usual under Anglo-conformity doctrine, however, children taught in this way are expected after a few years to complete the crossover to the English language and Anglo-American ways and to leave their ethnic culture permanently behind.

It is here that Anglo-conformity policy and pluralist policy differ. Cultural pluralists may agree that bilingual-bicultural education should give the child a full command of English and the customs and values of the dominant society. They will not agree, though, that the object of such an education should be to wean the children away from the parent culture. On the contrary, from the perspective of cultural pluralism, bilingual-bicultural education should ensure that minority children will not lose their ethnic heritage. It is expected that they will be assisted in preserving and elaborating their heritage in a full and appreciative way.

These differences in the educational policies favored by Anglo conformists and cultural pluralists should dispel any notion that the debate between them is purely academic. The public schools in America, as traditionally operated, clearly are instruments of Anglo conformity. Furthermore, it does not follow that any program of bilingual-bicultural education is pluralistic. The implementation of an educational program in the public schools that would genuinely meet the criteria of pluralism would require significant changes in the curriculum, teaching materials, training of teachers, and allocation of funds. Beyond this, of course, would be numerous smaller problems such as those encountered in the assignment of students and teachers to schools and classrooms. At what point should non-English speakers be placed in desegregated classrooms? If desegregation begins in kindergarten or the first grade, should the dominant-group children also be required to become bilingual? When should the minority children be shifted to classes taught exclusively in English? These and many other problems are certain to appear in any practical effort to pursue the goal of cultural pluralism.

But these changes, while large, controversial, and difficult to effect, are quite modest compared to the demands of the advocates of separatism. Under this doctrine, the minority children would not be required to master the language and customs of the dominant group. Indeed, in areas in which ethnic groups are a majority, the schools would be under their separate control, and any child of the dominant group who might attend such a school would be expected to conform to the standards of the given minority. Quite clearly, the aim of such a program would be "a transformation of American institutions rather than an inclusion into them" (Skolnick, 1975:573). Quite clearly, also, it would be extremely difficult to muster the support necessary to introduce such changes into education in modern America. Even cultural pluralists consider such far-reaching proposals extreme and unworkable.

Another example of the different social policies preferred by Anglo conformists and cultural pluralists may be found in the controversy surrounding the preservation of ethnic neighborhoods. As noted earlier in this chapter, Anglo conformists tend to view the continuation of white ethnic neighborhoods with suspicion. People who live there and struggle to maintain a distinctive ethnic culture are considered to be something less than full-fledged or "real" Americans. These "hyphenated" Americans, Anglo conformists believe, should be strongly encouraged by government policies covering such things as VA and FHA loans, urban renewal, and highway construction to move out of their neighborhoods and disperse throughout the cities.

We have seen that many minority-group members take a very different view of the matter. To them, the ethnic neighborhood does not represent a restraint on assimilation. It represents, rather, the way in which a group of people have chosen to express their Americanism. The neighborhood is a source of social morale and is the main link through which the individual is "plugged into" the society. The individual receives social and psychological support from family and friends in the neighborhood. The destruction of the neighborhood, therefore, does not signify the end of the foreign culture and the complete adoption of American culture. It may signify instead the destruction of a specific way of being an American.[8] It is not surprising, therefore, that many white ethnics object to the assumption by government officials that the old neighborhoods are slums and therefore oppose policies that further their deterioration.

This brief comparison of the social policy preferences of Anglo conformists and cultural pluralists should suffice to show that they do indeed differ—and in ways that most Americans consider to be of great importance. However, their disagreements—though large and significant—take place primarily within a mutually accepted economic and political framework. This does not mean that cultural pluralists are uncritical of the American economic and political system. Nor does it mean that the conflicts arising between Anglo conformists and pluralists in this connection are minor. What it does mean is that cultural pluralists believe the operating principles of American life afford, in Glazer's (1972:174) words "enormous scope for group diversity." Although the dominant group has long wished to convert the ideas of Anglo conformity into the law of the land—to *require* that everyone become "Americanized" along the lines they prefer—the official policy of the country in the long run always has rejected this approach as "un-American." It is true, as our historical review illustrates, that official discrimination has occurred against many of our ethnic groups, especially against the nonwhite groups, but our courts and legislatures have declared (even if slowly) that all of these acts are opposed to America's basic principles. Slavery was, at last, ended; the relocation of the Japanese was declared illegal; the blacks, Indians, and Japanese have become citizens; and discrimination on the basis of race, color, and national origins has been declared unconstitutional (Glazer, 1972:175). The basic faith of the cultural pluralists is that the consensus on the principles of American economic and political life does not require abject submission to the will of the dominant group. Even though the amount and severity of dominant-group discrimination in our history must give even an optimist pause, the main ethnic-group conflicts of the past have been settled on the side of the rights of minorities. Stated differently, the "tyranny of the majority," which Tocqueville warned might be the fatal flaw of democracy, has, so far, been forestalled, and cultural pluralists believe the institutions of this nation are sufficiently flexible to permit this pattern of group adjustments to continue.

The right to maintain a pluralist pattern, however, does not assure a group's actual success in doing so. Regardless of the desire of a group's members to have "the best of both," may it not be true, as discussed in chapter 1, that the forces behind the historical shift away from tradition and toward modernity will gradually erode the distinctiveness of the ethnic groups in American society? Will these groups, as Park's cycle theory insists, finally be "melted" into the dominant society?

Our analysis supports two basic conclusions. First, America's shift from an agrarian to an urban-industrial society has made it extremely difficult for primary ethnic groups to survive or be generated. During this century, the Chicanos have become much more nearly a secondary than a primary ethnic group. However, our second conclusion is that the adjustment of the colonial, old, and new immigrants from Europe demonstrates that ethnic ties never- theless typically persist for many generations within the American setting. While many groups have undergone a high degree of cultural and secondary structural assimilation within three generations, the third generation frequently has experienced a renewed interest in its ethnic heritage. Moreover, given the proper circumstances, even later revitalizations of ethnic ties may occur. Nevertheless, in time, even the secondary ethnic groups will succumb to the homogenizing pressures of America's industrial civilization. No one knows how long this outcome may take. Unless there are catastrophic changes in the world order, it seems almost certain that the white ethnics will disappear before the nonwhites; but taking history as our guide, some of the former could sustain themselves for several additional generations and the disap- pearance of the latter could take centuries.

Taken together these two conclusions suggest a third. While primary ethnic groups may be "obsolete" in modern societies, a "leftover" from times gone by, secondary ethnic groups are compatible with an urban- industrial society. Indeed, as most critics of Anglo conformity fondly note, America's great industrial might could not have been developed without the enormous contributions of her racial and ethnic minorities. Although the continued existence of these minorities may from time to time pose a problem for national unity, they also may help to sustain a sense of individual and social purpose for many Americans. Valued ethnic identities may serve as social insulation—what Handlin has called "contexts of belonging"—to prevent the anonymity and bewilderment that frequently develops within urban-industrial settings.[9]

A far greater problem than the continuing existence of ethnic groups is the continuing failure to afford the opportunity for secondary structural assimilation for all Americans who wish it. To reach this goal, we must moderate our long-standing preoccupation with prejudice and focus more directly on the reduction of discrimination. This step is essential to the realization of our people's finest impulses.

KEY IDEAS

1. The decline in the importance of ethnic identities in twentieth-century America has been more apparent than real. There has been a tendency to express ethnic concerns as religious concerns.

2. During the 1970s, the right of Americans to have and maintain an ethnic heritage other than the Anglo-American heritage was increasingly defended.

3. Considerable conflict was generated around the issue of the preservation of ethnic neighborhoods. Government and business policies that tended to identify such neighborhoods as slums were vigorously attacked. White ethnics also frequently fought desegregation of schools and neighborhoods on the ground that such efforts placed an unfair burden on them.

4. The occurrence of full Anglo-conformity assimilation has been much slower than is generally recognized. Very few American groups have achieved full merger with the dominant group within three generations. However, virtually complete merger has occurred for practically all white ethnic groups within eight generations. Hence, groups from the countries of the new immigration are unlikely to disappear in less than four generations, and they may continue for eight. This means that some new immigrant groups presently in the United States will persist for at least one more generation and perhaps for as many as five. It is not known whether the period of ethnic distinctiveness can be extended beyond this point.

5. Since no nonwhite group has experienced full Anglo-conformity assimilation, it is unknown whether this process can occur. However, some nonwhite immigrant groups (e.g., the Japanese Americans) have experienced a high level of cultural pluralism, showing that under some circumstances this assimilationist goal may be approximated by nonwhites within three generations.

6. Francis (1976) has presented a theory that relates conquest and immigration to ethnic-group formation. According to Francis, primary ethnic groups are viable corporate units whose members seek to maintain their group rather than to be accepted as equal members of the dominant society. Secondary ethnic groups form within the host society and serve, among other things, as instruments to assist the group's members to attain equal treatment. Primary ethnic groups are more likely to be formed through conquest, while secondary ethnic groups are more likely to arise through immigration.

7. Francis' analysis of primary and secondary ethnic groups may explain why heavily oppressed groups like the Chicanos and black Americans nonetheless adopt cultural pluralism or Anglo conformity as goals. For example, although the Chicanos originally were conquered and formed a primary ethnic group, their subsequent experiences have, for the most

part, transformed them into a secondary ethnic group. However, even though cultural pluralism is now widely accepted among Chicanos, the continuation of discrimination against them could lead to their retransformation into a primary ethnic group.

8. Unlike Chicanos, black Americans were not a fragment of some parent society, and they did not form a primary ethnic group. Consequently, despite the unspeakable oppression of slavery, black Americans generally have pursued Anglo conformity and cultural pluralism.

9. The main line of division between the Anglo-Americans and white ethnics concerns cultural pluralism. Anglo conformity is stronger among the former, and cultural pluralism is stronger among the latter.

10. Although separatist sentiment is stronger across the white-nonwhite line, the main division here also is between those who favor cultural pluralism or some alternative.

11. Anglo conformity and cultural pluralism, though both ideologies of assimilation, lead in many cases to noticeably different social policies and tactics of change. These differences nevertheless occur within a framework of broad agreement.

12. America's shift from an agrarian to an urban-industrial society has made it extremely difficult for primary ethnic groups to survive or be generated. Nevertheless, secondary ethnic groups may persist within American society for many generations.

13. While ethnic groups, even secondary ethnic groups, may pose a problem for national unity, they also assist to give meaning and purpose to people's lives.

14. The failure to grant equal opportunity to achieve secondary structural assimilation is a far more serious problem for America than the existence of ethnic divisions. Higher levels of secondary structural assimilation among minorities depend more on reductions in discrimination than in prejudice.

NOTES

1. Justice Thurgood Marshall has made the point as follows: "The dream of America as the great melting pot has not been realized for the Negro; because of his skin color he never even made it into the pot" (*University of California Regents* v. *Bakke,* No. 76-811, Separate B:14).

2. Brink and Harris have found that in the middle 1960s low-income whites were more alienated than low-income Negroes (Brink and Harris, *Black and White,* p. 135).

3. The phrase "white ethnics" refers primarily to those of lower middle-class status. Although there is some evidence that the increases in ethnic consciousness have extended across social class lines, the lower middle-class has been the hardest hit and the most vocal.

4. Many *individuals,* of course, lost their ethnic identities. The speculations here refer entirely to groups.

5. Although we find here another example of the primary-secondary distinction we have used to divide structural assimilation into subprocesses, the terms here apply to groups rather than subprocesses.

6. For example, one presentation of the aims of the Chicano Movement stresses the need for various forms of education and the recognition of Chicano culture by the dominant group. And the list of priorities adopted by the first convention of La Raza Unida Party includes improvements in the areas of jobs, education, housing, health, and the administration of justice (Forbes, *Aztecas Del Norte,* pp. 292–294). La Raza Unida's goals also include, however, such separatist policies as community control of law enforcement, the schools, and the economy.

7. Like the Chicanos, Indian Americans clearly entered American society through conquest and illustrate the formation of primary ethnic groups. The various Indian societies were obviously viable social units before they were conquered. And afterward they definitely did not desire to be treated as citizens, preferring instead to be permitted to reconstruct their previous societies. Most tribes have steadfastly resisted assimilation into the dominant society for more than three centuries. Since they became citizens in 1924, however, the Indians have shown increasing signs of being transformed from a large number of primary ethnic groups into one, loosely-federated, secondary ethnic group. Like most other Americans, they have been unable to resist the pressures of urbanization and industrialization. To a much greater extent than is generally recognized, the Indians have moved into urban centers in a search for employment. They have not, though, readily broken their ties to the reservations or to other members of their tribes within the cities (Steele, in *Majority and Minority,* eds. Yetman and Steele, pp. 305–314). In general their movement toward the status of a secondary ethnic group has not been as great as among the Chicanos. They definitely are cool toward the prospect of full Anglo conformity, and they continue to be ambivalent about secondary structural assimilation. They nonetheless seem to be moving slowly toward a demand that they be admitted into American society on an equal footing with other citizens.

8. The disappearance of ethnic neighborhoods does not necessarily mean the ethnic community will disappear. In this connection see Michael Parenti, "Ethnic Politics and the Persistence of Ethnic Identification," pp. 717–726.

9. Quoted by Will Herberg, *Protestant-Catholic-Jew,* p. 43.

References

"ABS Statement Assails Book by Wilson," *Footnotes* 6 (December 1978):4.

Acuña, Rodolpho. *Occupied America*. San Francisco: Canfield Press, 1972.

Adam, Barry D. "Inferiorization and 'Self-Esteem,' " *Social Psychology* 41 (March 1978):47–57.

Adamic, Louis. *A Nation of Nations*. New York: Harper and Brothers Publishers, 1944.

Adams, Romanzo. "The Unorthodox Race Doctrine of Hawaii," in E. B. Reuter, ed. *Race and Culture Contacts*. New York: McGraw-Hill Book Co., 1934, pp. 143–160.

Adorno, T. W., Else Frenkel-Brunswik, Daniel J. Levinson, and R. Nevitt Sanford. *The Authoritarian Personality*. New York: Harper and Brothers, 1950.

Agresti, Barbara Finlay. "The First Decades of Freedom: Black Families in a Southern Country, 1870–1885," *Journal of Marriage and the Family* 40 (November 1978):697–706.

Allport, Gordon. *The Nature of Prejudice*. Garden City, N.Y.: Doubleday and Co., 1958.

Alvarez, Rodolfo. "The Psycho-Historical and Socioeconomic Development of the Chicano Community in the United States," *Social Science Quarterly* 53 (March 1973):920–942.

Alvírez, David, and Frank D. Bean. "The Mexican American Family," in C. H. Mindel and R. W. Habenstein, eds. *Ethnic Families in America: Patterns and Variations*. New York: Elsevier North-Holland Publishing Co., 1976, pp. 271–292.

Amir, Yehuda. "Contact Hypothesis in Ethnic Relations," *Psychological Bulletin* 71 (May 1969):319–342.

Anderson, Charles H. *White Protestant Americans*. Englewood Cliffs, N.J.: Prentice-Hall, Inc., 1970.

Asher, Steven R., and Vernon L. Allen. "Racial Preference and Social Comparison Processes," *Journal of Social Issues* 25 (No. 1, 1969):157–166.

Bache, R. Meade. "Reaction Time with Reference to Race," *Psychological Review* 21 (September 1895):475–486.

Baker, Ross K., ed. *The Afro-American*. New York: Van Nostrand Reinhold Co., 1970.

Ball, Harry V., George Eaton Simpson, and Kiyoshi Ikeda. "Law and Social Change: Sumner Reconsidered," *American Journal of Sociology* 57 (March 1962):532–540.

Bardolph, Richard. *The Negro Vanguard*. New York: Vintage Books, 1961.

Barker, Eugene C. "Native Latin American Contributions to the Colonization and Independence of Texas," *Southwestern Historical Quarterly* 46 (April 1943):317–335.

Baron, Robert A. *Human Aggression.* New York: Plenum Press, 1977.

Bean, Frank D., and W. Parker Frisbie. *The Demography of Racial and Ethnic Groups.* New York: Academic Press, 1978.

Becker, Gary S. *The Economics of Discrimination.* Chicago: University of Chicago Press, 1971.

Bell, Daniel. *The End of Ideology.* Glencoe, Ill.: The Free Press, 1960, pp. 115–136.

Benedict, Ruth. *Race: Science and Politics.* New York: The Viking Press, 1961.

Berelson, Bernard, and Patricia J. Salter. "Majority and Minority Americans: An Analysis of Magazine Fiction," *Public Opinion Quarterly* 10 (Summer 1946):168–190.

———, and Gary A. Steiner. *Human Behavior: An Inventory of Scientific Findings.* New York: Harcourt, Brace & World, 1964.

Berger, Morroe. *Equality by Statute,* rev. ed. Garden City, N.Y.: Doubleday and Co., 1968.

Berkowitz, Leonard, ed. *Roots of Aggression: A Re-examination of the Frustration-Aggression Hypothesis.* New York: Atherton Press, 1969.

Berry, Brewton. *Race and Ethnic Relations,* 3rd ed. Boston: Houghton Mifflin Co., 1965.

Bierstedt, Robert. *The Social Order,* 3rd ed. New York: McGraw-Hill Book Co., 1970.

Billingsley, Andrew. *Black Families in White America.* Englewood Cliffs, N.J.: Prentice-Hall, Inc., 1968.

Blauner, Robert. *Racial Oppression in America.* New York: Harper and Row, Publishers, 1972.

Block, N. J., and Gerald Dworkin, eds. *The IQ Controversy.* New York: Pantheon Books, 1976.

Bogardus, Emory S. "A Social Distance Scale," *Sociology and Social Research* 17 (January-February 1933):265–271.

———. *Social Distance.* Yellow Springs, Ohio: Antioch Press, 1959.

Bonacich, Edna. "A Theory of Ethnic Antagonism: the Split Labor Market," *American Sociological Review* 37 (October 1972):547–559.

———. "A Theory of Middleman Minorities," *American Sociological Review* 38 (October 1973):583–594.

———. "Abolition, the Extension of Slavery, and the Position of Free Blacks: A Study of Split Labor Markets in the United States, 1830–1863," *American Journal of Sociology* 81 (November 1975):601–628.

———. "Advanced Capitalism and Black/White Race Relations in the United States: A Split Labor Market Interpretation," *American Sociological Review* 41 (February 1976):34–51.

Bonjean, Charles M., Richard J. Hill, and S. Dale McLemore. *Sociological Measurement.* San Francisco: Chandler Publishing Co., 1967.

Boyer, William H., and Paul Walsh. "Innate Intelligence: An Insidious Myth?" in Edgar A. Schuler, Thomas Ford Hoult, Duane L. Gibson, and Wilbur B. Brookover, eds. *Readings in Sociology,* 5th ed. New York: Thomas Y. Crowell Co., 1974, pp. 55–62.

Bradshaw, Benjamin S., and Frank D. Bean. "Intermarriage Between Persons of Spanish and Non-Spanish Surname: Changes from the Mid-Nineteenth Century to the Mid-Twentieth Century," *Social Science Quarterly* 51 (September 1970):389–395.

Brigham, Carl C. *A Study of American Intelligence.* Princeton: Princeton University Press, 1923.

———. "Intelligence Tests of Immigrant Groups," *Psychological Review* 37 (March 1930):158–165.

Brink, William, and Louis Harris. *Black and White.* New York: Simon and Schuster, 1966.

Broom, Leonard, and Norval D. Glenn. *Transformation of the Negro American.* New York: Harper and Row, Publishers, 1965a.

———, and ———. "When Will America's Negroes Catch Up?" *New Society* (March 25, 1965b): 6–7.

———, and John I. Kitsuse. *The Managed Casualty.* Berkeley and Los Angeles: University of California Press, 1956.

Browning, Harley L., and S. Dale McLemore. *A Statistical Profile of the Spanish-Surname Population of Texas.* Austin: University of Texas Bureau of Business Research, 1964.

Bryan, Samuel. "Mexican Immigrants on the Labor Market," in Wayne Moquin and Charles Van Doren, eds. *A Documentary History of the Mexican Americans.* New York: Bantam Books, 1972, pp. 333–339.

Bunche, Ralph J. "A Critical Analysis of the Tactics and Programs of Minority Groups," *Journal of Negro Education* 4 (July 1935):308–320; reprinted in August Meier, Elliott Rudwick, and Francis L. Broderick, eds. *Black Protest Thought in the Twentieth Century,* 2nd ed. Indianapolis and New York: Bobbs-Merrill Co., 1971, pp. 183–202.

Burma, John H. "Interethnic Marriage in Los Angeles, 1948–1959," *Social Forces* 42 (December 1963): 156–165.

———. "A Comparison of the Mexican American Subculture with the Oscar Lewis Culture of Poverty Model," in John H. Burma, ed. *Mexican-Americans in the United States.* Cambridge, Mass.: Schenkman Publishing Co., 1970a, pp. 17–28.

———, ed. *Mexican Americans in the United States.* Cambridge, Mass.: Schenkman Publishing Co., 1970b.

Burns, W. Haywood. *The Voices of Negro Protest in America.* New York: Oxford University Press, 1963.

Buss, Arnold H. "Instrumentality of Aggression, Feedback, and Frustration as Determinants of Physical Aggression," *Journal of Personality and Social Psychology* 3 (February 1966):153–162.

Butler, John Sibley, and Kenneth L. Wilson. "The American Soldier Revisited: Race Relations in the Military," *Social Science Quarterly* 59 (December 1978): 451–467.

Camejo, Antonio. "Texas Chicanos Forge Own Political Power," in Livie Isauro Duran and H. Russell Bernard, eds. *Introduction to Chicano Studies.* New York: The Macmillan Co., 1973, pp. 552–558.

Carmichael, Stokely. "Black Power," Chicago: Student Nonviolent Coordinating Committee, 1966; reprinted in Gilbert Qsofsky, ed. *The Burden of Race.* New York: Harper and Row, Publishers, 1968, pp. 629–636.

————, and Charles Hamilton. *Black Power.* New York: Vintage Books, 1967.

Cattell, J. Mck. "Mental Tests and Measurements," *Mind* 15 (July 1890):373–380.

Caudill, William, and George DeVos. "Achievement, Culture, and Personality: The Case of the Japanese Americans," *American Anthropologist* 58 (December 1956):1102–1126.

Clark, Kenneth B. *Prejudice and Your Child,* 2nd ed. Boston: Beacon Press, 1963.

————, and Mamie K. Clark. "The Development of Consciousness of Self and the Emergence of Racial Identification in Negro Preschool Children," *Journal of Social Psychology* 10 (November 1939):591–599.

————, and ————. "Racial Identification and Preference in Negro Children," in Eleanor E. Maccoby, Theodore M. Newcomb, and Eugene L. Hartley, eds. *Readings in Social Psychology.* New York: Henry Holt and Co., 1958, pp. 602–611.

Cole, Stewart G., and Mildred Wiese Cole. *Minorities and the American Promise.* New York: Harper and Brothers, 1954.

Connor, John W. "Acculturation and Family Continuities in Three Generations of Japanese Americans," *Journal of Marriage and the Family* 36 (February 1974):159–165.

Conroy, Hilary, and T. Scott Miyakawa, eds. *East Across the Pacific.* Santa Barbara, Calif.: American Bibliographical Center-CLIO Press, 1972.

Coward, Barbara E., J. Allen Williams, and Joe R. Feagin. "The Culture of Poverty Debate: Some Additional Data," *Social Problems* 21 (June 1974):621–634.

Cronon, Edmund David. *Black Moses.* Madison: The University of Wisconsin Press, 1968.

Cuéllar, Alfredo. "Perspective on Politics," in Joan W. Moore, *Mexican Americans,* 1st ed. Englewood Cliffs, N.J.: Prentice-Hall, Inc., 1970, pp. 137–156.

Daniels, Roger. *The Politics of Prejudice.* New York: Atheneum Publishing Co., 1969.

Darden, Joe T. "Black Inequality and Conservative Strategy," in Edgar A. Schuler, Thomas Ford Hoult, Duane L. Gibson, and Wilbur B. Brookover, eds. *Readings in Sociology,* 5th ed. New York: Thomas Y. Crowell Co., 1974, pp. 643–663.

Davie, Maurice R. *Negroes in American Society.* New York: McGraw-Hill Book Co., 1949.

DeFleur, Melvin L., and Frank B. Westie. "Verbal Attitudes and Overt Acts," *American Sociological Review* 23 (December 1958):667–673.

Delany, Martin R. "Destiny of the Colored Race: 1852," in Paul Jacobs and Saul Landau, eds. *To Serve the Devil,* vol. 1. New York: Vintage Books, 1971:148–157.

Deutsch, Morton, and Mary Evans Collins. "Interracial Housing," in William Petersen, ed. *American Social Patterns.* Garden City, N.Y.: Doubleday and Co., 1956, pp. 7–61.

Dinnerstein, Leonard, and Frederic Cople Jaher, eds. *The Aliens.* New York: Appleton-Century-Crofts, 1970.

————, and David M. Reimers, eds. *Ethnic Americans.* New York: Dodd, Mead and Co., 1975.

Dollard, John. *Caste and Class in a Southern Town,* 3rd ed. Garden City, N.J.: Doubleday and Co., 1957.

———, Leonard Doob, Neal Miller, O. H. Mowrer, and R. R. Sears. *Frustration and Aggression.* New Haven: Yale University Press, 1939.

Dowdall, George W. "White Gains from Black Subordination in 1960 and 1970," *Social Problems* 22 (December 1974):162–183.

Doyle, Bertram W. *The Etiquette of Race Relations in the South.* Chicago: University of Chicago Press, 1937.

Dreger, Ralph Mason, and Kent S. Miller. "Comparative Psychological Studies of Negroes and Whites in the United States," *Psychological Bulletin,* 57 (no. 5, 1960):361–402.

DuBois, W. E. B. "The Immediate Program of the American Negro," *The Crisis* 6 (April 1915):310–312; reprinted in August Meier, Elliot Rudwick, and Francis L. Broderick, eds. *Black Protest Thought in the Twentieth Century,* 2nd ed. Indianapolis and New York: Bobbs-Merrill Co., 1971, pp. 67–72.

Dunn, L. C., and Theodosius Dobzhansky. *Heredity, Race and Society.* New York: The New American Library, 1964.

Dworkin, Anthony Gary. "A City Founded, A People Lost," in Livie Isauro Duran and H. Russell Bernard, eds. *Introduction to Chicano Studies.* New York: The Macmillan Co., 1973, pp. 406–420.

Ehrlich, Howard J. *The Social Psychology of Prejudice.* New York: John Wiley and Sons, 1973.

———, and James W. Rinehart. "A Brief Report on the Methodology of Stereotype Research," *Social Forces* 44 (December 1965): 171–176.

Eitzen, D. Stanley. "Two Minorities: The Jews of Poland and the Chinese of the Philippines," *The Jewish Journal of Sociology* 10 (December 1968): 221–240.

Elkins, Stanley M. *Slavery,* 2nd ed. Chicago: University of Chicago Press, 1968.

Ellison, Ralph. *Shadow and the Act.* New York: Random House, 1964.

Elson, R. M. *Guardians of Tradition.* Lincoln: University of Nebraska Press, 1964.

Enloe, Cynthia. *Ethnic Conflict and Political Development.* Boston: Little, Brown and Co., 1973.

Farley, Reynolds. "Racial Integration in the Schools: Assessing the Effect of Governmental Policies," *Sociological Focus* 9 (January 1975):3–26.

———. "Trends in Racial Inequalities: Have the Gains of the 1960s Disappeared in the 1970s?" *American Sociological Review* 42 (April 1977):189–208.

———. "School Integration in the United States," in W. Parker Frisbie and Frank D. Bean, eds. *The Demography of Racial and Ethnic Groups.* New York: Academic Press, 1978, pp. 183–202.

———, and Albert Hermalin. "The 1960s: A Decade of Progress for Blacks?" *Demography* 9 (August 1972):353–370.

Farmer, James. *Freedom—When?* New York: Random House, 1965, pp. 60–62; reprinted in August Meier, Elliott Rudwick, and Francis L. Broderick, eds. *Black Protest Thought in the Twentieth Century,* 2nd ed. Indianapolis and New York: Bobbs-Merrill Co., 1971, pp. 183–202.

Faulkner, Harold Underwood. *American Political and Social History.* 5th ed. New York: Appleton-Century-Crofts, 1948.

Feagin, Joe R. "Indirect Institutionalized Discrimination," *American Politics Quarterly* 5 (April 1977):177–200.

————, and Nancy Fujitaki. "On the Assimilation of the Japanese Americans," *Amerasia Journal* 1 (February 1972):13–30.

————, and Harlan Hahn. *Ghetto Revolts*. New York: The Macmillan Co., 1973.

Featherman, David L., and Robert M. Hauser. *Opportunity and Change*. New York: Academic Press, 1978.

Feldstein, Stanley, and Lawrence Costello, eds. *The Ordeal of Assimilation*. Garden City, N.Y.: Anchor Press/Doubleday, 1974.

Festinger, Leon. *A Theory of Cognitive Dissonance*. New York: Harper and Row, Publishers, 1957.

Fogel, Robert William, and Stanley L. Engerman. *Time on the Cross: The Economics of American Negro Slavery*. Boston: Little, Brown and Co., 1974.

Foner, Laura, and Eugene D. Genovese, eds. *Slavery in the New World*. Englewood Cliffs, N.J.: Prentice-Hall, Inc., 1969.

Forbes, Jack D. *Aztecas Del Norte*. Greenwich, Conn.: Fawcett, 1973.

Ford, W. Scott. "Interracial Public Housing in a Border City: Another Look at the Contact Hypothesis," *American Journal of Sociology* 79 (May 1973): 1426–1447.

Fox, David Joseph, and Valerie Barnes Jordan. "Racial Preference and Identification of Black, American Chinese, and White Children," *Genetic Psychology Monographs* 88 (1973):229–286.

Francis, E. K. *Interethnic Relations*. New York: Elsevier Scientific Publishing Co., 1976.

Franklin, John Hope. *Reconstruction*. Chicago: University of Chicago Press, 1961.

Frazier, E. Franklin. *The Negro Family in the United States*. Chicago: University of Chicago Press, 1939.

————. *The Negro in the United States,* rev. ed. New York: The Macmillan Co., 1957.

Frisbie, Parker. "Illegal Migration from Mexico to the United States: A Longitudinal Analysis," *International Migration Review* 9 (Spring 1975):3–13.

Fujimoto, Isao. "The Failure of Democracy in a Time of Crisis," in Amy Tachiki, Eddie Wong, Franklin Odo, and Buck Wong, eds. *Roots: An Asian American Reader*. Los Angeles: The Regents of the University of California, 1971, pp. 207–214.

Galitzi, Christine A. *A Study of Assimilation Among the Roumanians in the United States*. New York: Columbia University Press, 1929.

Garrett, Henry E. "A Note on the Intelligence Scores of Negroes and Whites in 1918," *Journal of Abnormal and Social Psychology* 40 (July 1945a):344–346.

————. "Comparison of Negro and White Recruits on the Army Tests Given in 1917–1918," *American Journal of Psychology* 58 (October 1945b):480–495.

Garth, Thomas. *Race Psychology*. New York: McGraw-Hill Book Co., 1931.

Garvey, Amy Jacques. *Garvey & Garveyism*. London: Collier-Macmillan Ltd., 1970.

Garvey, Marcus. "An Appeal to the Conscience of the Black Race," in Gilbert Osofsky, ed. *The Burden of Race*. New York: Harper and Row, Publishers, 1968a, pp. 290–295.

————. "Declaration of Rights of the Negro Peoples of the World," in Gilbert Osofsky, ed. *The Burden of Race.* New York: Harper and Row, Publishers, 1968b, pp. 296–302.

Geen, Russell G., and Leonard Berkowitz. "Some Conditions Facilitating the Occurrence of Aggression After the Observation of Violence," *Journal of Personality* 35 (December 1967):666–676; reprinted in Leonard Berkowitz, ed. *Roots of Aggression: A Re-examination of the Frustration-Aggression Hypothesis.* New York: Atherton Press, 1969, pp. 106–118.

Genovese, Eugene D. *Roll, Jordan, Roll.* New York: Pantheon Books, 1974.

Gerard, Harold B., and Norman Miller. *School Desegregation: A Long-Term Study.* New York: Plenum Press, 1975.

————, Terrence D. Jackson, and Edward S. Conolley. "Social Contact in the Desegregated Classroom," in Harold B. Gerard and Norman Miller, eds. *School Desegregation: A Long-Term Study.* New York: Plenum Press, 1975, pp. 211–241.

Geschwender, James A. "Explorations in the Theory of Social Movements and Revolutions," *Social Forces* 47 (December 1968):127–135; reprinted in James A. Geschwender, ed. *The Black Revolt.* Englewood Cliffs, N.J.: Prentice-Hall, Inc., 1971.

Glazer, Nathan. "Blacks and Ethnic Groups: The Difference, and the Political Difference It Makes," *Social Problems* 18 (Spring 1971):444–461.

————. "America's Race Paradox," in Peter I. Rose, ed. *Nation of Nations.* New York: Random House, 1972, pp. 165–180.

————, and Daniel Patrick Moynihan. *Beyond the Melting Pot,* 1st and 2nd eds. Cambridge, Mass.: MIT Press, 1964 and 1970.

Glenn, Norval D. "Occupational Benefits to Whites from the Subordination of Negroes," *American Sociological Review* 28 (June 1963):443–448.

————, "White Gains from Negro Subordination," *Social Problems* 14 (Fall 1966):159–178.

Goff, Regina. "Educating Black Americans," in Mabel M. Smythe, ed. *The Black American Reference Book.* Englewood Cliffs, N.J.: Prentice-Hall, Inc., 1976, pp. 410–452.

Goldman, Peter. *Report from Black America.* New York: Simon and Schuster, 1970.

Gómez-Quiñones, Juan. "The First Steps: Chicano Labor Conflict and Organizing, 1900–20," in Manuel P. Servín, ed. *An Awakening Minority: The Mexican-Americans,* 2nd ed. Beverly Hills, Calif.: Glencoe Press, 1974, pp. 79–113.

Goodchilds, Jacqueline D., James A. Green, and Tora Kay Bikson. "The School Experience and Adjustment," in Harold B. Gerard and Norman Miller, eds. *School Desegregation: A Long-Term Study.* New York: Plenum Press, 1975, pp. 151–166.

Gordon, Milton M. *Assimilation in American Life.* New York: Oxford University Press, 1964.

————. *Human Nature, Class, and Ethnicity.* New York: Oxford University Press, 1978.

Gossett, Thomas F. *Race: The History of an Idea in America.* Dallas: Southern Methodist University Press, 1963.

Gould, C. W. *America, A Family Matter.* New York: Charles Scribner's Sons, 1922.

Grebler, Leo, Joan W. Moore, and Ralph C. Guzman. *The Mexican-American People.* New York: The Free Press, 1970.

Greeley, Andrew M. *Ethnicity in the United States.* New York: John Wiley and Sons, 1974.

————. *Why Can't They Be Like Us?* New York: E. P. Dutton and Co., 1971.

Green, James A. "Attitudinal and Situational Determinants of Intended Behavior Toward Blacks," *Journal of Personality and Social Psychology* 22 (April 1972):13–17.

Grodzins, Morton. *The Loyal and the Disloyal.* Chicago: University of Chicago Press, 1956.

Gurak, Douglas T., and Mary M. Kritz. "Intermarriage Patterns in the U.S.: Maximizing Information from the U.S. Census Public Use Samples," *Public Data Use* (March 1978):33–43.

Gutierrez, Armando, and Herbert Hirsch. "The Militant Challenge to the American Ethos: 'Chicanos' and 'Mexican Americans,'" *Social Science Quarterly* 53 (March 1973):830–845.

Gutman, Herbert G. *Slavery and the Numbers Game: A Critique of 'Time on the Cross.'* Urbana, Ill.: University of Illinois Press, 1975.

————. *The Black Family in Slavery and Freedom, 1750–1925.* New York: Pantheon Books, 1976.

Hamilton, Alexander, James Madison, and John Jay. *The Federalist Papers.* New York: The New American Library, 1961.

Hamilton, David L., and George D. Bishop. "Attitudinal and Behavioral Effects of Initial Integration of White Suburban Neighborhoods," *Journal of Social Issues* 32 (no. 2, 1976):47–67.

Handlin, Oscar. *Race and Nationality in American Life.* Garden City, N.Y.: Doubleday and Co., 1957.

Hansen, Marcus Lee. *The Problem of the Third Generation Immigrant.* Rock Island, Ill.: Augustana Historical Society, 1938.

————. *The Atlantic Migration, 1607–1860.* Cambridge, Mass.: Harvard University Press, 1945.

Hartz, Louis. *The Founding of New Societies.* New York: Harcourt, Brace and World, 1964.

Heer, David M. "Negro-White Marriage in the United States," *Journal of Marriage and the Family* 28 (August 1966):262–273.

Heiss, Jerold, and Susan Owens. "Self-evaluation of Blacks and Whites," *American Journal of Sociology* 78 (September 1972):360–370.

Herberg, Will. *Protestant-Catholic-Jew.* Garden City, N.Y.: Doubleday and Co., 1960.

Hernández, Jose, Leo Estrada, and David Alvírez. "Census Data and the Problem of Conceptually Defining the Mexican American Population," *Social Science Quarterly* 53 (March 1973):671–687.

Herskovitz, Melville J. *The American Negro: A Study in Racial Crossing.* New York: Alfred A. Knopf, 1928.

————. *The Myth of the Negro Past.* Boston: Beacon Press, 1958.

Hill, Robert B. *The Strengths of Black Families.* New York: Emerson Hall Publishers, 1971.

Hollingshead, August B. "Cultural Factors in the Selection of Marriage Mates," *American Sociological Review* 15 (October 1950):619–627.

Homans, George. "What Kind of a Myth is the Myth of a Value-free Social Science?" *Social Science Quarterly* 58 (March 1978):530–541.

Hoppe, Sue Keir, and Peter L. Heller. "Alienation, Familism, and the Utilization of Health Services by Mexican Americans," *Journal of Health and Social Behavior* 16 (September 1975):304–314.

Horowitz, E. L. "The Development of Attitude Toward the Negro," *Archives of Psychology* 29 (January 1936):5–47.

Horton, John. "Order and Conflict Theories of Social Problems as Competing Ideologies," *American Journal of Sociology* 71 (May 1966):701–713.

Hosokawa, Bill. *Nisei: The Quiet Americans.* New York: William Morrow and Co., 1969.

Hyman, Herbert H., and Paul B. Sheatsley. "Attitudes Toward Desegregation," *Scientific American,* July 1964, pp. 16–23.

Ichihashi, Yamato. *Japanese in the United States.* Palo Alto, Calif.: Stanford University Press, 1932.

Ichioka, Yuji. "Nisei: The Quiet Americans," in Amy Tachiki, Eddie Wong, Franklin Odo, and Buck Wong, eds. *Roots: An Asian American Reader.* Los Angeles: Regents of the University of California, 1971, pp. 221–222.

Institute for Research on Poverty. "Nature-Nurture Nonsense," *Focus* 1 (Spring-Summer 1976):1–4.

Institute for Social Research. "Cross-Racial Contact Increases in Seventies: Attitude Gap Narrows for Blacks and Whites," *ISR Newsletter,* Autumn 1975, pp. 4–7.

Iwata, Masakazu. "The Japanese Immigrants in California Agriculture," *Agricultural History* 36 (January 1962):25–37.

Jacobs, Paul, and Saul Landau, eds. *To Serve the Devil,* vol. 1. New York: Vintage Books, 1971.

Jensen, Arthur R. "How Much Can We Boost IQ and Scholastic Achievement?" *Harvard Educational Review* 39 (Winter 1969): 1–123.

————. "Race and the Genetics of Intelligence: A Reply to Lewontin," in N. J. Block and Gerald Dworkin, eds. *The IQ Controversy.* New York: Pantheon Books, 1976, pp. 93–106.

Johnson, James Weldon. "Description of a Race Riot in Chicago," in Gilbert Osofsky, ed. *The Burden of Race.* Harper and Row, Publishers, 1968, pp. 304–309.

Jones, Maldwyn Allen. *American Immigration.* Chicago: University of Chicago Press, 1960.

Jordan, Winthrop D. "Modern Tensions and the Origins of African Slavery," in Donald L. Noel, ed. *The Origins of American Slavery and Racism.* Columbus, Ohio: Charles E. Merrill Publishing Co., 1972, pp. 81–94.

Kagiwada, George. "Assimilation of Nisei in Los Angeles," in Hilary Conroy and T. Scott Miyakawa, eds. *East Across the Pacific.* Santa Barbara, Calif.: American Bibliographical Center-CLIO Press, 1972, pp. 268–278.

————. "Confessions of a Misguided Sociologist," *Amerasia Journal* 3 (Fall 1973):159–164.

Kallen, Horace M. *Culture and Democracy in the United States.* New York: Boni and Liveright, 1924.

Karlins, Marvin, Thomas L. Coffman, and Gary Walters. "On the Fading of Social Stereotypes: Studies in Three Generations of College Students," *Journal of Personality and Social Psychology* 13 (September 1969):1–16.

Karno, Marvin, and Robert B. Edgerton. "Perceptions of Mental Illness in a Mexican-American Community," in John H. Burma, ed. *Mexican-Americans in the United States*. Cambridge, Mass: Schenkman Publishing Co., 1970, pp. 343–351.

Katz, Daniel, and Kenneth W. Braly. "Racial Stereotypes of One Hundred College Students," *Journal of Abnormal and Social Psychology* 28 (October-December 1933):280–290.

Kennedy, Ruby Jo Reeves. "Single or Triple Melting-Pot? Intermarriage Trends in New Haven, 1870–1940," *American Journal of Sociology* 49 (January 1944):331–339.

Kibbe, Pauline R. *Latin Americans in Texas*. Albuquerque, N.M.: University of New Mexico, 1946.

Kikimura, Akemi, and Harry H. L. Kitano. "Interracial Marriage: A Picture of the Japanese Americans," *Journal of Social Issues* 29 (no. 2, 1973):67–81.

King, James C. *The Biology of Race*. New York: Harcourt Brace Jovanovich, 1971.

King, Martin Luther, Jr. "The Case Against 'Tokenism,'" *New York Times Magazine,* August 5, 1962, pp. 11ff.

———. *Why We Can't Wait*. New York: New American Library, 1964.

———. "The Use of Nonviolence," in Gilbert Osofsky, ed. *The Burden of Race*. New York: Harper and Row, Publishers, 1968, pp. 522–526.

———. "Our Struggle for an Interracial Society Based on Freedom for All," in August Meier, Elliott Rudwick, and Francis L. Broderick, eds. *Black Protest Thought in the Twentieth Century,* 2nd ed. Indianapolis and New York: Bobbs-Merrill Co., 1971a, pp. 291–302.

———. "We Still Believe in Black and White Together," in August Meier, Elliott Rudwick, and Francis L. Broderick, eds. *Black Protest Thought in the Twentieth Century,* 2nd ed. Indianapolis and New York: Bobbs-Merrill Co., 1971b, pp. 584–595.

Kitano, Harry H. L. *Japanese Americans*. Englewood Cliffs, N.J.: Prentice-Hall, Inc., 1969.

Klineberg, Otto. *Negro Intelligence and Selective Migration*. New York: Columbia University Press, 1935.

———. "Mental Tests," *Encyclopedia of the Social Sciences,* vol. 10. New York: The Macmillan Co., 1937, pp. 323–329.

———. "Pictures in Our Heads," in Edgar A. Schuler, Thomas Ford Hoult, Duane L. Gibson, and Wilbur B. Brookover, eds. *Readings in Sociology,* 5th ed. New York: Thomas Y. Crowell Co., 1974, pp. 631–637.

Kluckhohn, Florence. "Dominant and Variant Value Orientations," in Clyde Kluckhohn, Henry A. Murray, and David M. Schneider, eds. *Personality in Nature, Society, and Culture,* 2nd ed. New York: Alfred A. Knopf, 1956, pp. 342–357.

Krickus, Richard J. "White Ethnic Neighborhoods: Ripe for the Bulldozer?" in Stanley Feldstein and Lawrence Costello, eds. *The Ordeal of Assimilation*. Garden City, N.Y.: Anchor/Doubleday, 1974, pp. 434–439.

Kriegel, Leonard. "Last Stop on the D Train: In the Land of the New Racists," in Stanley Feldstein and Lawrence Costello, eds. *The Ordeal of Assimilation*. Garden City, N.Y.: Anchor/Doubleday, 1974, pp. 418–434.

Kristol, Irving. "The Negro Today Is Like the Immigrant of Yesterday," in Peter I. Rose, ed. *Nation of Nations*. New York: Random House, 1972, pp. 197–210.

LaPiere, Richard T. "Attitudes vs. Actions," *Social Forces* 13 (December 1934): 230–237.

LaViolette, Forrest E. *Americans of Japanese Ancestry*. Toronto: Canadian Institute of International Affairs, 1945.

Lazarus, Emma. *Poems*. Boston: Houghton Mifflin, 1889.

Lea, Tom. *The King Ranch*, vol. 1. Boston: Little, Brown and Co., 1957.

Lee, Everett S. "Negro Intelligence and Selective Migration: A Philadelphia Test of the Klineberg Hypothesis," *American Sociological Review* 16 (April 1951):227–233.

Leighton, Alexander. *The Governing of Men*. Princeton: Princeton University Press, 1946.

Lerner, Richard M., and Christie J. Buehrig. "The Development of Racial Attitudes in Young Black and White Children," *Journal of Genetic Psychology* 127 (September 1975):45–54.

Levine, Gene N., and Darrel M. Montero. "Socioeconomic Mobility Among Three Generations of Japanese Americans," *Journal of Social Issues* 29 (no. 2, 1973):33–48.

Levine, Lawrence W. *Black Culture and Black Consciousness*. New York: Oxford University Press, 1977.

Lewis, Oscar. *La Vida*. New York: Random House, 1965.

Lewontin, Richard C. "Race and Intelligence," in N. J. Block and Gerald Dworkin, eds. *The IQ Controversy*. New York: Pantheon Books, 1976a, pp. 78–92.

———. "Further Remarks on Race and the Genetics of Intelligence," in N. J. Block and Gerald Dworkin, eds. *The IQ Controversy*. New York: Pantheon Books, 1976b, pp. 107–112.

Leyburn, James G. "Frontier Society," in Leonard Dinnerstein and Frederick Cople Jaher, eds. *The Aliens*. New York: Appleton-Century-Crofts, 1970, pp. 65–76.

Lieberson, Stanley. "A Societal Theory of Race and Ethnic Relations," *American Sociological Review* 26 (December 1961):902–910.

———, and Glenn V. Fuguitt. "Negro-White Occupational Differences in the Absence of Discrimination," *American Journal of Sociology* 73 (September 1967):188–200.

Liebow, Elliot. *Tally's Corner*. Boston: Little Brown and Co., 1967.

Light, Ivan H. "Kenjin and Kinsmen," in Rudolph Gomez, Clement Cottingham, Jr., Russell Endo, and Kathleen Jackson, eds. *The Social Reality of Ethnic America*. Lexington, Mass.: D. C. Heath and Co., 1974, pp. 282–297.

Lincoln, C. Eric. *The Black Muslims in America*. Boston: Beacon Press, 1961.

Linn, Lawrence S. "Verbal Attitudes and Overt Behavior: A Study of Racial Discrimination," *Social Forces* 43 (March 1965):353–364.

Loehlin, John C., Gardner Lindzey, and J. N. Spuhler. *Race Differences in Intelligence*. San Francisco: W. H. Freeman and Co., 1975.

Lohman, Joseph D., and Dietrich C. Reitzes. "Note on Race Relations in Mass Society," *American Journal of Sociology* 57 (November 1952):240–246.

Lopreato, Joseph. *Italian Americans.* New York: Random House, 1970.

McCarthy, John, and William Yancey. "Uncle Tom and Mr. Charlie: Metaphysical Pathos in the Study of Racism and Personal Disorganization," *American Journal of Sociology* 76 (January 1971):648–672.

McCone, John A. "The Watts Riot," in Gilbert Osofsky, ed. *The Burden of Race.* New York: Harper and Row, Publishers, 1968, pp. 608–621.

Macias, Ysidro Ramon. "The Chicano Movement," in Wayne Moquin and Charles Van Doren, eds. *A Documentary History of the Mexican Americans.* New York: Bantam Books, 1971, pp. 499–506.

McKitrick, Eric L., ed. *Slavery Defended.* Englewood Cliffs, N.J.: Prentice-Hall, Inc., 1963.

McLemore, S. Dale. "Ethnic Attitudes Toward Hospitalization: An Illustrative Comparison of Anglos and Mexican Americans," *Southwestern Social Science Quarterly* 43 (March 1963):341–346.

————. "The Origins of Mexican American Subordination in Texas," *Social Science Quarterly* 53 (March 1973):656–670.

MacLeish, Archibald. *A Time to Act.* Boston: Houghton Mifflin, 1943.

McWilliams, Carey. *California: The Great Exception.* New York: A. A. Wyn, Publisher, 1949.

————. "Getting Rid of the Mexicans," in Wayne Moquin and Charles Van Doren, eds. *A Documentary History of the Mexican Americans.* New York: Bantam Books, 1972, pp. 383–387.

————. *North from Mexico.* New York: Greenwood Press, Publishers, 1973.

Malcolm X. "Malcolm X Founds the Organization of Afro-American Unity," in August Meier, Elliott Rudwick, and Francis L. Broderick, eds. *Black Protest Thought in the Twentieth Century,* 2nd ed. Indianapolis and New York: Bobbs-Merrill Co., 1971, pp. 412–420.

————, and James Farmer. "Separation or Integration: A Debate," in August Meier, Elliott Rudwick, and Francis L. Broderick, eds. *Black Protest Thought in the Twentieth Century,* 2nd ed. Indianapolis and New York: Bobbs-Merrill Co., 1971, pp. 387–412.

Marumoto, Masaji. " 'First Year' Immigrants to Hawaii & Eugene Van Reed," in Hilary Conroy and T. Scott Miyakawa, eds. *East Across the Pacific.* Santa Barbara, Calif.: American Bibliographical Center-CLIO Press, 1972, pp. 5–39.

Masaoka, Mike. "The Japanese American Creed," *Common Ground* 2 (Spring 1942):11.

Matsumoto, Gary M., Gerald M. Meredith, and Minoru Masuda. "Ethnic Identity: Honolulu and Seattle Japanese-Americans," in Stanley Sue and Nathaniel Wagner, eds. *Asian-Americans.* Ben Lomand, Calif.: Science and Behavior Books, 1973, pp. 65–74.

Meer, Bernard, and Edward Freedman. "The Impact of Negro Neighbors on White Home Owners," *Social Forces* 45 (September 1966):11–19.

Meier, August, Elliott Rudwick, and Francis L. Broderick, eds. *Black Protest Thought in the Twentieth Century,* 2nd ed. Indianapolis and New York: Bobbs-Merrill Co., 1971.

Meister, Richard J., ed. *Race and Ethnicity in Modern America.* Lexington, Mass.: D. C. Heath and Co., 1974.

Merton, Robert K. "Discrimination and the American Creed," in Robert M. MacIver, ed. *Discrimination and National Welfare*. New York: Harper and Row, Publishers, 1949, pp. 99–126.

Metzger, L. Paul. "American Sociology and Black Assimilation: Conflicting Perspectives," *American Journal of Sociology* 76 (January 1971):627–647.

Middleton, Russell. "Ethnic Prejudice and Susceptibility to Persuasion," *American Sociological Review* 25 (October 1960):679–686.

Mikulski, Barbara. "Who Speaks for Ethnic America?" in Stanley Feldstein and Lawrence Costello, eds. *The Ordeal of Assimilation*. Garden City, N.Y.: Anchor Press/Doubleday, 1974, pp. 440–443.

Miller, Neal E. "The Frustration-Aggression Hypothesis," *Psychological Review* 48 (July 1941):337–342; reprinted in Leonard Berkowitz, ed. *Roots of Aggression: A Re-Examination of the Frustration-Aggression Hypothesis*. New York: Atherton Press, 1969, pp. 29–34.

Milner, Lucille B. "Letters from a Segregated Army," in Gilbert Osofsky, ed. *The Burden of Race*. New York: Harper and Row, Publishers, 1968, pp. 414–420.

Mintz, Sidney W. "Slavery and Emergent Capitalisms," in Laura Foner and Eugene D. Genovese, eds. *Slavery in the New World*. Englewood Cliffs, N.J.: Prentice-Hall, Inc., 1969, pp. 27–37.

Mittlebach, Frank G., and Joan W. Moore. "Ethnic Endogamy—The Case of Mexican Americans," *American Journal of Sociology* 74 (July 1968):50–62.

Miyamoto, S. Frank. *Social Solidarity Among the Japanese of Seattle*. Seattle: University of Washington Press, 1939.

———. "An Immigrant Community in America," in Hilary Conroy and T. Scott Miyakawa, eds. *East Across the Pacific*. Santa Barbara, Calif: American Bibliographical Center-CLIO Press, 1972, pp. 217–243.

Monahan, Thomas P. "An Overview of Statistics on Interracial Marriage in the United States, with Data on Its Extent from 1963–1970," *Journal of Marriage and the Family* 38 (May 1976):223–231.

Montaigne, M. E. de. *Selections from the Essays of Montaigne,* translated by Donald M. Frame. New York: F. S. Crofts and Co., 1948.

Moore, Joan W. *Mexican Americans,* 1st and 2nd eds. Englewood Cliffs, N.J.: Prentice-Hall, Inc., 1970 and 1976.

Moquin, Wayne, and Charles Van Doren, eds. *A Documentary History of the Mexican Americans*. New York: Bantam Books, 1971.

Morland, J. Kenneth. "A Comparison of Race Awareness in Northern and Southern Children," *American Journal of Orthopsychiatry* 36 (January 1966):22–31.

Moynihan, Daniel Patrick. *The Negro Family*. Washington, D.C.: U.S. Department of Labor, 1965.

Murguía, Edward. *Assimilation, Colonialism, and the Mexican American People*. Austin: University of Texas Center for Mexican American Studies, 1975.

———, and W. Parker Frisbie. "Trends in Mexican American Intermarriage: Recent Findings in Perspective," *Social Science Quarterly* 58 (December 1977):374–389.

Myrdal, Gunnar. *An American Dilemma,* 2 vols. New York: McGraw-Hill Book Co., 1964.

Nash, Gary B. *Red, White, and Black.* Englewood Cliffs, N.J.: Prentice-Hall, Inc., 1974.

National Advisory Commission. *Report of the National Advisory Commission on Civil Disorders.* New York: The New York Times Co., 1968.

Newman, William M. *American Pluralism.* New York: Harper and Row, Publishers, 1973.

Noel, Donald L. "A Theory of the Origin of Ethnic Stratification," *Social Problems* 16 (Fall 1968):157–172.

————. *The Origins of American Slavery and Racism.* Columbus, Ohio: Charles E. Merrill Publishing Co., 1972.

Nostrand, Richard L. " 'Mexican American' and 'Chicano': Emerging Terms for a People Coming of Age," *Pacific Historical Review* 62 (August 1973):389–406.

Novak, Michael. *The Rise of the Unmeltable Ethnics.* New York: The Macmillan Co., 1971.

Novotny, Ann. *Strangers at the Door.* Toronto: Bantam Pathfinders Edition, 1974.

Okimoto, Daniel. "The Intolerance of Success," in Amy Tachiki, Eddie Wong, Franklin Odo, and Buck Wong, eds. *Roots: An Asian American Reader.* Los Angeles: Regents of the University of California, 1971, pp. 14–19.

Osofsky, Gilbert, ed. *The Burden of Race.* New York: Harper and Row, Publishers, 1968.

Parenti, Michael. "Ethnic Politics and the Persistence of Ethnic Identification," *American Political Science Review* 61 (September 1967):717–726.

Park, Robert E. "The Concept of Social Distance," *Journal of Applied Sociology* 8 (July-August 1924):339–344.

————. *Race and Culture.* New York: The Free Press of Glencoe, 1964.

————, and Ernest W. Burgess. *Introduction to the Science of Sociology.* Chicago: University of Chicago Press, 1921.

Parkman, Margaret A., and Jack Sawyer. "Dimensions of Ethnic Intermarriage in Hawaii," *American Sociological Review* 32 (August 1967):593–607.

Parsons, Talcott. "Full Citizenship for the Negro American?" *Daedalus* 95 (Fall 1965):1009–1054.

Patchen, Martin, James D. Davidson, Gerhard Hofmann, and William R. Brown. "Determinants of Students' Interracial Behavior and Opinion Change," *Sociology of Education* 50 (January 1977):55–75.

Patterson, Orlando. "Slavery," in Alex Inkeles, ed. *Annual Reviews of Sociology.* Palo Alto, Calif: Annual Reviews, Inc., 1977, pp. 407–449.

Penalosa, Fernando. "The Changing Mexican-American in Southern California," in John H. Burma, ed. *Mexican-Americans in the United States.* Cambridge, Mass.: Schenkman Publishing Co., 1970, pp. 41–51.

Petersen, William. *Japanese Americans.* New York: Random House, 1971.

————. "Success Story: Japanese American Style," *New York Times Magazine* (January 9, 1966):20–43.

Pettigrew, Thomas F. *Racially Separate or Together?* New York: McGraw-Hill Book Co., 1971.

————. "A Sociological View of the Post-Milliken Era," in U.S. Commission on Civil Rights, *Milliken v. Bradley: The Implications for Metropolitan Desegregation.* Washington, D.C.: U.S. Government Printing Office, 1974.

————. *Racial Discrimination in the United States.* New York: Harper and Row, Publishers, 1975.

Proshansky, Harold. "The Development of Intergroup Attitudes," in Lois Wladis Hoffman and Martin L. Hoffman, eds. *Review of Child Development Research,* vol. 2. New York: Russell Sage Foundation, 1966, pp. 311–371.

Rainwater, Lee, and William L. Yancey. *The Moynihan Report and the Politics of Controversy.* Cambridge, Mass.: MIT Press, 1967.

Randolph, A. Philip. "Address to the Policy Conference," in August Meier, Elliott Rudwick, and Francis L. Broderick, eds. *Black Protest Thought in the Twentieth Century,* 2nd ed. Indianapolis and New York: Bobbs-Merrill Co., Inc., 1971a, pp. 224–233.

————. "A. Philip Randolph Urges Civil Disobedience Against a Jim Crow Army," in August Meier, Elliott Rudwick, and Francis L. Broderick, eds. *Black Protest Thought in the Twentieth Century,* 2nd ed. Indianapolis and New York: Bobbs-Merrill Co., 1971b, pp. 233–238.

Reich, Michael. "The Economics of Racism," in David M. Gordon, ed. *Problems in Political Economy.* Lexington, Mass.: D. C. Heath, 1971.

Rendon, Armando B. "Chicano Culture in a Gabacho World," in Livie Isuaro Duran and H. Russell Bernard, eds. *Introduction to Chicano Studies.* New York: The Macmillan Co., 1973, pp. 350–362.

Rives, George Lockhart. *The United States and Mexico, 1821–1848.* New York: Charles Scribner's Sons, 1913.

Roche, John P., and Milton M. Gordon. "Can Morality Be Legislated?" in Kimball Young and Raymond W. Mack, eds. *Principles of Sociology,* 3rd ed. New York: American Book Co., 1965, pp. 332–336.

Rodman, Hyman. "Technical Note on Two Rates of Mixed Marriage," *American Sociological Review* 30 (October 1965):776–778.

Romano, Octavio Ignacio. "The Anthropology and Sociology of the Mexican Americans," *El Grito* 2 (Fall 1968), pp. 13–26.

Rosenberg, Morris, and Roberta Simmons. *Black and White Self-Esteem: The Urban School Child.* Washington, D.C.: American Sociological Association, 1972.

Rostow, Eugene V. "Our Worst Wartime Mistake," *Harper's Magazine* (September 1945):193–201.

Rubenstein, Richard E. *Rebels in Eden.* Boston: Little, Brown and Co., 1970.

Rustin, Bayard. ". . . A Workable and Christian Technique for the Righting of Injustice," in August Meier, Elliott Rudwick, and Francis L. Broderick, eds. *Black Protest Thought in the Twentieth Century,* 2nd ed. Indianapolis and New York: Bobbs-Merrill Co., 1971, pp. 233–238.

Ryan, William. *Blaming the Victim.* New York: Vintage Books, 1971.

St. John, Nancy H. *School Desegregation Outcomes for Children.* New York: John Wiley and Sons, 1975.

Samora, Julian, ed. *La Raza: Forgotten Americans.* South Bend, Ind.: University of Notre Dame Press, 1966.

Sampson, William A. "Black Sociologist Backs Wilson," *Footnotes* 6 (December 1978):4.

Sanchez, George I. "Pachucos in the Making," in Wayne Moquin and Charles Van Doren, eds., *A Documentary History of the Mexican Americans.* New York: Bantam Books, 1972, pp. 409–415.

Saunders, Lyle. *Cultural Difference and Medical Care.* New York: Russell Sage Foundation, 1954.

Schermerhorn, Richard A. *These Our People.* Boston: D. C. Heath and Co., 1949.

————. *Comparative Ethnic Relations.* New York: Random House, 1970.

Schmid, Calvin F., and Charles E. Nobbe. "Socioeconomic Differentials Among Nonwhite Races," *American Sociological Review* 30 (December 1965):909–922.

Schuman, Howard, and Michael P. Johnson. "Attitudes and Behavior," in Alex Inkeles, ed. *Annual Reviews of Sociology.* Palo Alto, Calif.: Annual Reviews Inc., 1976, pp. 161–207.

————, and Shirley Hatchett. *Black Racial Attitudes: Trends and Complexities.* Ann Arbor: University of Michigan Institute for Social Research, 1974.

Scott, Robin Fitzgerald. "Wartime Labor Problems and Mexican-Americans in the War," in Manuel P. Servín, ed. *An Awakening Minority: The Mexican-Americans,* 2nd ed. Beverly Hills, Calif.: Glencoe Press, 1974, pp. 134–142.

Sheldon, Paul M. "Community Participation and the Emerging Middle Class," in Julian Samora, ed. *La Raza: Forgotten Americans.* South Bend, Ind.: University of Notre Dame Press, 1966, pp. 125–157.

Shuey, Audrey M. *The Testing of Negro Intelligence,* 2nd ed. New York: Social Science Press, 1966.

Siegel, Paul M. "On the Cost of Being a Negro," *Sociological Inquiry* 35 (Winter 1965):41–57.

Simmel, Georg. "The Stranger," in Kurt H. Wolf, translator, *The Sociology of Georg Simmel.* Glencoe, Ill.: The Free Press, 1950, pp. 402–406.

Simpson, George Eaton, and J. Milton Yinger. *Racial and Cultural Minorities,* 4th ed. New York: Harper and Row, Publishers, 1972.

Singer, Lester. "Ethnogenesis and Negro Americans Today," *Social Research* 29 (Winter 1962):419–432.

Skinner, B. F. *About Behaviorism.* New York: Alfred A. Knopf, 1974.

Sklare, Marshall. "American Jewry: Social History and Group Identity," in Norman R. Yetman and C. Hoy Steele, eds. *Majority and Minority,* 2nd ed. Boston: Allyn and Bacon, 1975, pp. 261–273.

Skolnick, Jerome H. "Black Militancy," in Norman R. Yetman and C. Hoy Steele, eds. *Majority and Minority,* 2nd ed. Boston: Allyn and Bacon, 1975, pp. 557–577.

Smith, James P., and Finis Welch. *Race Differences in Earnings: A Survey and New Evidence.* Santa Monica, Calif.: The Rand Corp., 1978.

Smith, Lillian. *Killers of the Dream.* Garden City, N.Y.: Doubleday and Co., 1963.

Smythe, Mabel M. ed. *The Black American Reference Book.* Englewood Cliffs, N.J.: Prentice-Hall, Inc., 1976a.

————. "The Black Role in the Economy," in Mabel M. Smythe, ed. *The Black American Reference Book.* Englewood Cliffs, N.J.: Prentice-Hall, Inc., 1976b, pp. 207–250.

Sørensen, Annmette, Karl E. Taeuber, and Leslie Hollingsworth, Jr. "Indexes of Racial Residential Segregation for 109 Cities in the United States, 1940–1970," *Sociological Focus* 8 (April 1975):125–142.

Steele, C. Hoy. "The Acculturation/Assimilation Model in Urban Studies: A Critique," in Norman R. Yetman and C. Hoy Steele, eds. *Majority and Minority,* 2nd ed. Boston: Allyn and Bacon, 1975, pp. 305–314.

Stonequist, Everett V. *The Marginal Man.* New York: Charles Scribner, 1937.

"Success Story: Outwhiting the Whites," *Newsweek* (June 21, 1971):24–25.

Sugimoto, Howard H. "The Vancouver Riots of 1907: A Canadian Episode," in Hilary Conroy and T. Scott Miyakawa, eds. *East Across the Pacific.* Santa Barbara, Calif.: American Bibliographical Center-CLIO Press, 1972, pp. 92–126.

Sumner, William Graham. *Folkways.* Boston: Ginn and Co., 1906.

Szymanski, Albert. "Racial Discrimination and White Gain," *American Sociological Review* 41 (June 1976):403–414.

Tachiki, Amy. "Introduction," in Amy Tachiki, Eddie Wong, Franklin Odo, and Buck Wong, eds. *Roots: An Asian American Reader.* Los Angeles: Regents of the University of California, 1971, pp. 1–5.

Taeuber, Karl E., and Alma F. Taeuber. "The Negro as an Immigrant Group: Recent Trends in Racial and Ethnic Segregation in Chicago," *American Journal of Sociology* 69 (January 1964):374–394.

———. *Negroes in Cities.* New York: Atheneum, 1969.

———. "The Black Population of the United States," in Mabel M. Smythe, ed. *The Black American Reference Book.* Englewood Cliffs, N.J.: Prentice-Hall, Inc., 1976, pp. 159–206.

Takagi, Paul. "The Myth of 'Assimilation in American Life,' " *Amerasia Journal* 3 (Fall 1973): 149–158.

Taylor, D. Garth, Paul B. Sheatsley, and Andrew M. Greeley. "Attitudes Toward Racial Integration," *Scientific American,* June 1978, pp. 42–49.

Taylor, Paul S. *An American-Mexican Frontier.* Chapel Hill, N.C.: University of North Carolina Press, 1934.

tenBroek, Jacobus, Edward N. Barnhart, and Floyd W. Matson. *Prejudice, War and the Constitution.* Berkeley and Los Angeles: University of California Press, 1954.

Thomas, Dorothy Swaine. *The Salvage.* Berkeley and Los Angeles: University of California Press, 1952.

———, and Richard S. Nishimoto. *The Spoilage.* Berkeley and Los Angeles: University of California Press, 1946.

Thompson, Charles H. "The Conclusions of Scientists Relative to Racial Differences," *Journal of Negro Education* 19 (July 1934):494–512.

Thurow, Lester. *Poverty and Discrimination.* Washington, D.C.: The Brookings Institution, 1969.

Tinker, John N. "Intermarriage and Ethnic Boundaries: The Japanese American Case," *Journal of Social Issues* 29 (no. 2, 1973):49–66.

Trotter, Monroe. Editorial, Boston *Guardian,* December 20, 1902; reprinted in August Meier, Elliott Rudwick, and Francis L. Broderick, eds. *Black Protest Thought in the Twentieth Century,* 2nd ed. Indianapolis and New York: Bobbs-Merrill Co., 1971, pp. 32–36.

Turner, Frederick Jackson. *The Frontier in American History*. New York: Henry Holt and Co., 1920.

Tussman, Joseph, ed. *The Supreme Court on Racial Discrimination*. New York: Oxford University Press, 1963.

Tyler, Leona. *The Psychology of Human Differences*. New York: Appleton-Century-Crofts, 1965.

U.S. Bureau of the Census. *Historical Statistics of the United States, Colonial Times to 1957*. Washington, D.C.: U.S. Government Printing Office, 1960.

————. *U.S. Census of Population: 1950*. Vol. 2, "Characteristics of the Population," part 1, United States Summary. Washington, D.C.: U.S. Government Printing Office, 1953.

————. *U.S. Census of Population: 1960*. Vol. 1, "Characteristics of the Population," part 1, United States Summary. Washington, D.C.: U.S. Government Printing Office, 1964.

————. *U.S. Census of Population: 1970*. Vol. 1, "Characteristics of the Population," part 1, United States Summary—section 2. Washington, D.C.: U.S. Government Printing Office, 1973.

————. *U.S. Census of Population: 1950*. Vol. 4, part 3, chapter c, "Persons of Spanish Surname." Washington, D.C.: U.S. Government Printing Office, 1953.

————. *U.S. Census of Population: 1960*. Subject Reports PC(2)–1B, "Persons of Spanish Surname." Washington, D.C.: U.S. Government Printing Office, 1973.

————. *U.S. Census of Population: 1970*. Subject Reports PC(2)–1D, "Persons of Spanish Surname." Washington, D.C.: U.S. Government Printing Office, 1973.

————. *U.S. Census of Population: 1970*. Subject Reports. Final Report PC(2)–1G, "Japanese, Chinese, and Filipinos in the United States." Washington, D.C.: U.S. Government Printing Office, 1973.

U.S. Commission on Civil Rights. *Milliken v. Bradley: The Implications for Metropolitan Desegregation*. Washington, D.C.: U.S. Government Printing Office, 1974.

U.S. Department of Health, Education, and Welfare. "Social Mobility in America," in Edgar A. Schuler, Thomas Ford Hoult, Duane L. Gibson, and Wilbur B. Brookover, eds. *Readings in Sociology*, 5th ed. New York: Thomas Y. Crowell Co., 1974, pp. 342–352.

University of California Regents v. *Bakke*, No. 76–811, Supreme Court of the United States (June 28, 1978).

Vaca, Nick C. "The Mexican-American in the Social Sciences," *El Grito* 4 (Fall 1970), pp. 17–51.

van den Berghe, Pierre L. *Race and Racism*. New York: John Wiley and Sons, 1967.

Van Til, Sally Bould, and Jon Van Til. "The Lower Class and the Future of Inequality," in Edgar A. Schuler, Thomas Ford Hoult, Duane L. Gibson, and Wilbur B. Brookover, eds. *Readings in Sociology*, 5th ed. New York: Thomas Y. Crowell Co., 1974, pp. 313–321.

Van Valey, Thomas L., Wade Clark Roof, and Jerome E. Wilcox. "Trends in Residential Segregation: 1960–1970," *American Journal of Sociology* 82 (January 1977):826–844.

Wagley, Charles, and Marvin Harris. *Minorities in the New World.* New York: Columbia University Press, 1958.

Ware, Caroline F. "Immigration," *Encyclopedia of the Social Sciences,* vol. 7. New York: The Macmillan Co., 1937, pp. 587–594.

War Relocation Authority. *WRA, A Story of Human Conservation.* Washington, D.C.: U.S. Government Printing Office, 1946.

Warner, Lyle G., and Melvin L. DeFleur. "Attitude as an Interactional Concept: Social Constraint and Social Distance as Intervening Variables Between Attitudes and Action," *American Sociological Review* 34 (April 1969):153–169.

Warner, W. Lloyd, and Leo Srole. *The Social Systems of American Ethnic Groups,* 2nd ed. New Haven: Yale University Press, 1946.

Washington, Booker T. *Up from Slavery.* New York: Bantam Books, 1959.

Wattenberg, Ben J., and Richard M. Scammon. "Black Progress and Liberal Rhetoric," in Edgar A. Schuler, Thomas Ford Hoult, Duane L. Gibson, and Wilbur B. Brookover, eds. *Readings in Sociology,* 5th ed. New York: Thomas Crowell Co., 1974, pp. 643–653.

Weaver, Jerry L. "Mexican American Health Care Behavior: A Critical Review of the Literature," *Social Science Quarterly* 54 (June 1973):85–102.

Westie, Frank R. "Race and Ethnic Relations," in Robert E. L. Faris, ed. *Handbook of Modern Sociology.* Chicago: Rand McNally and Co., 1964, pp. 576–615.

Wilkins, Roy. "Address to NAACP Convention, 1966," in August Meier, Elliott Rudwick, and Francis L. Broderick, eds. *Black Protest Thought in the Twentieth Century,* 2nd ed. Indianapolis and New York: Bobbs-Merrill Co., 1971, pp. 596–598.

Wilkinson, Doris Y. "Toward a Positive Frame of Reference from Analysis of Black Families: A Selected Bibliography," *Journal of Marriage and the Family* 40 (November 1978):707–708.

Williams, Allen J., Jr., "Reduction of Tension Through Intergroup Contact," *Pacific Sociological Review* 7 (Fall 1964):81–88.

Williams, John E., and J. Kenneth Morland. *Race, Color, and the Young Child.* Chapel Hill, N.C.: University of North Carolina Press, 1976.

Williams, Robin M., Jr. *The Reduction of Intergroup Tensions.* New York: Social Science Research Council, 1947.

———. *Strangers Next Door.* Englewood Cliffs, N.J.: Prentice-Hall, Inc., 1964.

Wilner, Daniel M., Rosabelle P. Walkley, and Stuart W. Cook. *Human Relations in Interracial Housing: A Study of the Contact Hypothesis.* Minneapolis: University of Minnesota Press, 1955.

Wilson, William J. "Race Relations Models and Explanations of Ghetto Behavior," in Peter I. Rose, ed. *Nation of Nations.* New York: Random House, 1972, pp. 259–275.

———. *The Declining Significance of Race.* Chicago: University of Chicago Press, 1978.

Wirth, Louis. "The Problem of Minority Groups," in Ralph Linton, ed. *The Science of Man in the World Crisis.* New York: Columbia University Press, 1945, pp. 347–372.

Wittke, Carl. *We Who Built America,* 3rd ed. Englewood Cliffs, N.J.: Prentice-Hall, Inc., 1964.

Wood, Ralph, ed. *The Pennsylvania Germans*. Princeton, N.J.: Princeton University Press, 1942.

Woodrum, Eric. "Japanese American Social Adaptation over Three Generations." Ph.D. dissertation, University of Texas at Austin, 1978.

Woodward, C. Vann. *The Strange Career of Jim Crow*. New York: Oxford University Press, 1957.

Woodworth, R. S. "Racial Differences in Mental Traits," *Science* (February 4, 1910):171–186.

Works, Ernest. "The Prejudice-Interaction Hypothesis from the Point of View of the Negro Minority Group," *American Journal of Sociology* 67 (July 1961):47–52.

Yerkes, Robert M., ed. *Psychological Examining in the United States Army*, vol. 15. Washington, D.C.: *Memoirs of the National Academy of Sciences*, 1921.

Yetman, Norman R., and C. Hoy Steele, eds. *Majority and Minority*, 2nd ed. Boston: Allyn and Bacon, 1975.

Zangwill, Israel. *The Melting Pot*. New York: Macmillan Publishing Co., 1909; abridged in Richard J. Meister, ed. *Race and Ethnicity in Modern America*. Lexington, Mass.: D. C. Heath and Co., 1974, pp. 15–21.

Index of Names

Abernathy, Ralph D., 291
Acuña, Rodolpho, 205
Adam, Barry D., 124
Adamic, Louis, 49, 55, 98
Adams, John Quincy, 23, 209
Adams, Romanzo, 90
Adorno, T. W., 152
Agresti, Barbara Finlay, 320
Alger, Horatio, 156, 264, 265
Allen, Vernon L., 123
Allport, Gordon W., 74, 105, 111, 113,
    124, 125, 128, 136, 138, 151,
    152
Alvarez, Rodolfo, 6, 206, 217, 218, 219,
    229
Alvírez, David, 243, 244, 252
Amir, Yehuda, 139, 142
Anderson, Charles H., 40
Asher, Steven R., 123
Austin, Moses, 210
Austin, Stephen Fuller, 210
Ayres, E. D., 226

Bache, R. Meade, 79, 80
Baker, Ross K., 280
Ball, Harry V., 144
Banneker, Benjamin, 78
Bardolph, Richard, 78, 262
Barker, Eugene, C., 211
Barnhart, Edward N., 158, 159, 160,
    161, 173, 177, 199, 200
Baron, Robert A., 110
Bean, Frank D., 243, 244
Becker, Gary S., 117, 119
Bell, Daniel, 66
Benedict, Ruth, 84, 99

Berelson, Bernard, 107, 135, 138, 152
Berger, Morroe, 143, 146
Berkowitz, Leonard, 110, 151
Berry, Brewton, 20
Biddle, Francis, 175
Bierce, Ambrose, 102
Bierstedt, Robert, 77
Bikson, Tora Kay, 141
Billingsley, Andrew, 302
Binet, Alfred, 80
Bishop, George D., 140
Blauner, Robert, 205, 217, 252, 267
Block, N. J., 99
Blumenbach, Johann Friedrich, 73, 74
Bogardus, Emory S., 108
Bonacich, Edna, 115, 116, 117, 129,
    160, 195
Bonjean, Charles M., 151
Boyer, William H., 88
Bradshaw, Benjamin S., 244
Braly, Kenneth W., 106, 107
Brigham, Carl C., 82, 83
Brink, William, 341
Broderick, Francis L., 278, 279
Broom, Leonard, 152, 181, 185, 200
Brown, William R., 141
Browning, Harley L., 231
Bruner, Frank G., 80
Bryan, Samuel, 216
Buehrig, Christie J., 124
Buffon, Georges L. L. de, 74, 78
Bunche, Ralph J., 284
Burgess, Ernest W., 48
Burma, John H., 189, 200, 313, 320
Burns, W. Haywood, 291
Buss, Arnold H., 110
Butler, John Sibley, 152

Camejo, Antonio, 252
Carmichael, Stokely, 133, 296–297
Caudill, William, 192
Churchill, Winston, 45
Clark, Kenneth B., 122, 123, 124, 288
Clark, Mamie K., 122, 123, 124
Clark, Tom C., 176
Coffman, Thomas L., 107
Cole, Mildred Wiese, 48
Cole, Stewart G., 48
Collins, Mary Evans, 139, 145
Connor, Eugene "Bull," 291
Connor, John W., 186
Conolley, Edward S., 141
Cook, Stuart W., 140
Coon, Carleton S., 74
Cortina, Juan N., 207, 213–214
Costello, Lawrence, 61, 325, 328
Coward, Barbara E., 320
Crevecoeur, Jean de, 51
Cronon, Edmund David, 281
Cuéllar, Alfredo, 206, 207, 228, 229

Daniels, Roger, 158, 159, 160, 161,
    162, 169, 171, 199
Darden, Joe, 305, 307
Darwin, Charles, 78, 79
Davidson, James D., 141
Davie, Maurice R., 261, 263, 267, 271,
    275, 276, 319
Davies, James C., 296
DeFleur, Melvin L., 131
Delany, Martin, 261, 266, 319
Deniker, Joseph, 74
Deutsch, Morton, 139, 145
DeVos, George, 192
DeWitt, John L., 173, 174, 176, 183
Díaz, José, 225
Díaz, Porfírio, 214, 215
Dinnerstein, Leonard, 48, 49, 67, 330
Dobzhansky, Theodosius, 73, 74, 76
Dollard, John, 110, 111, 119
Doob, Leonard, 110, 111
Douglas, Kirk, 111
Douglas, William O., 183
Douglass, Frederick, 261
Dowdall, George W., 117, 118
Doyle, Bertram W., 119

Dreger, Ralph Mason, 86
DuBois, W. E. B., 255, 278, 279, 281
Dunn, L. C., 73, 74, 76
Dworkin, Anthony Gary, 224
Dworkin, Gerald, 99

Edgerton, Robert B., 248
Ehrlich, Howard, J., 105, 106, 107, 151
Eitzen, D. Stanley, 201
Elkins, Stanley M., 260, 263, 264, 265,
    301, 314, 315, 319
Ellison, Ralph, 265, 302
Elson, R. M., 108
Endo, Mitsuye, 184
Engels, Friedrich, 296
Engerman, Stanley L., 264, 265
Enloe, Cynthia, 20
Estrada, Leo, 252

Fard, W. D., 282
Farley, Reynolds, 303, 305, 306, 307,
    308, 310
Farmer, James, 285, 286
Faulkner, Harold Underwood, 48, 61,
    212, 268
Feagin, Joe R., 133, 186, 188, 200, 297,
    298, 320
Featherman, David L., 311
Feldstein, Stanley, 61, 325, 328
Festinger, Leon, 112
Fillmore, Millard, 61
Fogel, Robert William, 264, 265
Forbes, Jack D., 343
Ford, W. Scott, 139
Fox, David Joseph, 123
Francis, E. K., 48, 56, 98, 332, 333, 341
Franklin, Benjamin, 40
Franklin, John Hope, 268, 269
Frazier, E. Franklin, 256, 257, 258, 260,
    261, 263, 267, 272, 273, 275,
    276, 299, 300, 301, 315, 319
Frenkel-Brunswik, Else, 152
Frisbie, Parker, 232, 234, 244
Fuguitt, Glenn V., 152
Fujimoto, Isao, 187
Fujitaki, Nancy, 186, 188, 200

Galitzi, Christine A., 48
Galton, Francis, 78, 79
Garcia, Macario, 224
Garrett, Henry E., 85
Garvey, Amy Jacques, 281
Garvey, Marcus, 255, 280–282, 293,
    317
Geen, Russell G., 110
Genovese, Eugene D., 262
Gerard, Harold B., 140, 141
Geschwender, James A., 295, 296
Gilbert, G. M., 107
Glazer, Nathan, 1, 4, 90, 323, 325, 327,
    330, 332, 339
Glenn, Norval D., 114, 117, 118, 119,
    129, 152
Goff, Regina, 307
Goldman, Peter, 320, 323
Gómez-Quiñones, Juan, 216, 219, 220
Goodchilds, Jacqueline D., 141
Gordon, Milton M., 18, 25, 38, 39, 48,
    49, 91, 92, 94, 144, 146, 190,
    191, 198, 204, 237, 303, 320
Gossett, Thomas F., 31, 73, 78, 79
Gould, C. W., 82
Grant, Ulysses S., 62
Grebler, Leo, 216, 220, 221, 222, 223,
    235, 237, 240, 241, 242, 243,
    252
Greeley, Andrew M., 20, 98, 135, 152,
    313, 323, 329, 331, 337
Green, James A., 131, 141
Grodzins, Morton, 200
Gurak, Douglas T., 190, 313
Gutierrez, Armando, 252
Gutman, Herbert G., 264, 265, 300, 302
Guzman, Ralph C., 216, 220, 221, 222,
    223, 235, 237, 240, 241, 242,
    243, 252

Hahn, Harlan, 297–298
Hamilton, Alexander, 43
Hamilton, Charles V., 133
Hamilton, David L., 140
Handlin, Oscar, 256, 257, 258, 259, 340
Hanihara, Masanao, 170, 171
Hansen, Marcus Lee, 5, 48, 56, 57
Harlan, John Marshall, 273, 274

Harris, Louis, 342
Harris, Marvin, 48
Hartz, Louis, 19
Hatchett, Shirley, 320
Hauser, Robert M., 311
Heer, David M., 313
Heiss, Jerold, 123, 124
Heller, Peter L., 249
Herberg, Will, 91, 324, 325, 343
Hernández, Jose, 252
Herskovitz, Melville J., 299, 320
Hill, Richard J., 151
Hill, Robert B., 302
Hirabayashi, Gordon, 182, 183
Hirsch, Herbert, 252
Hitler, Adolph, 84, 176
Hofmann, Gerhard, 141
Hollingshead, August B., 324
Hollingsworth, Leslie, Jr., 310
Homans, George, 20
Hoppe, Sue Keir, 249
Horowitz, E. L., 123
Horton, John, 18, 92, 94, 319
Hosokawa, Bill, 172, 173, 177, 184,
    187, 200
Hughes, Charles Evans, 170, 171
Hyman, Herbert H., 133

Ichihashi, Yamato, 159, 162, 163, 164,
    168, 172
Ichioka, Yuji, 187
Ikeda, Kiyoshi, 144
Iwata, Masakazu, 169

Jackson, Andrew, 59
Jackson, Robert H., 183
Jackson, Terrence D., 141
Jacobs, Paul, 260, 261, 319
Jaher, Frederick Cople, 49
Jefferson, Thomas, 78, 209, 211
Jensen, Arthur R., 86, 87, 88, 99, 318,
    320
Johnson, Andrew, 268
Johnson, James Weldon, 280
Johnson, Lyndon B., 292
Johnson, Michael P., 152
Johnston, Harry, 319

Jones, Maldwyn Allen, 36, 48, 55, 59, 60, 61, 62, 71
Jordan, Valeri Barnes, 123
Jordan, Winthrop D., 319

Kagiwada, George, 157, 188, 189, 200
Kallen, Horace M., 51, 91
Karlins, Marvin, 107
Karno, Marvin, 248
Katz, Daniel, 106, 107
Kearny, Stephen, 212
Kennedy, John F., 292
Kennedy, Ruby Jo Reeves, 189, 243, 324, 325
Kibbe, Pauline R., 211
Kikumura, Akemi, 190
King, James C., 74, 76
King, Martin Luther, Jr., 144, 147, 152, 285, 290–292, 297, 298
Kitano, Harry H. L., 167, 171, 173, 185, 186, 187, 188, 190, 192, 196, 199, 200
Kitsuse, John, 181, 185, 200
Klineberg, Otto, 80, 85, 105
Kluckhohn, Florence R., 246–247, 248, 320
Korematsu, Fred, 183
Krickus, Richard J., 328
Kreigel, Leonard, 328
Kristol, Irving, 332
Kritz, Mary M., 190, 313

Landau, Saul, 260, 261, 319
LaPiere, Richard T., 130, 132
LaViolette, Forest E., 163, 166, 167
Lazarus, Emma, 1
Lea, Tom, 213, 214
Lee, Everett S., 85
Leighton, Alexander, 176, 178, 200
Lerner, Richard M., 124
Levine, Gene N., 197
Levine, Lawrence W., 300
Levinson, Daniel J., 152
Lewis, Oscar, 314
Lewontin, Richard C., 88
Leyburn, James G., 49
Lieberson, Stanley, 152, 252

Liebow, Elliot, 315, 316
Light, Ivan, 166
Lincoln, Abraham, 51, 62, 212, 267, 268
Lincoln, C. Eric, 280, 282
Lindzey, Gardner, 74, 76, 86, 87
Linn, Lawrence S., 131
Linnaeus, Carolus, 73, 74
Lippman, Walter, 99, 105
Little, Malcolm. *See* Malcolm X
Lodge, Henry Cabot, 170, 171
Loehlin, John C., 74, 76, 86, 87
Lohman, Joseph D., 130, 132, 142
London, Jack, 161
Lopreato, Joseph, 65, 66, 67

McCarthy, John, 123
McCone, John A., 294, 295
McKitrick, Erick L., 319
MacLeish, Archibald, 1
McLemore, S. Dale, 151, 231, 248, 252
McWilliams, Carey, 156, 158, 215, 222, 223, 224, 225, 226, 227
Madison James, 43
Malcolm X, 283, 293–294
Marshall, Thurgood, 342
Martínez, José P., 227
Marumoto, Masaji, 199
Marx, Karl, 114, 117, 296
Masaoka, Mike, 155
Masuda, Minoru, 186
Matson, Floyd W., 158, 159, 160, 161, 173, 177, 199, 200
Matsumoto, Gary M., 186
Meier, August, 278, 279
Meister, Richard J., 91
Mendel, Gregor, 75
Meredith, Gerald M., 186
Merton, Robert K., 132, 142
Metcalf, Victor, 162
Metzger, L. Paul, 96
Middleton, Russell, 136, 137
Mikulski, Barbara, 326, 328
Miller, Neal E., 110, 111
Miller, Norman, 141
Miller, Ralph Mason, 86
Milner, Lucille B., 287
Mintz, Sidney W., 264

Mittlebach, Frank G., 244
Miyamoto, S. Frank, 163, 164, 166, 194, 199
Monahan, Thomas P., 313, 320
Montaigne, M. E. de, 101
Montero, Darrel M., 197
Montezuma, 207
Moore, Joan W., 205, 213, 216, 220, 221, 222, 223, 235, 237, 240, 241, 242, 243, 244, 252
Moquin, Wayne, 212, 213
Morland, J. Kenneth, 123
Morse, Samuel F. B., 60
Mowrer, O. H., 110, 111
Moynihan, Daniel Patrick, 4, 90, 301, 302, 314, 315, 323, 325, 327, 330
Muhammad, Elijah, 282, 283, 293
Murguía, Edward, 99, 207, 244, 253
Murieta, Joaquin, 207
Murphy, Frank, 183
Músquiz, Ramón, 210
Myrdal, Gunnar, 17, 18, 103, 115, 125, 128, 143, 284, 299, 300

Nash, Gary B., 32, 33
Navarro, José Antonio, 210
Newman, William M., 91
Nishimoto, Richard S., 181, 200
Nixon, E. D., 290
Nixon, Richard M., 328
Nobbe, Charles E., 157
Noel, Donald L., 213
Nostrand, Richard L., 252
Novak, Michael, 323, 327, 329
Novothy, Ann, 65, 69, 70

Okimoto, Daniel, 197
Osofsky, Gilbert, 123, 280, 286, 287, 288, 292
Owens, Susan, 123, 124

Parenti, Michael, 343
Park, Robert E., 23, 24, 25, 33, 36, 37, 39, 46, 48, 108, 185, 190, 191, 204, 215, 237, 330, 340

Parkman, Margaret A., 190
Parks, Rosa, 290
Parsons, Talcott, 19
Pastorius, Franz Daniel, 49
Patchen, Martin, 141
Patterson, Orlando, 264, 319
Penalosa, Fernando, 203, 244
Penn, William, 36
Pershing, John J. "Blackjack," 215
Petersen, William, 156, 163, 166, 167, 169, 184, 191, 193, 194, 201
Pettigrew, Thomas F., 145, 308, 309
Phelan, J. D., 159, 199
Phillips, Ulrich B., 259, 260, 263
Polk, James K., 212
Poole, Elijah. *See* Muhammad, Elijah
Proshansky, Harold, 152
Prosser, Gabriel, 262, 281, 317

Quatrefages de Bréau, J. L. A., 74

Rainwater, Lee, 302
Randolph, A. Phillip, 282, 284, 285, 287, 291
Reich, Michael, 117, 118
Reimers, David M., 48, 67, 331
Reitzes, Dietrich C., 130, 132, 142
Rendon, Armando B., 203
Rice, Thomas D., 319
Rinehart, James W., 107
Rives, George Lockhart, 211
Roberts, Owen J., 178
Robinson, James R., 285
Roche, John P., 144, 146
Rodman, Hyman, 200
Romano, Octavio Ignacio, 248, 249
Roof, Wade Clark, 310
Roosevelt, Franklin D., 173, 285, 328
Roosevelt, Theodore, 162
Root, Elihu, 162
Rosenberg, Morris, 124
Ross, E. A., 160
Rostow, Eugene V., 174, 175, 184
Rubenstein, Richard E., 43
Rudwick, Elliot, 278, 279
Rustin, Bayard, 285, 287

Rutledge, Wiley B., 183
Ryan, William, 320

St. John, Nancy H., 141
Salter, Patricia, 107
Sampson, William A., 311
Sanchez, George I., 203, 224, 252
Sanford, R. Nevitt, 152
Santa Anna, Antonio Lopez de, 211
Saunders, Lyle, 246, 247, 248
Sawyer, Jack, 190
Scammon, Richard M., 305
Schermerhorn, Richard A., 19, 65, 66,
    67, 68, 69, 99, 131
Schmid, Calvin F., 157
Schuman, Howard, 152, 320
Schurz, Carl, 59
Scott, Robin Fitzgerald, 227, 228
Scott, Winfield, 212
Sears, R. R., 110, 111
Sheatsley, Paul B., 133, 135, 152, 313,
    337
Sheldon, Paul M., 248
Shuey, Audrey M., 85, 99
Siegel, Paul M., 320
Simmel, Georg, 108
Simmons, Roberta, 124
Simon, Thomas, 80
Simpson, George Eaton, 113, 115, 144,
    151
Singer, Lester, 98
Skinner, B. F., 152
Sklare, Marshall, 67, 68
Skolnick, Jerome H., 94, 338
Smith, James P., 306, 307
Smith, Lillian, 119
Smythe, Mabel M., 306
Sørenson, Annmette, 310
Speed, Joshua F., 51
Spuhler, J. N., 74, 76, 86, 87
Srole, Leo, 19
Steele, C. Hoy, 343
Steiner, Gary A., 135, 138, 152
Stern, Wiliam, 80
Stevenson, Coke, 224
Stonequist, Everett V., 19
Sugimoto, Howard H., 199

Sumner, William Graham, 48, 101, 120,
    121, 143, 144, 145, 146
Szymanski, Albert, 117, 118

Tachiki, Amy, 155, 157
Taeuber, Alma F., 240, 241, 253, 307,
    309, 310
Taeuber, Karl E., 240, 241, 253, 307,
    309, 310
Takagi, Paul, 157, 197
Taylor, D. Garth, 135, 152, 313, 337
Taylor, Paul S., 211, 213, 214
Taylor, Zachary, 212
TenBroek, Jacobus, 158, 159, 160, 161,
    173, 177, 199, 200
Terman, Lewis, M., 99
Thomas, Dorothy Swaine, 181, 200
Thompson, Charles H., 83
Thurow, Lester, 117, 119, 129
Tinker, John N., 190
Tocqueville, Alexis de, 296, 339
Togo, Heihachiro, 162
Trotter, Monroe, 278
Truman, Harry S., 287
Truth, Sojourner, 261
Tubman, Harriet, 261
Turner, Frederick Jackson, 89
Turner, Nat, 262, 281, 317
Tussman, Joseph, 178, 183, 273, 274,
    288
Tyler, Leona, 77

Vaca, Nick C., 248, 249
Van den Berghe, Pierre, 309
Van Doren, Charles, 212, 213
Van Reed, Eugene, 199
Van Til, Jon, 320
Van Til, Sally, 320
Van Valey, Thomas L., 310
Vesey, Denmark, 262, 281, 317
Villa, Francisco "Pancho," 215

Wagley, Charles, 48
Walker, David, 261
Walkley, Rosabelle P., 140
Wallace, George, 329

Walsh, Paul, 88
Walters, Gary, 107
Ware, Carolyn F., 81
Warner, Lyle G., 131
Warner, W. Lloyd, 19
Warren, Earl, 288
Washington, Booker T., 255, 277–280
Washington, George, 43
Wattenberg, Ben, 305
Weaver, Jerry L., 248, 253
Welch, Finis, 306, 307
Westie, Frank R., 131
Wilcox, Jerome E., 310
Wilkins, Roy, 255
Wilkinson, Doris Y., 302
Williams, John E., 123
Williams, J. Allen, Jr., 152, 320
Williams, Robin M., Jr., 19, 121, 122
Wilner, Daniel M., 140

Wilson, Kenneth L., 152
Wilson, William J., 310, 311, 312, 319
Wilson, Woodrow, 215
Wirth, Louis, 19, 95
Wittke, Carl, 40, 55, 65, 67, 68
Woodrum, Eric, 186, 188, 189, 190
Woodward, C. Vann, 271, 272, 273, 319
Woodworth, Robert, 80
Works, Ernest, 140

Yancey, William L., 123, 302
Yerkes, Robert M., 82, 99
Yetman, Norman R., 343
Yinger, J. Milton, 113, 115, 151

Zangwill, Israel, 89

Index of Subjects

Abolition(ism), 59, 62
Accommodation (*see* Assimilation, stages of)
Acculturation (*see* Assimilation, cultural)
Affirmative action, 147
Afro-Americans (*see* Black Americans)
Alien and Sedition Acts, 42 (*see also* Immigration, regulation of)
American Creed, The, 18, 103, 143
Americanization (*see* Assimilation)
American Revolution (*see* Ethnic groups, participation in American Revolution)
Anglo-Americans (*see* Majority)
Anglo conformity, ideology of, 33–35, 47, 71–72, 336–339, 341 (*see also* Assimilation, ideologies of)
Articles of Confederation, 43
Asiatic Exclusion League, 161, 163
Assimilation (*see also* Ethnic groups; Inclusion):
  of blacks, 45–46, 298–314
  of Chicanos, 230–244
  of cultural groups, 12
  of Dutch, 30
  of Germans, 41, 47
  ideologies of, 25, 33–35, 45–48, 71–72, 89–98, 207–208, 318, 323–340
  of Indians, 33, 45–46, 208–209
  of Irish, 37–39
  of Italians, 65
  of Japanese, 184–191, 198
  of Jews, 67–68
  of racial groups, 12
  of Scotch-Irish, 38–39

  resistance to, 33
  stages of, 24–25, 37
  subprocesses of
    attitude receptional, 49
    behavior acceptional, 49
    civic, 49
    cultural, 38–39, 46, 67, 70, 184, 187, 198, 234–237, 251, 298–303, 318
    identificational, 49
    marital, 38–39, 70, 189–190, 198, 243–244, 251, 312–314, 318, 324–325
    primary structural, 39, 70, 188–189, 198, 242–243, 251, 312, 318
    secondary structural, 38–39, 47, 49, 70, 187–188, 198, 237–242, 251, 303–312, 318
    structural, 38–39
  three generations process of, 4, 11, 16, 24, 70, 191, 330–332
  time required for, 18, 329–332, 341
Association of Black Sociologists, 311
Assumptions (*see* Theories)

Bakke case (*see University of California Regents* v. *Bakke*)
Belonging, sense of (*see* Community, cohesion of; Family, cohesion of)
Birds of Passage, 195 (*see also* Sojourners)
Black Americans, 255–320
  African survivals among, 299–300

Black Americans (*continued*)
    associations of, 278–298, 290–294,
        336
    civil rights movement of, 277–298
    as colonized minority, 265–267, 316
    culture of, 299–303
    education of, 307–309 (*see also*
        Integration, of schools)
    emancipation of, 267
    family of, 299, 301–303, 315
    as immigrant minority, 275–277, 316
    legal segregation of, 271–275
    occupations of, 276–277, 303–307
    as primary ethnic group, 336
    during Reconstruction, 267–270
    as secondary ethnic group, 336
    slave revolts, 261–262
    slavery, 78, 256–265, 299–300, 317
    values, 315–316
Black Muslims, 282–284, 293–294
Black Panther party, 297 (*see also*
        Black Americans, associations
        of)
Black Power Movement, 293–298
Blacks (*see* Black Americans)
Boomerang effect, 136, 150
Bracero program (*see* Chicanos)
Brown v. *Topeka Board of Education,*
        133, 287–289, 308, 317, 318
Burgesses, House of, 28

Catharsis, 151
Catholics and Catholicism, 35, 55–56,
        98 (*see also* Majority, hostility
        of toward foreigners)
Charters, royal, 27–28
Chicanismo, 206
Chicanos, 203–253
    associations of, 229
    Border Patrol and, 216, 222
    bracero program and, 223–224, 251
    "charity deportations" of, 222, 251
    as colonized minority, 209–215
    education of, 239–240
    family and, 235, 247–249
    health care of, 246–249
    "historical primacy" and, 217
    as immigrant minority, 215–219

    immigration of, 219–230
    occupations of, 237–239
    "Operation Wetback" and, 223, 251
    population of, 231–234
    prejudice toward, 219–230
    as primary ethnic group, 334–335,
        340–341
    as secondary ethnic group, 335, 340–
        342
    Texas Rangers and, 214
    values of, 245–249
    Zoot-Suit Riots and, 225–227, 251
    See also Assimilation, of Chicanos
Chinese:
    exclusion of, 71, 80, 116, 159, 168,
        216
    prejudice toward, 130, 158–159, 199
Civil Rights Act of 1866, 268–269
Civil Rights Act of 1964, 292, 318
Civil War, 62–63
Cognitive dissonance theory, 112–113,
        145
Cohesion (*see* Community, cohesion
        of; Family, cohesion of)
Colonial analogy, 95, 204–215, 249–
        250, 251, 252, 265–267, 319,
        332, 334, 336
Colonial Germans (*see* Germans)
Colonial Irish (*see* Scotch-Irish)
Colonialism, internal (*see* Colonial
        analogy)
Colonization:
    of Dutch, 27, 29
    of English, 25–31
    of Spanish, 25, 207–209, 250
Community:
    cohesion of, 12–13
    loyalty to, 13–14
Community Service Organization, 229
        (*see also* Chicanos, associations
        of)
Competition (*see* Assimilation, stages
        of)
Concord, The, 49
Conflict (*see also* Assimilation, stages
        of; Majority, hostility of toward
        foreigners; Prejudice, group
        gains theory of; Riots):
    historical result of, 329

nonviolent, 18, 147, 150, 179–180, 290–293, 318
probability of, 19–20, 145–146
violent, 32–33, 36, 62, 71, 147, 161, 205, 210, 269–270, 286–287, 291, 294–298, 318
Congress of Racial Equality, 285–286, 290, 294, 336 (*see also* Black Americans, associations of)
Constitutional Convention, 43
Contact (*see* Assimilation, stages of)
Contact hypothesis, 138, 141
Core group (*see* Majority, composition of)
Creed-deed discrepancy, 129–132
Cultural assimilation (*see* Assimilation, subprocesses of)
Cultural pluralism, 91–91, 323–341 (*see also* Assimilation, ideologies of)
Culture of poverty thesis, 314–315, 318–319
Cultures (*see* Ethnic groups)

Desegregation (*see* Integration)
Dillingham Commission, 98
Discrimination:
   cultural transmission of, 126–128, 150
   definition of, 101–102
   group gains and, 128–129, 150
   institutional, 133–134, 150
   prejudice and, 125–126, 130–132, 142, 149, 150, 152
   reduction of (*see* Prejudice, reduction of; *see also* Theories)
   situational pressures and, 129–132, 142, 150
Disruptive pressure, 18, 31 (*see also* Conflict)
Dolls test, 122–123
Dominant group (*see* Majority)
Dred Scott case, 259

Ellis Island, 3, 65
Endo v. *United States*, 184

Ethnic groups:
   cohesion of, 10, 41, 68, 165, 174, 185, 193, 196–197, 206, 240
   creation of 56, 66–67, 96, 209, 250, 341
   distinctions within, 58, 66–68
   distinctiveness of, 11, 14, 36, 40, 57, 64–65, 68–69, 340, 343
   diversity of, 17 (*see also* Cultural pluralism)
   future of, in America, 334–340
   identity of, 1–2, 4, 33, 38, 66, 200, 228–229, 324–329, 340, 341
   involuntary entrance of, 6–10, 203–204, 249, 333
   loyalty of, 61–62, 181–182, 227
   loyalty to, 13–14, 18, 66, 121–122
   names of, 19, 252
   participation in American Revolution, 41–45
   primary, 333–334, 340–341
   secondary, 333–334, 340–341
   similarities of, 30, 40–41, 68–69, 237–239
   voluntary entrance of, 6–10, 18, 203–204, 333
   white, 325–329, 339–342
Ethnocentrism, 48, 121–122
Ethnogenesis, 98, 304 (*see also* Ethnic groups, creation of)

Family:
   cohesion of, 13
   loyalty to, 13, 18
Federalist Papers, 43
Feudal societies (*see* Traditional societies)
"First Year Men," 199
Folk societies (*see* Traditional societies)
Folkways, 144
Foreigners, hostility toward (*see* Majority; Nativism)
Foreign group, definition of, 30–31, 47
Forty-Eighters, 57–60
Frontier thesis, 44, 89–90
Frustration-aggression hypothesis, 110–114, 149

Generation, length of a, 19
Gentlemen's Agreement, 162–163, 165,
    169–171, 198, 216
German Reformed Church, 42
Germans:
    colonial, 39–41, 48
    nineteenth-century, 56–59
G.I. Forum, 229 (*see also* Chicanos,
    associations of)
Guadalupe Hidalgo, treaty of, 212–213,
    215, 218, 250

Hansen's thesis, 5, 187, 188, 191
Heredity, laws of, 75–77
Hirabayashi v. *United States,* 182–183
Hispanos (*see* Chicanos)
Housing, interracial, 139–140 (*see also*
    Assimilation, subprocesses of,
    secondary structural)

Ideals (*see* Values)
Immigrant analogy, 215–219, 250, 251,
    265–267, 332, 334
Immigration:
    changing patterns of, 63–74
    factors affecting, 51–52, 54
    first great stream of, 53–59, 96
    regulation of, 42, 61, 71, 80–81, 83,
        97, 170, 216, 220–221
    second great stream of, 64–70, 96
    size of, 52–55, 64, 71, 216, 221–222
Inclusion (*see also* Assimilation):
    as a goal, 6–9
    model of, 23–25
    rate of, factors affecting, 6–12, 18,
        30, 40
Indian Americans, 31–33, 48, 203, 206–
    209, 255–256, 343
In-group, 120
Integration (*see also* Assimilation,
    subprocesses of, secondary
    structural):
    attitudes toward, 133, 136
    definition of, 49, 237
    of military services, 287, 317
    of neighborhoods, 240–242, 308–

    310, 318, 327–329, 338–339,
        341
    of schools, 140–141, 145–146, 287–
        289, 307–309, 317, 318, 341
Intelligence:
    differences in, 78–89, 97, 99
    heritability of, 87–88
Internal colonialism (*see* Colonial
    analogy)
Involuntary entrance (*see* Ethnic
    groups, involuntary entrance of)
I.Q. controversy (*see* Intelligence)
Irish:
    colonial (*see* Scotch-Irish)
    nineteenth-century, 53–56
    rent system, 54
Iroquois Confederacy, 32
Italians, 65–67

Jamestown, founding of, 27–29, 32
Japanese (*see* Japanese Americans)
Japanese American Citizens League,
    172–173 (*see also* Japanese
    Americans, associations of)
Japanese American Research Project,
    186, 189, 190
Japanese Americans, 155–201 (*see also*
    Assimilation, of Japanese)
    alien land laws and, 168–169
    associations of, 166–167, 172–173
    citizenship of, 168, 199–200
    emigration of, 159
    exclusion of, 170–171, 198
    evacuation of, 172–184
    family and community of, 164–173,
        193–195, 198
    immigration of, 157–164
    as "model" minority, 156–157
    occupations of, 168–169
    picture brides and, 164
    prejudice toward, 157–164, 198
    relocation, 174–182, 198
    school board crisis and, 161–162
    values, 166, 191–193, 199
Japanese Association, 167 (*see also*
    Japanese Americans, associa-
    tions of)

Jews, Jewish, 31, 67–70, 136–137
"Jim Crow" system, 271–275, 295, 309, 319
jus sanguinis, 200
jus soli, 199

Know-Nothing party, 61–62
Korematsu v. *United States,* 183–184
Ku Klux Klan, 269–270, 280, 288

La Raza Unida party, 343 (*see also* Chicanos, associations of)
League of United Latin American Citizens, 229 (*see also* Chicanos, associations of)
Lowndes County Freedom Organization (*see* Black Panther party)
Loyalty (*see* Community, loyalty to; Ethnic groups, loyalty to; Family, loyalty to)
Lutherans, 41–42

Majority:
   composition of, 25–26, 29–30, 45–48, 108
   formation of, 25–31, 39, 42–46
   goals of, 18–19, 34–35, 150
   hostility of toward foreigners, 7, 35–36, 40, 55–56, 59–63, 66, 70–71, 96
   power of, 7–8, 18
   size of, 7–8, 10
"Manifest Destiny," 209, 212
March on Washington Movement, 284–285, 356 (*see also* Black Americans, associations of)
Marginal position, 3, 19, 172
Marital assimilation (*see* Assimilation, subprocesses of)
Mayflower Compact, 29
Melting Pot, 89–91, 324 (*see also* Assimilation, ideologies of)
Mennonites, 41, 46
Mexican American Political Association, 229 (*see also* Chicanos, associations of)

Mexican American Study Project, 242
Mexican American Youth Organization, 229 (*see also* Chicanos, associations of)
Mexican Americans (*see* Chicanos)
Mexicans (*see* Chicanos)
"Middleman" minority, 195
Milliken v. *Bradley,* 308, 320
Minority, Minorities (*see also* specific groups):
   goals of, 18–19, 135, 150, 184, 229–230, 235, 251, 280, 293, 314
   power of, 7–8, 18
   size of, 7–8, 10, 20, 148, 204
Modern societies (*see also* Traditional societies):
   characteristics of, 12–13, 18, 65, 311
   historical tendency of, 11, 340, 342
   historical trend toward, 13–14
Mores, 144

Napoleonic Wars, 44, 53
National Association for the Advancement of Colored People, 278–279, 290, 317, 336 (*see also* Black Americans, associations of)
National Urban League, 319, 336
Nationality (*see* Ethnic groups, identity of)
Native American party, 61
Native group, definition of, 30
Nativism (*see* Immigration, regulation of; Majority, hostility of toward foreigners)
Naturalization, 42, 60–61 (*see also* Immigration, regulation of)
Negroes (*see* Black Americans)
New immigration (*see* Immigration, second great stream of)

Old immigration (*see* Immigration, first great stream of)
"Operation Wetback" (*see* Chicanos)
Out-group, 121
Ozawa v. *United States,* 168

"Pennsylvania Dutch," 40

Plessy v. *Ferguson,* 199, 273–275, 277, 287, 317

Pluralism (*see* Assimilation, ideologies of; Cultural pluralism)

Plymouth, founding of, 27–29

Population, growth of, 52–53

Potato famine, 54–57

Power (*see* Majority, power of; Minority, power of)

Prejudice:
    cultural transmission of, 105–109, 149
    definition of, 101–102
    discrimination and, 102–103, 124–125, 130–132, 149, 150
    group gains and, 114–120, 149, 160
    group identification and, 120–124, 149
    personality and, 109–114, 149, 151–152
    reduction of,
        by contact, 138–142, 150
        by information, 135–138, 150
        by law, 143–147, 150
        by protest, 147–148, 151
        by vicarious experience, 136–138, 150
    social class and, 117, 120, 135–136

Presbyterians, 35

Primary relations, 38–39

Primary structural assimilation (*see* Assimilation, subprocesses of)

Protest (*see* Conflict)

Protestants (*see* Majority, composition of; *see also* separate listings)

Quotas, immigation, 81, 170 (*see also* Immigration, regulation of)

Race relations:
    cycle of, 23–25, 33, 46, 204–205, 215, 340
    etiquette of, 119, 269

Races, definition, numbers, and significance of, 72–77, 96–97, 155–156

Racial differences:
    beliefs about, 31, 72–74, 77–79, 96–97
    in intelligence (*see* Intelligence, differences in)

Racial groups (*see* Ethnic groups)

Racism, 79, 88–89, 96

Reconstruction Acts, 268–269

Relative deprivation hypothesis, 294–295

Reservation system, 33

Rise and drop hypothesis, 296

Rising expectations hypothesis, 295

Riots, 62, 163, 180, 294–298 (*see also* Conflict, violent)

Scapegoat, 111, 113

Scotch-Irish:
    assimilation (*see* Assimilation, of Scotch-Irish)
    immigration, 35–39, 47–48

Secession(ism), 94–95, 125, 206, 266, 280, 322, 336

Secondary relations, 38

Secondary structural assimilation (*see* Assimilation, subprocesses of)

Segregation (*see* Integration)

Self-esteem; Self-hate, 122–124, 140

"Separate but equal," doctrine of, 161 (*see also Plessy* v. *Ferguson*)

Separatism, 92, 94–95, 125, 206, 293, 323, 336, 338, 342, 343

Servants, indentured, 27–28, 34, 256–265

Slavery (*see* Black Americans, slavery)

Social distance, 108–109, 155

Social mobility (*see* Success)

Social stratification, 101 (*see also* Assimilation, subprocesses of)
    environmentalist view, 72
    hereditarian view, 72
    of ethnic groups, 213

Sojourners, 160, 195 (*see also* Birds of Passage)

Solidarity (*see* Community, cohesion of; Ethnic group, cohesion of; Family, cohesion of)

Southern Christian Leadership Conference, 290–293, 336 (*see also* Black Americans, associations of)
Split labor market theory (*see* Prejudice, group gains and)
Stereotypes, 66, 105–108, 134, 135, 260, 264, 265
Student Nonviolent Coordinating Committee, 290, 296 (*see also* Black Americans, associations of)
Structural assimilation (*see* Assimilation, subprocesses of)
Subordinate groups (*see* Minority, Minorities)
Success:
  assimilation and, 96, 156–157
  environmentalist views of, 96
  theories of, 156–157, 191–198, 245–249; 251, 314–316, 319

Tejanos, 211
Theories (*see also* Assimilation, ideologies of):
  practical importance of, 14, 15–17, 18, 25, 34–35, 120, 125–126, 129, 134–148, 312, 337–339, 342
Three generations process (*see* Assimilation, three generations process of)
Traditional societies (*see also* Modern societies):
  changes in, 26
  characteristics of, 12, 18
Transmuting Pot, 91
Turnvereine, 58–59, 67

Unity (*see* Community, cohesion of)
Universal Negro Improvement Association, 280–282 (*see also* Black Americans, associations of)
University of California Regents v. *Bakke,* 147, 152, 342
Urban League (*see* National Urban League)

Values (*see also* Success, theories of):
  ideal, 17
  premises, 17–18, 245
Vicious circle, theory of, 128, 133, 149, 150
Voluntary entrance (*see* Ethnic groups, voluntary entrance of)
Voting Rights Act of 1965, 292, 318

Whites (*see* Majority)
White supremacy, doctrine of, 31, 71–72, 77, 97 (*see also* Racial differences, beliefs about)

"Yellow peril," 158, 199